Attacks on Christendom
in a World Come of Age

Princeton Theological Monograph Series

K. C. Hanson, Charles M. Collier, D. Christopher Spinks,
and Robin Parry, Series Editors

Attacks on Christendom in a World Come of Age

Kierkegaard, Bonhoeffer, and the Question of "Religionless Christianity"

Matthew D. Kirkpatrick

With a Foreword by Geffrey B. Kelly

PICKWICK *Publications* · Eugene, Oregon

ATTACKS ON CHRISTENDOM IN A WORLD COME OF AGE
Kierkegaard, Bonhoeffer, and the Question of "Religionless Christianity"

Princeton Theological Monograph Series 166

Pickwick Publications
An Imprint of Wipf and Stock Publishers
199 W. 8th Ave., Suite 3
Eugene, OR 97401

www.wipfandstock.com

ISBN 13: 978-1-60899-550-9

Cataloging-in-Publication data:

Kirkpatrick, Matthew D.

  Attacks on Christendom in a world come of age : Kierkegaard, Bonhoeffer, and the question of "religionless Christianity" / Matthew D. Kirkpatrick ; foreword by Geffrey B. Kelly.

  Princeton Theological Monograph Series 166

  xviii + 240 p. ; 23 cm. Includes bibliographical references and indexes.

  ISBN 13: 978-1-60899-550-9

  1. Bonhoeffer, Dietrich, 1906–1945. 2. Kierkegaard, Søren, 1813–1855. 3. Church and the world. 4. Christianity and culture. I. Kelly, Geffrey B. II. Title. III. Series.

BR115.W6 K61 2011

Manufactured in the U.S.A.

For Kate

Contents

Foreword

Wɪᴛʜ ᴛʜᴇ ʀᴇɴᴇᴡᴀʟ ᴏꜰ widespread interest in the life and writings of Dietrich
Bonhoeffer new studies have appeared that trace the formative influences—philosophical, theological, and biographical—that inspired Bonhoeffer from his early writings
to his resistance of the Nazi dictatorship. This interest has been sparked in recent years by
the appearance of the English language translations of the collected works of Bonhoeffer
in new critical editions accomplished in collaboration with the German editors of the
original texts. These translations—published as the Dietrich Bonhoeffer Works English
Edition—are now nearing completion with the publication in 2010 of the long awaited
Letters and Papers from Prison.

Among the formative influences that have shaped Bonhoeffer's heroic resistance to the
Nazi dictatorship, few stand out more than that of the Danish writer, Søren Kierkegaard.
His influence on Bonhoeffer has been widely recognized through studies on both authors and attested to by none other than Bonhoeffer himself. On two separate occasions,
Bonhoeffer spoke of his indebtedness to his standing "in the tradition of Paul, Luther and
Kierkegaard." Yet this recognition has been limited to brief footnoted references in studies
of Bonhoeffer's theology and to the occasional paper at scholarly conferences. For this
reason, Matthew D. Kirkpatrick's comprehensive study of the amazing spiritual connect-
edness of these two giants in religious literature stands out as one of the most important
contributions to Bonhoeffer scholarship to appear in recent years.

Kirkpatrick has demonstrated the various respects in which Bonhoeffer adopted and
adapted the theological insights and ecclesio-political commitments of Kierkegaard to
his own life and biographical situation. Kirkpatrick makes a convincing case for his contention that Kierkegaard and Bonhoeffer both regarded the established "Christendom"
as a corruption of the authentic Christian witness, to which ecclesiastical leaders paid
homage, and followers of Christ succumbed. As the title of his book suggests, Kirkpatrick
convincingly argues that Bonhoeffer's existential testimony and personal investment to
the role of Christian faith in a "world come of age" qualifies him as a "fulfillment" of
Kierkegaard's own witness that an individual Christian must live even at great risk to his
life and ecclesio-political status. Despite the paucity of Bonhoeffer's direct references to
Kierkagaard—throughout his authorship, only *Fear and Trembling*, *Works of Love*, and
his *Sickness unto Death* are directly cited—Kirkpatrick shows that Bonhoeffer found in
Kierkegaard "a kindred soul." But Kirkpatrick is adept in stepping beyond direct relationship between Kierkegaard and Bonhoeffer to lay the foundation for his using them as
interpretive tools for understanding each other and their relevance for "a world come
of age." Though their historical climates were so very different, Kirkpatrick reveals that

Bonhoeffer was able to extend and redirect Kierkegaard's works and manages, unlike so many other interpreters, to overcome the simple juxtaposition of Kierkegaard's individualism with Bonhoeffer's Christocentric ecclesiology. Kirkpatrick presents compelling evidence to demonstrate that their "attacks" on Christendom, though of different centuries, bear much similarity to each other.

Kirkpatrick identifies Kierkegaard's "attack on Idealism" as what impressed Bonhoeffer most in Kierkegaard's works. Both Kierkegaard and Bonhoeffer allege that the intellectual hegemony of "Idealism" in their countries had pernicious effects on their philosophical bearings, their ethics, their Christology, and their similar concepts of Christian discipleship.

Kirkpatrick takes his readers on a highly informative journey into Kierkegaard's experience of the destructive effects of the Danish Revolution of 1848. He shows how Kierkegaard suffered as he witnessed the so-called "revolutionaries" undermining the spiritual liberation that he had attempted to promote, and his church's failure to intervene. This was for him a typical act of cowardice that he would later repudiate in his "attack on Christendom"—an attack that would intersect with Bonhoeffer's dramatic critique of his own church's craven self-seeking in the prison letters. These destructive effects of the 'revolution' on the Danish church find their parallel in Nazism's appeal to the concept of a German *Volk* and a *volkish* church that seduced so many parishioners and their sycophantic leaders. Kirkpatrick references Kierkegaard's *Concept of Anxiety, Fear and Trembling*, and his *Concluding Unscientific Postscript*, to mark a significant influence on Bonhoeffer's analysis of the ecclesiology of *Sanctorum Comunio* and the epistemology of *Act and Being*. Kirkpatrick uses the markings in Bonhoeffer's copy of *Concept of Anxiety* to highlight his having adopted Kierkegaard's understanding of "the moment" and the power of "original sin" in his dissertations but also in tandem with his firm links with Luther, in his attack on idealism.

It is clear from Kirkpatrick's analyses that Bonhoeffer's central themes in his spiritual classic, *Discipleship*, find many parallels in the writings of Kierkegaard, such as *Fear and Trembling*, and several other works evidenced in Bonhoeffer's library. Kirkpatrick explains in gripping detail how both writers emphasized the mandate for Christians of a wholehearted "imitation" of Christ as they both sought to rescue Jesus Christ from the shackles of idealist thought while rejecting the notion of Christ as mere "idea" or "doctrine." Kirkpatrick notes likewise that Bonhoeffer's descriptions of Christ as "paradox," "incognito," "offense," and "contemporaneity" are rooted in Kierkegaard's original attempts to depict the appeal of Christ to Christian faith and life. Both writers also emphasize the notion of "imitation" in constructing their arguments for the relevance of Jesus Christ's gospel to the issue of how to live one's Christianity authentically by obedience to Jesus Christ. Finally, Kirkpatrick coordinates the various strands of the theological critique of idealism common to both Kierkegaard and Bonhoeffer in terms of Kierkegaard's "Attack on Christendom" and Bonhoeffer's pungent criticism of the fecklessness of the church leaders in the Nazi era. In this matter of ecclesio-political timidity and hypocrisy, their biographies intersect. Kirkpatrick concludes that, for both creative thinkers, a key feature of their witnessing to the truth of the Christian gospel meant witnessing against the cultural collusion of church and state wherein each saw Christ's instruction to love God and neighbor diluted and co-opted by nationalist ideology and political expediency. Herein lies the concept of religion that Bonhoeffer criticized with Barthian emphasis because of the role religion had played in the churchy acclamation of Adolf Hitler as Germany's political messiah. His critique of religion and indictment of the churches for their complicity in the rise to power of Hitler dovetails with Kierkegaard's sharp attack on the deterioration of Christianity into an ecclesio-political Christendom. In his monumental study of these two giants of Christian thought, Kirkpatrick reveals that while proclaiming discipleship as the principal of witnessing to the truth would finally lead Bonhoeffer to the gallows, his reading of Kierkegaard would escort him through his own life of discipleship and prepare him for the heroic sacrifice that Kierkegaard had unflinchingly challenged his contemporaries to emulate.

Kirkpatrick's book, *Attacks on Christendom in a World Come of Age: Kierkegaard, Bonhoeffer, and the Question of "Religionless Christianity,"* is the most comprehensive study of these two inspirational writers, offering a comprehensive analysis of their authorships, and demonstrating the profound influence Kierkegaard could exert on the hero of German resistance. Matthew D. Kirkpatrick has achieved an original and substantial contribution not only to scholarship on the writings of these two seminal thinkers but also to the history of Christian thought in both the nineteenth and twentieth centuries. This book is indispensable for any future studies of the contribution to religious history of these two seminal thinkers. Kirkpatrick has shown conclusively that the writings of these two distinguished authors are significant for their attacks on their miscreant religious institutions and for their spirited attempt to reform Christianity for a world of authentic faith. However, in addition, he has revealed their joint endeavors to release Christian faith from its enchainment to an ecclesio-political world where systemic injustice and hypocrisy had impeded Christians and their churches from radiating Jesus Christ and his gospel to the world where, despite the risks, Christ was to be followed and their faith emboldened.

Geffrey B. Kelly, Professor of Systematic Theology, Department of Religion, La Salle University, former two-term President of the International Bonhoeffer Society, English Language Section, author of *Liberating Faith: Bonhoeffer's Message for Today*, and co-author of *A Testament to Freedom: The Essential Writings of Dietrich Bonhoeffer*.

Acknowledgments

I AM GREATLY INDEBTED TO A NUMBER OF PEOPLE WHO HAVE MADE THIS PROJECT POSsible. I would like to express my gratitude to various people around the world who very kindly went out of their way to help me track down sources and find works that were otherwise out of my reach. These include Ruth Cameron and Seth Kasten at the Burke Library in New York, Dorothea Barfknecht and her colleagues at the Staatsbibliothek zu Berlin, and especially Cynthia Lund at the Howard and Edna Hong Kierkegaard Library in Minnesota. I also received extremely generous help from various experts in Germany, including Prof. Dr. Christiane Teitz, Enno Obendiek, and Dr. Ferdinand Schlingensiepen.

I have benefited greatly from the camaraderie of members of the Angus Library at Regent's Park College, who provided much needed discussion and distraction. In particular I would like to thank Dr. Clint Bass for his friendship and support over a number of years. Also at Regent's Park, I would like to express my gratitude to Dr. Pamela Sue Anderson for her constant advice and support throughout the project.

I am of course deeply indebted to Canon Prof. George Pattison for supervising the project, providing his gentle but incisive direction to everything I have done, correcting and editing copious reams of material and bringing out the best in my work.

Finally, I would also like to thank Dr. Joel Rasmussen for his perceptive contributions and Prof. Geffrey B. Kelly for his extremely generous support in the writing, editing, and publishing of this work.

Abbreviations

Works by Søren Kierkegaard

ACR   *Ausgewählte christliche Reden*. Translated by Julie von Reincke. Giessen: A. Topelmann, 1923

ASA   *Sören Kierkegaards agitatorische Schriften und Aufsätze: 1851 bis 1855, Sören Kierkegaards Angriff auf die Christenheit, Erster Band: Die Akten.* Translated and edited by Christoph Schrempf and August Dorner. Stuttgart: Frommanns, 1896.

AUN   *Abschliessende unwissenschaftliche Nachschrift*: Teil 2, *Gesammelte Werke* 7. Translated and edited by Christoph Schrempf. Jena: Diederichs, 1910.

BA   *Der Begriff der Angst, Gesammelte Werke* 5. Translated and edited by Christoph Schrempf. Jena: Diederich, 1923.

CA   *The Concept of Anxiety*. Translated and edited by Reidar Thomte. Kierkegaard's Writings VIII. Princeton: Princeton University Press, 1980.

CD   *Christian Discourses*. Translated and edited by Howard V. Hong and Edna H. Hong. Kierkegaard's Writings XVII. Princeton: Princeton University Press, 1997.

CI   *The Concept of Irony*. Translated and edited by Howard V. Hong and Edna H. Hong. Kierkegaard's Writings II. Princeton: Princeton University Press, 1989.

CUP   *Concluding Unscientific Postscript to "Philosophical Fragments."* 2 vols. Translated and edited by Howard V. Hong and Edna H. Hong. Kierkegaard's Writings XII. Princeton: Princeton University Press, 1992.

COR   *The Corsair Affair*. Kierkegaard's Writings XIII. Translated and edited by Howard V. Hong and Edna H. Hong. Princeton: Princeton University Press, 1982.

EC   *Einübung in Christentum, Gesammelte Werke* 9. Translated and edited by Christoph Schrempf. Jena: Diederichs, 1924.

EK	*Der Einzelne und die Kirche.* Translated and edited by Wilhelm Kütemeyer. Berlin: Kurt Wolff / Der Neue Geist, 1934.
EL	*Das Evangelium der Leiden. Christliche Reden.* Translated by Wilhelm Kütemeyer. München: Chr. Kaiser, 1933.
E/O (P)	*Either/Or.* Translated and edited by Alastair Hannay. London: Penguin, 1992.
E/O	*Either/Or: Part 1 and 2.* Translated and edited by Howard V. Hong and Edna H. Hong. Kierkegaard's Writings III–IV. Princeton: Princeton University Press, 1988.
E/O (U)	*Entweder-Oder, ein Lebensfragment.* Translated by Otto Gleiß. Dresden: Ungelenk, 1927.
EPW	*Early Polemical Writings.* Translated and edited by Julia Watkin. Kierkegaard's Writings I. Princeton: Princeton University Press, 1990.
EUD	*Eighteen Upbuilding Discourses.* Translated and edited by Howard V. Hong and Edna H. Hong. Kierkegaard's Writings V. Princeton: Princeton University Press, 1992.
FSE/JFY	*For Self-Examination/Judge For Yourself!* Translated and edited by Howard V. Hong and Edna H. Hong. Kierkegaard's Writings XXI. Princeton: Princeton University Press, 1991.
FT/R	*Fear and Trembling/Repetition.* Translated and edited by Howard V. Hong and Edna H. Hong. Kierkegaard's Writings VI. Princeton: Princeton University Press, 1983.
FT	*Fear and Trembling.* Translated by Alastair Hannay. London: Penguin, 1985.
JP	*Søren Kierkegaard's Journals and Papers.* 7 vols. Translated and edited by Howard V. Hong and Edna H. Hong. Bloomington: Indiana University Press, c. 1967–1978.
KZT	*Die Krankheit zum Tode, Gesammelte Werke* 8. Translated and edited by Christoph Schrempf. Jena: Diederich, 1911.
LD	*Letters and Documents.* Translated by Henrik Rosenmeier. Kierkegaard's Writings XXV. Princeton: Princeton University Press, 1978.
LR	*A Literary Review.* Translated by Alastair Hannay. London: Penguin, 2001.
M	*The Moment and Late Writings.* Translated and edited by Howard V. Hong and Edna H. Hong. Kierkegaard's Writings XXIII. Princeton: Princeton University Press, 1998.

Abbreviations

Pap	*Papirer*. 11 vols. Edited by P. A. Heiberg, V. Kuhr, and E. Torsting. Kiøbenhaven: Gyldendal, 1909–1948.
PC	*Practice in Christianity*. Translated and edited by Howard V. Hong and Edna H. Hong. Kierkegaard's Writings XX. Princeton: Princeton University Press, 1991.
PF/JC	*Philosophical Fragments/Johannes Climacus*. Translated and edited by Howard V. Hong and Edna H. Hong. Kierkegaard's Writings VII. Princeton: Princeton University Press, 1985.
PV	*The Point of View*. Translated and edited by Howard V. Hong and Edna H. Hong. Kierkegaard's Writings XXII. Princeton: Princeton University Press, 1998.
SLW	*Stages on Life's Way*. Translated and edited by Howerd V. Hong and Edna H. Hong. Kierkegaard's Writings XXI. Princeton: Princeton University Press, 1988.
SUD	*The Sickness Unto Death*. Translated by Alastair Hannay. London: Penguin, 1989.
SSS	*So spricht Sören Kierkegaard; aus seinen Tage- und Nächtebüchern ausgewählt*. Translated and edited by Robert Dollinger. Berlin: Furche, 1930.
T	*Die Tagebücher*. Translated and edited by Theodor Haecker. Innsbruck: Brenner, 1923
TBA	*The Book of Adler*. Translated and edited by Howard V. Hong and Edna H. Hong. Kierkegaard's Writings XXIV. Princeton: Princeton University Press, 1998.
UDVS	*Upbuilding Discourses in Various Spirits*. Translated and edited by Howard V. Hong and Edna H. Hong. Kierkegaard's Writings XV. Princeton: Princeton University Press, 1993.
WA	*Without Authority*. Translated and edited by Howard V. Hong and Edna H. Hong. Kierkegaard Writings XVIII. Princeton: Princeton University Press, 1997.
WL	*Works of Love*. Translated and edited by Howard V. Hong and Edna H. Hong. Kierkegaard's Writings XVI. Princeton: Princeton University Press, 1995.
ZFG	*Im Zwange des freien Gewissens: Gedanken über Gott und Mensch aus den Tage- und Nächtebüchern*. Translated and edited by Robert Dollinger. Berlin: Furche, 1938.

Works by Dietrich Bonhoeffer

AB   *Act and Being: Transcendental Philosophy and Ontology in Systematic Theology.* Edited by Wayne Whitson Floyd Jr. Translated by Martin Rumscheidt. DBWE 2. Minneapolis: Fortress, 1996.

B   *Berlin 1932–1933.* Edited by Larry L. Rasmussen. Translated by Isabel Best and David Higgins. DBWE 12. Minneapolis: Fortress, 2009.

BBA   *Barcelona, Berlin, New York 1928-1931.* Edited by Clifford J. Green. Translated by Reinhart Staats and Hans Christoph von Hase. DBWE 10. Minneapolis: Fortress, 2007.

C   *Christology.* Translated by John Bowden. London: Collins, 1974.

CF   *Creation and Fall: A Theological Exposition of Genesis 1–3.* Edited by John de Gruchy. Translated by Douglas Stephen Bax. DBWE 3. Minneapolis: Fortress, 1996.

CCIG   "Concerning the Christian Idea of God." *Journal of Religion* 12:2 (April 1932) 177–85.

D   *Discipleship.* Edited by Geffrey B. Kelly and John D. Godsey. Translated by Barbara Green and Reinhard Krauss. DBWE 4. Minneapolis: Fortress, 2001.

D (SCM)   *The Cost of Discipleship.* Translated by R. H. Fuller. London: SCM, 1959.

E   *Ethics.* Edited by Clifford J. Green. Translated by Reinhard Krauss, Charles C. West, and Douglas W. Scott. DBWE 6. Minneapolis: Fortress, 2005.

E (SCM)   *Ethics.* Translated by Neville Horton Smith. London: SCM, 1998.

GS   *Gesammelte Schriften* I–IV. Edited by Eberhard Bethge. Munich: Chr. Kaiser, 1958–61.

ITF   *Illegale Theologenausbildung: Finkenwalde 1935–1937.* Edited by Otto Dudzus and Jürgen Henkys, with Sabine Bobert-Stützel, Dirk Schulz, and Ilse Tödt. DBW 14. Gütersloh: Chr. Kaiser/Gütersloher, 1996.

ITS   *Illegale Theologenausbildung: Sammelvikariate 1937–1940.* Edited by Dirk Schulz. DBW 15. Gütersloh: Chr. Kaiser/Gütersloher, 1998.

L   *London 1933–1935.* Edited by Keith Clements. Translated by Isabel Best and Douglas W. Scott. DBWE 13. Minneapolis: Fortress, 2007.

LT   *Life Together/Prayerbook of the Bible.* Edited by Geffrey B. Kelly. Translated by Daniel W. Bloesch and James H. Burtness. DBWE 5. Minneapolis: Fortress, 1996.

LPP
Letters and Papers from Prison. Edited by John de Gruchy. Translated by Isabel Best, Lisa E. Dahill, Reinhard Krauss, and Nancy Lukens. DBWE 8. Minneapolis: Fortress, 2010.

LPP (SCM)
Letters and Papers from Prison. Edited by Eberhard Bethge. London: SCM, 1971.

NRS
No Rusty Swords: Letters, Lectures, and Notes, 1928–1936. Translated and edited by Edwin H. Robertson and John Bowden. London: Collins, 1965.

OUP
Ökumene, Universität, Pfarramt 1931–1932. Edited by Eberhard Amelung and Christoph Strohm. DBW 11. Gütersloh: Kaiser/ Gütersloher, 1994.

SC
Sanctorum Communio: A Theological Study of the Sociology of the Church. Edited by Clifford Green. Translated by Reinhard Krauss and Nancy Lukens. DBWE 1. Minneapolis: Fortress, 1998.

SC (K)
Sanctorum Communio: Eine dogmatische Untersuchung zur Soziologie der Kirche. Edited by Joachim von Soosten. DBW 1. Munich: Chr. Kaiser, 1986.

TF
A Testament to Freedom: The Essential Writings of Dietrich Bonhoeffer. Translated and edited by Geffrey B. Kelly and F. Burton Nelson. San Francisco: HarperSanFrancisco, 1990.

WF
The Way to Freedom: Letters, Lectures, and Notes, 1935–1939. Translated and edited by Edwin H. Robertson and John Bowden. London: Collins, 1966.

Other Works

LW
Luther's Works. 55 vols. Edited by Jaroslav Pelikan and Helmut T. Lehmann. Philidelphia: Fortress.

All works quoted from German and Danish sources are translated by the author.

Introduction

In yet a little while
I shall have won;
Then the whole fight
Will at once be done.
Then I may rest
In bowers of roses
And unceasingly, unceasingly
Speak with my Jesus.[1]

Kierkegaard, Bonhoeffer, and the Problem of Influence

KIERKEGAARD'S INFLUENCE ON BONHOEFFER HAS BEEN WIDELY RECOGNIZED BY SPECIAL-
ists of both authors. Indeed, near the beginning of his authorship Bonhoeffer twice described his own academic lineage, standing "in the tradition of Paul, Luther, Kierkegaard,
in the tradition of genuine Christian thinking."[2] And yet this recognition has occurred
exclusively in footnotes, digressions, and the occasional paper. No comprehensive study
has been conducted thus far.[3] Furthermore, the little scholarship that does exist has
been plagued by several stereotypes. First, discussion is often limited to an analysis of
Bonhoeffer's *Discipleship*. Second, Kierkegaard has been identified as an individualist and
acosmist who rejected the church. This has lead many to consider Bonhoeffer, the ecu-
menist and ecclesiologist, as selectively agreeing with Kierkegaard, but ultimately rejecting his overall stance. I will argue that neither stereotype is true. Rather I will show that
Kierkegaard's influence can be found throughout Bonhoeffer's work and that, although a
more stereotypical perspective may be present in *SC*, by the end of his life Bonhoeffer had
gained a far deeper understanding across the breadth of Kierkegaard's work.

Before beginning, I should add a certain disclaimer. The concept of "influence" is
itself deeply problematic. Without an author's direct and explicit declaration, discerning
influences must remain extremely speculative. It is not simply a matter of establishing a

---

1. The poem that adorns Kierkegaard's gravestone, by H. A. Brorson, translated from Danish by Alastair Hannay, in Hannay, *Kierkegaard*, 418.

2. *NRS*, 361; *CCIG*, 184.

3. Indeed, Peter Frick argues that the whole area of study into Bonhoeffer's influence is woefully lacking (cf. Frick, *Formation*, 2).

direct relationship, which is itself a challenge. One must contend with a whole web of possible relationships and influences. One must ask whether Bonhoeffer received Kierkegaard directly, or through other "Kierkegaardian" writers such as Barth, Bultmann, and Tillich. If Bonhoeffer did read Kierkegaard directly, was he reading through the interpretation of others or the stereotypes of the day? Furthermore, when Bonhoeffer and Kierkegaard were heavily influenced not only by Paul and Luther, but also a Herrnhut background, one needs to consider how much is direct influence and how much simply similarity.[4]

A further layer of obscurity arises in the reactions of an author to his influences. In his seminal work, *The Anxiety of Influence*, Harold Bloom suggests the potentially Freudian relationship a son has to his intellectual father(s), desiring above all else to break free and establish his own originality and, ultimately, his own self. Bloom suggests that its most common manifestation is in the son's denial or omission of the father's work from his own, mentioning him only by way of critique.

Given the limited nature of the secondary sources and the problems of influence, this work has a lot to overcome. Before looking at the primary sources themselves, I will begin by setting the scene. This will include a summary of the scholarship thus far, an examination of the evidence for Bonhoeffer's direct relationship to Kierkegaard, and an overview of the Kierkegaardian climate in which Bonhoeffer found himself.

Secondary Sources

References

A number of works discuss Kierkegaard and Bonhoeffer together without addressing their relationship to one another. As both were confirmed Lutherans who undertook a strong social and ecclesiological critique, it isn't surprising that they should be used as foils and comparisons for each other. For instance, in his overview of Bonhoeffer's work, André Dumas dedicates a chapter to the comparison of *Discipleship* and *LT* to a number of Kierkegaard's later works. Likewise, in *Beyond Religion*, Daniel Jenkins uses both Bonhoeffer and Kierkegaard as primary sources in developing his ideas on religion.

A comparison is equally used from the perspective of Kierkegaardian scholarship in relation to Kierkegaard's later works. Consequently, the *International Kierkegaard Commentary* on *FSE* and *JFY* contains two articles, by David Law and Murray Rae, which contrast Kierkegaard's ideas with Bonhoeffer's concepts of "discipleship" and "cheap grace," as well as his attack on Christendom. Indeed, both here and in his later article, "Kierkegaard's Anti-Ecclesiology," Law comes out strongly in favor of Bonhoeffer against what he perceives to be Kierkegaard's Gnostic form of Christianity. Vernard Eller, in his pietist interpretation of Kierkegaard, also makes the comparison without the connection. This is particularly surprising as he entitles two of his chapters "Religionlessness" and "Nachfolge" respectively, mentioning Bonhoeffer only enough to criticize his attack on

---

4. Although Kierkegaard research has developed an understanding of the influence of the Herrnhut movement, it receives sparse mention in the Bonhoeffer secondary literature. Two notable exceptions are: Tödt, *Authentic Faith*, 153, and Bethge, *Bonhoeffer*, 35. It is clear that a Moravian influence continued in both writers' adult lives.

Christendom as inconsistent in its claim to hold both religiousness and a high ecclesiology.[5] Similarly, Craig Hinkson describes Kierkegaard's attack on Luther's followers as having adopted "cheap grace," but does not make any reference to Bonhoeffer.[6] Stacey Ake has also written on the comparison of Kierkegaard and Bonhoeffer's more aesthetic thoughts, without making an explicit link.

From the Kierkegaardian side the link is explicitly, if briefly, made. In his abovementioned article, Murray suggests that Bonhoeffer moved towards Kierkegaard where Barth ultimately moved away. In his analysis of Kierkegaard's attack on Christendom, John Elrod also makes the connection. However, his argument is somewhat undermined in suggesting that Kierkegaard influenced the young German pastors, including Barth and Bonhoeffer, who wrote the Barmen declaration.[7]

Explicit Discussions

A handful of commentators have sought to highlight Bonhoeffer's use of Kierkegaard beyond these footnotes and allusions, presented here in chronological order.

Wenzel Lohff

The first recognizable attempt occurs in a short article from 1963, entitled "Justification and Ethics," by Wenzel Lohff. Lohff's argument is tangential, drawing on Kierkegaard in the last few paragraphs to argue that where the systematization of justification might breed moral laxness, so this was overcome through Kierkegaard, whose work "became effective, in different ways, especially through the early work of Dietrich Bonhoeffer."[8] However, Lohff's analysis extends no further than four cross-references in the footnotes concerning "cheap grace," the true nature of grace as the "result" of faith rather than its presupposition, and the need for "imitation."

Heinrich Traugott Vogel

Following Lohff's cursory attempt, Vogel is perhaps the first to offer a serious analysis of the relationship. And yet even here it occurs in a short appendix, entitled "Traces of Kierkegaard in Bonhoeffer's *Discipleship*," at the end of his doctoral thesis.

Although his focus is clearly *Discipleship*, Vogel argues that at the beginning of Bonhoeffer's authorship, "Kierkegaard was well known to him at that time, and his relationship to the developing contemporary situation."[9] Specifically, he suggests that Bonhoeffer's critique of idealism in *SC* "is recognizably parallel" to Kierkegaard's, but in the place of

---

5. Eller, *Discipleship*, 333.

6. Hinkson, "Real Martin Luther," 39.

7. John Elrod, *Christendom*, 48. Barth was Swiss and Bonhoeffer, although one of its strongest champions, did not write the Barmen Declaration.

8. Lohff, "Rechtfertigung," 317.

9. Vogel, "Christus," 297.

Kierkegaard's "rejection of the idea of the church," Bonhoeffer uses "the I-Thou school of thought" to establish the community.[10]

Turning to *Discipleship*, Vogel briefly discusses Bonhoeffer's description of the movements of faith, the need for a "first step" on the part of the individual, and so the reversal of the Lutheran conception of works following on from faith. Vogel argues that Bonhoeffer's argument is decidedly weak on this point as he is not so much thinking for himself but injecting Kierkegaard's argument into his.[11]

From a textual analysis (Bonhoeffer's library was not available to him) Vogel argues that there are strong similarities between *Discipleship* and Wilhelm Kütemeyer's collection of Kierkegaard's journals, *EK*, specifically concerning such terms as the "first step," "cheap grace," and the life of the "extraordinary."[12]

However, Vogel is also very keen to point out the differences between Bonhoeffer and Kierkegaard, and in a brief and condensed paragraph he offers three points. First, Vogel argues that Bonhoeffer's Christology, of Christ as "*lex pro nobis impleta*," stands against Kierkegaard's "ethics of imitation," which is in effect "the realization of a derelict ideal."[13] Secondly, he argues that against Kierkegaard's individualism, Bonhoeffer forges a church community through imitation of Christ in his truly human nature. Finally, Vogel argues that against Kierkegaard's attacks on Paul, Bonhoeffer held together the objective identities of both the Gospel and apostolic announcements.

Unfortunately, Vogel does not expand or clarify these brief and fragmentary descriptions. But it is clear that he rests his views on the individualist stereotype of Kierkegaard. While it is unclear how Kierkegaard ends up attacking Paul, and fails to balance the Gospel New Testament witness, I will further argue that the concept of Christ as "*pro nobis*" and the rejection of ethical abstraction are central to Kierkegaard's ethics of imitation.

Ernst Feil

Feil discusses Kierkegaard in a number of footnotes, particularly in reference to *Discipleship*. Feil's understanding appears to come from both Lohff and Vogel, and he adds a list of the various catchphrases he believes Bonhoeffer took directly from Kierkegaard, such as "immediacy," "result," "direct assault," "extraordinary," "imitation," "situation," "cloister," and "either/or." Furthermore, Feil identifies in *Discipleship* an "anti-worldly" theme (in contrast to the "worldliness" of *LPP*) and argues that this "might not have been conceived without Kierkegaard's influence."[14] Sadly, many of these references have been cut from the English version of Feil's work, and are only found in the original.

10. Ibid.

11. Ibid, 298.

12. *JP*, 1142/*Pap*, X4 A 114; *EK*, 158—strangely, concerning the "first step" Vogel does not make the link with *JFY* where this concept is most clearly expounded.

13. Vogel, "Christus," 303.

14. Feil, *Theologie*, 277 n. 39.

Geffrey B. Kelly

Geffrey B. Kelly has conducted the most consistent work on Kierkegaard and Bonhoeffer. In his 1972 doctoral dissertation, Kelly briefly analyzes the relationship alongside Bonhoeffer's other philosophical influences, including Kant, Hegel, Nietzsche, Feuerbach, and Troeltsch. This was followed up two years later with a short article in the *Irish Theological Quarterly* entitled, "The Influence of Kierkegaard on Bonhoeffer's Concept of Discipleship." Finally, Kelly considerably expanded these earlier thoughts in his contribution to *Bonhoeffer's Intellectual Formation*. Throughout these works Kelly draws on a wide range of Kierkegaard texts and, although focusing on the concept of discipleship, covers a number of other topics. These focus heavily on both authors' perceptions of Luther, but also their mutual appreciation of the "two Kingdoms," the issue of "cheap grace," the need for "simple obedience," the nature of discipleship as "imitation," and the concept of the "extraordinary."

While many of these themes have been observed by other commentators, Kelly is perhaps the first to have suggested the influence of Kierkegaard's Christology on both *Discipleship* and Bonhoeffer's Christology lectures.[15] Furthermore, Kelly looks beyond the stereotypical differences between Kierkegaard's individualism and Bonhoeffer's concept of community to highlight the Kierkegaardian theme of solitude and isolation standing behind Bonhoeffer's *Gemeinschaft*.[16] Indeed, much of Kelly's analysis revolves around Kierkegaard and Bonhoeffer's interactions with the church and their cultural and ecclesiological critiques. Kelly draws on Jenkins' work to argue for the association of the "knight of faith" with Bonhoeffer's "non-religious Christianity" and his understanding of the church in "realizing the universally human."[17]

Kelly's dissertation is thoroughly researched and includes in the index an interview with Eberhard Bethge in which Bethge refers Kelly to Vogel's dissertation and the direct influence of *EK* on *Discipleship*—in particular the concept of "cheap grace."[18] Kelly was able to look through Bonhoeffer's own copy of *EK* to analyze his markings and states, "It is now certain that Bonhoeffer was not only strongly influenced by Søren Kierkegaard in developing *The Cost of Discipleship*, but also that he used Kierkegaard's *Der Einzelne und die Kirche . . .* as a direct source."[19]

Kelly's analysis is not uncritical, and expounds on the various explicit criticizms that Bonhoeffer himself makes of Kierkegaard's thought. However, Kelly believes that Bonhoeffer was deeply impressed by Kierkegaard, grasping hold of his concepts and extending them.[20] Despite their differences, Bonhoeffer saw in Kierkegaard a thinker after his own heart.[21]

---

15. Kelly, "Kierkegaard as 'Antidote,'" 156f.

16. Ibid., 158.

17. Kelly, "Revelation in Christ," 56f.

18. Ibid., Appendix II, 33f; cf. 309 nn. 63, 64.

19. Ibid., 310 n. 64.

20. Cf. Kelly, "Kierkegaard as 'Antidote,'" 152, 155, 160.

21. Ibid., 150.

Kelly's articles and chapters cover much the same ground and are extremely condensed. However, he shows a far greater knowledge and appreciation of Kierkegaard than other commentators, and many of his insights will be drawn upon in the following analysis.

Jörg Alfred Rades

In the 1980s a doctorate was begun at the University of Aberdeen by Jörg Rades, analyzing Bonhoeffer's various intellectual influences. Alongside Luther, Hegel, Nietzsche, and metaethics more generally, it included a chapter on Kierkegaard. Tragically, in March 1989 Rades died of cancer before the completion of his thesis, leaving behind various draft manuscripts, which are now held in the Bonhoeffer Archive at the Burke Library in New York. Although the chapter on Kierkegaard is a second draft, it is far from complete. Therefore, the analysis Rades' work receives here is prefaced by the acknowledgment that his thoughts were very much a work in progress.

Rades provides one of the broadest analyses of the relationship of our two subjects. His chapter considers eleven key passages from across Bonhoeffer's work. Sadly, the draft is only half complete, and includes the preliminary textual analysis but not the final discussion of "the relation between the philosopher and the theologian Bonhoeffer in a more conceptual form," that he describes in its introduction. Consequently, Rades' opening question concerning how much one can really know about this relationship remains unanswered. From the general tone of these eleven sections, one suspects that his answer would either have been "not very much," or at least that Bonhoeffer knew, but substantially rejected or altered, Kierkegaard's thought.

As it stands, the draft is somewhat superficial in its analysis. This is perhaps inevitable in attempting to treat this relationship in such a short piece. However, it is also present in Rades' reading of Kierkegaard, which is derived exclusively from secondary sources. Unfortunately, this leads Rades into painting a Kierkegaardian caricature, epitomized by an acosmic, individualistic thought that not only denies the church but actively works against it. Rades may well have gone on to overcome this problem. But, in its present state, Rades' thesis reveals once again the stereotype that is so easily applied to Kierkegaard, which this book seeks to overcome.

David H. Hopper

In a paper presented to the AAR conference in November 1989, and its brief summary in the article, "Metanoia: Bonhoeffer on Kierkegaard," David Hopper provides a relatively diverse treatment of our subject. Although his analysis is once again centered on *Discipleship*, Hopper also describes the context of this relationship by looking at Bonhoeffer's use of Kierkegaard in his earliest works, as well as in his final *LPP*.

Hopper's main aim is to criticize Bethge's suggestion that ideologically Bonhoeffer's work is essentially consistent, divided only by a profound conversion experience in 1931 shortly after his return from America.[22] In contrast, Hopper argues that "Bonhoeffer's

22. Cf. Bethge, *Bonhoeffer*, 202–6.

thought is at best described as episodic, driven by certain personalistic concerns that make that thought fragmentary and something less than persuasive."[23] Furthermore, he argues that the real transition in Bonhoeffer's thought occured much later during his imprisonment, epitomized in his reflection,

> I thought I myself could learn to have faith by trying to live something like a saintly life. I suppose I wrote *Discipleship* at the end of this path. Today I clearly see the dangers of that book, though I still stand by it. Later on I discovered, and am still discovering to this day, that one only learns to have faith by living in the full this-worldliness of life. (*LPP*, 486)

Hopper argues that the divide is between a pious, religious striving on the one hand (epitomized in *Discipleship* and a legalistic adherence to pacifism) and a worldly drive on the other, defined by a form of natural theology (as found in *LPP* and his active resistance). Hopper argues that the first stage was created through the influence of Kierkegaard (specifically on *Discipleship*), and therefore the second by Bonhoeffer's rejection of him.

Hopper references *EK* (through Vogel), and suggests that its emphasis on the "later Kierkegaard" and his attack on Christendom was particularly important in influencing Bonhoeffer's striving for the "holy life."[24] Hopper argues that before *Discipleship*, "one finds a few scattered references [to Kierkegaard] but that is all,"[25] all of which come from a vague familiarity through secondary sources, and deal "largely with Kierkegaardian generalities."[26] Indeed, Hopper declares, "there is no evidence of a first hand reading of Kierkegaard in either the *Communion of Saints* (1972) or *Act and Being* (1930)."[27] Furthermore, Hopper suggests that although Bonhoeffer may have read *FT*, his treatment of it is entirely uncritical and fails to appreciate its nuances.[28] After *Discipleship*, Kierkegaard is dropped and finds no place in his *Ethics* other than as the general forefather of situationist ethics.[29] Therefore, Bonhoeffer's use of the late Kierkegaard during *Discipleship* is essentially an uncritical flash in the pan that led to thoughts he later regretted. Indeed, Hopper argues that had Bonhoeffer read Kierkegaard more widely and carefully, he would not have been led into what he describes as the exclusive, acosmic, "ghetto mentality" of *Discipleship*,[30] nor the natural-theological "world come of age" of *LPP*, both of which Kierkegaard criticized.[31]

This book disagrees with the majority of Hopper's arguments concerning the content and scope of Bonhoeffer's familiarity with Kierkegaard, as well as Hopper's overall interpretation of both authors. Hopper's central attack on Bonhoeffer's consistency is par-

---

23. Hopper, "Metanoia," 71.

24. Cf. Hopper, "Kierkegaard Question," 9. However, certain concerns already open up concerning Hopper's familiarity and reading of Kierkegaard as he includes such works as *SUD* in his description of the "early Kierkegaard."

25. Ibid., 13.

26. Ibid., 14.

27. Ibid., 70.

28. Ibid., 11ff.

29. Ibid., 42.

30. Ibid., 33.

31. Hopper, "Metanoia," 73.

ticularly problematic, and significantly overplays Bonhoeffer's above-quoted reflection on *Discipleship* from *LPP*, and the discrepancy concerning his "pacifism." Hopper refers to Bonhoeffer's "later view," of the need to be a spoke in the wheel of the state to bring it to a halt, as standing in opposition to the earlier pacifist thoughts of *Discipleship*.[32] However, the "spoke" analogy was first coined in Bonhoeffer's paper, "The Church and the Jewish Question," written in 1933, four years before the publication of *Discipleship* (*NRS*, 225). Furthermore, the ideas that preclude the legalistic adherence to any ethical principle, so clearly present in *Ethics* and *LPP*, were already outlined in the paper, "Basic Questions of a Christian Ethic" written in 1929. These examples alone significantly undermine Hopper's argument and point towards a certain unifying coherence in Bonhoeffer's work. Furthermore, as will be discussed in chapter 3, the need to overcome his pious self-control concerned Bonhoeffer throughout his life. Not only does Bonhoeffer affirm the content of *Discipleship* in this passage from *LPP*, so suggesting that it is not the transition Hopper suggests, but one gets the sense that every time Bonhoeffer looked back on his life he saw this pious striving. As will be discussed in Chapters 6 and 7, when the end of human striving is an "unconscious discipleship," every act viewed in retrospect is pious self-control.

Ann L. Nickson

In *Bonhoeffer on Freedom*, Nickson's analysis of Kierkegaard and Bonhoeffer is something of a digression. Indeed, the point is not to analyze Kierkegaard at all, but rather to attack Hopper's paper to the AAR, as falsely perpetrating the "myth of individualism" surrounding *Discipleship*. However, Nickson shows clear knowledge of the debate, referencing Rades, Kelly's short *ITQ* article, as well as Hopper. In debunking Hopper, therefore, Nickson argues that Kierkegaard was not the "flash in the pan" at the time of writing *Discipleship* that Hopper makes out, but also that Bonhoeffer showed a critical and developed appreciation from the time of *SC* onwards.

Stephen J. Plant

At the beginning of *Bonhoeffer*, Plant analyzes some of Bonhoeffer's main influences, including Kierkegaard. However, in this brief treatment, Plant presents a rather negative account of the relationship. As he comments, "Bonhoeffer rarely discusses Kierkegaard's writings at any length and the precise role and significance of Kierkegaard for Bonhoeffer is therefore moot. In particular, commentators are not agreed whether Bonhoeffer had grasped Kierkegaard's thought thoroughly or superficially."[33]

While seriously acknowledging the difficulty of the term "influence," I will paint a more hopeful picture. Plant discusses Bonhoeffer's qualified appropriation of the "teleological suspension of the ethical," and Bonhoeffer's criticizms that Kierkegaard places the individual higher than the community. However, Plant never gets beyond *SC* in his analysis, and consequently concludes that, like Barth, Bonhoeffer was interested in Kierkegaard's work during his youth, but ultimately left him there.

32. Hopper, "Kierkegaard Question," 32.

33. Plant, *Bonhoeffer*, 46.

The Direct Relationship

Bonhoeffer's Direct References

A first port of call when seeking to discern the "direct relationship" is to analyze the works that Bonhoeffer actually cites. One of the great problems of discerning Kierkegaard's influence, is that Bonhoeffer only references three of his texts: *FT*, *WL*, and *SUD*.

Fear and Trembling/Repetition

In a footnote near the end of *SC*, Bonhoeffer rejects Calvin's basis for excommunication as neither Abraham nor Hosea would have escaped. As evidence, Bonhoeffer references *FT* (*SC*, 258 n. 130). However, earlier on, while discussing solitude as the foundation of community and the whole created order, Bonhoeffer offers the footnote, "Kierkegaard, who knew how to speak of the burden of loneliness like few others, comes out from there to the rejection of the idea of the church (cf. *Furcht und Zittern*, Diederichs, p. 171). 'As soon as the single one [*Einzelne*] has entered the paradox, he does not arrive at the idea of the church' (p. 106)" (*SC (K)*, 104 n. 20 (*SC*, 162 n. 20)—author's translation).[34]

Coupled together, these references would suggest a direct and intimate knowledge of *FT*. It will certainly be argued later that this is one of the key texts that remained in Bonhoeffer's mind throughout his life. However, there are grounds for questioning how critically Bonhoeffer actually understood the text at this point in his authorship. First, as the editors of *DBW* rightly comment, Bonhoeffer's page references are not actually correct. The second should read p. 67 rather than 106, and the first leads to a seemingly unrelated passage in the second work of the combined volume, *Repetition*. Secondly, Bonhoeffer's commentary on Kierkegaard is curious. In the passage Bonhoeffer cites, Kierkegaard makes no comment on "the concept of the church," let alone its rejection. His point is that in the movement of faith, the individual is alone before God, and cannot defer this responsibility out of obedience to the church. In context, it could be suggested that Kierkegaard's argument is that the individual owes an absolute duty towards God, and only a relative one towards the church. This is Bonhoeffer's own argument in *SC* where he describes the absolute authority of the Word of God in conflict with the relative authority of the church (*SC*, 251).

Works of Love

While arguing that the "person who loves God must, by God's will, really love the neighbor," Bonhoeffer offers an extended footnote critiquing Barth's notion of love that Bonhoeffer argues makes the neighbor a tool through which the individual loves God. After using Bultmann in support of his own ideas, and then returning once again to Barth, Bonhoeffer adds the somewhat ambiguous comment, "Regarding the entire argument see Kierkegaard, *Works of Love*" (169 n. 28). It is therefore unclear whether Bonhoeffer associates Kierkegaard positively with his own argument or negatively with that of Barth. Although Kelly suggests

---

34. The page numbers refer to Schrempf's 1909 *Gesammelte Werke* edition.

the latter,[35] it could be argued that Bonhoeffer is aligning himself with Kierkegaard, noting the source of his own argument only at the end, as he did with his attack on idealism earlier in *SC*. Kierkegaard's notion of God as the "middle term" of love in *WL*, standing between the individual and his neighbor, is in clear distinction to Bonhoeffer's reading of Barth (cf. *WL*, 106–7, 260). For Kierkegaard, the individual cannot truly love his neighbor, but in loving God is brought into love for the neighbor. The individual therefore loves the neighbor with God's love, rather than the idealistic love created through his own mind and emotions. This stands in strong agreement with Bonhoeffer's notion of "mediation," as described in such places as *SC*, *Discipleship*, and *LT*, as the necessary term through which idealistic love is overcome (cf. *SC*, 168; *D*, 92–99; *LT*, 10–15). Furthermore, in *FT*, in the paragraph before Bonhoeffer's quotation (as cited above), Kierkegaard's argument rests on the reality of Abraham's love of Isaac (*FT*, 101). Consequently, the paradoxical tension of Abraham's love for God and Isaac stands in agreement with Bonhoeffer's own argument.

The Sickness Unto Death

The final reference appears in Bonhoeffer's lecture series on "Theological Psychology," delivered in the Winter Semester of 1932/33 (*B*, 214–32). Although his original texts have been lost, its overall content can be seen from his students' notes. To the question, "Is reflection already mankind's fall?" Bonhoeffer offers five different answers of which the last is, "The sinner and transgressions (*desperatio* in Luther and Kierkegaard)—dichotomy and trichotomy in Paul—the individual and individuality—Schelling—Kierkegaard" (215). The lecture, entitled "Sin and Transgression," delivered on 8 February 1933, compares Kierkegaard's concept of despair, sin, consciousness, and existence to that of Luther. Although it is unclear from these sparse and incomplete notes who was more favorably considered (although one suspects Bonhoeffer presented an amalgamation of the two) Bonhoeffer reveals a seemingly critical understanding of *SUD* across the breadth of its various arguments (228f.).

Bonhoeffer's Library

As a background to these references, Bonhoeffer owned an extensive collection of Kierkegaard's works. Following his death, Bonhoeffer's library was given to Eberhard Bethge, and its contents compiled by Dietrich Meyer in cooperation with Bethge in the volume, *Nachlass Dietrich Bonhoeffer*. However, since 1996, his library has resided in the *Staatsbibliothek* in Berlin. Bonhoeffer made numerous underlinings and marginal lines throughout these works, alongside the occasional annotation. Again, although the details of these books will be dealt with in the appropriate chapters, their overall scope will be discussed here.

---

35. Kelly, "Kierkegaard as 'Antidote,'" 161–63; "Influence of Kierkegaard," 152.

Concluding Unscientific Postscript, Part 2 (Gesammelte Werke 7)

Part two of the *Gesammelte Werke* version of *CUP* begins in Chapter III of Section II entitled, "Actual Subjectivity, Ethical Subjectivity; the Subjective Thinker." Bonhoeffer's marks are consistently frequent throughout the first two sections of this chapter, picking up particularly on the issues of Hegel and the confrontation between pure thinking and existence, underlining such phrases as "an individual existing human being" (*AUN*, 12; *CUP*, 313), "pure thinking is a phantom" (*AUN*, 13; *CUP*, 314), the desire for "diversion" (*AUN*, 21; *CUP*, 232), and the distinction between the "particular" and the "universal" (*AUN*, 24; *CUP*, 326). Bonhoeffer also pays particular attention to Kierkegaard's definition of existence as investment and risk, and its relationship to faith. Although the marks become less frequent from this point on, they appear at steady intervals until the end of the work, particularly when Kierkegaard discusses such topics as the distinction between the individual and the mass (*AUN*, 51; *CUP*, 355), the difference between Christianity and doctrine (*AUN*, 74; *CUP*, 379), the concept of inwardness and the "life-view" (*AUN*, 125–6; *CUP*, 434–5), the nature of the individual before God (*AUN*, 158; *CUP*, 469), the three stages of life (*AUN*, 187; *CUP*, 501), and the concept of the comic (*AUN*, 198; *CUP*, 513).

The Concept of Anxiety (Gesammelte Werke 5)

There are a few marks within this volume that may not be from Bonhoeffer's own hand. However, his distinctively heavy, dark pencil marks can be found throughout the book, with numerous margin lines and underlining present on almost every page, suggesting his particular appreciation of this work.

The Sickness Unto Death (Gesammelte Werke 8)

There are a small number of marks throughout this work, beginning in Part I, Section B, where Kierkegaard describes despair as the root of selfhood, and so the greatest providence (*KZT*, 23; *SUD*, 56). Bonhoeffer then marks the beginning of section C and the description of the nature of the individual's despair and willfulness as defined through his self-consciousness (*KZT*, 26; *SUD*, 59). This is followed shortly after by the concept of silence promoting both despair and inwardness (*KZT*, 31; *SUD*, 64). Bonhoeffer's marks reappear at the beginning of Part Two, Section A, where Kierkegaard describes despair as sin, and its presence within the escapism of the poet-existence (*KZT*, 72; *SUD*, 109).

Practice in Christianity (Gesammelte Werke 9)

Of the three parts to *PC*, Bonhoeffer's markings appear throughout Part I and II, as well as sections I and II of Part III. From this point on (page 179 onwards) there are no further markings and the pages appear pristine and unbent, suggesting perhaps that they remain unread.

However, while not as frequent as in *CA*, in the earlier sections the marks appear regularly. They show Bonhoeffer's particular interest in Kierkegaard's Christology, for instance the earthly and historical nature of Christ in his abasement (*EC*, 18, 133; *PC*, 24, 154), his identity as the extraordinary in servitude (*EC*, 36; *PC*, 42), and the image of the sorrowful Christ (*EC*, 85; *PC*, 99). In terms of discipleship, Bonhoeffer marks such issues as offence (cf. *EC*, 34, 96; *PC*, 39, 110), the need for contemporaneity with Christ (*EC*, 31; *PC*, 37), the path of suffering (*EC*, 94–95; *PC*, 108–9), and the message and presence of Christ freely drawing the follower in (cf. *EC*, 132; *PC*, 153). Furthermore, Bonhoeffer notes the blasphemy of the triumphant preaching and message of the church (cf. *EC*, 93; *PC*, 107).

Entweder-Oder

Although *E/O* is within the Bonhoeffer library, it appears to have been a gift from Bonhoeffer to Bethge himself, inscribed at the front, "E. Bethge von D. Bonhoeffer Dez. 1935," and includes several markings near the end by Bethge. However, that Bonhoeffer should have given Bethge this work is itself significant towards Bonhoeffer's appreciation of it. Furthermore, two potential references to it are found at the very beginning and end of his authorship: in "Jesus Christ and the Essence of Christianity," delivered in Barcelona in December 1928, Bonhoeffer argues that Christ demands that "we commit to him in an abrupt either-or" (*BBNY*, 342); in *LPP* Bonhoeffer comments on Kierkegaard's concept of the aesthetic life (*LPP*, 268).

Das Evangelium der Leiden—Christliche Reden

Within this short volume, the section that caught Bonhoeffer's particular attention is entitled, "The Joy of It That The School of Sufferings Educates for Eternity." As a meditation on Heb 5:8—"Although he was a son, he learned obedience from what he suffered"— Bonhoeffer makes four marks, highlighting three of the latter paragraphs. These concern the relationship between faith, obedience, and suffering. In particular, Bonhoeffer marks Kierkegaard's concluding summary, focusing on the Christology of his chosen verse, and the necessity of our appreciation of Christ's nature in abasement: divine and yet truly learning through his obedience and suffering.

Ausgewählte christliche Reden

ACR contains extracts of the first two parts of *CD*. The first, "Anxieties of the Heathens," contains all sections apart from the fifth form of anxiety: "The anxiety of Self-Torment." The second, "states of Mind in the Strife of Suffering," includes the first three sections as well as the fifth. Of particular interest is the Appendix: "Søren Kierkegaard's Family and Private Life: original extracts from the once only printed manuscript and, therefore, little known Danish writings of Søren Kierkegaard's niece, Miss H (K) Lund." None of Bonhoeffer's other books appear to contain any substantially biographical details of Kierkegaard's life. It is significant, therefore, that he should have had access to these details, in particular through Henriette Lund, whose testimony reveals a far more tender and personal side to Kierkegaard's life than that expressed through his many commentators. However, there are no markings within this volume.

Der Einzelne und die Kirche

This volume contains a selection of Kierkegaard's journal entries by Wilhelm Kütemeyer, from across the breadth of his life, as well as editions one and nine of *The Moment*. Apart from this final section, *EK* contains a number of markings spread sporadically through-out. Although fewer in number to some of the other volumes (such as *CA* and *PC*), many of the markings reveal a stronger impression on Kierkegaard, signified by double lines in the margin as well as frequent single or even double exclamation marks. The issues that particularly stood out for Bonhoeffer were the misrepresentation of Luther (cf. *EK*, 132; *JP*, 2542/*Pap*, X4 A 451), the transformation of Christianity away from imitation into secularization and the misunderstanding of church and state relations (cf. *EK*, 131, 136, 143, 144; *JP*, 1908/X4 A 459, 4209/X4 A 126, 2760/X4 A 531, 1912/X4 A 500), the conversion of Christ into idea and doctrine (*EK*, 145; *JP*, 1904/*Pap*, X4 A 354), and therefore the untruthful proclamation of the church (*EK*, 53; *JP*, 660/*Pap*, IX A 198).

Die Tagebücher

Die Tagebücher is a two-volume collection of Kierkegaard's journals by Theodor Haecker. It contains no markings.

Sören Kierkegaards agitatorische Schriften und Aufsätze: 1851 bis 1855

This is a large and extremely comprehensive collection of Kierkegaard's later works edited by Christoph Schrempf, and includes *FSE* and *JFY*, all of Kierkegaard's overtly autobio-graphical works including *PV*, *The Individual*, *About my Work as an Author*, and even "A First and Last Explanation," taken from the end of *CUP*, as well as all ten editions of *The Moment*. However, perhaps most impressively, it contains all of Kierkegaard's newspaper articles, starting with "[An open letter] [O]n the occasion of a statement about me by Dr. Rudelbach" in 1851, and includes the responses made by Bishop Martensen, Rasmus Nielsen, and various anonymous writers. A small number of marks can be found in *About my Work as an Author*, *FSE*, and *The Moment* 4.[36] However, in part two of *JFY* we find a large number of markings. These concentrate on such issues as Kierkegaard's ideas on the impact of the Middle Ages and the corruption of Luther's thought (*ASA*, 571; *JFY*, 192), the juxtaposition of the Monastery and solitude (*ASA*, 549; *JFY*, 169), the similarities between the monk and the present day professor as the extraordinary (*ASA*, 574; *JFY*, 195), the fundamental position of imitation and heterogeneity with the world (*ASA*, 570; *JFY*, 191), and the relationship between faith and obedience (*ASA*, 570; *JFY*, 191).

Bonhoeffer and Germany's Kierkegaard

As discussed, this thesis will argue that by the end of his life Bonhoeffer had gained a deep, personal understanding of Kierkegaard. However, it is important also to understand the image of Kierkegaard presented at the time that may have either directed Bonhoeffer

---

36. Contrary to the comment in *Nachlass Dietrich Bonhoeffer* that they occur only later in the volume, from 549ff. (Bethge, *Nachlass*, 219).

towards Kierkegaard, or even colored his own interpretation of him. Little can be directly known as the only secondary source we know Bonhoeffer read was Heinrich Barth's article, "Kierkegaard der Denker," whose interpretation he critiques in *SC*.[37] However, Bonhoeffer's own library offers us some important insights.

By the turn of the century, the German-speaking world had been exposed to various different "Kierkegaards." In 1871, Kierkegaard's old adversary, H. L. Martensen, published his *Christian Ethics* in German, in which he offers a guarded affirmation of Kierkegaard's individualism, but vehemently refutes the religious and ecclesiological application Kierkegaard had given it.[38] In the 1870s Georg Brandes sought to remove the spiritual elements of Kierkegaard's works to appropriate him for secular humanism.[39] Again, in 1896 Harold Høffding's influential *Sören Kierkegaard als Philosoph* placed Kierkegaard firmaly within the field of philosophy, even though disagreeing with both Martensen and Brandes. However, according to Malik, Høffding presented Kierkegaard through a subjectivity that merged into a form of subjectivisim.[40] During this time, it was perhaps only Pastor Albert Bärthold, who provided some of the first German translations of Kierkegaard's work, who sought to emphasize Kierkegaard as a religious thinker, specifically through the concept of "personality" [*persönlichkeit*].

Despite the various angles interpreters had taken, according to Malik's exhaustive survey, by the turn of the twentieth century Kierkegaard had become known in particular through a heavy individualism and subjectivism. This context is extremely relevant to our study, and will prove particularly significant in our analysis of *SC* and its more stereotyped portrayal of Kierkegaard. However, as Bonhoeffer read more of Kierkegaard's works, it was the editors of these volumes who provided a more direct influence than the above-mentioned commentators.

Christoph Schrempf

Many of the Kierkegaard works Bonhoeffer owned were edited and translated by Christoph Schrempf. Not only was he the editor of *ASA*, but also the predominant translator and the editor of the first *Gesammelte Werke* series.

Schrempf is somewhat infamous within the history of Kierkegaard scholarship. Indeed, Malik goes so far to describe him as a "spiritually confused and intellectually unstable man,"[41] "ostentatious, self-centered, and prolific, especially in his writing about himself,"[42] whose influence on Kierkegaard studies was "deplorable."[43] It is universally recognized that his translations are blighted by inaccuracies and omissions, colored by his

---

37. Cf. *SC*, 42 n. 6.

38. Malik, *Receiving Kierkegaard*, 222.

39. Ibid., 230.

40. Ibid., 331.

41. Ibid., 337.

42. Ibid., 311.

43. Ibid., 313.

own interpretation and disposition, and smothered in his own inciteful comments and notes.

As Schrempf reveals in his introduction to *ASA*, it was through reading Kierkegaard that he was "compelled to settle accounts with myself and the church, whereby I first had to throw off my parish, and in addition was then also impelled to revoke my confirmation vow as a misunderstanding."[44] Indeed, Malik argues that "the Schrempf Affair" proved to be something of a well-known scandal at the time.[45] Given this personal commitment, it is not surprising that Schrempf gave particular emphasis to Kierkegaard's later writings and his attack on Christendom. Indeed, Schrempf suggests that *ASA* is really an opportunity to showcase *The Moment* in its wider context.[46] Schrempf argues that Kierkegaard's "methods and methodology of moral-religious thinking and work" are important for Germany's present context, particularly in terms of the "problem of the truth-witness."[47] However, he declares that Kierkegaard did not go far enough in his deconstructive attack as he "simply accepted Christian belief or Christian understanding as given."[48] For Schrempf, Kierkegaard's attack needs to be taken to its logical conclusion to challenge the very existence of Christendom and the Christian truths to which it holds. Although he refuses to say any more on how this might happen, he urges his readers to go beyond Kierkegaard's desires and to stop only with what "Governance" actually wanted from him.[49]

In further clarifying his position Schrempf goes through the previous Kierkegaardian literature. Here he aligns himself strongly with the religious interpretation of Bärthold against Brandes whose aesthetic interpretation he argues is a total misunderstanding. Finally, he also suggests his agreement with the "penetrating and sympathetic study" by Høffding who he believes also appreciated Kierkegaard's relationship to Christianity against Brandes' aestheticism.[50]

As described, Schrempf was extremely influential for Kierkegaard's reception at the beginning of the twentieth century. And his radically anti-clerical stance was promoted through other commentators such as the Catholic philosopher, essayist, cultural critical, and physiognomist, Rudolf Kassner who, influenced in particular by Schrempf's *ASA* and his translation of *CA*, wrote several high-profile pieces discussing the provocative relation of "*der Einzelne*" to Christendom.[51]

44. Schrempf, "Einleitung," xvi.

45. Malik, Receiving *Kierkegaard*, 332.

46. Schrempf, "Einleitung," xvi–xvii.

47. Ibid., xiii.

48. Ibid., xv.

49. Ibid., xvi.

50. Ibid., xxii–xxiii.

51. Malik, *Receiving Kierkegaard*, 357–60.

Theodor Haecker

Theodor Haecker was first introduced to Kierkegaard through such figures as Schrempf and Høffding.[52] However, as his knowledge of Kierkegaard grew he became frustrated with these earlier writers. Indeed, in his later biography of Kierkegaard, Haecker shows a basic contempt for Brandes, Høffding, and Schrempf.[53] Consequently, Haecker embarked on his own translations. One of these was *Die Tagebücher* that Bonhoeffer owned.

Early in his career, Haecker emphasized Kierkegaard's concept of "inwardness" (*Innerlichkeit*) and saw in Kierkegaard a profound social and ecclesiological critic for his time.[54] This perspective gained enormous influence through his publication of the third section of *LR*, "The Present Age," under the title *Kritik der Gegenwart*, just two weeks before the beginning of the First World War. This was backed up by a fiery "Nachwort" that drew stark parallels between Kierkegaard's works and Germany's current situation, and published in the influential journal, *Der Brenner*.[55]

Over time, however, Haecker's views began to change.[56] This was particularly influenced through translating *TBA* as well as the work of Cardinal Newman. In contrast to his earlier fire, Haecker began to see Kierkegaard's attack as not so much directed at the church itself, but rather its relationship to the state. Consequently, in the "Nachwort" to *TBA*, and particularly in his later biography, Haecker recanted of previous statements that undermined the nature and authority of the church.

In his forward to *Die Tagebücher*, published six years later, something of this shift can be seen. Haecker reveals the central theme of his selection to be Kierkegaard's attack but couched in its proper context to mediate its shocking harshness. As he comments, his most important aim is to "allow the continuity of Kierkegaard's spiritual [*geistigen*] development to become visible, to let him give a picture of the slow, steady, but unceasing growth of the weather clouds, which led to the catastrophe and which neither the contemporaries, nor we, see as such from the main works, so that the flash and thunder would not be a sudden surprise."[57] Malik goes so far as to suggest that Haecker's selection is an attempt to harmonize Kierkegaard and Newman.[58]

In 1921 Haecker finally converted to Catholicism, the same year *Die Tagebücher* was published. Despite Haecker's attempts to alter the perception of Kierkegaard, it was his earlier work that had influenced the "Brenner Circle," and in particular Carl Dallago, a "self-styled Nietzschean poet-turned-social-critic," who had co-founded the journal.[59] Malik suggests that Dallago became somewhat obsessed with Kierkegaard, and in particular his attack on the church. Consequently, as Haecker backed away, Dallago became

---

52. Ibid., 377.

53. Cf. Haecker, *Søren Kierkegaard*, 9, 49, 57.

54. Cf. Janik, "Haecker," 195ff.

55. Commentators have suggested that *Der Brenner*'s subscribers included Jaspers, Heidegger, Husserl, Buber (Malik, *Receiving Kierkegaard*, 387, 391–92), Wittgenstein, and Adorno (Janik, "Haecker," 219–20).

56. Janik, "Haecker," 193; Malik, *Receiving Kierkegaard*, 382ff; Dru, "Introduction," xiii.

57. Haecker, "Vorwort," v.

58. Malik, *Receiving Kierkegaard*, 385.

59. Janik, "Haecker," 192.

firmer in his stance, publishing his opinion of the church as a "murderess" in the same year as Haecker's conversion,[60] and a year later conducting an attack on the Catholic Church.[61]

It is also worth mentioning that Haecker was known for his academic contribution, but also his activism against the Nazi regime. Not only had he strong connections with the resistance and the "White Rose" movement, with which it has been suggested Bonhoeffer was also personally familiar,[62] but he had been banned from public speaking from the moment Hitler had taken power.[63] It may be that this had an effect, not simply on Bonhoeffer's appreciation of Haecker as a Kierkegaard interpreter, but also as an example of how Kierkegaard's influence might be acted out.

Wilhelm Kütemeyer

In Malik's account, Kütemeyer receives only passing attention as something of a great pretender. Malik describes how Kütemeyer reaped Haecker's anger in translating *CI* before he could, and adds the comment that Kütemeyer "wanted to imitate Haecker and become the principle transmitter of Kierkegaard into German."[64] Certainly, in the introduction to *EK*, Kütemeyer is disparaging of Haecker's selection in *Die Tagebücher*, arguing that his own in *EK* is partly to "correct the false impression aroused intentionally or unintentionally in Haecker's choice."[65] However, Kütemeyer attacks outright the whole Kierkegaardian tradition that had gone before him—including Bärthold, Haecker, Dallago, and *Der Brenner*[66]—and offers praise to Schrempf for at least being "man enough" to properly embody Kierkegaard, rather than undermining his attack by transferring it into theological niceties.[67]

At the beginning of *EK*, Kütemeyer offers a long preliminary discussion that sets out and expands Kierkegaard's attack. Although the key points will be addressed in later chapters, it is interesting that he particularly emphasizes such concepts as the "bargain" made between the world and Christianity and Kierkegaard's financial language to this effect, grace as "result," Christianity as "doctrine," its absorption into "worldliness," and even the inability to discern "light from darkness," all of which prove important for Bonhoeffer.[68]

Of particular interest is Kütemeyer's belief in Kierkegaard's importance for his day and age. On the publisher's sleeve, surrounding the book and its cover, it declares, "Is this book a current contribution to the religious crisis? That it most assuredly is. It concerns more than just Kierkegaard's lifetime." Kütemeyer translates Kierkegaard's discussion very much into the political and historical climate describing how Protestantism has delighted

---

60. Cf. Dallago, "Augustine, Pascal und Kierkegaard."

61. Cf. Dallago, *Der Christ Kierkegaards.*

62. Cf. Dumbach and Newborn, *Sophie Scholl*, 7.

63. Cf. Dru, "Introduction," xivf; Dumbach and Newborn, *Sophie Scholl*, 73ff.

64. Malik, *Receiving Kierkegaard*, 381 n. 148.

65. Kütemeyer, "Anfang," 33.

66. Ibid., 31.

67. Ibid., 29.

68. Cf. Kütemeyer, "Vorbesprechung," 6, 7, 10–11.

the world through "the union of throne and alter, God and petrol, poisonous Gas and Holy Ghost."[69] Furthermore, not only does he suggest that had Nietzsche read Kierkegaard in the winter of 1888/89—as he had planned—both his destiny and that of Germany itself would have taken a different course, but also that "without the remedy, historically identified by the name of Kierkegaard, a quick and awful downfall will overtake Europe."[70]

Summary

As suggested above, Bonhoeffer's library is not complete, and we are left very much in the dark concerning what other sources Bonhoeffer may have been exposed to. By the start of the Second World War several influential volumes existed in Germany concerning Kierkegaard. These included the substantial *Sören Kierkegaard im Kampfe mit der Romantik, der Theologie und der Kirche,* by F. A. Voigt, as well as various volumes by Emanuel Hirsch. Vogel further suggests that Bonhoeffer may well have been aware of the collection of Kierkegaard's journals, *ZFG,* collected by Robert Dollinger. Further to these sources, of particular note is the work of Eduard Geismar. Daphne Hampson recollected that she had been told by Bonhoeffer's close friend, Franz Hildebrandt, that at the time of writing *Discipleship* Bonhoeffer had been reading the article on Kierkegaard in *Religion in Geschichte und Gegenwart* written by Geismar, then the Professor of Theology at the University of Copenhagen.[71] Indeed, Hildebrandt further clarified that it was from this article that Bonhoeffer had chosen the title, "Nachfolge." In addition, it is possible that Bonhoeffer was familiar with Geismar's other works on Kierkegaard, including the two volume, *Sören Kierkegaard: seine Lebensentwicklung und seine Wirksamkeit als Schriftsteller,* published in 1929, which David Swenson suggests to have been be both "widely read" and "the most comprehensive and the most judicial that has yet seen the light."[72]

Before considering the textual analysis of the following chapters, it is clear that far more can already be said than the stereotypes present in the majority of secondary sources, most of which simply regurgitate the same information. By the end of his life, Bonhoeffer's knowledge of Kierkegaard was extensive. Bonhoeffer owned a large proportion of Kierkegaard's works. Furthermore, *FT,* which was perhaps the most influential, does not appear in his library, demonstrating that the list we do have is incomplete. In addition, from the wide range of issues highlighted throughout these works, Bonhoeffer's interest goes far beyond the issues simply dealt with in *Discipleship,* or presented in *EK.*

Of particular note in the secondary sources is the lack of adequate description of a progression in Bonhoeffer's understanding of Kierkegaard. This is to be expected given the brevity of these accounts. However, it is a significant omission. It is clear that Bonhoeffer did not own all of these works from the start, and that his understanding of Kierkegaard in his earliest works is far less than it was later. It is significant that of the four direct references to Kierkegaard's works, the first three, all from *SC,* point towards ambiguities in his

69. Ibid., 13.

70. Ibid., 31.

71. Prof. Daphne Hampson, in correspondence with the author, January 8, 2009.

72. Swenson, "Editor's Introduction," xi.

understanding, and it is only the last, referenced much later, that shows a comprehensive knowledge. When the Kierkegaardian stereotypes of the time were so strongly in the direction of individualism and subjectivity, it is not surprising that Bonhoeffer should be led in that direction at the beginning, but gain his own understanding as his direct knowledge grew. Most of the secondary sources never allow Bonhoeffer to progress beyond the understanding of *SC*. It is not easy to say at what point Bonhoeffer read the various works discussed. However, this progression must still be dealt with as best it can.

The image of Kierkegaard in Germany appears curiously split. Kierkegaard had clearly been defined by individualism and subjectivism. However, Bonhoeffer was also exposed to a very different perspective. Although Schrempf, Haecker, and Kütemeyer all disapproved of each other, their main thrust remained the same: each saw Kierkegaard's importance in healing the catastrophic times in which they lived. Kierkegaard's critique was not simply theological, but social and political. Consequently, when many commentators relegate Kierkegaard behind a form of "worldlessness" in *Discipleship*, Bonhoeffer was also introduced to a Kierkegaard more akin to a revolutionary healer than a Gnostic. As will be shown, Bonhoeffer's interpretation changed over time, and it was the later interpretation that gained the upper hand.

A Theory of Bonhoeffer's Influence

Bonhoeffer has not helped this book by offering so few direct references. However, this treatment should not be considered abnormal. Across the board, Bonhoeffer does not reference many of his sources. Indeed, the footnotes of the *DBW* editions are littered with the editors' suggestions of sources from which Bonhoeffer might have drawn his ideas. This makes Bonhoeffer's declaration in *SC* that his attack on idealism has been taken from Kierkegaard somewhat unique. Rather, Bonhoeffer tends to critique and develop those he references. Bloom would argue that Bonhoeffer's anxiety is manifested through his omission of their influence, and discussion of their work only by way of critique. However, one does not have to agree with Bloom to affirm the complex relationships an author has with his influences. It is uncontested that Bonhoeffer was an extremely wilful individual, passionately committed to the search for real, existential truth. He did not sit in an ivory tower but placed himself at the cutting edge of theology and "reality." He relished the acquisition of truth and immersed himself in thinkers whose work he believed embodied it. Consequently, it can be argued that when he was clearly influenced by these writers, he did not simply use them but rather wrote from within them. From this it should perhaps be argued that Bonhoeffer did not represent an "anxiety of influence" but quite the opposite: an ambivalence or irrelevance of influence.

An example from 1934 perhaps illustrates our point. During his brief stay in London, Bonhoeffer preached the sermon on Matt 11:28–30, "Come to me, all you who are weary and burdened, and I will give you rest" (*L*, 371–75). This is the same text with which Kierkegaard begins Part I of *PC*, and the markings within Bonhoeffer's own copy show his interest in this section. Bonhoeffer does not cite, reference, or show any external sign that Kierkegaard is his influence. And yet the tone and direction of the sermon strongly resemble Kierkegaard. Bonhoeffer draws on the universality of Christ's call, the absurdity of judging an individual's spiritual need by externals, and the truly human nature of Christ, learning through the yoke of suffering, all of which are central to Kierkegaard's short discussion. In terms of Kierkegaard's influence, the point is not that Bonhoeffer is copying Kierkegaard, writing with a copy of *PC* next to him. Rather, Bonhoeffer immersed himself in Kierkegaard, found himself in Kierkegaard, and therefore wrote his own words from within Kierkegaard. For Bonhoeffer the anxiety concerns truth not originality.

As Kelly suggests, Bonhoeffer found in Kierkegaard "a kindred soul."[73] This becomes strikingly clear in this sermon. At its end, discussing the final rest of eternity, Bonhoeffer quotes the lines by the Danish hymn writer, Hans Adolf Brorson, which are quoted at the beginning of this chapter. These words are carved on Kierkegaard's gravestone.[74] This information is not in any of the primary or secondary sources we know Bonhoeffer read, revealing again the fragmentary nature of the information we do have. It has also been entirely ignored by the secondary sources. However, it reveals the close, personal bond between Bonhoeffer and Kierkegaard that stood alongside Bonhoeffer's intellectual admiration. Bonhoeffer's sermon revolves around the response of the individual to Christ, of taking hold of his yoke, and following him along the path of suffering. It is one of obedience, sacrifice, fulfilment, and ultimately rest. And it is with Kierkegaard in mind that Bonhoeffer wrote it.

Beyond Influence

Interpretive Tools

The issue of influence is obviously significant. However, the importance of this study is also to step beyond Kierkegaard and Bonhoeffer's direct relationship, to lay the foundation for their use as interpretive tools for each other. Understanding Kierkegaard as lying behind Bonhoeffer makes Kierkegaard an obvious tool for Bonhoeffer. However, given their very different historical climates, with different emphases and concerns, Bonhoeffer takes Kierkegaard's work in different directions and extensions, forcing Kierkegaard to answer questions that did not concern him at the time. In *LPP*, drawing on comments in *EK* as well as *JFY*, Bonhoeffer commented to his parents, "Already one hundred years ago Kierkegaard said that Luther today would say the opposite of what he said back then. I think that is true—*cum grano salis*" (*LPP*, 173).[75] As both writers agreed concerning Luther, through the lens of Bonhoeffer we are led to understand Kierkegaard not statically, through the literal declarations of his work, but rather as a thinker responding to his own situation, and who may still speak into new and diverse situations to which he was not party. Through Bonhoeffer we may ask what Kierkegaard "would say" when confronted

---

73. Kelly, "Kierkegaard as 'Antidote,'" 150.

74. The German Bonhoeffer uses is a "somewhat free" version of the Danish. Interestingly, it does not appear in Bonhoeffer's library or in any of the secondary sources that we know Bonhoeffer read (*L*, 375; cf. *ITS*, 219).

75. Cf. *EK*, 105, 135, 139; *JP*, 2518. (X3 A 153 n.d., 1850), 4976. (X4 A 406 n.d., 1851), 530. (X4 A 115 n.d., 1851); cf. *JFY*, 196.

with different situations. In asking how much Bonhoeffer is "like" Kierkegaard we are not simply trying to compare documents but men. It is not enough to simply juxtapose Kierkegaard's individualism with Bonhoeffer's ecclesiology.

Furthermore, Bonhoeffer will also be shown to be an important interpretive tool against the Kierkegaardian stereotypes of individualism and acosmism. Kierkegaard was in most part a polemicist and "auditor" of culture and Christendom. His task was far more deconstructive than constructive. Consequently, these stereotypes have been forged in large part through his silence concerning the church and the world. When one reads Kierkegaard in the light of Bonhoeffer, when one sees Kierkegaard's notions standing behind Bonhoeffer's understanding of the church and the world, when one considers their mutual presuppositions and asks the same questions of Kierkegaard that Bonhoeffer faced, one is granted a new window through which to interpret Kierkegaard away from these stereotypes.

Bonhoeffer as Reformer

Perhaps one of the key differences between Kierkegaard and Bonhoeffer is that Bonhoeffer was not bound to Kierkegaard's indirect, Socratic method. Unlike Kierkegaard, Bonhoeffer was not fettered from going out beyond himself, from declaring God's word to its height. Consequently, a new question arises concerning the relationship between Kierkegaard and Bonhoeffer. Despite his final declarations concerning Christendom, Kierkegaard maintained that he could never be a reformer. Rather, in what appear as somewhat prophetic declarations, Kierkegaard spoke of the "reformer" (*JFY*, 211–3) or "missionary" (*JP*, 2004/ *Pap*, VIII1 A 482; *EK*, 32) who would achieve what he denied himself. Alluding to Luther, Kierkegaard argued, "When the Church needed a reformation, no one reported for duty, there was no crowd to join up; all fled away. Only one solitary man, the reformer, was disciplined in all secrecy by fear and trembling and much spiritual trial for venturing the extraordinary in God's name" (*JFY*, 213). So he declares,

> If anyone among us dares to undertake to walk ethically in the character of what is suggested here, also appealing as a single individual to an immediate relationship with God, then I shall at once . . . be on duty to undertake what I understanding before God as my task. My task will be: to escort him, the reformer, step by step, never leaving his side, in order to see if he step by step is in the character, is the extraordinary. (211)

When both Kierkegaard and Bonhoeffer's work is fulfilled in their parallel attacks on Christendom, we are led to ask, "Is Bonhoeffer Kierkegaard's reformer?" "Concerning influence, do we find Kierkegaard escorting Bonhoeffer in his character of the extraordinary?" In a journal entry from as early as 1847, Kierkegaard argued,

> When he, the missionary, comes, he will use this category [of the single individual]. If the age is waiting for a hero, it waits in vain; instead there will more likely come one who in divine weakness will teach men obedience—by means of their slaying him in impious rebellion, him, the one obedient to God. (*JP*, 2004/*Pap*, VIII1 A 482; *EK*, 32)

In Bonhoeffer's life do we find a weakness in obedience through which God's strength was manifest? In Bonhoeffer's death do we find the martyrdom that Kierkegaard demanded as its sign? In Bonhoeffer do we find the essence of the extraordinary?

Attacks on Idealism and Christendom

Sadly, it is not possible in this work to consider every area of influence. Kierkegaard and Bonhoeffer's relationship is extremely rich, and many parallels deserve far more treatment than the present work can offer. The aim of this book therefore is to focus on the trajectory of their thought towards their final attacks. Consequently, such fertile areas as Kierkegaard and Bonhoeffer's more psychological thought, their mutual understanding of sin, as well as their descriptions of love, receive only a glancing analysis here but fully merit their own individual study.

Despite their very different historical settings, it is striking that their attacks on Christendom bear such similarity. However, both have received considerable criticism, with Kierkegaard being considered "unbalanced in mind" by the end of his life,[76] and Bonhoeffer becoming "overwhelmed by events" and writing "under the influence of imprisonment."[77] The aim of this book is to suggest that the attacks stand not as unfortunate endings to otherwise profound careers but as the fulfilment of their thought. Against the sporadic use of Kierkegaard that many of the secondary sources suggest, the proceeding chapters will reveal Bonhoeffer's systematic adoption of Kierkegaard, leading Bonhoeffer from his earliest thought into his final attack.

One of the central themes that ties Bonhoeffer's thought together is an attack on idealism. As will be demonstrated in chapter 3, it was an idealism that for Bonhoeffer stood against true obedience to the Word of God and made Hitler's seduction of the churches possible. Although many of the secondary sources acknowledge that Bonhoeffer drew his attack on idealism from Kierkegaard in SC, few recognize the continued influence throughout Bonhoeffer's work. For both authors, the attack on idealism cannot simply be limited to their epistemology, but defines their ethics, Christology, discipleship, and finally also their attacks. In this way, Bonhoeffer was continually drawn back to Kierkegaard as he proceeded in his authorship through these themes. It will be argued that through the attack on idealism we gain a view of Kierkegaard and Bonhoeffer's work that reveals the continuity between their earliest thought and their attacks on Christendom.

Before proceeding into a comparative analysis, it is important that the scene be set. To this end, chapters 2 and 3 will offer biographical outlines to show the context and motivations behind each author's work.

---

76. *Fædrelandet*, November 23, 1855, as quoted in Croxall, *Glimpses and Impressions*, 85.

77. As argued by Wilhelm Niesel, in Zimmermann and Gregor-Smith, *I Knew Dietrich Bonhoeffer*, 147.

2

1848 and All That

The Road to Kierkegaard's Attack on Christendom

Introduction

IN THE PROCEEDING CHAPTERS THE ANALYSIS WILL DISCUSS AND COMPARE KIERKEGAARD and Bonhoeffer's work equally, following the issues of epistemology, ethics, Christology, and discipleship, and then finally their attacks. Although there is something of an internally consistent progression of ideas running throughout Bonhoeffer's thought, his work is categorized into these different topics. Consequently, although the subject of this thesis is both Kierkegaard and Bonhoeffer, the following chapters will essentially follow a systematic progression through Bonhoeffer's individual works, while drawing on the wealth of material from Kierkegaard's whole authorship.

This methodology fits naturally with a discussion of "influence" as one must already have a relatively complete understanding of the issues of the first author in order to look for them in the second. This does not, however, provide us with an adequate methodology in which to understand Kierkegaard's ideas as a whole, or the progression that runs through his thought. The aim of this chapter is to overcome these issues by providing an overview of Kierkegaard's thought to show its progression, but also to contextualize the issues that will be dealt with in later chapters. This overview will reveal the importance of Kierkegaard's attack as the authentic fulfilment of his earlier thought, but also the inconsistency of the Kierkegaardian stereotypes when considered within Kierkegaard's thought as a whole.

Kierkegaard and the Problems of Biography

In reaction to the more literal interpretations of Kierkegaard's pseudonymous writings by such figures as Walter Lowrie, much recent scholarship has called into question the autobiographical content of Kierkegaard's work, and the possibility of gaining an objective picture of Kierkegaard and the context for his work. This has particularly affected the interpretation of Kierkegaard's journals and autobiographical writing. Joakim Garff has suggested that Kierkegaard's personal declarations are a "documenta(fic)tion" of the constantly changing and re-creating 'I's of his overly reflective and refracted personality.[1]

---

1. Cf. Garff, "Eyes of Argus," 86f.

Such works may never be described as *auto*biographical, or treated separately from the pseudonyms, with whom Kierkegaard himself declared his distinction. Indeed, as Julia Watkin points out, it is the vein of much scholarship to disavow anything Kierkegaard might say about himself.[2] Such positions have frustrated discussion of a coherent progression within Kierkegaard's works, but also led to a subordination of his later, post-1848, religious writings as a growing and overly reflective eccentricity. Written under his own name, it is inevitable that these later, direct works should be treated with such suspicion.

Others, such as Louis Mackey and Benjamin Daise, have taken the issue even further to suggest that one should not even look for unifying themes within Kierkegaard's works, as this fails to appreciate Kierkegaard's nature as a poet-artist. Still others, perhaps most vehemently Henning Fenger, have denied the legitimacy of any "theological" reading to Kierkegaard, denounced Kierkegaard as a "falsifier of history," and rejected his later works with deep distrust.

This thesis will take Kierkegaard's use of pseudonymity seriously, acknowledging Kierkegaard's desired focus on the reader rather than the identity and intentions of the writer, his concern at being associated with the words of his pseudonyms, as well as the complexity of Kierkegaard's identity. However, this thesis denies such deconstructivist positions as not taking seriously Kierkegaard's own association with the pseudonyms, his overwhelming desire to fulfil a specific task, and the progression and consistency of themes clearly present within his work. To ignore the substantial weight of this material is as incorrect an abstraction as Lowrie's pseudonymous neglect.[3] Furthermore, the comprehensive rejection of the possibility of a consistent and "natural" Kierkegaardian "I" within the journals fails to take their complexity seriously. Alongside the many literary forms, including sections with clear pseudonymous or poetic intent, passages with a consistent, personal "I" may be discerned in contrast. For someone so inwardly directed and isolated as Kierkegaard, it should not surprise us that his journals became his closest companion, critic and counsellor, described like self-illuminating letters posted to an intimate friend (*JP*, 5241/*Pap*, II A 118). With this weight of potential it could be suggested that those who pass over Kierkegaard's journals to concentrate on the pseudonyms are like those who "know a little about the scholarly King's Highway but absolutely nothing about the lanes and by-ways and their unsung glories and vistas" (*JP*, 5243/ *Pap*, II A 120).

Consequently, while paying careful attention to the potholes and murky puddles that such country paths afford, this investigation will seek to discern and take seriously the personal "I" of Kierkegaard's journals in outlining a progression of his thought from 1848 until his attack.

2. Watkin, *Kierkegaard*, 1ff.

3. We are here essentially agreeing with Stephen Backhouse that one must reject both extreme positions as failing to take seriously the idea of "stages on life's way" within Kierkegaard's authorship—of a growing progression that, although stands in consistency with his earlier works, moves beyond them.

PART 1
KIERKEGAARD AND THE EVENTS OF 1848

Throughout Kierkegaard's journals, no year is emphasized more than 1848. Near the end of 1849 Kierkegaard dramatically comments, "In one sense 1848 has raised me to another level. Another sense has shattered me, that is, it has shattered me religiously, or to say it in my own language: God has run me ragged" (*JP*, 6501/*Pap*, X2 A 66). In 1853 he again writes, "Then came 1848. Here I was granted a perspective on my life that almost overwhelmed me. As I perceived it, I felt that Governance had guided me, that I actually had been granted the extraordinary" (*JP*, 6843/ *Pap*, X5 A 146).

This chapter will suggest the importance of 1848 in understanding the progression of Kierkegaard's thought leading to his attack and argue: (a) that during this period Kierkegaard experienced enormous personal strife and anxiety, (b) that where Kierkegaard's polemical style had previously been aimed at a vague and somewhat anonymous foe, these events made his object clear, and (c) that both of these provoked an awakening that acted as the foundation for Kierkegaard's attack on Christendom. This chapter will therefore describe Kierkegaard's progression from the indirectness of pseudonymity, through Anti-Climacus, to a direct communication that paved the way for his attack, suggesting not only a continuity to his work, but also that his later works are the fruition of his earlier thought. Along the way, this chapter will also highlight and contextualize many of the themes that will be drawn upon in the later chapters.

1848 and the Danish Revolution

The first half of the 19th century was a period of enormous upheaval for Denmark. Through their neutral prevarications during the Napoleonic War, Denmark had been economically devastated. By 1813, the year of Kierkegaard's birth, a state of national bankruptcy had been declared. Furthermore, the revolutionary rumblings around Europe during this period had also had a profound effect on Denmark's social climate. Denmark had experienced an absolute monarchy since the 1660s. However, through the influence of the French Revolution at the end of the eighteenth century, and in particular its continuation in the July Revolution of 1830, the Danish monarchy had come under threat. Despite its attempts at reform, under the influence of the German Revolution of the same year, in 1848 Denmark underwent its own "revolution" in which the King abdicated his absolute monarchy and established a limited constitutional democracy.

These events profoundly affected Kierkegaard, and provoked two distinct and yet related reactions within his work. The first concerns the authenticity of the revolution, and the second the consequences of the revolution.

The Authenticity of the Revolution and the "Life-View"

On 28 November 1835, almost five years after the monarchy had established provincial assemblies in order to stem the tide of revolutionary fervor, Kierkegaard took part in a University Union debate. The topic concerned the role of the liberal press in having fought for the freedoms of the people against the oppression of the absolute monarchy. In his address, entitled "Our Journalistic Literature: A Study From Nature in Noonday Light," Kierkegaard did not simply attack journalism but the whole climate of revolutionary feeling that was sweeping through Denmark. Kierkegaard argued that the Liberal "revolutionaries" had made two fundamental errors.

First, such individuals were hailing the beginning of a new age of freedom and prosperity before it had even started. Kierkegaard argued that this age "like(s) to dwell on the first appearance of an idea in world history," drawing people in from every direction to worship it and to "let a mighty tree spring forth from the factually given mustard seed" (*EPW*, 36). However, there was no evidence or reason to believe that this would occur. For Kierkegaard, these revolutionaries were looking at things through the partial and romanticized light of dawn, and not in the clarity of noonday light that would reveal the truth. Kierkegaard also criticized the Conservatives who, in supporting the King, were overly pessimistic about changes. For Kierkegaard, the true path lay in actuality rather than either a positive or negative idealism (37).

Secondly, Kierkegaard suggested that the revolutionary zeal was not natural to Denmark and its history, but rather simply adopted from France. These "revolutionaries" were simply jumping on the bandwagon and applying the circumstances and needs of France to those of Denmark, which were clearly different. Quite in contrast to the oppressive tendencies of the French monarchy, Kierkegaard argued that it was the Danish monarchy that made the first steps towards reform and not the "revolutionaries" or liberal press. Like forcing a key into the wrong lock, to apply these foreign but extreme notions to Denmark could be potentially disastrous. As Kierkegaard declared, one cannot "travel in Sjælland with a map of France" (48).

In *From the Papers of One Still Living*, published almost three years later, Kierkegaard expanded these ideas to show their foundation in a willful misunderstanding of Hegel's concept of "beginning again from the beginning." Adopting Hegel's optimistic understanding of the progression of history, Kierkegaard argued that his generation "misunderstands the deeper significance of an historical evolution and clings curiously enough, as if in a fight for its life, to the cliché that the world always becomes wiser" (63). Its twofold error is to have arrogantly believed that it simply is wiser than the past without appropriating its riches and, consequently, to have perceived and promoted abstract manifestos hailed as successful truth. Rather, Kierkegaard argued that when the past is the "actual" (64), it is only through its existential appropriation that one can ever enter into the realm of actuality.

The essential error of such "revolutionaries" was the lack of what Kierkegaard defines as a "life-gymnastic," "world-view" or "life-view." For Kierkegaard a "life-view" is gained through the combining of immediate, sensory experience with the reflection of one's past, to weave a tapestry of understanding from which "an unshakeable certainty in oneself won from all experience" is gained (77). As such, for one who,

> . . . does not allow his life to fizzle out too much but seeks as far as possible to lead its single expressions back to himself again, there must necessarily come a moment in which a strange light spreads over life without one's therefore even remotely need-

ing to have understood all possible particulars, to the progressive understanding of which, however, one now has the key. There must come a moment, I say, when, as Daub observes, life is understood backward through the idea. (78)

Through surveying one's own growing history, one undergoes a "transubstantiation of experience" (77), perceiving the ideal and so something of the truth of all life and experience. The "life-view" is the perception of objective truth expressed through the subjectivity of the individual life, established through the subjectivity of individual experience. Each person views the same ideal, even if their unique experiences offer different angles from which to view it. True art, as it manifests the ideal, should reach out as if with "an evangelistic tinge," extending, establishing, and exciting the reader or viewer in their own perception of the ideal (66).[4]

A passivity is implied in describing the ideal like a "strange light" that "spreads over life without one's therefore even remotely needing to have understood all possible particulars." This is further explained in a journal entry written only a few months later:

> The development of *a priori* basic concepts is like a prayer in the Christian sphere, for one would think that here a person is related to God in the freest, most subjective way, and yet we are told that it is the Holy Spirit that effects prayer, so that the only prayer remaining would be to be able to pray, although upon closer inspection even this has been effected in us—so also there is no deductive development of concepts or what one could call that which has some constitutive power—man can only concentrate upon it, and to will this, if this will is not an empty, unproductive gift, corresponds to this single prayer and like this is effected, so to speak, in us. (*JP*, 2257/*Pap*, II A 301)

Through the gift of his will, humankind is to prepare himself to receive knowledge from God's hand, "effected" within him. Its improper use is the "deductive development of concepts" and "constitutive power," the sagacity and speculation of the mind, capturing and defining the world around it.

In a second journal entry written eight months later, Kierkegaard attacks the speculation rife within the philosophical, and aesthetic world:

> The philosophers think that all knowledge, yes, even the existence of the deity, is something man himself produces and that revelation can be referred to only in a figurative sense in somewhat the same sense as one may say the rain falls down from heaven, since the rain is nothing but an earth-produced mist; but they forget, to keep the metaphor, that in the beginning God separated the waters of the heaven and of the earth and that there is something higher than the atmosphere. (*JP*, 2266/*Pap*. II A 523)

---

4. In order to make believable the many characters (pseudonyms etc.) used throughout his writing, Kierkegaard had to give them genuine "life-views." Without these, they would have neither the similarity of ideal perception with the reader required to penetrate his heart and mind, nor the personal perspective required to convince the reader of the characters" true and consistent identity. Both enemy (Levin) and friend (Brøchner) describe Kierkegaard as taking on the character of these individuals for substantial periods, in order to understand their visions and life-views.

What might be called an "active passivity" is made clear in Kierkegaard's comments in the margins of both, and links the two above-quoted passages together. In the first Kierkegaard writes, "One can therefore also say that all knowing is like breathing, a *re-spiratio*" (*JP*, 2258/*Pap*. II A 302), and in the second, "The contrast to [the arrogant method of the philosophers] I have expressed in one of my other journals by the statement that all knowledge is *re-spiratio*" (*JP*, 2267/*Pap*, II A 524).

This passivity is described as a "breathing in" of knowledge, of opening one's life, all one's senses, to the air of truth, allowing it to give life, removing it from the control of the breather. In using the term "*re-spiratio*," Kierkegaard is again drawing our attention to the nature of knowledge as of God. In Danish the verb "to breathe"—"*at aande*," is unmistakably related to the word for "spirit"—"*Aanden*." To receive knowledge one must lay one's reason to rest, to quell the noise of the mind's processes, and to rest before God in the silence that affords one's ability to receive.

These thoughts find summary in a journal entry from 1840. Here, Kierkegaard reflects on *Meno* and Plato's suggestion that "all knowledge is recollection," drawn out from within the individual, giving rise to "a polemic against the world with the object of subjugating knowledge of the external world in order to bring about the stillness in which these recollections become audible." Explaining further the nature of "active passivity," Kierkegaard therefore writes,

> But we ought not therefore remain stationary. On the contrary, here in the world of knowledge there rests upon man a curse (blessing) which bids him eat his bread in the sweat of his brow, but just as it does not mean that in the physical realm he must give the earth germinating power etc. but that he is to do everything in order that it can express itself, so it is with knowledge, and we can therefore say that the finite spirit is as it is, the unity of necessity and freedom (it is not to determine through an infinite development what it is to become, but it is to become through development that which it is), and thus it is also the unity of consequence and striving (that is, it is not to produce through development a new thing but it is to acquire through development what it has). (*JP*, 2274/*Pap*, III A 5)

For Kierkegaard, the ideal is not an objectified externality to be grasped at arms length, but that which is found within oneself. In a further entry from 1840, Kierkegaard argues that the only way to gain understanding is "to do everything in order that [knowledge] can express itself," through opening one's life to its experiences (*JP*, 2274/*Pap*, III A 5). Knowledge is a self-knowledge drawn from all that one already has within one's life and experiences, an existential category, a "life-view,"

Kierkegaard returns to the concept of a "life-view" in *LR*, written as he looked over the proofs of *CUP* in 1846. Despite this term gaining little interest within the secondary sources, it would appear to have been extremely important for Kierkegaard. Not only is it the central concept in the two works that bracket his "first authorship"—Kierkegaard had initially planned to finish his authorship with *CUP*—but both of these works are published under his own name.

Affirming his thoughts in *From the Papers of One Still Living*, Kierkegaard argues that for an author to gain a "life-view" and so to write with the power of "persuasion" (*LR*,

16), he or she must be "twice-matured": first by an investment in life and experience, and second by an ability to let this experience work within him (13). Furthermore, this "life-view" is the reception of the eternal. As he argues, "the possibility of being to yield such a work, is the reward God has bestowed on the author, since, twice matured, he has gained something eternal in a life-view. It is because he is an author who isn't looking for himself, but one who found himself before he became an author, that he can be a guide" (13). The sense of "active-passivity" is once again affirmed as Kierkegaard describes this "life-view" as a gift from God (13), like "the real pearl, which is formed, as is known, inside the oyster by the absorption of dew" (44).

By 1846 it is clear that Kierkegaard was fully aware of the possibility of the impending revolution. In *LR* he presents not simply a critique of literature, but also the distinction between the authentically "revolutionary age" and the "present age." For Kierkegaard, the revolutionary age is defined by individuals who are passionately related to a single idea, who may be violent, uncurbed, wild, and ruthless, but only so in absolute commitment to that idea (54). In contrast, the present age is "*sensible, reflective, dispassionate, eruptive in its fleeting enthusiasms and prudently indolent in its relaxation*" (60). It is an age that is devoid of passion and is rather like a "stagnant lake" (54). It is an age defined not by passionate commitment, but by "eruptive enthusiasm" and "apathetic indolence" (65)—what he had previously referred to back in 1835 as a "bustling busyness," "a fitful fumbling," and a "restless rambling" (*EPW*, 48). For Kierkegaard, the Danish "revolutionaries" had sought to embrace the revolutionary zeal of France, defined by a true passion and commitment that they themselves did not manifest. The French revolutionaries were prepared to die for their cause; the Danish "revolutionaries" were never going to be asked to do so because the situation in Denmark was so much milder. Their "revolution" was therefore a farce, in seeking the heroic appearance of overthrowing the "tyrannical" monarch," whilst still enjoying the comforts that it afforded. As Kierkegaard comments,

> A passionately tumultuous age wants to *overthrow everything, subvert everything*. A revolutionary but passionless and reflecting age changes the manifestation of power into a dialectical sleight-of-hand, *letting everything remain but slyly defrauding it of its meaning; it culminates, instead of in an uprising, in the exhaustion of the inner reality of the relationships, in a reflecting tension that nevertheless lets everything remain, and it has transformed the whole of existence into an equivocation which, in its facticity, is—whereas privately a dialectical fraud surreptitiously substitutes a secret way of reading—that it is not.* (*LR*, 68)

The central point in "Our Journalistic Literature," "From the Papers of One Still Living," and *LR*, is that the Danish "revolutionaries" simply lacked any sense of a "life-view." Indeed, Kierkegaard argues that the evidence of this lack, and that they could never embody the unifying passion of true revolutionaries, was that these "revolutionaries" were so disunified as to what the "revolution" should actually be.

The Consequences of the Revolution and the "Common Man"

For Kierkegaard, the Danish "revolution" was a cataclysmic event with devastating implications for the spiritual health of the nation. The reason for this is most intimately caught up in the notion of the "common man," and their corruption at the hands of the "revolutionaries." Before 1848, Kierkegaard's journals only have two references to the "common man." From 1848 onwards it is a recurring theme. So important does this issue become that Kierkegaard declares in 1849, "the common man is my task" (*JP*, 6498/*Pap*, X2 A 48). Why this sudden emphasis? The answer lies in both who the "common man" is, but also his relationship to the "revolution."

The Identity of the Common Man

Despite the frequency with which Kierkegaard uses the term, he does not go into detail as to who the "common man" actually is. Kierkegaard uses a number of social categorizations, referring to the cultured elite, the liberals, bourgeois philistines, pastors, reformers, professors, and assistant professors etc. As polemical terms, each is defined by certain stereotypical behavior that separates such people from God and the truth. Consequently, it could be argued that the "common man" is simply the person who is as yet uncorrupted by these manmade manifestos, standing in a state of simple innocence. This is certainly true in part. However, the "common man" is not simply Kierkegaard's "individual," but a specific social class. In his journals, Kierkegaard refers to them as the "ordinary class" (*JP*, 6354/*Pap*, X1 A 131), who keep company on the "streets and avenues" (*JP*, 1056/*Pap*, X1 A 650). Furthermore, he reveals the distinction when he actually appeals to "those few single individuals who really relate themselves to spirit" to come to the aid of the "common man" (*JP*, 2083/*Pap*, XI2 A 149).

The error of each of the flawed personalities mentioned above is that like the "revolutionaries" they created and projected realities for themselves. They all failed to invest in their lives, and to gain an authentic "life-view" by allowing their existence to speak to them. As will be discussed in chapter 4, each has become deaf to the voice of the eternal, drowned out by the "busy, clamorous noise" of their own minds (*JP*, 2274/*Pap*, III A 5). According to Kierkegaard, it is rather only the "common man" who has the ability to gain an authentic "life-view" through the simplicity of his life. These ideas are made clear in both *CUP* and *LR*. Here Kierkegaard discusses the difference between the "simple" and the "wise" man. Inspired by a Socratic understanding of knowledge, Kierkegaard argues that the mind of the wise man is crowded by everything that he "knows" and the realities he has created for himself. Consequently, to actually know something is far easier for the simple person. As Kierkegaard declares,

> *Is it not precisely the simple that is most difficult for the wise man to understand?* The simple person understands the simple directly, but when the wise person is to understand it, it becomes infinitely difficult . . . The more the wise person thinks about the simple . . . the more difficult it becomes for him. Yet he feels gripped by a deep humanness that reconciles him with all of life: that the difference between the wise person and the simplest person is this little evanescent difference *that the simple*

person knows the essential and the wise person little by little *comes to know* that he knows it or *comes to know* that he does not know it, but what they know is the same. (*CUP*, 1:160)

In *LR* Kierkegaard declares that the strength of the wise "goes to waste on the futility of reflection" (*LR*, 58). For Kierkegaard, the present age is defined by the promotion of multifarious man-made, abstract ideas. As Johannes de Silentio declares at the beginning of *FT*, "Not just in commerce but in the world of ideas too our age is putting on a veritable clearance sale. Everything can be had so dirt cheap that one begins to wonder whether in the end anyone will want to make a bid" (*FT*, 41). The present age lacks a "life-view" and so each person creates their own ideas that fail to "evangelize," to "persuade," and so to unify people behind a common cause. In contrast to the revolutionary age, which fights for a single purpose, in *LR* Kierkegaard describes the present age as undertaking the process of "levelling," of stifling and impeding everything that is an extreme. Everything is made gray. This is why simple issues cannot be simply embraced by the wise as they must always say "maybe" and "perhaps" before they can accept it. The simple person, the common man, remains within the realm of the black and white, the objects of "contradiction," knowing good from bad, right from left, and so action from inaction. Free from speculation and sagacity, he is simply able to receive the ideal that is always within him and requires no "cultivating" for its legitimate understanding—he simply embodies it. When the cultured and elite in society look down on the common man and refer to him as an "animal creature" because of his simplicity, so Kierkegaard declares just a few weeks before his death, "if any class of men deserves to be called animals in comparison with the rest of us, it is preachers and professors" (*JP*, 1940/*Pap*, XI2 A 434). The common man is the only one who can be truly revolutionary, to be passionate, and unified behind a common cause.

The Common Man and the Revolution

The "revolutionaries'" proclamation of the new constitution as the "promised land" for Denmark's destiny incited Kierkegaard and caused what he saw as the greatest danger. Not only was this not the revolution Kierkegaard craved, but their proclamation threatened to destroy the last vestiges of its possibility in Denmark. For Kierkegaard, true revolution was required in finding liberation to stand as individuals "before God," unchained from the tolerant, watered-down "Christianity" of the Danish Church. As discussed, Kierkegaard believed that Denmark did not have a context that justified a political revolution in line with that of France and Germany. Denmark's history and socio-political situation was too mild and its monarch too paternalistic to ever contextualize these revolutionary feelings. However, in terms of spiritual bondage and suffering, Kierkegaard believed that Denmark had a history ripe for revolution.

When the ideal, and so fulfillment, can only be manifest existentially from an internal "life-view," the conditions of the individual's external life become relatively irrelevant. Consequently, an external revolution is not only irrelevant but fundamentally harmful if its proclamation distracts from a revolution of internality. In the lead up to the events of the "revolution," in 1847 Kierkegaard declares,

> A poor woman who weeds the gardens of the rich can say, "I am doing this work for a dollar a day, but that I do it very carefully is for the sake of conscience." In truth, these are kingly words! But a person must remember that he must have such words for himself—with God. This is real magnificence. For this reason it is very fatuous to want to make the poorer class impatient with their condition. The small worldly alteration that may be achieved is nevertheless as nothing, but this phrase and this thought—for the sake of conscience—is a transformation of language, is the Archimedean point outside the world, and with this, when it is in deep inward silence before God, the weeder-woman can say that she moves heaven and earth. (*JP*, 683/*Pap*, VIII1 A 60)

Before God all are equal and defined by their relationship to him, not by their physical circumstances. Indeed, the movements of mankind on earth are of such secondary significance to God that Kierkegaard even discards war as merely "some nonsense we human beings cook up among ourselves," and not at all the interest of God or eternality (*JP*, 2571/*Pap*, XI2 A 55; cf. *JP*, 2570/*Pap*, XI2 A 54).

For Kierkegaard, the liberal revolutionaries had simply whipped up and used the common man for their own ends, enticing them with hollow promises of universal male suffrage. Consequently, when they could have been made to see the desire for spiritual revolution, they were enticed to see one only of externals. As Elrod argues, Kierkegaard saw the individual being lost in the "illusion that his spirit was being improved by his participation in the modernization of Denmark."[5] So Kierkegaard laments,

> The representation of the concerns of the spirit, of the idea, of Christianity, homogenized, please note, with finitude, has also contributed to the demoralization which is Christendom. Therefore what should have helped to lift society or at least to awaken a memory that there is something higher, now strengthens the finite and finite striving in its finitude, yes, in such a way that these very representatives of the idea and of Christianity villainously exploit the finite understanding of the common man to oppose anything, if it did appear, which really bears the idea or is borne by the idea and is really related to Christianity. (*JP*, 4531/*Pap*, XI1 A 431)

KIERKEGAARD AND THE COMMON MAN

In the aftermath of the "revolution" Kierkegaard described his belief that before God there is no difference between a servant girl and the most eminent genius, and his "exaggerated sympathy towards ordinary people, the common man" (*JP*, 236/*Pap*, X1 A 135). He further lamented that the common man has "rarely had anyone who has Christianly loved him more disinterestedly than I have" (*JP*, 6354/*Pap*, X1 A 131), and admitted his desire to give everything up to become a pastor in the country. Kierkegaard's preferential perception of the "common man" has been well documented in Jurgen Bukdahl's *Søren Kierkegaard and the Common Man*. However, Bukdahl's more straightforward reading is criticized by commentators such as Joakim Garff, who question the factual veracity of Kierkegaard's altruistic claims. However, whether Kierkegaard was deluded, or at least optimistic about his

---

5. Elrod, *Christendom*, xii.

concerns, the "common man" is a constantly recurring theme that profoundly influenced his authorship.

Kierkegaard's perception of the "common man" may be idealized in the sense of his perception of the idyll of their simple lives, but not in terms of their relationship to truth. The point for Kierkegaard was not that the "common man" did, or necessarily would, embody the hope for Denmark's spiritual revival. They were simply the only ones in Kierkegaard's mind who had the potential to embody it. As mentioned above, the "common man" is not the same as the "individual," who fully embodies the "life-view" and relationship to truth. Rather, the "common man" needs such a figure to lead them into the truth. The revolutionaries had seduced and abused the "common man." Perhaps one of the strongest figures of the Liberal movement who managed to bring the peasants and farmers on board the "revolution" was Orla Lehmann.[6] Kierkegaard's niece, Henrietta Lund recalled her brief admiration with Lehmann at the age of twelve when he rode through the streets with great aplomb, followed by cheering crowds and children eating "Orla Lehmann" branded sweets.[7] While the common man can perhaps be likened to a child in Kierkegaard's treatment, conveying a sense of paternal superiority over them, in Kierkegaard's mind such "revolutionaries" as Lehmann appealed to this childlike simplicity in order to ensnare them without concern for their well-being or potential.

When Kierkegaard conceives his task as introducing both the individual and Christianity into the present age of Christendom, to answer the problem of how the individual might become a Christian, so the revolution of 1848 delivered its complete opposite. However, where one could expect such groups as politicians and the elite intelligentsia to use and abuse the "common man," Kierkegaard's most profound anger rested with those who *should* have defended them: the Crown and, in particular, the Church. In Kierkegaard's mind, not only was 1848 a "catastrophe" for Denmark, but reflecting back from a year later he comments,

> Then I was horrified to see what was understood by a Christian state (this I saw especially in 1848); I saw how the ones who were supposed to rule, both in Church and State, hid themselves like cowards while barbarism boldly and brazenly raged; and I experienced how a truly unselfish and God-fearing endeavor (and my endeavor as an author was that) is rewarded in the Christian state. That seals my fate. Now it is up to my contemporaries how they will list the cost of being a Christian, how terrifying they will make it. (*JP*, 6444/*Pap*, X1 A 541)

These frustrations at the Church's betrayal occupied Kierkegaard's authorship until his death, and are the foundation for its progression.

The Corsair Affair

Through a long-standing and acrimonious duel with the *Corsair* newspaper, Kierkegaard believed he was personally confronted with the Liberal press' abilities to corrupt the com-

---

6. Kierkegaard had clashed with Lehmann at the very beginning of his authorship in 1936 in a series of newspaper articles, accusing him of political deceit.

7. As cited in Kirmmse, *Encounters*, 163.

mon man. Although beginning as early as the end of 1845, the self-destructive battle raged until the beginning of 1848, leaving both Kierkegaard and the *Corsair's* authors counting its cost.[8] Kierkegaard's suffering reached its climax in the *Corsair's* later portrayals of his physical demeanor and its ridicule of his peculiar dress. These descriptions, complete with cartoons, convinced Kierkegaard that he met the mocking stares of both middle class and common man with every turn.

Kierkegaard experienced both a profound anger at the common man because of his sense of superiority, but also distress: from 1848 onwards his journals repetitively reference his heartfelt desire and interaction with them. Indeed, to the stoic distance he kept from the upper classes he declares, "O, but this is not my life at all":

> But the common man whom I loved! It was my greatest joy to express some measure of love to the neighbor; when I saw this loathsome condescension towards less important people, I dared say to myself, "I do not live like that." It was my consolation to alleviate this when possible; it was my pleasure, my blessed diversion. My life was made for that. So when I have to bear the derision of the common man it saddens me indescribably. There was in fact hardly anyone around here who loved the common man this way—and now to see him turned against me in hostility. A journalist who tricks the common man out of his money and in return gives him confused concepts is regarded as a benefactor—and the person who sacrificed so much, every advantage of solidarity with the upper class, is represented as an enemy of the common man, as someone to insult. (*JP*, 6611/*Pap*, X3 A 13)

Kierkegaard's journals are punctuated by lamenting descriptions of his personal interactions, taking the effort and initiative to greet all people, wholeheartedly rejecting "the callousness and cruelty of class distinctions that ordinarily underlie associations with the common man" (*JP*, 6504/*Pap*, X2 A 88). Following these attacks Kierkegaard, however, felt obliged to isolate himself, greeting them with half absent looks and impersonality (*JP*, 6384/*Pap*, X1 A 258).

Despite doubts concerning the facticity of Kierkegaard's interactions with the "common man," and idyllic perception of them, evidence suggests that he was somehow significant to the lower classes of society, as witnessed at his funeral. Henriette Lund describes a peculiar scene, "where the tightly packed mass of people surged like an angry sea," and the coffin became surrounded by a ring of "unpleasant-looking characters."[9] Bishop Hans Martensen commented in like manner from his distant window that "the cortege was primarily composed of young people and a large number of obscure personages."[10] The newspaper reports following the funeral also bear witness to the diversity of people present.[11] These members of the lower classes must have felt enough

---

8. Cf. Kirmmse, *Encounters*, 75, 79.

9. As cited in Kirmmse, *Encounters*, 173.

10. As cited in Bukdahl, *Common Man*, 129. Hans L. Martensen had been one of Kierkegaard's professors, and later succeeded Bishop Jacob Mynster as Danish Primate. Throughout his journals and final attack Martensen reaps nothing but disdain from Kierkegaard. Alongside ridicule for his academic abilities, Martensen embodied for Kierkegaard the shallow professor and clergyman, searching only for his own comfort and promotion, who stood at the heart of Christendom's corruption.

11. Cf. Croxall, *Glimpses*, 84ff.

affection for Kierkegaard to wish to see his final departure. Indeed, Glebe-Møller suggests that Kierkegaard's funeral lives out his thought in *WL* where love is proved to be true when it is love of one who is dead.[12]

In contrast to the favorable, lamenting descriptions of the "common man" in his journals following 1848, in the heat of battle of 1846 Kierkegaard expresses anger and frustration with the "riff-raff" and the indignation he felt at receiving ridicule from those who "cannot think two thoughts together and are able to understand only what is willow and paltry" (*JP*, 5915/*Pap*, VII1 A 128). In agreement with the suggestions of the previous section, this distinction perhaps suggests that it is only from 1848—as he became aware of the significance of the "revolution," the potential of the "common man," and their abuse—that Kierkegaard's perception towards them radically changed. Consequently, Kierkegaard reflects from 1854, "I cannot stop being fond of the common man, even though journalistic scurrility has done everything to confuse him" (*JP*, 2971/*Pap*, XI1 A 234).

Finances

Another influential issue of 1848 concerns the state of Kierkegaard's finances. Kierkegaard lived his life off a sizable inheritance and financed his own publications. However, it was not his original intention to remain unemployed, and he describes his earliest publications as digressions from entering the church. Although financial concerns are apparent around the time of *CUP*, they were perhaps overshadowed by the "Corsair Affair," and so resurface again with greater urgency in 1848. From this time on Kierkegaard's journals reveal a raging tension between his task as an author and these external needs, as he believed his authorial nature as a polemicist would be fatally compromised were he to become attached to any social, political or ecclesiological body. If he could not guarantee his impartiality and polemical integrity, his work was over.

However, as with our understanding of Kierkegaard's desire for the common man, the desire to take an appointment in a country parish held far more attraction to him than the purely financial. Returning to a recurring theme, Kierkegaard comments,

> I have always urged that Christianity is properly for poor people who perhaps toil and sweat the whole day and are scarcely able to make a daily living. The greater the advantages the more difficult it is to become a Christian, for reflection can so very easily take a wrong turn. My desire has always been to preach to the common man. But when the journalism of mob vulgarity did everything to present me to the common man as being demented, I had to give up the desire for a time, but I will return to it again. (*JP*, 991/*Pap*, X3 A 714)

While ideological tensions clearly caused him much concern, it can also be suggested that for such a mind as Kierkegaard's, chained within his imagination, reflection, and sense of enormous intellectual superiority, any possibility of being forced into a conditioned relationship to society must have also presented consternation for more practical reasons.

---

12. Glebe-Møller, "Recollecting One Who Is Dead," 534.

Health

A final concern that plays an important role in 1848 is Kierkegaard's health. Only the year before, Kierkegaard had been shocked to survive beyond his 34th birthday. There has been much speculation concerning the various sinister beliefs of the Kierkegaard family. One story is that Michael Pedersen cursed God from a lonely hillside in Sjæland as a child, bringing a curse upon the family that none of his children would live beyond the age of thirty-four and so outlive Christ. This belief is somewhat contexualized by the Herrnhut emphasis on the seismic implications of each individual's guilt and the belief in providential signs in all life's events.[13] Given that only Søren and his older brother, Peter Christian, had so far survived out of the seven siblings (two others having been struck down at the age of thirty-three, and three of them dying along with their mother within the space of two years) this belief becomes more understandable. As Lowrie points out, it is noteworthy that Kierkegaard entitled his first work, written shortly after the death of his father, *From the Papers of One Still Living*.[14] In one of "the most disputed of all Kierkegaard's journal entries,"[15] Kierkegaard describes the experience of a "great earthquake" through which he came to understand his family:

> Then it was that the great earthquake occurred, the frightful upheaval which suddenly drove me to a new infallible principle for interpreting all the phenomena. Then I surmised that my father's old-age was not a divine blessing, but rather a curse, that our family's exceptional intellectual capacities were only for mutually harrowing one another; then I felt the stillness of death deepen around me, when I saw in my father an unhappy man who would survive us all, a memorial cross on the grave of all his personal hopes. A guilt must rest upon the entire family, a punishment of God must be upon it: it was supposed to disappear, obliterated by the mighty hand of God, erased like a mistake . . . (*JP*, 5430/*Pap*, II A 805)

Kierkegaard's journals also describe a son who accidentally discovers some terrible secret about his father (*JP*, 5720/*Pap*, V A 108). Furthermore, Kierkegaard recounts the story of an old man who cannot forget the moment in his youth when, hungry and cold, he cursed God from a lonely hillside, even though he is now eighty-four—the age at which Michael Pedersen died (*JP*, 5874/*Pap*, VII1 A 5). As recounted by a number of commentators, when Peter Christian was questioned about this passage after Kierkegaard's death, he confirmed that it was indeed about Michael Pedersen and the Kierkegaard family.[16] However, to combine all of these mysterious passages is extremely speculative. If the "earthquake passage" does relate to a specific sin by the father, there is nothing to confirm that it was this specific sin.[17]

13. Cf. Kirmmse, *Golden Age*, 32ff. Garff refers to the family's "partiality for numerological mysticism," and "unfathomable logic of coincidences"—Garff, *Kierkegaard*, 136.

14. Lowrie, *Kierkegaard*, 24.

15. Garff, *Kierkegaard*, 132. Garff points out the real difficulties in assessing the "earthquake" text, in terms of when and why it was written. Garff particularly points out the confusion that was created by the less than scientific approach taken by Kierkegaard's first editor, H. P. Barford.

16. Lowrie, *Kierkegaard*, 22; Dupré, *Kierkegaard as Theologian*, 10; Garff, *Kierkegaard*, 136.

17. Michael Pedersen married his illiterate housekeeper (who would become the father of all the

Whether or not the story of the curse is true does not concern us here. What is important is that Kierkegaard shows clear signs that he believed he would not make it past thirty-four. Kierkegaard's friend, Hans Brøchner, recorded that just the day after his birthday Kierkegaard checked in the parish birth records to make sure there was no mistake.[18] A little afterwards, Kierkegaard rather understatedly comments, "strange that I have lived out thirty-four years. I cannot fathom it; I was so sure of dying before that *Geburtstag* or on it that I actually am tempted to assume that the date of my birth is a mistake and that I will still die on my thirty-fourth" (*JP*, 5999/*Pap*, VIII1 A 100). Consequently, although his thirty-fourth birthday was in 1847, thoughts of his impending death are formidably resurrected in 1848. As Kierkegaard writes just after his birthday, "My health is failing day by day; soon I may very well be released but I do not fear death; just like the Roman soldiers, I have learned that there are worse things" (*JP*, 6194/*Pap*, IX A 492).

Throughout this year Kierkegaard's journals are full of references to his health and approaching demise. Whether this was because of the curse, or simply in addition to these fears, is unclear. However, it is only by the following year that these concerns appear to subside.

Governance at Work

Each of these events reach their climax in 1848 and add to the overwhelming burden Kierkegaard felt at this time. However, it should not surprise us that such suffering should have a profound effect upon his authorship. Kierkegaard believed that it was through suffering that he gained greater proximity and sensitivity to God. As he declared, suffering is "the condition for my intellectual work" (*JP*, 6507/*Pap*, X2 A 92). Kierkegaard reflects from 1848,

> How often this same thing has happened to me that now has happened to me again! I am submerged in the deepest suffering of despondency, so tied up in mental knots that I cannot get free, and since it is all connected with my personal life I suffer indescribably. And then after a short time, like an abscess it comes to a head and breaks—and inside is the loveliest and richest creativity—and the very thing I must use at the moment. (*JP*, 6230/*Pap*, IX A 217)

This is clearly revealed during the "Corsair Affair," which Kierkegaard describes as an "essentially Christian collision," or "spiritual trial," through which he not only received an understanding of Governance within his life, but God captured him (*JP*, 6384/*Pap*, X1 A 258). Indeed, so significant was the "Corsair Affair" that Kierkegaard reveals his only other collision, an "erotic collision," occurred in his engagement to Regine Olsen (*JP*, 6385/*Pap*, X1 A 260).[19] Through each, God made him captive to his will in obedience and dependence. As Kierkegaard declares in 1849,

---

Kierkegaard children) only a year after the death of his first wife when it became clear that she was several months pregnant. Garff goes to pains to keep this possible interpretation open (Garff, *Kierkegaard*, 135f.).

18. As cited in Kirmmse, *Encounters*, 240.

19. Kierkegaard was engaged to Regine Olsen in September 1840, until he broke it off a year later. As will be discussed later, Kierkegaard offers no unequivocal reason why. However, Regine continued to play upon his thought and work until his death.

> I was meant to be captured. And I had to be captured in such a manner that, in the deepest sense, I had to come into conflict with myself . . . So it was I was captured, or I was forced to make myself captive to the God relationship. After it happened, it was as if Governance said: . . . you are trapped in the responsibility and captive to me. (*JP*, 6488/*Pap*, X2 A 3)

Indeed, the enlightenment Kierkegaard received was so great that in 1854, of three things he retrospectively praises God for, the third is precisely "that I voluntarily exposed myself to being abused by the Corsair" (*JP*, 6935/*Pap*, XI2 A 248).

Through the suffering and collisions of 1848 Kierkegaard speaks of understanding the hand of Governance within his life, gaining a knowledge of himself, the world, and "a proper relation to Christianity," that was otherwise beyond him (*JP*, 6594/*Pap*, X2 A 586). Kierkegaard argued that from this he received a new desire to continue his authorship following *CUP*.[20] The aim of the rest of this chapter is to discern what Kierkegaard understood the revelation of Governance to be for his life, how this effected such a radical change in his authorship after *CUP*, and why he entered such a prominent silence between 1851 and his final attack. To do this, four different periods of his authorship will be outlined, examining the effects of 1848 for his authorial progression, and so the foundation for his attack.

PART 2
KIERKEGAARD AND THE EFFECTS OF 1848

Period I: Penitence and Pseudonymity 1843–c. 1847

From his relationship with his father and Herrnhut upbringing, a crucial part of Kierkegaard's life concerns his identity as a penitent "before God." Indeed, Kierkegaard described the world like a "penitentiary," in which to work out his sins (*JP*, 4057/*Pap*, XI2 A 161), and himself like the thief on the cross, imitating Christ in his deepest suffering while accepting it as just punishment (*JP*, 424/*Pap*, II A 83).

It is, therefore, no surprise that Kierkegaard's high living as a young man should contribute to the guilt he felt as an adult. These thoughts resurfaced especially strongly as he reflected on his broken engagement to Regine. There are many theories concerning this relationship. However, an important factor was his belief in the essentially honest nature of marriage, and so the inevitability that Regine should be "initiated into terrible things," including "my going astray, my lusts and debauchery" (*JP*, 5664/*Pap*, IV A 107)—events the disclosure of which he pathologically feared (*JP*, 6372/*Pap*, X1 A 183). It can be suggested that it was most profoundly in his engagement that Kierkegaard suddenly became aware of his sins and their implications for his life.

---

20. Once we have understood the need for a passive reception of knowledge from God's hands, the requirements of a "life-view" in retrospective education, and the philosophical notion that "life is understood backward through the idea," that Kierkegaard should gain an understanding and meaning of his life through retrospection should not be considered a sudden attempt at self-justification—as has been suggested by Joakim Garff—but rather as consistent with his philosophical methodology.

Kierkegaard's sin and penitential nature profoundly influenced his first pseudony-mous authorship, describing his writing as partly an attempt to compensate for his sins (cf. *JP*, 5913/*Pap*, VII1 A 126; *JP*, 6002/*Pap*, VIII1 A 119). Against the belief of certain Romantic poets that they alone embodied and revealed the ideal for those who could not reach it,[21] Kierkegaard described himself as a "dialectical poet" who presented the ideal, while recognising its absence in both his own sinful life and that of the world. Such a poet cannot demand that others conform to the ideal but simply recognize how far they fall short of it (*JP*, 6227/*Pap*, IX A 213). Kierkegaard feared being considered a hypocrite, or of being led beyond his nature as a penitent by his own ambitious arrogance.

Kierkegaard's indirect communication has two central motivations. First, Kierkegaard believed that it was crucial for his reader to existentially appropriate his message. Secondly, it was also the method through which he overcame his fears of both hypocrisy and arro-gance. In this earliest period of authorship, it was the first motive that Kierkegaard em-phasized. However, as will be suggested, it is the second that is of greater significance to his later work. In these later periods, one does not find a change in his understanding of the reader, but rather of his own internal state—a change that allowed him to embrace a direct authorship.

Period II: The Direct Pseudonym c. 1848–1850

In a journal entry from the beginning of 1848 we find Kierkegaard's certainty and secu-rity concerning his method in pieces. Here Kierkegaard describes a sudden realization concerning "the relation between direct communication and decisive Christianity" and the interpretation of indirect communication (*JP*, 6248/*Pap*, IX A 265). Specifically, he became aware that he had used indirectness more out of methodological "uncertainty" than conviction, and considers it inappropriate for what he must now do. What that is, and why these thoughts have suddenly arisen, is unstated. However, his journals bear witness to the enormous internal strife they created.

At the beginning of 1849 light is shed on these questions. Through his suffering at the hands of society, and especially fears concerning his health and finances, Kierkegaard recalls that from the beginning of 1848 he believed that his authorial task was to end suddenly, devastatingly, and in a profound directness towards this ungrateful and cor-rupt society. Because "rabble barbarism has interfered somewhat with my incognito and tended to force me to be direct instead of dialectical," he reflects that he came danger-ously close to making "a complete turnabout" with respect to his method (*JP*, 6327/*Pap*, X1 A 78). This turnabout was to have been the publishing of *PV*, *SUD*, and what would later become *PC*, in one volume under his own name, dropped as a "incendiary" into the midst of Christendom while he disappeared from view—whether through death or an ap-pointment in the country. When both Kierkegaard's polemical object and message became more clearly defined through the "chaos" and "catastrophe" of 1848 (cf. *JP*, 6721/*Pap*, X4 A

---

21. Cf. Henrik Steffens' notion of the poet who alone creates "holy, radiant images of the eternal," as cited in Pattison, *Aesthetic and the Religious*, 6; cf. Adam Oehlenschlager and the notion of the "rare few" as discussed in Kirmmse, *Golden Age*, 90.

6; *JP* 6370/*Pap*, X1 A 167), through this "incendiary," Kierkegaard intended to vindicate his life and work through *PV*, as well as to wreak his retribution on society by expressing at its height the true revolutionary message that Christianity no longer exists in Christendom. In Kierkegaard's mind, no more devastating or direct a communication could be made.

Although stopped at the eleventh hour by "Governance," the impact of 1848 concerning the nature of his foe, the content of his task, and so the form of communication required, created confusion as to what Kierkegaard should therefore do. What he had written in *SUD* and *PC* was not only true but, as he would later reflect in 1849, "the most perfect and truest thing I have ever written" (*JP*, 6501/*Pap*, X2 A 66). However, it stood in painful tension with his penitential nature and refusal to go beyond himself that, after the heat of the moment, again returned as an influential concern.

Caught within this tension, Kierkegaard's journals reveal his fear that should he return to his indirect method it would be purely out of hypochondriacal insecurity (cf. *JP*, 6391/*Pap*, X1 A 281; *JP*, 6394/*Pap*, X1 A 309). Furthermore, he laments the place of the "dialectical poet" within society, and his fear stopping him from being anything more.

However, by the summer of 1849, a certain peace has returned concerning indirectness and his task, as he writes,

> All communication of truth has become abstract; the public has become the authority; the newspapers call themselves the editorial staff, the professor calls himself speculation; the pastor is meditation—no man, none, dares to say I. But since without qualification the first prerequisite for the communication of truth is personality, since "truth" cannot possibly be served by ventriloquism, personality had to come to the fore again. But in these circumstances, since the world was so corrupted by never hearing an I, it was impossible to begin at once with one's own I. So it became my task to create author-personalities and let them enter into the actuality of life in order to get men a bit accustomed to hearing discourse in the first person. Thus my task is no doubt only that of a forerunner until he comes who in the strictest sense says: I. But to make a turn away from this inhuman abstraction to personality—that is my task. (*JP*, 6440/*Pap*, X1 A 531)

While acknowledging the need for a direct communicator, Kierkegaard appears to regain a confidence in seeing his role as its John the Baptist, turning the hearts of people towards its message. Indeed, a few entries later Kierkegaard reveals a newfound zeal for this task, and goes so far as to define his pre-1848 method as a passivity towards society, gently and humorously revealing their lack of earnestness, in contrast to the challenge he now embraces, attacking society with whatever force it should require (*JP*, 6440/*Pap*, X1 A 541).

This newfound peace arrives in the form of Anti-Climacus, through whom Kierkegaard believed he could inject the full height of Christianity back into Christendom. Kierkegaard perceived in Anti-Climacus a mediator of this tension, remaining within indirectness and yet satisfying something of the demand for directness. While still a pseudonym, Anti-Climacus essentially transcended his earlier pseudonymity. Indeed, Kierkegaard would later reflect from 1852 that Anti-Climacus was almost too extreme, even for himself (cf. *JP*, 6813/*Pap*, X4 A 604).

Interestingly, Kierkegaard shows particular concern in emphasizing Anti-Climacus' works as coming from the traumatic period of 1848 and not the more peaceful 1849, stressing the works published in the interim, such as *The Lily of the Fields* and *Two Ethical-Religious Essays*, to be something quite distinct (cf. *JP*, 6457/*Pap*, X1 A 583; *JP*, 6487/*Pap*, X1 A 678). Kierkegaard's thought at this time suggests his desire to conclude his authorship with Anti-Climacus, but the sense of regret concerning these stray publications perhaps stems from his desire that the works of the "incendiary" should remain uninterruptedly linked with the events of 1848 and act as his ultimate and final response to them. These other works disrupt that link and perhaps soften the strength of his personal feelings towards society that his 1848 works clearly express.

By the end of 1849, during a time of peace at the thought of his authorship concluding with Anti-Climacus, we find a long passage in which Kierkegaard summarizes much of his position:

> I understood myself to be what I must call a poet of the religious, not however that my personal life should express the opposite—no, I strive continually, but that I am a "poet" expresses that I do not confuse myself with the ideal. My task was to cast Christianity into reflection, not poetically to idealize (for the essentially Christian, after all, is itself the ideal) but with poetic fervor to present the total ideality at its most ideal—always ending with: I am not that, but I strive . . . [F]or a time I misunderstood myself, although not for long. I wanted to publish this book. The understanding of my life as an author and of myself was, if I may say so, a gift of Governance to me, encouraging me to go ahead with becoming more truly a Christian—and the misunderstanding was that I wanted to publish it, forgetting that this would be an overstepping of my limits. (*JP*, 6511/*Pap*, X2 A 106)

In a following entry, Kierkegaard again affirms indirectness as his "native element," but through the events of 1848 "also acquired a deeper understanding of indirect communication—the new pseudonym" (*JP*, 6532/*Pap*, X2 A 195).

Period III: The Turning of the Tide 1850–1851

By the beginning of 1851, following the publishing of *PC*, consternation concerning his method again arose, creating something of an "inner frontier struggle" within Kierkegaard:

> I am a poet. But long before I became a poet I was intended for the life of religious individuality. And the event whereby I became a poet was an ethical break or a teleological suspension of the ethical. And both of these things make me to want to be something more than "the poet," while I also am learning ever more anxiously to guard against any presumptuous arrogance in this, something God also will surely watch over. (*JP*. 6718/*Pap*, X3 A 789)

This passage throws fascinating light on both Kierkegaard's progression and the events surrounding his broken engagement. It is his belief that it was always his intention to be direct as a religious individual. However, through this "ethical break"—the broken engagement to Regine—he was forced to become indirect, writing *E/O* in order to take the blame himself, because of his deep religious sense. While this remained his method for the reasons already discussed, Kierkegaard suggests that this initial desire for directness remained with him.

By May 1851, these thoughts had taken root. On Sunday the 18th, Kierkegaard mused over the possibility of preaching "ex tempore" by reading aloud one of Bishop J. P. Mynster's sermons, adding description of how it affected him to demonstrate the sermon's existential importance (*JP*, 6768/*Pap*, X4 A 322).[22] However, as he reflected later, the moment he considered actually taking this method on he also realized the risk that such an approach would have, placing himself directly before the congregation to reveal something of his own abilities and religious progression. To preach in such a way therefore meant "accentuating Christianity existentially as far out as possible," as if in public confession (*JP*, 6769/*Pap*, X4 A 323).

Kierkegaard describes falling seriously ill the following day, with "the dismaying, agonizing pain which constitutes my personal limits, something which had not happened to me for a long, long time." With each pendulous desire to either entertain this idea (and so to risk going too far out) or to cast it aside (and so risk giving in to fear) the pain simply increased. After a week of suffering Kierkegaard describes its culmination:

> On Sunday, the one following May 18, I read one of Mynster's sermons as usual, and the text for the day was about the thorn in the flesh: Let my grace be sufficient for you. That struck me.
>
> Meanwhile I was still reluctant to give up my idea [of preaching "ex tempore"], even contemplated forcing myself to do it. Now my torment increased. So I changed my mind, saw that once again I had wanted to go beyond my limits, and now I rest in the thought: Let my grace be sufficient for you. Inward deepening is my task, and there is much of the poetic in me.
>
> On the morning of Sunday the eighteenth I had prayed God that something new might be born in me (I do not know myself how it occurred to me); even then the thought pressed in on me that just as parents bring up their children and finally bring them to confirmation, in the same way this was the confirmation to which God was bringing me.
>
> And in a way that has happened. Something new has been born in me, for I see my task as an author in a different way—it is now dedicated in a quite different way to advancing religion directly. And I have been confirmed in this, and this is how it is with me. (*JP*, 6769/*Pap*, X4 A 323)

The concept of the "thorn in the flesh" played a crucial part in Kierkegaard's self-understanding. He described it as an obsessive reflectivity or "misrelation between my mind and my body," which manifested itself in overwhelming melancholy (*JP*, 5913/*Pap*, VII1 A 126). Although manifesting itself in an acute awareness of sin and guilt, Kierkegaard also saw it as a divine blessing through which he had become dependent on God. Up until this point, both here and in other expositions, Kierkegaard's emphasis on 2 Cor 12:9 always lay on the first declaration, "Let my grace be sufficient for you." When Kierkegaard understood God's grace to be his melancholic, penitential nature, this passage was interpreted as backing up his abhorrence of going out beyond this nature into direct communication (cf. *JP*, 4644/*Pap*, X2 A 246).

22. The Primate of the Church of Denmark at the time, well known to Kierkegaard through his father, and the figure who would bare the brunt of Kierkegaard's attack in *The Moment*.

Kierkegaard does not say much more about Mynster's sermon, and specifically why it should have such a profound effect. However, further suggestions can be made if we turn to its content. Entitled, "Our Duty To Be Content With God's Mercy," many of its themes and exhortations could well have been written by Kierkegaard himself, and it is perhaps this feature that allowed the sermon to speak so much into Kierkegaard's life, as if he were exhorting himself. Although discussing the sufficiency of God's grace, Mynster paid far more attention to the second half of God's declaration, "for my power is made perfect in weakness":

> . . . the thorn gnaws away and will not allow itself to be drawn out, so as to humiliate us, to remind us of our weakness, remind us that this strength, which expresses itself in us, is God's and not our own; for we are not strong when we think that we prevail upon all others by ourselves, but, as the Apostle says, when we are weak then we are powerful; when we feel ourselves and our state as it is, then we turn ourselves to him whose strength is perfected in our weakness, and in belief and confidence in him we become first strong, invincible.[23]

This affirmed Kierkegaard's initial apprehensions about direct communication in his desire to prevail upon society through the "incendiary." But the sense of "invincibility" through weakness must have spoken into Kierkegaard's concerns that he used indirectness only out of hypochondriacal fear. Furthermore, Mynster declares vanity to be found as strongly in buckling under the weight of the thorn as in seeking to overcome it, and warns that God will demand an accounting for all one's actions.

Ironically, Mynster may well have unwittingly convinced Kierkegaard of his responsibility towards direct communication, but also of its need. Mynster declares, "If the Spirit was always illuminated, its activity unhindered, then we might grasp an ill reliance on ourselves, and superficial thoughts might displace [the Spirit's light and works], as only mature in serious reflection, in doubt and dispute."[24] Mynster riles here against a future that Kierkegaard believed was already present—where the light and work of the Spirit remains unheard through the clamor of the human mind.

Over this week, Kierkegaard experienced an awakening of God's grace binding individuals to Himself by destroying their abilities, *so that* they might be equipped with God's strength to fulfill His tasks beyond their limits. In this understanding of grace Kierkegaard found the answer to the tension between his desire to speak directly and his nature as a penitent: affirming both. Through grace Kierkegaard was to remain a poet, and yet granted the strength to transfer his key phrase, "I am not that, but I strive," from the mouth of his pseudonyms to his own. Therefore, shortly after this revelation Kierkegaard declares, "I came by way of further reflection to the realization that it perhaps is more appropriate for me to make at least an attempt once again to use my pen but in a different way, as I would use my voice, consequently in direct address to my contemporaries, winning men, if possible." (*JP*, 6770/*Pap*, X6 B 4:3). A short while later, Kierkegaard goes so far as to discuss the "dubious qualities" of indirect communication, describing it as a "transitional"

---

23. Mynster, *Prædikener*, 197.

24. Ibid., 199.

method at best. Kierkegaard understood that when this grace, of both conviction of sin and affirmation through God's strength, had to be the content of Christianity, it could not remain hidden in indirectness (*JP*, 6783/*Pap*, X4 A 395).

Up until this point, Kierkegaard's journals reveal his methodological dilemma, even after the apparent peace of Anti-Climacus. However, from this point on he presents a far greater conviction, which, although punctuated by fears and concerns, never ultimately wavers. As a direct consequence of this conviction we therefore find a flow of writing, including *On My Work as an Author*, *Two Discourses on the Communion of Fridays*, *FSE* and *JFY*, leaving pseudonymity behind to proclaim grace directly under his own name.

In an entry from 1852 Kierkegaard presents something of a confession of his authorship thus far, as he writes:

> . . . the highest is not to understand the highest but to do it. Of course I had been aware of this from the beginning and therefore am different from an author in the usual sense. But I had not so clearly perceived that by having private means and being independent I could more easily express existentially what was understood. When I perceived this, I was willing to declare myself a poet . . . But here it comes again: the highest is not to understand the highest but to do it and, please note, with all the weights laid on. Only then did I properly understand that "grace" had to be introduced; otherwise a person is shattered the minute he is supposed to begin. (*JP*, 6801/*Pap*, X4 A 545)

Despite understanding existential necessity from the beginning, Kierkegaard was only able to manifest this through pseudonymity. Even when his understanding grew, this only led to what may be described as his direct pseudonym, Anti-Climacus. Only once grace had been injected to carry the implications of sin did he "properly understand" his task in directness.

Period IV: Silence and The Moment 1851–1855

However, following this flurry of publications, Kierkegaard went silent for more than three years. If Kierkegaard understood both his task and method, why did he stop, and only embark on *The Moment* so much later? Although Kierkegaard had relative peace concerning which method he should be using, the new direct authorship presented a new "inner frontier struggle."

Regine and the Common Man

In 1849 Kierkegaard describes the terrible predicament of the penitent. As discussed, the penitent is one who is captured by God and cannot escape. He is bound to God's bidding. This bidding, as Kierkegaard understood it for himself, was to present the highest dialectical contradiction of Christendom, to reveal Christianity's total absence from Danish society. Mirroring Faust, Kierkegaard believed his message to be one that would rock the very foundations of humankind's systems and reality, and could potentially lead to suicide (*JP*, 1791/*Pap*, X3 A 525). However, just as Johannes de Silentio argued that Abraham's sacrifice could only be enacted through faith if he truly loved Isaac with his whole heart

(*FT*, 101), so Kierkegaard understood that in order to proclaim God's message he must also love the world that his message was about to destroy. Given Kierkegaard's love of the common man and their simple life, his predicament was terrible (*JP*, 6306/*Pap*, X5 A 158). Those who listened to Kierkegaard would either reap a share in his melancholy or revel in pouring further ridicule and estrangement on him. Although he believed that his message was particularly aimed at the wise, the elite, the professors, pastors and journalists who promoted the deception of Christendom, Kierkegaard felt that the common man could not escape.

Kierkegaard's position is further revealed around the time of Anti-Climcus as he writes, "I love being human,"

> I never dare directly charge others, for it seems that the first thing I have to do is to make them unhappy, and I cannot do that, I who—all the worse, as the rigorous Christian would say—still so love to see others have a purely human joy in life, something for which I have a more than ordinary eye, because I have a poet's eye for it. Moreover, I am a penitent—and again I cannot take it upon myself to compel others to be that, but certainly I am that myself. (*JP*, 6616/*Pap*, X3 A 77; cf. 6834/X5 A 46)

These concerns explain something of the inner turmoil Kierkegaard experienced in his translation to directness from 1848. Indeed, he suggests that in using indirectness he was like one who ran away to the monastery in order to remain silent. Even after his final revelation of grace, the pain of his task is still overwhelmingly clear when he writes in 1853,

> I now live in melancholy's chamber set apart—but I dare to rejoice upon seeing the joy of others, and I dare Christianly to sanction it. To be loved by a woman, to live in a happy marriage, enjoying life—this is denied me; but when I emerge from my chamber set apart I dare to rejoice upon seeing the happiness of others, I dare to encourage them in their thought that to rejoice in life and to enjoy life are acceptable to God. To be healthy and strong, a complete man with the expectation of a long life—this was never granted to me. But when I emerge from my solitary pain and move among the happy ones, I believe I dare have the sad joy of encouraging them in their joy in life. O, but it must be told that dying to the world, to be loved by God, means to suffer, and that to love God means to suffer; therefore I must disturb the happiness of all the others, and I cannot have the sad joy of rejoicing in their happiness, the sad joy of being loved by them. (*JP*, 6837/*Pap*, X5 A 72)

However, it is not the "common man" who is Kierkegaard's greatest concern, but Regine, for whom he maintained strong feelings throughout his life. To preach this direct message to society in general was one thing, but to Regine it is quite another. In a tantalizing reflection from 1849 Kierkegaard comments, "when a hardened sinner in the last days of his life suddenly awakens to repentance and the pangs of sin-consciousness, send for me—with God's help I will be sure to preach. But a young, light-hearted, lovable girl, as yet without any deep impression—and then Christianity! Here I did not know how to preach. And yet she is no doubt much, much purer than I" (*JP*, 6469/*Pap*, X1 A 644).

It is no coincidence that thoughts on Regine resurface around 1848. Concerning his task Kierkegaard describes the pain he would feel, because he would inevitably become "alienated from her" (*JP*, 6771/*Pap*, X4 A 339). Kierkegaard believed that she had "no inkling of this kind of Christianity." Consequently, by 1853 he feared that his direct communication would create both a "religious disparity" between them, but also a belief in his arrogance (*JP*, 6843/*Pap*, X5 A 146). In 1849, following the death of her father, Kierkegaard considered a reconciliation with Regine. However, he came to regret having just published *SUD* as he believed that even through Anti-Climacus such a barrier was put in place (*JP*, 6762/*Pap*, X4 A 299).

When a true relationship with God can only occur through a complete break with the world, to keep the "common man" and Regine from suffering was essentially to keep them from God. From the moment of his awakening to grace, Kierkegaard expresses his lament concerning Regine and the "common man." However, each is always qualified by the declaration that it must still be fulfilled. Mynster's sermon may well have helped with this tension as he comments, "If the love within us never becomes wounded, if it is always happy on earth—as the children who are brought up too tenderly soon only demand to be cradled throughout life," so the weak and useless self-love, "might take that true loves' place, which forgets itself in the other."[25]

This goes a long way to explaining Kierkegaard's continued reticence and internal strife about embracing a direct method. However, one further event may help illuminate Regine's influence on Kierkegaard's silence. In his final attack on Christendom in *The Moment*, and specifically his mauling of the dead Mynster, Kierkegaard created an enormous scandal. On 17 March 1855, Regine left for the West Indies with her husband, Johan Frederik Schlegel. On the day she left, she passed Kierkegaard in the street and uttered the only words exchanged between them following the breaking of their engagement, "God bless you—may all go well with you," to which Kierkegaard could only stutter back a meager pleasantry.[26] Although Kierkegaard had already begun his attack in *Fædrelandet*, it had not yet reached its height. It could well be suggested that Kierkegaard had in part delayed his attack in full until she had left. On his deathbed Kierkegaard revealed to his nephew, Henrik Lund, the enormous comfort he had in knowing that his "little governess" was married, happy, and away from all that he had done in the last months of his life.[27]

Mynster

Kierkegaard's task inevitably involved attacking the church, and so also Mynster. Through the events of 1848, Kierkegaard became acutely aware of how far short Mynster and the church came to imitating Christ, and the proclamation of the Gospel. Mynster's words may have been abstractly correct, but they found no existential legitimation. As Kierkegaard declared in March 1854, concerning the events of 1848, "It was a catastrophe. In a catastrophe like that, the Christianity Bishop Mynster's proclamation represents is utterly untenable" (*JP*, 6854/*Pap*, XI3 B 15). Instead of proclaiming the true situation in Denmark and the need for internal, spiritual revolution, the church had fought for its own survival within

25. Ibid., 200.

26. Kirmmse, *Encounters*, 38.

27. Ibid., 42.

the "revolution." As Mynster was "a representation who carries a country," who "carried a whole age," Kierkegaard believed Mynster could have brought the country to its knees before God (*JP*, 6844/*Pap*, XI3 B 15; *JP*, 6853/*Pap*, XI1 A 1).

Kierkegaard understood his task with fear and trembling, not least because he knew that it had to be completely fulfilled before he died. In a long journal entry from 1853 Kierkegaard reflects that the moment he enters eternity he will be asked, "Have you carried out your errand, have you very specifically said the specific something you were to say? And if I have not done it, what then?" (*JP*, 6842/*Pap*, X6 B 232). Alongside a "morbid love" for Mynster through the influence of his father (*JP*, 6842/*Pap*, X6 B 232), Kierkegaard understood that as long as Mynster was alive his confession might still occur and bring that redemption to Denmark. If it was left to Kierkegaard it could only be achieved through violence and upheaval. As Kierkegaard reflects from 1854 following Mynster's death,

> If Bishop M. could have been prevailed upon, what could not have been achieved, what an awakening! And also how beautifully it could have been achieved, how solemnly, with what an elevating effect, without any commotion, which now perhaps can hardly be avoided, although it still may be only a misunderstanding. And how gently, how peacefully, how reconcilingly, whereas now there perhaps must be a battle and only God knows how violent. (*JP*, 6854/*Pap*, XI3 B 15; cf. *JP*, 6853/ *Pap*, XI1 A 1)

The works that followed Kierkegaard's awakening of 1850/51, although direct, do not express the full directness that Kierkegaard understood his task to require. But to proclaim the full message required attacking Mynster as the figurehead of Denmark's delusion. Consequently, Kierkegaard felt obliged to wait until Mynster either made his confession or died. Therefore, following Mynster's confessionless death, Kierkegaard embraced his unambiguous task, and having removed the barriers that previously held him back, committed himself to an undignified violence on society.

CONCLUDING REMARKS

1848 was deeply significant for Kierkegaard. During this year Kierkegaard's suffering reached a crescendo as he battled the personal concerns of his health, finances, and the fall-out of the "Corsair Affair," but also witnessed the "revolutionaries" undermine the spiritual liberation that he believed Denmark desperately needed. Furthermore, he watched the Church fail to intervene. When Kierkegaard believed that he received his most profound insights through the suffering of Governance, it is therefore not surprising that this year should prove so fruitful in both revealing his task and transforming his method. Although Kierkegaard continued to be plagued by his own limits and conditions, the works that follow 1848 reveal a progression as he slowly but surely came to realize his task and the full extremity of its expression. Whether one agrees with Kierkegaard's final attack on Christendom, or consider it too extreme, what has been shown is that it stands in continuity with his earlier work, and follows a consistent progression of his ideas as he became more and more aware of his task and his abilities to embody it.

3

Bonhoeffer and the German *Volk*

Introduction

BONHOEFFER'S LIFE HAS BEEN WELL DOCUMENTED. ALONGSIDE EBERHARD BETHGE'S magnum opus, a significant number of works have appeared in recent years, such as Elizabeth Raum's *Called by God*, Eric Metaxas' *Pastor, Martyr, Prophet, Spy*, and Ferdinand Schlingensiepen's *Martyr, Thinker, Man of Resistance*. These general biographies have been supplemented by more specific analyses of Bonhoeffer's relationship to the Nazi regime and the German resistance, such as John A. Moses' *The Reluctant Revolutionary*, and Sabine Dramm's *Dietrich Bonhoeffer and the Resistance*. The aim of this chapter is not to offer an exhaustive account of Bonhoeffer's life, nor to further scholarship in this area. Furthermore, it should also be clarified that the task is not to provide a complete analysis of the influences on Germany under the Nazis or reasons for the Second World War. The aim, rather, is to highlight a number of the substantial themes that were present during this period that had a significant impact on the German people, and Bonhoeffer's theological and emotional state. To this end, the chapter will first look at these themes in Part 1, before analyzing Bonhoeffer's interaction with them in Part 2.

PART 1
GERMANY AND ITS INFLUENCES

One of the most significant dates in German history is 30th January 1933: the day on which Adolf Hitler was sworn in as Chancellor. By 23rd March, Hitler had pushed through the "Reichstag Fire Decree" and the "Enabling Act," transforming his once ramshackle party into a totalitarian dictatorship. The speed with which Hitler was able to grasp control may appear incomprehensible to our twenty-first-century minds, especially considering the vicious behavior the National Socialists had already shown before 1933. However, Hitler's rise to power becomes more comprehensible given the issues that concerned the German people at the time—issues that had been brewing for more than a century.

Influences

Luther

One of the most significant influences on the German political mindset was Martin Luther, and in particular his understanding of the *Zweireichlehre*—the doctrine of the "two kingdoms." The *Zweireichlehre* is perhaps the most widely debated area of Lutheran scholarship. This is partly because it is not a directly formulated doctrine in itself, but an idea gleaned from Luther's wider writing. Indeed, the term itself is not Luther's but was first used by Karl Barth in 1922.[1]

In contrast to the extreme dualism of Augustine's *City of God*, in the treatise *Temporal Authority* Luther argues that God has not simply created a spiritual kingdom on earth in the church, but also poured out his creative love into the rest of the world. In particular, Luther proposed that God had created *Ordnungen*, or "orders of creation," which order human existence and allow it to live in peace and some sense of fulfilment. These orders cover all aspects of human life including roles in the family, business, civil service, servanthood, and government.[2]

Incorporated into the two kingdoms, therefore, is the further notion of the "two governments." Drawing on Paul's description in Romans 13, Luther argued that God's governing hand is exercised not simply through the church, but also through the state. Where the church's responsibility is concerned with proclaiming the Word of God for the sake of people's souls, so the state has responsibility to wield the sword of justice for the sake of their physical preservation.[3] For Luther, therefore, the two realms are entirely distinct. It is not the state's remit to prescribe rules concerning souls and the conscience, nor does the church have the ability to wield justice.[4] As Althaus comments, "we should separate [the church and state] as far from each other as heaven is separated from earth," as only disaster can arise from their confusion.[5]

For Luther, therefore, the Christian is in a curious position. As both a child of God and a citizen of the state, he or she is subject to both spiritual and earthly authority. Consequently, while the Christian accepts a certain ethic when in the isolation of the church, in the public realm he or she must be obedient to the state. The Christian is "two persons," each answering to a different lord.[6] As Althaus elaborates, "a Christian man is indeed a double person functioning in a twofold office and living under a twofold law."[7] The disparity is mediated for Luther by the idea that, because God created the state out of love for the world, obedience to it, even in ambiguous situations, is to take part in God's loving design and action. When in the church the Christian may embrace an ethic of pacifism, outside these confines he or she must support the state, even so far as to take up the role

---

1. Lohse, *Luther's Theology*, 154.
2. Cf. Althaus, *Ethics*, 47; Lohse, *Martin Luther*, 188.
3. Althaus, *Ethics*, 37; Lohse, *Luther's Theology*, 319.
4. *LW* 45, 104ff.
5. Althaus, *Ethics*, 60.
6. Ibid., 62; Lohse, *Luther's Theology*, 321.
7. Althaus, *Ethics*, 66

of executioner should it be required.[8] The two forms of life may look entirely different, but their meaning is the same, finding a "unity in love."[9]

The basic position of the *Zweireichlehre* provides a theology that affirms the state as the instrument of God, and a source of good in the world. Furthermore, it describes a forceful ethic of dutiful obedience. Without further elaboration one can already sense the significance of this doctrine for Germany under Nazi rule. However, the *Zweireichlehre* creates further consequences that are deeply important to this period.

War

For Luther, warfare is one of the tools of the state for the defence of its people. In the treatise *Whether Soldiers, Too, Can Be Saved*, Luther argues that an aspect of obedience to the state is to fight in its wars.[10] Consequently, Luther declares, "war and killing along with all the things that accompany wartime and martial law have been instituted by God."[11] Although such acts may seem terrible, they are a work of love, in keeping with God's plan for the world.[12] In a just setting, "it is both Christian and an act of love to kill the enemy without hesitation, to plunder and burn and injure him by every method of warfare until he is conquered."[13]

It should be pointed out that Luther believed that warfare is only just when it is waged in defence of a people. *Whether Soldiers, Too, Can Be Saved* is explicit in condemning warmongers, and those with ulterior motives. Indeed, Luther argues that anyone who actually starts a war will end up losing it, and that history has shown that seldom has anyone been beaten who acted purely in self-defence.[14] While this may seem somewhat optimistic, inherent in Luther's thought is the idea that God is acting in history, and such acts as war are not simply allowed to play out according to chance or human intention. For Luther there is a divine limiting, or policing, placed on human action.

Rebellion

It should be fairly clear from the preceding analysis that Luther does not condone rebellion against the state. Luther does aim to paint a realistic picture of the "godless tyrants and enemies of God" who sit in positions of authority, arguing that a good prince is "a mighty rare bird."[15] However, an evil tyrant does not justify rebellion. Only when the wishes of the state directly oppose those of God is one allowed to resist. However, when this resistance may take the form of refusal, it cannot be manifest in revolution. In *Whether Soldiers, Too, Can Be Saved*, Luther once again calls upon the action of God in history to argue that it is

8. *LW* 45, 95.

9. Althaus, *Ethics*, 70.

10. *LW* 46, 99.

11. *LW* 46, 95.

12. *LW* 46, 96.

13. *LW* 45, 125.

14. *LW* 46, 96, 117.

15. *LW* 46, 115; *LW* 45, 113.

not our responsibility to police the state, but rather God's. If He wants the state removed He will be the one who does it.[16] If people take that responsibility upon themselves, they will simply open the gates for a far worse ruler to take power.

Luther's affirmation of the state's divine appointment and task is such that resistance requires absolute conviction that the state's will is in opposition to that of God. If there is the slightest doubt, the individual is to obey the state, even concerning matters as grave as supporting its wars.[17] Even if the state does oppose the gospel, Christians should either suffer or move to a more tolerant region, rather than undermine the state's authority. Indeed, Luther argues that he has "never known of a case in which [rebellion] was a just action, and even now I cannot imagine any."[18]

History

As has already been mentioned, the *Zweireichlehre* reveals something of God's action within history. At the heart of Luther's views lies a certain natural theology such that "God can be known to a certain extent even where the biblical revelation, the word, and faith are not known."[19] Although it is a "superficial knowledge," and non-salvific, through natural reason humankind can know of God through his works of creation and history.[20] For Luther, history is the battleground between God and Satan. Despite the clouding of sin, faith allows one to discern something of these forces struggling for the lives of humankind.[21]

A further aspect of Luther's interpretation of history is outlined by Althaus. At the very end of *The Ethics of Martin Luther*, Althuas dedicates a whole chapter to "Great Men in Political History." Here Althaus describes God's action in giving humankind great men, not only in salvation history or the history of the church, but in political history.[22] God has not simply created the institution of government, but actually intervenes in politics to bring about his will. Such "heroes" and "wondrous men" have been ordained and gifted by God to the nations. As he summarizes, "Just as the individual person must wait for God to give him a new nature, so a nation must wait for God to give it a great man who has the kind of greatness that is beyond all the possibilities of human education and training."[23]

On 18th April 1939, these ideas were powerfully expressed in a text published in the official journal of the German Evangelical Church, by its president, Friedrich Werner, to celebrate Hitler's birthday—"In [Hitler] God has given the German people a real miracle worker; thus Luther named those who were truly great, whom God has sent out from time to time according to his free counsel and will, that they may work powerfully in the

---

16. *LW* 46, 107f.
17. *LW* 45, 126; *LW* 46, 131.
18. *LW* 46, 104.
19. Althaus, *Theology*, 15.
20. Ibid., 18.
21. Lohse, *Martin Luther*, 194.
22. Althaus *Ethics*, 155.
23. Ibid., 159.

breadth and depth of history, showing their people and the world new goals, paving the way to a living future and bringing in a new age."[24]

Volk

A final consequence of the *Zweireichlehre* to be discussed here concerns the question of which aspects of life are considered divinely ordained orders. According to Luther, obedience to God is found in living within his orders. However, this is not simply a general guideline, but a declaration that people should seek to embrace the orders that they find themselves in. Faithfulness and obedience are, for Luther, not a matter of where one is in society, but rather of how one acts within it. Although Luther does not preclude social advancement within the orders, unless one feels specifically called by God to do so the motive is more than likely to be selfish gain.

Luther's understanding of vocation is therefore to embrace the existence God has called one into being within. However, this must lead to the question of "how much" of this context, of the individual's social identity, is created and designed by God. For many in Germany it extended along national lines to the concept of *das Volk*.

Das Volk is a difficult concept to define. It is not necessarily racial, or even exclusively nationalistic, but often defines a group of people according to their communal attributes. *Das Volk* has a metaphysical element to it that unites a people beyond political or man-made divisions. As Moses describes, it is a concept that speaks of the soul of a people, of their tribal spirit, or *Volksgeist*.[25] Although this may seem vague, it is intimately linked to the history of a nation that had only been unified since 1871. Before then, the Germanic peoples had been disparate tribes. And yet they felt a significant bond that remained untarnished by the lines of division between them. The term "culture" in English describes attributes that define a group along intellectual, artistic and behavioral lines. As Moses describes, the German word "*Kultur*," intimately linked to the nature of *das Volk*, means much more, embracing the historical and mystical elements that define the Germanic peoples.[26]

For many who embraced Luther's *Ordnungen* in the 1920s, it seemed only natural to consider both the state and its specific people as orders of creation.[27] To fulfil one's vocation, therefore, was to live within and for one's own *Volk*.

Hegel

Hegel believed that his philosophy was simply the perfecting of Luther's ideas. It is no surprise, therefore, that one finds in Hegel a strong influence on the perception of *das Volk* and nationalism as a whole.

Further details of Hegel's dialectic will be discussed in later chapters. Here it is sufficient to say that for Hegel, existence is not static but in a constant progression towards

---

24. As quoted in Schlingensiepen, *Bonhoeffer*, 225.

25. Moses, *Reluctant Revolutionary*, 19.

26. Ibid., 18.

27. Althaus, *Ethics*, 113.

perfection. Specifically, history is progressing towards the fulfilment of the Idea: the single theme that unites and explains all existence. Throughout history, humanity has created and embodied forms through which the Idea is perceived and manifest. These forms have given way to new forms that fulfil this task more perfectly. In his *Lectures on Aesthetics*, therefore, Hegel argues that the more rudimentary form of architecture has given way to sculpture, which has given way to painting, and music, until it has reached the most perfect aesthetic form of poetry. However, art has itself given way to religion. And religion has given way to the highest form of the Idea, philosophy. History is always progressing forward until it reaches its end in the Idea. Nothing in existence is exempt from this system. The most dramatic example can be seen on the political stage. Here, progression is most obviously manifest through warfare and the overcoming of one state by another more powerful.

Hegel's somewhat evolutionary system does two important things. First, it offers a justification, or perhaps even an obligation, for warfare. Secondly, through an understanding of the perfecting of the forms through history, it allows for the possibility of reaching a perfect state. It is here that nineteenth-century Germany enters the picture. As argued by Moses, Hegel's ideas were developed and adopted by Germany, forging its identity as *the* "World Historical Nation," leading the rest of the world to fulfilment.[28] Germany came to believe in itself as God's chosen people, administering his will and justice to other nations. Consequently, as Moses comments, "Germany had a prior right from God to impose its *Kultur* upon the world for the benefit of all humankind."[29]

One of the consequences of Hegel's ideas was the notion of the *Machtstaat*—the "power state"—defined by strong leadership and duty. In the West today we tend to consider liberal democracy the obvious platform for human freedom. However, this was certainly not the case in Germany at the start of the twentieth century. An explanation is found in Hegel's understanding of the relationship between freedom and duty. According to Hegel, the progressive understanding and embodiment of the Idea maximizes human freedom. However, this is not the liberal freedom that conceives of itself as simply the ability to do what one wants. For Hegel, such freedom is a chimera as we are all constituted by different influences and pressures. Acting according to the emotions is simply to be moved and manipulated by external forces. Hegel argued that at the center of existence lies rationality. Consequently, the only way to be free is to choose what is rational and, therefore, universal. Freedom, is to submit to a system of dutiful obedience.

Up to this point, Hegel has been following Kant. However, he breaks away by arguing that a deontology based on "duty for duty's sake" fails to satisfy the problem of motivation—that is, "Why should I be moral?" In contrast, Hegel set up a deontology bound to each individual's personal satisfaction. The concept of liberal freedom understands people as abstract, isolated individuals. In contrast, Hegel argued that each person is created by his or her community. Consequently, the community not only creates but also fosters the individual's desires. Quite apart from acting as an obstacle or limit, by working for the

28. Moses, *Reluctant Revolutionary*, 8, 11.

29. Ibid., 11.

community through obedience to the state, one is actually promoting one's desires and self-satisfaction.

Hegel reacted strongly against representative democracy as he believed that it was far too influenced by individual, emotional choice. In contrast, he affirmed the concept of a constitutional monarch, a strong ruler at the head of a rational society, acting in everyone's best interests. When one considers the history of Germany's formation, the Golden age ruled over by Kaiser Wilhelm I and Otto von Bismark as Prime Minister, it is easy to see why Hegel's political theory should have been so influential in promoting the strong leadership of the *Machtstaat*.

Hegel was, of course, not the only philosophical influence on Germany during this period. Metaxas particularly points towards Nietzsche, and it is easy to see such ideas as the will to power and the *Übermensch* playing important roles.[30] However, where Nietzsche effected the mentality of the period, so Hegel provided a principled basis for its growth.

The First World War and the Treaty of Versailles

AN UNJUST DEFEAT

Following the end of the First World War and the Paris Peace Conference, on 28th June 1919 Germany signed the Treaty of Versailles. The Treaty was politically and economically debilitating. Not only was Germany forced to pay reparations to the sum of 132 million marks, but the treaty demanded the reduction of Germany's armed forces to 100,000—a number that rendered them helpless to external attack, and handicapped to civil unrest.

The Treaty was clearly a terrible burden for Germany. However, two further clauses would leave particular scars. First, Germany lost a significant amount of land. While this had obvious economic consequences, it was also wounded Germany's *völkisch* mindset. Germany's boundaries in 1919 had been in the majority defined by Bismark when he had united the Germanic peoples. These boundaries were far more significant than political lines. To Germany, the removal of these lands was not a loss but an amputation. Secondly, Germany was forced to take full responsibility for the war. For many, this was the most difficult of the conditions since the Allies had not only defeated them, but their demands were considered deeply dishonourable.

ANTI-SEMITISM

Given Hegel's understanding of the *Machtstaat* and the inevitable progression towards perfection, as Moses points out, it is interesting that Germany's defeat did not dent their belief in being the "World Historical Nation."[31] However, part of the reason for this is that Germany believed that it hadn't truly lost the war, but had been stabbed in the back. Specifically, it had been betrayed by the Jews, who had sapped German strength during the war, and masterminded its mistreatment at Versailles afterwards. As Scholder describes,

---

30. Metaxas, *Bonhoeffer*, 168f.

31. Moses, *Reluctant Revolutionary*, 34.

The thought of a Jewish world conspiracy against Germany was, of course, absurd. But it did not seem more absurd to many Germans than a beaten army, a scuttled fleet, street battles in Berlin, a government of worker's councils in Munich, a continuing flood blockade and a progressive devaluation of the currency. And anyone who had once given way to these thoughts immediately found evidence for them everywhere. Jews in France, in England and America; Jews in Berlin and Munich, on the stock exchange, in the press, and at the universities—was that not proof enough?[32]

Moses offers an in-depth, statistical analysis of Jews in Germany in the earlier part of the twentieth century, and comes to the conclusion that although the majority of Jews were upper and middle class, with small numbers who were both far poorer and richer, this was a different profile to the rest of the population.[33] Despite their efforts to become assimilated into the wider community, the Jews continued to stand out as a more privileged people. When one couples to this the anti-Semitic declarations of Luther in his infamous "Concerning the Jews and their Lies," as well as the association of Judaism with Marxism through its leader, it is perhaps not surprising that they should have been made the scapegoat. Certainly, it should be noted that anti-Semitism and the "stab-in-the-back" belief was widespread before Hitler's virulent statements in *Mein Kampf*. Moses goes so far as to argue that "after the enforced signing of the Treaty of Versailles, most middle- and lower-middle-class Germans, at least, regarded the Jews more than ever as "Germany's misfortune.""[34]

Weimar Republic

The Weimar Republic was created after the German Revolution and abdication of the Kaiser following the end of the First World War. It came to be deeply resented by many people, and blamed for having capitulated to the Treaty of Versailles and Germany's impoverished situation. This perception was not helped by the catastrophic effects of the Wall Street Crash.

However, the Weimar Republic was not only unpopular for its acts, but for its very nature. As a democratic republic, it was perceived as a foreign imposition that undermined the concept of the *Machtstaat* and the strength of German *Kultur*. The Weimar democracy was considered both weak and corrupt in promoting a relativism, pluralism, and secularism that Ericksen defines as a "crisis of modernity."[35] The march of industrialism, the growth of travel and transportation, and the creation of the modern city, were seen as threats to religious, community, and family values.[36] Furthermore, the intellectual positivism of the nineteenth century gave way to pessimism and nihilism, embodied in such anarchistic movements as Dadaism, which rejected reason, nationalism and war, and the all-important bourgeoisie.

32. Scholder, *Third Reich*, I:79.

33. Moses, *Reluctant Revolutionary*, 49ff.

34. Ibid., 52.

35. Ericksen, *Theologians*, 2.

36. Ibid.

The Völkisch Movement

As Scholder describes, the spread of the *völkisch* movement was one of the most important social developments to occur following the First World War.[37] As has been described in the previous chapter, at the turn of the nineteenth century Denmark underwent significant political and economic upheaval following the catastrophe of the Napoleonic Wars. It was in this moment of darkness that Denmark entered its Golden Age and, in particular, saw the revival of Scandinavian mythology. In the same way, in the wake of its defeat, Germany experienced a profound revival of Nordic mythology and *völkisch* sentiment. For both countries, it was a matter of returning to past glory, of seeking to revive true national and racial identity, of stripping away the corruption and disease that had forged the nation's failures.

Against the industrialism and secularism of the Weimar Republic the *völkisch* movement saw a return to core values in family, community, and religion, and a return to the strong leadership of the *Machtstaat*. Furthermore, in contrast to the Republic's pluralism, the *völkisch* movement emphasized an ethical dualism between light and dark, good and evil, idealism and materialism, bravery and cowardice, purity and corruption. In this way, the *völkisch* movement further emphasized a dualism of race between Aryan and Jew. Playing on historical anti-Semitic imagery, the *völkisch* movement further emphasized the corruptive character of the Jews as defined by egotism, mammonism, and materialism. In contrast to the goodness and purity of the Aryan peoples, destined as the hope for the human race, the Jews were parasites, draining its host nations of their spiritual and economic wealth.

THEOLOGY AND THE VÖLKISCH MOVEMENT

The *völkisch* movement had a particularly strong effect on theology. German theology had already undergone some important changes in the nineteenth century. Against the more intuitive ideas of Schleiermacher, the rationality and scientific method of the nineteenth century came to the fore. This methodology was particularly influential in the area of biblical studies where the historical critical approach gained prominence in seeking to get behind the texts of faith and the community to find the real, historical Jesus. This can be seen particularly in such famous works as David Friedrich Strauss' *Life of Jesus* (1835), William Wrede's *The Messianic Secret* (1901), and Albert Schweitzer's *The Quest for the Historical Jesus* (1906).

This methodology provided the perfect foundation for the *völkisch* movement. The historical critical method provided legitimacy to the stripping away of the corruptive Jewish elements of biblical narrative. Not only was the Old Testament rejected but, once rescued from the interpretation of the Jew Paul, Jesus was no longer considered the Jew who allowed himself to be crucified, but a warrior who spent his life struggling against the Jews before being betrayed and crucified by them. Removed from all doctrinal context, Jesus was interpreted as justifying the racial theories of the *völkisch* movement, even being considered by some to be Aryan himself.

37. Scholder, *Third Reich*, I:74.

The most prominent of the *völkisch* religious movements was that of the "German Christians." Heavily loyal to Hitler's NSDAP (*Nationalsozialistische Deutsche Arbeiterpartei*) they sought to bind Christianity to the Nazi racial ideals, and called for a united and dynamic *Volkskirche*. In its "Guiding Principles," published on May 26, 1932, the German Christians called for a "truly national faith in Christ, in the Germanic spirit of Luther and of heroic piety." In drawing upon Luther's *Ordnungen*, point 7 declares, "In race, nation, and cultural heritage we see the orders of existence which God has given us in trust; it is the law of God that we should be concerned to preserve them. Therefore, racial admixture is to be opposed . . . faith in Christ does not destroy the race, it deepens and sanctifies it."[38] As it continues, not only are the Jews specified as the danger in "foreign marriage," but it "demands that the nation be protected from the feckless and inferior."[39]

As will be seen, the German Christians were never subtle, and Hitler was forced on many occasions to distance himself from them. In a rally on the November 13, 1933, held at the Berlin Sports Palace, the leader of the Berlin Nazi Party, Dr Reinhard Krause, declared without equivocation that Christianity must be "liberated from the Old Testament with its Jewish recompense ethic, from all stories about cattle-dealers and pimps." As he continues, "Our provincial church will also have to see to it that all obviously distorted and superstitious reports should be expunged from the New Testament, and that the whole scape-goat and inferiority-type theology of the Rabbi Paul should be renounced in principle."[40] As Schlingensiepen describes, although it caused outrage amongst the majority of the Christian community in Germany, none of the Ministry of Church Affairs officials or bishops of the Reich Church made any protest to such statements.[41]

Summary

Hitler did not rise to power on a wave of nationalistic and racial fervour. In the election of 6th November 1932, Hitler received only one third of the votes cast. Furthermore, the decision to bring the Nazi party into a coalition government, and to make him Reich Chancellor, was a move of expediency on the part of the other party leaders.[42] First, it was considered to be a way of keeping him close at hand and so under control. Secondly, it was felt that Hitler would quickly show his inability to rule and so lose his popularity. As history reveals, neither hope could have been less well realized.

Many in Germany were wary of this extreme character. However, when he came to power, as Schlingensiepen comments, people reacted with "a mixture of apprehension and dim hope."[43] Very few at that time could have embraced the full weight of his ideas, and plans for war and the final solution only appeared much later. But Hitler appealed to people's fears and hopes. Many felt concerned by the violent nature of the Nazi party

38. Matheson, *Christian Churches*, 5.

39. Ibid., 6.

40. Matheson, *Christian Churches*, 39.

41. Schlingensiepen, *Bonhoeffer*, 148.

42. Ibid., 114; Metaxas, *Bonhoeffer*, 145.

43. Ibid.

and the brutality of his SA militia. However, against the backdrop of Versailles and the Weimar Republic, the importance of Luther's *Zweireichlehre* and Hegel's historical progression, and ultimately the desire for strong leadership, his emphasis on *das Volk* and the future glory of the nation was hard to resist for many people, even if it meant accepting more unsavoury elements. At this point, Hitler did not necessarily require followers, but only sympathizers who would swallow the bitter pill. The church itself was relieved to see the back of the Weimar Republic, which had sought to undermine its responsibilities and authority. Furthermore, Hitler appealed to its firmly Lutheran and nationalistic roots to encase himself in theological identity and promise.

Paul Althaus—A Case Study

From a somewhat ignominious start, over the course of his reign many came zealously to accept Hitler's ideas. While we will consider the church in greater detail in Part 2, the theological realm was certainly not immune. Indeed, given the foundation of Lutheran doctrine as already described, theology was, perhaps amongst all other academic disciplines, the most susceptible to embracing Hitler. For some it was a very small step to consider him not simply the divinely ordained leader of the secular world, but also as a "great man of history," anointed and gifted by God to fulfil his will. Individual theologians, such as Gerhard Kittel and Emanuel Hirsch, accepted the full weight of Nazi ideology and imbued their theology with nationalism and anti-Semitism. However, whole faculties underwent profound transformations. Heschel offers a fascinating analysis of the nazification of the theology faculty at the University of Jena. Here, not only were unsympathetic professors removed, but the entire nature of theology was transformed into a "*völkisch* theology," destroying all Jewish influence, and converting Jesus into the Aryan "warrior God." The faculty at Jena sought to become the center of *völkisch* religion, demanded that students read *Mein Kampf* and the works of Alfred Rosenberg before they were allowed to sit their exams. Furthermore, they were to use only the *Volkstestament*: a translation of the Bible produced by an associate department of the Jena theology faculty—the Institute for the Study and Eradication of Jewish Influence on German Religious Life.[44] At Jena, it was only Bonhoeffer's friend, Gerhard von Rad, who offered a dissenting voice.

Although painting a vivid picture, these are certainly examples at the extreme end. However, as emphasized by both Ericksen and Heschel, the most dangerous theologians were not the radicals but rather the "neutrals" or moderates. It was those who offered a plausible theological face who were far more influential. Although offering an analysis of Kittel and Hirsch, it is the considerably more moderate Paul Althaus that Ericksen argues was by far the most dangerous.[45]

The above analysis of Luther already shows some of Althaus' interpretation drawn, in particular, from his famous later works, *The Theology of Martin Luther* (1962) and *The Ethics of Martin Luther* (1965). In the light of his relationship to National Socialism, both

---

44. Heschel, "University of Jena," 377.

45. Ericksen, *Theologians*, 116.

appear not simply as overviews of Luther's ideas, but also perhaps as a defence of Althaus' earlier position.

As Ericksen argues, Althaus was a theologian through and through. His ideas were not inspired by a latent nationalism or anti-Semitism, but more by what he considered theologically coherent. Where Heschel argues that theology began to use "present-day experience" as the "hermeneutical key to truth," Althaus continued to put theology as the primary interpretive tool.[46] Although emphasizing the theological significance of *das Volk*, he stood in critical opposition to the German Christians and *völkisch* theology.

It should be noted here that there is a profound distinction between *Volk* and *völkisch*. Where the former is simply the affirmation of a people, the latter essentially defines a process of assimilation. The first is a concept, the second is an ideology. As Scholder comments, many who sought to oppose the German Christians, and National Socialism more generally, constantly had to walk the fine line of attacking the *völkisch* movement without coming across as anti-German.[47] In this way, Althaus was a firm supporter of *das Volk*. As described above, he believed that it was a firm part of God's *Ordnungen*, and therefore of legitimate concern within the individual's sense of vocation. Althaus never affirmed a nationalism that considered one *Volk* as necessarily better than another. In this way, Althaus was Lutheran but not Hegelian. Rather, he believed that the realm of individual responsibility was for one's own *Volk*, in distinction to any other. The responsibility of the church, therefore, if it is to be responsible for the lives of its people, must therefore be concerned for, and promote, its specific *Volk*.

Althaus believed that the Weimar Republic was deeply corruptive.[48] Consequently, he greeted the victory of Hitler and National Socialism with gusto, believing it to be the will of God in bringing the German people back to their true identity in health, vitality, discipline, reverence, and respect. As Erickson documents, Athaus saw in the rise of Hitler "the virtual pointing finger from God."[49] National Socialism wasn't simply a political movement, but one that was directed spiritually, and sought to affirm the spirituality of the German people. Consequently, for Althaus, affirming it was not simply a political decision but rather a moral one.

Given this background, Althaus publically legitimated the removal of Jews from positions of authority, not on anti-Semitic grounds, but rather as a defence of the specificity of the German *Volk*. As he rationalized it, the uniqueness of the German *Volkgeist* was best defended and promoted when Germans held the positions of influence.

A final important issue concerns Althaus' understanding of revelation. As described above, Althaus interpreted Luther as defining God's revelation as not simply through Scripture, but also through reason and the interpretation of history. This placed him in violent opposition to the thought of Karl Barth and the dialectic school of thought. As will be described in later chapters, Barth affirmed the distinction between God and humankind, established through sin. Consequently, quite apart from a natural theology, there

---

46. Heschel, "University of Jena," 376.

47. Scholder, *Third Reich*, I:99ff.

48. Ericksen, *Theologians*, 84.

49. Ibid., 97.

was no way of humankind gaining understanding of God and his will except through his direct self-revelation. The only "object" of revelation was Scripture, and even here humility and submission were required. Althaus did not hold to the pure natural theology of the German Christians, but considered a middle ground between them and Barth. Consequently, he argued that there are two different forms of revelation accessible to humankind: the primary *Heilsoffenbarung*, found in the revelation of Christ in Scripture, and the *Ur-offenbarung*, God's activity in history and nature that points towards Christ. However, even as a mediation between the two views, as Ericksen argues, "the fundamental, though unexpressed, premise of *Ur-offenbarung* as developed by Althaus is that God created and approves the current political status quo."[50]

This point was not lost on Barth. Barth's understanding of revelation underpinned the Barmen declaration—often considered the most important document of the Church's resistance to Hitler. Here Barth outlined the position of submission and obedience to God through Scripture alone, and not to worldly institutions that were overrun by sin. Although accepting the sinfulness of the world, Althaus argued that the *Ordnungen* were still created by God. Consequently, society is also holy. Just two weeks after the publication of the Barmen Declaration, Althaus added his theological weight to the *Ansbacher Ratschlag*, written by his University of Erlangen colleague, Werner Elert. This document affirmed the will of God as meeting each person in their context, binding them to family, *Volk*, and race. Furthermore, it described *das Volk* and National Socialism as the creation of God, and defined responsibility before God in assisting the work of the *Führer*. When it was published, the document was pounced upon by the German Christians and printed as the "official" word on the matter from the Lutheran church in opposition to the renegade Barmen.

Althaus was perhaps motivated more by theological integrity than Nazi ideology. However, as will be discussed in Part 2, one finds in Althaus an example of someone who was neither a Nazi or anti-Semite who, nonetheless, was seduced by Hitler through social desires and theological convictions. Furthermore, Althaus represents the man of moderation and Christian integrity who crippled the theological conviction of the Confessing Church. As will be shown, Bonhoeffer's struggle, at least initially, was not against the Nazis, but against those reasonable people who, nonetheless, muddied the waters of theological conviction to make all confessions of faith and statements of fact against the Nazis powerless.

PART 2

BONHOEFFER AND HIS CONTEXT

From his childhood, Bonhoeffer was an individual who forged his own path, often to the consternation of his family and professors. While he was no stranger to anxiety and doubt, he was a man of profound conviction who, when he recognized the truth, would simply not give it up. He would not bend, break, or keep quiet. To both friend and foe he became

---

50. Ibid., 100.

the voice of conscience, condemning and soothing in equal measure. These qualities are wonderfully summarized in the reflections of a fellow student after the Second World War, where Bonhoeffer is described as someone who "did not merely study and absorb words and writings of some master, but who thought for himself and already knew what he wanted and also wanted what he knew."[51]

Alongside this dogged determination, one of Bonhoeffer's most significant qualities was his ability to see the situation in Germany clearly before others. While this was an influence of his family—the Bonhoeffer household was staunchly anti-Nazi from the beginning—Bonhoeffer was also unusual in being so internationally minded.[52] Before Hitler came to power, Bonhoeffer had already made significant trips to Italy, Spain, America, Cuba, and Mexico. This was clearly of great importance in Bonhoeffer's involvement with the ecumenical movement, but it also immunized him against the nationalist seduction that was a real possibility in his youth.[53]

Moses describes Bonhoeffer as a "reluctant revolutionary." While Bonhoeffer embraced his challenge head on it is clear that almost all Bonhoeffer's work was a reaction against the period and the dangers and pressures Christians faced in Germany under Nazi rule. Bonhoeffer took a revolutionary stand against the influences described in Part 1.

Sanctorum Communio and the Word of God

Bonhoeffer's revolutionary nature can be witnessed at the very beginning of his academic life. Bonhoeffer was one of the top students at Berlin, and there were a number of professors who vied for his attention, including such illustrious figures as Adolf von Harnack, Karl Holl, Adolf Diessman, and Reinhold Seeberg. For his doctoral studies, Bonhoeffer opted for the latter. However, it was a somewhat odd match. Politically, Seeberg had supported the furthest expansion of the German border during the First World War and was ardently nationalist. Theologically, his ideas were a synthesis of Hegel and Schleiermacher, embracing both the unity of all existence, and the ability to perceive God through emotions and experience. As will become clear throughout this study, Bonhoeffer stood poles apart from his supervisor and, as Bethge describes, remained throughout Seeberg's "polite but stubborn" pupil.[54]

This division between tutor and pupil is crucially important. If Bonhoeffer had not been the dogged individual, and maintained his differences, his life and involvement in the resistance could have been entirely different. For in *Sanctorum Communio*, Bonhoeffer's first doctoral dissertation, Bonhoeffer nailed his colours to the mast. As discussed, theological resistance in Germany defined its battleground according to the nature of revelation and the Word of God. Seeberg, as with so many others, stood alongside Althaus in affirming a natural theology that ultimately legitimated the Nazi regime and the "conversion" of the Bible to fit the age. In contrast, Bonhoeffer stood alongside Barth and a

---

51. Bethge, *Bonhoeffer*, 67.
52. Cf. Metaxas, *Bonhoeffer*, 143.
53. Moses, *Reluctant Revolutionary*, 74.
54. Bethge, *Bonhoeffer*, 70.

dialectical theology. For Bonhoeffer, humankind is defined by sin and the chasm that remains between humankind and God. Revelation is not something that can be imagined or interpreted from below, but must always remain that which is given, directly, in the moment, from God himself. Where Althaus and Seeberg presented a theological idealism, Barth and Bonhoeffer sought to place God as the subject of all human thought and action, free from the corruptive control of the human ego.

These ideas rest at the heart of *SC*, but also define Bonhoeffer's thought in general. On his first trip to the United States, Bonhoeffer found a similar problem, where the Word of God had been transformed into a social gospel. For Bonhoeffer, the Americans were using the same hermeneutic tool as Althaus and the German Christians. Although it was bringing them to humanitarian ends, Bonhoeffer argued that it was still leading towards a "secularization of Christianity" (*NRS*, 91). Consequently, near the end of his time at Union Theological Seminary in 1931, Bonhoeffer presented a seminar paper, entitled "The Theology of Crisis and Its Attitude toward Philosophy and Theology," in which he promoted Barth and dialectical theology as in the "tradition of Paul, Luther, Kierkegaard, in the tradition of genuine Christian thinking" (*BBNY*, 463).

Barth and Bonhoeffer's attitude towards Scripture was not uncritical, but was still defined by humble obedience as the Word of God. At the end of August 1932, at the joint youth conference of the World Alliance and the Ecumenical Council, Bonhoeffer declared that "we are no longer obedient to the Bible." As continues, "We are more fond of our own thoughts than of the thoughts of the Bible. We no longer read the Bible seriously, we no longer read it against ourselves, but for ourselves" (*NRS*, 185). Here we find the crux of the matter. Although Bonhoeffer revealed in America and at this ecumenical conference that this is a universal problem, the situation in Germany had been created because people were more concerned about their own thoughts, than those of God. These are the sentiments at the heart of Bonhoeffer's *Discipleship*, where he declares in the opening lines, "It is not ultimately important to us what this or that church leader wants. Rather, we want to know what Jesus wants" (*D*, 37). Speaking more directly about the German church situation, in a sermon preached in the Kaiser Wilhelm Memorial Church in Berlin on May 28, 1933, Bonhoeffer described the presence of two different churches—the church of Moses, and the church of Aaron (*NRS*, 243ff.). The first is defined by the prophet, without pomp or rhetoric, who simply seeks the will and Word of God directly, and proclaims it to the people in all truth and honesty. The second is that of the priest, dressed in full regalia, who serves the people by creating a god for them to worship, to satisfy their impatient desires for both security and piety. Although the Confessing Church and the *Reichskirche* had not yet been established, this sermon shows what the dividing line would be.

To return to *SC*, it should be noted that Bonhoeffer did not simply accept Barth's ideas. Furthermore, he was also not so stubborn as to miss the genuine contribution that Seeberg and liberal theology were making. According to Bonhoeffer, Barth had moved God so far out of human history and experience as to make God impassive to his creation. For Bonhoeffer, Barth's dialectical chasm was so large that it was unclear why God himself ever crossed it. In a now famous passage, Bonhoeffer therefore declared that God is not "free from" humankind, as he believed Barth to be suggesting, but is rather "free for" humankind. Despite humankind's separation from God through sin, God has not fully separated himself from humankind. Rather, he has given himself to us in the form of the church. As will be shown in chapter 4, this was to be a radical ecclesial statement.

Nationalism

Bonhoeffer completed his doctoral thesis in 1927. In an unexpected move, revealing Bonhoeffer's equal commitment to both academia and ministry, Bonhoeffer decided to take up the role of pastoral assistant to the German congregations in Barcelona. This post was for a year, starting in February 1928.

Far from an intellectual break, Bonhoeffer had time to reflect further on his developing theology and to offer lectures to the members of his congregation. These lectures reveal issues that would continue to play an important role in his later thought—most significantly, in the realm of ethics. As will be discussed further in chapter 5, in the lecture entitled "Basic Questions of a Christian Ethic," delivered on February 8, 1929, just before his return to Berlin, Bonhoeffer sets forth the nature of Christian ethics, binding an individual to God's direct and timely commands. Against an ethics of principles that distract the individual from God's will for the here and now, the individual is to seek God directly. The only ethical law is that of freedom and responsibility before God. In his final analysis, therefore, even such ideas as murder cannot necessarily be ruled out.

However, the significance of this lecture is not simply in revealing the foundations of Bonhoeffer's mature ethics, but also his youthfulness and relationship to his context. Bonhoeffer begins by arguing that principled ethics "is a matter of blood and history," and so different in every culture (*BBNY*, 362). From this, he describes an ethic of war as found in Luther's *Whether a Soldier, Too, Can Be Saved*. Pacifism, according to Bonhoeffer at this point, may look good as an argument, but as a principled ethic it fails to take into account the concrete situation and God's timely command. Rather, the commandment to love gives priority to defend others against the enemy (*BBNY*, 370f.). To do anything else would be to surrender one's brother and sister to these destructive forces. This position is not necessarily strange, and certain elements of it were preserved in Bonhoeffer's later thought. What is significant is that it is not the "victim" as a concept who Bonhoeffer describes as requiring defending, but rather one's *Volk*. Bonhoeffer acknowledges that Christianity levels the boundaries to make all people one's neighbour. However, he argues that just as one is given preferential love and responsibility or one's family, so also for one's *Volk*. At this point in his thought, *das Volk* was one of the *Ordnungen*, and bound to the concept of vocation. As he argues, "God gave me my mother, my people [Volk]. For what I have, I thank my people; what I am, I am through my people, and so what I have should also belong to my people; that is in the divine order [*Ordnung*] of things, for God created the peoples" (*BBNY*, 371).

Bonhoeffer's first conclusion is that it is one's responsibility to take up arms and defend one's *Volk*. Such killing may still be murder, but in such cases one is not presented with the choice between good and evil, but simply two evils. Consequently, "love for my people will sanctify murder, will sanctify war" (*BBNY*, 372).

Bonhoeffer then turns to the concept of a nation starting a war, and his ideas are even more surprising. In the realm of economics, Bonhoeffer argues that one person's wealth often means the poverty of another. And yet it remains a vocation to be a businessman, and to strive for success within this field (*BBNY*, 374f.). In the same way it is the responsibility of each *Volk* to become everything it can be, even though this may inhibit and encroach on others. Revealing the influence of Seeberg, Bonhoeffer shows his Hegelian side by arguing that it is the "divine will that guides world history," leading each nation to perform its role within it. In this significant passage Bonhoeffer declares,

> Every people . . . has within itself a call from God to create its history, to enter into a struggle that is the life of nations . . . God calls a people to diversity, to struggle, to victory . . . Now, should a people experiencing God's call in its own life, in its own youth, and in its own strength, should not such a people also be allowed to follow that call even if it disregards the lives of other people? God is the Lord of history; and if a people bends in humility to this holy will guiding history, then with God in its youth and strength it can overcome the weak and disheartened. Then God will be with it." (*BBNY*, 373)

At this point in his life, Bonhoeffer revealed that he was still very much a product of his time, standing alongside Althaus in embracing the priority of one's *Volk*, not on the grounds of necessary superiority, but precisely because it is one's own. However, Bonhoeffer also reveals an affirmation for the concept of *Lebensraum* that came to define the Nazi desire for expansion into foreign territories.

Just as many were captivated by the new birth of Germany, against the corruption and stagnation of the Weimar Republic, so Bonhoeffer also affirmed the youth of Germany and their struggle to break free from these old forms. Upon his return to Berlin Bonhoeffer argued that the younger generation are seeking to "mount an assault on a culture that in the broader sense has become inwardly untrue, and in so doing to break the binds that fetter truth" (*B*, 361). Without reservation Bonhoeffer makes clear that he does not believe that "everything in Germany today looks wonderful and full of hope," and that such a movement produces as much "filth" as truth (*BBNY*, 362). However, these passages reveal his desire for Germany, and at least the flickers of hope within the situation, if not its actualization. Consequently, they link Bonhoeffer to the hope for rebirth that many Germans felt, and which was exploited by the Nazis. Bonhoeffer adapted much of this material in a later speech, entitled "The Leader and the Individual in the Younger Generation," delivered the day after Hitler's appointment as Chancellor. It is significant to note that the hope for the younger generation witnessed here is no longer evident.

An American Revolution?

Bonhoeffer returned to a Germany in a state of turmoil. The Weimar Republic was increasingly unpopular due to Germany's economic situation and the Government's desire to be reconciled to the Western powers. Then, on October 29, 1929, the world experienced the Wall Street Crash. This threw Germany into further crisis, with violent clashes in the streets between police and protesters in every major city. Such anarchy and fear was the perfect feeding ground for the Nazis. On Bonhoeffer's return, the NSDAP only held 12 seats in the Reichstag. After the elections of September 14, 1930, it increased to 107.

During this time, Bonhoeffer undertook his post-doctoral thesis, *Act and Being*, which he completed on July 18, 1930. With this out the way, Bonhoeffer once again turned his mind abroad, and accepted the opportunity of a year's study at Union Theological Seminary in New York, through the German Academic Exchange Service. This year would prove to be one of real change and provide one of the first substantial transitions in Bonhoeffer's thought.

As already mentioned, Bonhoeffer was somewhat critical of the theological training he witnessed in America. While he may not have felt inspired in the lecture hall, Bonhoeffer faced challenges to his earlier views through his relationships. Of greatest significance was the influence of the Frenchman, Jean Lasserre. For in Lasserre, Bonhoeffer encountered, perhaps for the first time, a Christian pacifist of his own generation. As Bethge comments, Lasserre was a trained theologian who could not be dismissed.[55] And although he never became a "pacifist" in the formal sense, Bonhoeffer was convicted about his earlier thoughts. For although Bonhoeffer's work presented the necessity of humble obedience before the Word of God, Lasserre showed him that he was not truly embodying it. For Lasserre, Christ's peace commandments as found in the Sermon on the Mount could not simply be laid aside by separating the individual into Christian and citizen. Consequently, he challenged the possibility of being both Christian and truly nationalist. Such a position failed to take seriously that Christianity is about recognizing one's brothers and sisters in Christ across all national divides.

In a lecture on "War," delivered in November 1930, we find adumbrations of this transition in Bonhoeffer's thought. The material for this lecture is also found in a sermon he delivered on Armistice Day Sunday, November 9, 1930. In the opening of the sermon, Bonhoeffer declares that before the cross of Christ all people stand united as sinners, regardless of economic, moral, or national identities (*BBNY*, 580). Furthermore, the people of God belong to an "invisible community" that again overcomes all divisions of race, nationality, and custom (*BBNY*, 581). This does not make such concepts irrelevant, but clarifies their relationship within Christianity. Consequently, in both sermon and lecture, Bonhoeffer addresses his listeners as a Christian, but also a German who seeks to explain the situation in Germany and to offer a defence of its relationship to the First World War.

As discussed in Part 1, Germany felt dishonoured by the Treaty of Versailles—in particular at the assertion of Germany's guilt. In both sermon and lecture, Bonhoeffer unreservedly attacks this assertion as not only historically incorrect, but also "an injustice against our country," against which Germany has the right to protest (*BBNY*, 415). As he describes, this is the wound "which still is open and bleeds in Germany" (*BBNY*, 414).

As Schlingensiepen describes, as a youth Bonhoeffer had been deeply angered by the terms of the Treaty.[56] In reaction to the military conditions, drastically limiting Germany's army, Bonhoeffer had protested at university with many other students by undergo-

---

55. Bethge, *Bonhoeffer*, 153.

56. Schlingensiepen, *Bonhoeffer*, 15.

ing voluntary training with the Ulm Rifles troop in case the Reich should need them.[57] However, Bonhoeffer had also experienced the consequences of the massive reparations, which crippled the German economy and made the basic necessities of life a challenge. As a young boy, Bonhoeffer had become an expert on the black market in order to help his family get by. Consequently, in his addresses in America, Bonhoeffer set out the tremendously difficult situation in Germany, and the sense of hopelessness and despondency suffered by its people (*BBNY*, 416, 583).

These addresses offer us further insight into Bonhoeffer's relationship to the situation in Germany, and his firm understanding of the pressures people faced, which influenced the rise of the Nazism. However, they also reveal that Bonhoeffer was not yet aware of what the future held. For here he outlines the identity of the German people, in all strata of society, as committed to peace. As he describes,

> The youth movement, which started immediately after the war, was in its tendencies entirely pacifist. In deep religious feeling we recognize every people as brothers, as children of God. We wanted to forget all hard and bitter feeling after the war. We had anew discovered a genuine and true love for our home country and that helped us to get a great a deep love for other people, for the whole of mankind. You see, there are many various motives working for peace, but whatever motive it might be, there is one great aim and one great work; the peace movement in Germany is an enormous power." (*BBNY*, 417)

It is unclear whether these words were spoken out of youthful naiveté, a desire to win over his social-gospel inspired listeners, or as a projection of his own newfound desire for peace. Either way, they mark a break with the nationalist Barcelona thought, and reveal the transition towards peace that proved so important in Bonhoeffer's ministry within the ecumenical movement, as well as in his final decision towards active resistance.

Bonhoeffer became aware of the significance of his time in America on his life and thought. In 1935, Bonhoeffer wrote to his brother, Karl-Friedrich, "When I first started in theology, my idea of it was quite different—rather more academic, probably. Now it has turned into something else altogether . . . I think I am right in saying that I would only achieve true inner clarity and honesty by really starting to take the Sermon on the Mount seriously" (*L*, 284). These ideas are conveyed more forcefully in a now famous letter to Elizabeth Zinn, a distant cousin and fellow theologian, dated 1st January 1936:

> I plunged into my work in a very unchristian way, quite lacking in humility. I was terribly ambitious . . . Then something happened which has tossed about and changed my life to this day. For the first time I discovered the Bible . . . I had often preached, I had seen a great deal of the church, spoken and written about it—but I had not yet become a Christian. Instead, I had been my own master, wild and undisciplined . . . Then the Bible freed me from that, in particular the Sermon on the Mount. Since then everything has changed.[58]

---

57. Ibid., 20.
58. As quoted in Schlingensiepen, *Bonhoeffer*, 95.

This transition from master to servant, from academic to Christian, continued to be a constant concern and desire throughout Bonhoeffer's life. When reflecting on *Discipleship* from prison very near the end of his life, Bonhoeffer reveals the same sentiments when he comments, "I thought I myself could learn to have faith by trying to live something like a saintly life. I suppose I wrote *Discipleship* at the end of this path" (*LPP*, 486). When one considers Bonhoeffer's theology as binding the individual directly to God in simple obedience, removing all the religious principles that stand in the way of this relationship, and standing firmly against any form of idealism, it is only natural that the greatest hurdle in life should be in destroying one's identity as master. However, these letters reveal the impact of Bonhoeffer's trip to the United States, in particular the influence of Jean Lasserre and his commitment to the ethical requirements of the Sermon on the Mount.

A Return to Germany and the Ecumenical Movement

Upon his return from the United States in June 1931, Bonhoeffer threw himself back into life. Following a two week trip to Bonn to meet Karl Barth for the first time, in August 1931 Bonhoeffer took on responsibilities as an adjunct lecturer in systematic theology in Berlin. However, again keeping his intellectual and pastoral sides firmly in check, in November he was also ordained, taking on further responsibilities as chaplain to students at the Berlin Technical University, as well as a confirmation class for 42 underprivileged boys.

Despite these already heavy responsibilities, Bonhoeffer also became involved in the ecumenical movement. Bonhoeffer's ministerial formation had been overseen since 1925, when he was 19 years old, by the church Superintendent, Max Diestel. Up until this point Diestel had been one of the most significant influences on Bonhoeffer's life.[59] Diestel had immediately seen Bonhoeffer's potential and, out of a desire to protect and nurture his protégé, had suggested and facilitated Bonhoeffer's trips to both Barcelona and New York. Although Bonhoeffer would have been aware of the ecumenical movement through some of the Berlin faculty, it was through Diestel that Bonhoeffer was introduced to it. So on August 14, 1931, Diestel sent Bonhoeffer as a German delegate to the conference of the World Alliance for Promoting International Friendship through the Churches, held in Cambridge. So successful was Bonhoeffer that he returned as one of its three International Youth Secretaries, with responsibility for the youth work of the World Alliance in Scandinavia and Central Europe.

In the light of the Treaty of Versailles and Hegelian-Lutheran hermeneutic, the ecumenical movement in Germany faced significant opposition. In June 1931, in the build-up to the World Alliance conference, Hirsch and Althaus published an article in the *Hamburger Nachrichten*, under the headline, "Protestant Church and International Recognition," that condemned outright any such interaction:

> In this situation, in our judgment, there can be no understanding between us Germans and the victorious nations in the world war; we can only show them that as long as they continue the war against us, understanding is impossible . . . This

---

59. Schlingensiepen, *Bonhoeffer*, 33f.

lends weight to the demand (that we) break through all artificial semblance of cooperation and ruthlessly acknowledge that a Christian and church understanding and cooperation on the questions of rapprochement among the peoples is impossible so long as the others are waging a murderous policy against our people.

Whoever believes that understanding can be better served otherwise, denies the German destiny and confuses consciences at home and abroad, because this does not honor the truth.[60]

The article was reproduced on the front page of all right-wing newspapers, and was officially ratified by the German Evangelical Alliance.

Unperturbed, Bonhoeffer spent 1932 moving from one ecumenical conference to another. In April he attended a number of youth conferences in London and Berlin, and between July and August attended three further conferences in Westerburg (Germany), Ciernohorské Kúpele (Czechoslovakia), and Gland (Switzerland). Although he may have been relatively new to ecumenism, Bonhoeffer engaged himself with his typical tenacity and boldness. This can be seen particularly in his papers at Ciernohorské Kúpele and Gland in which he demanded clarity of both the ecumenical movement's identity and task.

Concerning the former, Bonhoeffer made two points. First, he argued that the role of the ecumenical movement was essentially useless unless it had a properly worked out theological basis upon which to found its discussions and decisions. Without it, "ecumenical thought has become powerless and meaningless" (*NRS*, 159). Secondly, Bonhoeffer challenged what the ecumenical movement believed itself to be. In Bonhoeffer's mind, there could be only one meaningful answer: the church. Only if the ecumenical movement took on its identity as the church itself could its theology and declaration have any meaning and power to the wider world. Why should anyone listen to it, whether individual Christian or world power, unless it claimed the authority of the church as proclaiming the word and command of God (*NRS*, 161ff.)? Bonhoeffer declared unreservedly, "We are not an organization to expedite church action, but we are a definitive form of the church itself" (*NRS*, 184).

Bound to this concept of identity, therefore, was the necessity of the church's task in speaking to the world. Bonhoeffer's first point is one that recurs throughout his authorship: The word of God is not a timeless principle, but spoken *hic et nunc*, here and now. To proclaim general principles is simply a way of evading taking a stand in current events. It is a way of leaving the ultimate decision up to the individual. As Bonhoeffer declares, "The church must be able to say the Word of God, the word of authority, here and now, in the most concrete way possible, from knowledge of the situation. The church may not therefore preach timeless principles however true, but only commandments which are true today. God is 'always' God to us 'today'" (*NRS*, 161).

Bonhoeffer was clearly heading for collision with the nationalism of the German Church, and in particular the German Christians. No greater position could be presented that showed the church as ambivalent to national divides. However, Bonhoeffer's second point confirmed this collision. To the question of how one discerns God's com-

---

60. Quoted in Bethge, *Bonhoeffer*, 195.

mand Bonhoeffer refuted Luther's "orders of creation." At the Berlin Youth Conference in April, Bonhoeffer had already gone head to head with a number of prominent delegates on this issue, arguing that the orders should be rejected as a "dangerous and fallacious basis" for Christian ethics (*NRS*, 180). At Ciernohorské Kúpele Bonhoeffer elaborated, arguing that anything can be defended using this doctrine. Understanding what is an order, and which orders gain priority over others, is simply a matter of human interpretation. At its heart, therefore, the doctrine fails to take seriously the fallenness of the world and the human mind.

Bonhoeffer's position was not a wholesale rejection of the "orders of creation," but rather a rediscription. This he presented as the "orders of preservation." Orders in the world exist; however they are not good in themselves, but only as they are "directed towards Christ," work "against sin in the direction of the gospel," and serve God in preserving humankind (*NRS*, 166f.). Where they fail in this task or clash with the gospel message they have lost their worth and must be rejected. Bonhoeffer's interpretation very much depends upon his dialectical theology of the Word of God, against the more natural theology of Althaus and others. It is a matter of finding the commandment of God, directly, in and from the person of Christ.

This background set up Bonhoeffer's most significant statement to the ecumenical church. Struggle within the world is, or at least can be, an order of preservation. It is by nature the quality of Christ within the sinful world. However, as the "certain self-annihilation of both combatants," as that which "today destroys both soul and body," and so a direct opposition to the gospel, warfare can no longer be considered an order of preservation (*NRS*, 170). Consequently, not only must the ecumenical church "utterly reject" war, but it must do so publicly and authoritatively. As he declares,

> Today there must be no more war—the cross will not have it. Man must realize that nothing happens without strife in the world fallen from God, but there must be no more war. War in its present form annihilates the creation of God and obscures the sight of revelation . . . The church renounces obedience should she sanction war. The church of Christ stands against war for peace among men, between nations, classes and races." (*NRS*, 187)

Bonhoeffer's message was bold and fiery. However, when it was delivered in 1932—before Hitler had even come to power—it would have appeared extremely foreign. Before so many others, Bonhoeffer came to believe that should the Nazis gain power, a war would be the consequence. In Gland, Bonhoeffer describes the situation where "Events are coming to a head more terribly than ever before," defined by "desperate men who have nothing to lose but their lives," and "humiliated nations who cannot get over their shame," a situation with "*political extreme against political extreme, fanatic against fanatic*, idol against idol, and behind it all a world which bristles with weapons as never before" (*NRS*, 186). Although veiled as a general description of "the world," this passage represents Bonhoeffer's understanding of Germany and the path ahead. From as early as 1932, Bonhoeffer believed that war and peace must be the central concern of the "ecumenical church."

Before moving on to discuss the events of 1933 and beyond, a further statement about the church and peace is needed. Despite the absolute conviction that the church can do nothing but condemn war, Bonhoeffer was not a pacifist. This apparent contradiction is overcome when we understand the difference between the church and the individual. When discussing his newfound understanding of the Sermon on the Mount in a letter to his brother, Karl-Friedrich, on 14th January 1935, Bonhoeffer declared, "Here alone lies the force that can blow all this hocus-pocus sky-high" (*L*, 284f.). However, the peace command of the Sermon on the Mount finds its power and authority in the church, not in life of the isolated individual. In a footnote, Pugh suggests that "it is immensely difficult being a solitary pacifist because this form of resistance is too difficult without the support and discipline of the community of Christ."[61] However, one can go a step further to suggest that for Bonhoeffer it is not simply a matter of practicality, but rather of authority. At one of his final ecumenical meetings at Fanö, Denmark, in 1934, Bonhoeffer declared concerning peace,

> The individual cannot do it. When all around are silent, he can indeed raise his voice and bear witness, but the powers of this world stride over him without a word. The individual church, too, can witness and suffer—oh, if it only would!—but it is suffocated by the power of hate. Only the one great Ecumenical Council of the holy church of Christ over all the world can speak out so that the world, though it gnash its teeth, will have to hear, so that the peoples will rejoice because the church of Christ in the name of Christ has taken the weapons from the hands of their sons, forbidden war, proclaimed the peace of Christ against the raging world. (*NRS*, 291)

For Bonhoeffer, if the church began to read the Bible against itself, took seriously the Sermon on the Mount, and became obedient to God's commands for the here and now, it could bring down any state. This is how a pacifism that struggled against the sinful world finds its power and authority. It is here that we find what Bonhoeffer believed should have happened. However, as an ethicist of responsibility, bound to God's present command rather than abstract principles, once it was clear that Plan A would not materialize, he began to search for Plan B, a task for the individual, quite unfettered by the church's call for peace.

Bonhoeffer and the Rise of Nazism

Bonhoeffer's roles as both lecturer and chaplain allowed him first hand experience of the Nazi movement. Before Hitler became Chancellor, the most important group of people that the NSDAP sought to convert were students. So successful was this programme that Heschel argues that "students took the lead in promoting the Nazi campaign at the universities."[62] The *Nationalsozialistischer Deutscher Studentenbund* ("National Socialist German Students Association") gained immense support even as early as 1931, when one of its members was elected as chair of the *Deutsche Studententag* (German Student Assembly).[63] So, in 1931, when the faculty at Heidelberg offered the chair in Practical

---

61. Pugh, *Religionless Christianity*, 34 n. 64.

62. Heschel, "University of Jena," 367.

63. Bethge reports that even in 1930, at one university up to 90% of the students attending lectures wore Nazi badges (Bethge, *Bonhoeffer*, 207).

Theology to the socialist and pacifist Günther Dehn, right wing students caused so many problems that the offer was withdrawn. When Dehn accepted the chair at Halle, he was unable to deliver his inaugural lecture as students of the NSDStB shouted him down. Dehn was then sent on leave when the students threatened a boycott unless he was removed.

Bonhoeffer also faced challenges first hand. Though less severe, his role as chaplain at the Technical College was a constant uphill struggle as two-thirds of the students already belonged to the NSDStB. Within his lectures, Bonhoeffer developed a small but loyal following as he sought to stand apart from the nationalistic academic scene. It is here, in the winter semester of 1932/33 that Bonhoeffer delivered his lectures on "Creation and Sin" (published as *Creation and Fall*), expounding on the decidedly un-Aryan Old Testament, and again emphasizing a dialectical theology of sin versus idealism. With his gentle but earnest style, Bonhoeffer was even afforded opportunities to speak with the German Student Christian Movement.[64]

It was during this time that Hitler finally gained power, and once again Bonhoeffer showed his incredible understanding of the time, and opposition to the marching forces. On February 1, two days after Hitler's appointment as Chancellor, Bonhoeffer delivered a radio address entitled, "The *Führer* and the Individual in the Younger Generation." In contrast to his earlier descriptions in New York of the younger generation, and their desire for internationalism and peace, Bonhoeffer begins by arguing that in the face of the difficulties and corruption of the post-war period, the younger generation is simply looking for a strong leader. When one considers the description in Part 1 of the Weimar Republic, Bonhoeffer comments that for this younger generation, "individualism, liberalism, personality became terms of denigration," embodying the secular subjectivity that had destroyed true *Kultur* and *Volk* (B, 272). In reaction they sought to regain a true concept of community and authority. Previously, leadership had been considered a given order or office, handed down from above, and therefore carefully defined. However, the younger generation, in its haste and desperation, has established not an office but an individual: the *führer* who becomes a creation from below, an ideal of the people, a projection of their own ego and desires. The *führer* becomes the object of their salvation—a "political-messianic idea"—in whom they entrust their identity and hopes (B, 278). They transfer their rights onto him, and deny all true sense of their own individuality. As Bonhoeffer explains,

> The individualistic remnants of the youth movement have been overcome. That is to say, a strange transfer has occurred. The individual sees his duty in unconditional obedience to the leader. The individual is totally dissolved; he becomes a tool in the hands of the leader; the individual is not responsible; it is the leader who is responsible. In his faith in the leader, the individual surrenders ultimate responsibility to the leader . . . The individual is renounced in favor of the leader. (B, 277)

Where the office of leadership is created for the good of the people, so the people create the *führer* who becomes the *telos* at the expense of all others. The office gives, the *führer*

---

64. Ibid., 208.

takes. Through the office, the individual is established before God. Through the concept of the *führer*, the individual is destroyed (*B*, 281).

Bonhoeffer's thoughts were deeply perceptive and penetrating. It is no surprise that he was disconnected before he could finish. Bonhoeffer was one of the few to see so clearly so early on. Even those who would later recognized the horror of the Nazi regime and stand against it were rejoicing in 1933. At the same time Bonhoeffer was delivering his radio address, Martin Niemöller, who established the Emergency Pastors League and Confessing Church, and strived like few others to preserve and further the work of the church resistance, was preaching the dawning of a new age and the *führer* as a "gift from God."[65] As Bentley describes, Niemöller had been a U-Boat captain during the First World War and had not only suffered the humiliation of watching his fleet scuppered, but as a husband and father had also experienced the suffering and hardship of the post-war years in a profound way. He resented the secularism of the Weimar republic and longed for a strong leader to rescue the nation. Furthermore, as will be seen, he was also susceptible to a latent anti-Semitism.[66] Niemöller fit the prefect demographic. However, he was also a man of conscience and theology. Very soon it would be impossible for such men to maintain their enthusiasm and allegiance.

The Beginnings of the Church Struggle

In 1933, two things occurred that established the church resistance. First, Hitler sought to unify the church into a single *Reichskirche*, under the guidance of a *Reichsbishof*. Up until that point, the Protestant churches in Germany were split into 28 independent provincial churches. The basic principle of unification was not in itself unwelcome, and before the rise of Nazism it might have been relatively unproblematic.[67] However, the rise of the *völkisch* movement and the German Christians created a tension and insurmountable division within the Protestant ranks. The German Christians were so unsubtle and feverish in their support of Nazism, nationalism, and anti-Semitism, that they were even an embarrassment and obstacle to Hitler's subtle propaganda machine, let alone "orthodox" Christianity. The question therefore shifted from "unification," which was impossible, to dominance—which side would gain control? Despite the attempts of the old church to appoint its own *Reichsbishof*, the new government decreed their decision illegal and, with just nine days warning, Hitler called elections for church leadership positions to be held on 23rd July 1933. This threw all sides of the divide into chaos, but allowed Hitler to install Ludwig Müller, a firm Nazi supporter, in place as the *Reichsbishof* nominee for the German Christians. As well as orchestrating the support of the student movement, the day before the election Hitler made a radio address unequivocally promoting the German Christians in their support of National Socialism. Inevitably, it was a landslide. The German Christians won 70 percent of the vote across the board, securing the vast majority of leadership positions, and turning almost all districts into German Christian churches.

65. Bentley, *Niemöller*, 41, 42.

66. Ibid., 45, 62ff.

67. Cf. Metaxas, *Bonhoeffer*, 176.

Only in Hanover and the Southern German provinces of Bavaria and Württemberg, under the control of Bishops Marahrens, Meiser, and Wurm respectively, did the German Christians not gain the majority.

Within six months Hitler had successfully converted the official German church to his cause. However, there was another, far more sinister move afoot. On 7th April, Hitler had pushed through the "Law on the Reconstruction of the Professional Civil Service." The third clause, now referred to as the infamous "Aryan paragraph," decreed that all those not of Aryan race (such as the Jews) should be barred from holding positions in public office. Although its implementation within the church was not immediate, it caught the imagination of many within the *Reichskirche* who sought to bring it in, and it was clear that it was only a matter of time.

Both issues represented a clear contravention of the *Zweireichlehre*. So influential was Luther's theology that this was enough to wake many Christians up to what might be going on.[68] Bonhoeffer was again one of the first to respond.[69] Just a week after the implementation of the "Aryan paragraph" Bonhoeffer had completed the manuscript, "The Church and the Jewish Question," published that June. Here Bonhoeffer reaffirms the principles of the *Zweireichlehre* and the separation between church and state. Concerning the relationship of the church to the state, Bonhoeffer argues that it was marked by three steps: a) to question the state concerning its actions; b) to bind the wounds its victims; c) to put a spoke in the wheel of the state in bring it to a grinding halt (*B*, 365; *NRS*, 225). At this early point in 1933, Bonhoeffer is drawing the church's attention to the possibility of a *status confessionis*—a moment when the gospel confession is at risk and requires active protection—and the need to stand against the state. Most importantly, he argues that "the obligatory exclusion of baptized Jews from our Christian congregations or a ban on missions to the Jews" represents such a moment (*B*, 366).

Bonhoeffer immediately went into action. Along with his close friend Franz Hildebrandt, himself a Jew, Bonhoeffer called upon pastors opposed to the German Christians to go on strike, refusing, amongst other things, to conduct any funerals until the church's rights had been restored. This could have been a crucial blow to Hitler in revealing that Germany was not fully behind him.[70] Occurring at the same time as the signing of the concordat between Hitler and the Vatican, it would have made an impressive statement from the Protestant church—one that Schlingensiepen believes would have forced Hitler to yield. However, no one would consider the proposal.

One of the main problems was that ultimately Bonhoeffer was on a different page to the majority of the church—even those who opposed Hitler. For the church opposition, the primary impulse was the contravention of the *Zweireichlehre*; for Bonhoeffer it was the Jewish question from which followed the problem of state imposition. There are at least two reasons for the former position. First, the number of pastors that this would effect was relatively small. Secondly, many in the church not only believed that the Jews became irrelevant to salvation history after Christ's death, but that they were cursed for having

68. Bentley, *Niemöller*, 60.

69. Schlingensiepen, *Bonhoeffer*, 125.

70. Ibid.; Metaxas, *Bonhoeffer*, 179.

crucified him. In essence, they believed that any misfortune that befell the Jews, whether by their hand or not, was simply God's punishment.[71] For many within the church opposition, the Aryan paragraph was of far less significance than the state's involvement in the church elections. Even Niemöller entertained the idea that Jewish Christians should either set up their own churches or at least remain invisible within the church.[72] For Bonhoeffer the situation was different. Not only was Bonhoeffer first among his colleagues to see the full consequences of the Nazi Jewish policy for the churches, but he believed that how the churches chose to deal with the Jews defined whether the church truly remained the church.[73]

Despite the church's reticence, as he had done with the ecumenical church, Bonhoeffer believed the church resistance needed a confession that would unite it in making an authoritative statement to the state. Consequently, Bonhoeffer and the Lutheran pastor Hermann Sasse retired to Bethel to forge such a document. The final draft, completed in August 1933, expounded the gospel message as it related to the authority of Scripture and the importance of the Reformation, the nature of God and the significance of sin, as well as once again juxtaposing the revelation of Christ with that of the *Ordnungen*. Finally, it turned to a discussion of the relationship between church, state, and *Volk*, and set out clearly the continued anointing of the Jewish people and the error of the Nazi persecution. The Bethel confession was overarching and bold. However, when it was circulated to twenty different theologians for ratifying, including Paul Althuas, it was substantially watered down—in particular the section on the Jews. The final product was so far from the statement Bonhoeffer wanted from the church that he refused to sign it, and Niemöller had to be cajoled by others into publishing it himself instead.[74]

1933 was a year of significant disappointment for Bonhoeffer. The church as an official organization had been so easily conquered and, despite Bonhoeffer's tireless attempts throughout that year, the church resistance had remained silent. "On all sides, Bonhoeffer and Hildebrandt's radical proposals fell on dead ears."[75]

London and the Rise and Fall of the Confessing Church

In October 1933, Bonhoeffer moved to London to take up the pastorate of two German parishes. Although he had been made the offer in July that year, it seems likely that Bonhoeffer's decision was influenced by his frustration with the church resistance.[76] It

---

71. It should be noted that Bonhoeffer also considered the Jews to be under a curse. However, where this curse drove the majority to reject the Jews, it revealed to Bonhoeffer that the Jews were still in relationship with God, and remained deeply significant to salvation history. Instead of vilifying the Jews, the church is to consider them with empathy, fear, hope, and a watchfulness for the fulfilment of their destiny. Cf. "The Church and the Jewish Question" (*B*, 367).

72. Cf. Bentley, *Niemöller*, 62f.; Moses, *Reluctant Revolutionary*, 155.

73. Cf. Moses, *Reluctant Revolutionary*, 109, 116; Schlingensiepen, *Bonhoeffer*, 127; Metaxas, *Bonhoeffer*, 156.

74. Bentley, *Niemöller*, 65.

75. Schlingensiepen, *Bonhoeffer*, 141.

76. Cf. Bethge, *Bonhoeffer*, 325; Schlingenspiepen, *Bonhoeffer*, 136; Metaxas, *Bonhoeffer*, 186.

should be pointed out that a month before leaving, Bonhoeffer had helped Niemöller establish the Pastor's Emergency League—an organization that would form the backbone of the church resistance. By January 1934, it had gained a membership of at least 7,000 pastors, close to half Germany's total number. The Pastor's Emergency League was a cause for hope. However, just two days before leaving for London, Bonhoeffer was given a taste of things to come. On 14th October, Hitler had withdrawn Germany from the League of Nations in protest against its refusal to award Germany full membership. To this Niemöller, representing the hopes of so many others, sent a telegram to the *Führer* in the name of the Pastor's Emergency League, "expressing gratitude and swearing loyal allegiance."[77] For Bonhoeffer the situation was that of a *status confessionis*. Moving away from Hegel, it was not so much of "world historical" significance but of salvation historical significance. As Bonhoeffer would later express from Finkenwalde, this was a battle between Christ and anti-Christ (*NRS*, 337). As can be seen even in his earlier predictions of war, Bonhoeffer recognized that the dangers were not just ecclesial but affected every corner of life. For so many others the contravention of the *Zweireichlehre* was really a matter of church administration. One could therefore oppose Hitler here, and yet praise him still as the gift of God. As described in Part 1, one of the major problems was the desire to maintain both Christianity and *Volk* at the same time. Bonhoeffer clearly rejected the alliance of Christianity and nationalism following his trip to America. And yet this was not the case for the majority of the church resistance. As will be shown, this compromised their opposition as each outcry was tempered by the refusal to appear anti-*Volk*.

During Bonhoeffer's time in London there were a number of successes within the German church resistance. Most significantly, the Pastor's Emergency League undertook what Bonhoeffer had desired for so long and created a firm confession of faith, and with this the Confessing Church came into being.[78] At the end of May 1934, 139 delegates from Lutheran, United, and Reformed churches from around Germany came together and ratified the Barmen Declaration, written in most part by Karl Barth. Here the church resistance declared its objection to the foreign influences of the German Christian Movement, and to the Reich Church government, both of which were "wreaking havoc in the church."[79] In a series of six statements it then went on to outline the independence of the church from the state, its ultimate authority and obedience in God, and the humility of the world in sin.

Following the attempt by the *Reichskirche* to dismiss Bishops Wurm and Meiser, the Confessing Church held a further synod at Dahlem, where its statement was bolder still. It condemned the actions of the *Reichskirche* and *Reichsbishof*, and the incorporation of the *Führer* principle into the church, to be unconstitutional and a threat to the gospel. Consequently, it proclaimed that the German Evangelical Church had collapsed and no longer existed as a legitimate authority. Those within its leadership were cut off from the Christian Church. As its *coup de grâce*, it declared that "we have to proclaim today that a state of emergency exists and that the church has the right to act in order to remedy it."[80]

77. Bethge, *Bonhoeffer*, 323.

78. Bentley, *Niemöller*, 101.

79. Matheson, *Christian Churches*, 46.

80. Ibid., 50.

These were the kind of statements Bonhoeffer had been after for so long, and he took them incredibly seriously. In a paper published in August 1935 entitled "The Confessing Church and the Ecumenical Movement," Bonhoeffer declared the confessions of Barmen and Dahlem to be authoritatively binding, and demanding either a "Yes" or "No" (*NRS*, 329). Exactly a year later, Bonhoeffer took up these themes in an article entitled "The Question of the Boundaries of the Church and Church Union." Here he declared, first, that the confessions of Barmen and Dahlem had revealed the *Reichskirche* to be independent of the Christian Church; secondly, that one could not remain neutral to these confessions—any prevarication was effectively a "No"; and thirdly, as a consequence, "Whoever knowingly cuts himself off from the Confessing Church in Germany cuts himself off from salvation" (*WF*, 93).

In such statements, Bonhoeffer was not seeking to add to these confessions but simply to implement them. However, once again Bonhoeffer's calls were not only unheeded but vehemently criticized as far too extreme.[81] Bonhoeffer, it seems, had taken the confessions far more seriously than many who forged them. One of the main problems, as stressed by both Schlingensiepen and Matheson, is that the church opposition was not forged through a common commitment, but rather a common enemy. It was only because of the persecutions that they stood together. Hitler's most significant weapon was not to crush the church but to seduce it. Frustrated with the brazen incompetence of Müller, in the summer of 1935 Hitler appointed Hanns Kerrl as head of the newly created Ministry for Church Affairs. Kerrl promptly abolished the authority of all church governing bodies, including that of the *Reichsbishof*, and created committees to oversee each of the provincial churches, sitting underneath a further committee for the whole German Evangelical Church. The Confessing Church, and such figures as Niemöller, were too popular to simply crush. Consequently, Kerrl used a far more subtle tactic. Under the guise of protecting the church, Kerrl centralized all of the church's resources under the authority of the committees. If one wanted to receive a salary, take up offerings and raise money, make use of legal council, or even publish newsletters and other literature, it had to be done through the committees. Otherwise, all such activities were illegal. This severely drained the resources of the Confessing Church, and made a minefield of rules through which Confessing Church pastors could be arrested in droves. However, most significantly, it caused a fatal split. As discussed earlier, in the church elections of 1933, the majority of the church districts had come under German Christian control. However, in a few areas, Hanover, Bavaria, and Württenberg, the churches had remained out of German Christian hands (referred to as the "intact" churches). In this way they could be members of the Confessing Church while also under the auspices of the committees. They were protected by the state and could only gain from distancing themselves from the Confessing Church.

Although never finally separating, on March 18, 1936, the "intact" churches eventually set up their own Lutheran Council in distinction to the leadership of the Confessing Church, the Council of Brothers, and sought further agreement with the committees. In hindsight this dual alliance was fatal to the church resistance. Because these "intact"

---

81. Bethge, *Bonhoeffer*, 524f.

churches fought for themselves, and only sought real union with the Council of Brothers when under persecution, each time the Confessing Church sought to take a stand, compromise and division crept in. Even Bonhoeffer's struggles within the ecumenical movement were somewhat thwarted as it became almost impossible for foreign eyes to discern who, out of the committees, Council of Brethren, Lutheran Council, and the German Christians, was the true "German Church" with whom they were meant to be in discussion.[82] This alliance with the committees also allowed many pastors to be seduced into thinking they could remain a part of the opposition and yet retain their nationalism and salary. Consequently, many left the ranks of the official Confessing Church and became "legalized." In 1936, Niemöller had described the future of the Confessing Church as "cloudy," and by the time the Lutheran Council and Council of Brethren once again convened in the summer of 1937, following a new round of persecutions, it was already too late.[83] During this time, the *Reichskirche* had auctioned off the church youth groups to the Hitler Youth, embraced the Aryan paragraph, installed a "muzzling decree" that made illegal all discussion of the church struggle in church buildings or publications, and shown capitulation to *völkisch* theology at every stage. To all of these the church resistance had proved ineffective.

When Bonhoeffer made the decision to go to London, it was not without anxiety at leaving the front line. However, as he revealed in a letter to Barth eight days after his arrival, Bonhoeffer felt as if he were alone, and had constantly been opposed. Although Bonhoeffer never stopped fighting for the Confessing Church, he comments here that even if he had stayed, "it probably would not have taken long until I was forced to a formal parting of the ways with my friends" (*L*, 23). Already at this early stage, there is a sense of separation between Bonhoeffer and the church resistance. Although Barth responded in no uncertain terms that Bonhoeffer should be in Berlin "with all guns blazing," in hindsight it is unclear what Bonhoeffer could have done to such fickle and divided opposition (*L*, 39). Bonhoeffer was considered a "zealot,"[84] "legalist,"[85] "pessimist,"[86] an "inconvenient Cassandra,"[87] a "lightning rod for controversy,"[88] and even a heretic by many in the church resistance.[89] Given his frustrations and sense of isolation, it was perhaps important that Bonhoeffer withdrew in order to recharge his fighting spirit.

While in London, Bonhoeffer continued to work tirelessly for the resistance. He not only succeeded in uniting the expatriate churches around England against the injustices of the *Reichskirche*, but led the churches to bombard it with telegrams and petitions. Hitler's plans relied upon presenting a united and positive image to the foreign press. Consequently, the expatriate community were extremely important. So disturbing

---

82. Cf. ibid., 493.

83. Bentley, *Niemöller*, 122.

84. Bethge, *Bonhoeffer*, 569.

85. Ibid., 521f.

86. Schlingensiepen, *Bonhoeffer*, 167.

87. Ibid., 127.

88. Metaxas, *Bonhoeffer*, 278.

89. Bethge, *Bonhoeffer*, 521f.

were these protests from the English Germans that emissaries, including theologians and lawyers, were sent to convert them to the *Führer's* way of thinking. However, they came up against Bonhoeffer who thwarted every attempt. Without wasting a moment, he had declared in the first meeting that in the face of the failures of the church and its bishop, "the most urgent church-political task was secession from such a church, rather than an attempt to achieve unified organization whatever the circumstances."[90] On 4th November 1934, the expatriate churches did just that.

The expatriate churches were not as diverse, or perhaps even as nationalistic, as those in the fatherland. However, in London Bonhoeffer saw the impact that even a small number of churches could achieve with a unity of faith and will. It is hard to imagine that this must have been bittersweet as he considered the difficulties of the wider church resistance.

Finkenwalde and Resistance

During this time Bonhoeffer continued to work energetically within the ecumenical movement, as well as lend support to the Confessing Church itself. In April 1935, Bonhoeffer accepted the post of leading the Confessing Church seminary, first at Zingst on the Baltic Sea, before moving to Finkenwalde in what is now Poland. In that significant letter to his brother, Karl-Friedrich, written while still in London on January 14, 1935, Bonhoeffer commented that "The restoration of the church must surely depend on a new kind of monasticism, which has nothing in common with the old but a life of uncompromising discipleship, following Christ according to the Sermon on the Mount" (*L*, 285). At Finkenwalde he was able to put this into practice. Although some would add "monkish" to his list of accolades, Bonhoeffer sought to create a truly spiritual community, of shared hope, faith, and confession. In such difficult times, this was the trust and unity Bonhoeffer believed the church must have if it was to be effective and even survive with its identity intact.[91] Sadly, the experiment was short lived. On December 2, 1935, Kerrl made illegal the hiring and training of ordinands outside of the committees. In many respects, it is amazing that it survived as long as it did; it was almost two years later, in September 1937, that the Gestapo finally arrived. By November, 27 of his seminarians were in prison. This did not spell the end of the Confessing Church seminaries. From the end of 1937 until 1940 Bonhoeffer moved to East Pomerania where he continued to teach several seminary pastorates under the radar. However, it marked the end of Bonhoeffer's desire for a truly Christian community. Despite its short life, Finkenwalde produced two of the twentieth-century's spiritual classics: *Discipleship*, delivered as lectures to the seminarians, and *LT*, Bonhoeffer's later reflections of the community life, published 1937 and 1939 respectively. Both works continued to be of immense importance and encouragement to the Confessing Church pastors and seminarians scatted throughout Germany and the front line.

Meanwhile, things had worsened in the church resistance. At the beginning of 1938, the church president, Dr Friedrich Werner, demanded that all Protestant pastors swear an oath of allegiance to Hitler to mark his forty-ninth birthday. Refusal would mean in-

90. Ibid., 349.
91. Schlingensiepen, *Bonhoeffer*, 182.

stant dismissal. As Pugh comments, 85 percent of Confessing Church pastors capitulated.[92] Furthermore, in the summer that year the Confessing Church and Lutheran Council had again sought reconciliation. However, this could only be attempted by limiting the Barmen and Dahlem Declarations. As Schlingensiepen comments, when the synagogues burned on 9th November 1938, "the Confessing Church no longer had the strength to protest," and remained silent.[93]

Bonhoeffer found himself in a difficult position. Resistance through the church was no longer a possibility. Consequently, it was unclear to him how to proceed. The situation was further complicated as he himself had been targeted by the state. In January 1938 he had been banned from residing in Berlin and Brandenburg. On August 22, 1940, he was then banned from public speaking. And then on March 19, 1941, he was banned from publishing. In many ways it was surprising he had maintained such liberty as long as he had. However, he now found his wings firmly clipped.

However, a further issue had arisen. Although not a pacifist, Bonhoeffer had believed for some time that war was inevitable and, equally, that he would refuse to fight. Not only would this have meant certain execution, but he would find no support for his actions within a still nationalistic church that had no theology of conscientious objection.[94] In June 1939, Bonhoeffer therefore accepted the invitation from Reinhold Niebuhr to come to New York. However, before he had even docked, he felt deeply uncertain about the decision to leave Germany and, by July 27, he had arrived back.

The "solution" to Bonhoeffer's problem came in the form of his brother-in-law, Hans von Dohnanyi. As a brilliant lawyer, von Dohnanyi had risen through the ranks of the civil service. Without accident he ended up in Department Z of the foreign office of the Military Intelligence (*Abwehr*) as special aid to Colonel Hans Oster, under the overall supervision of Admiral Wilhelm Canaris. All three had been opposed to Hitler for a long time—von Dohnanyi had been keeping a file of Nazi atrocities since 1933—and Department Z became the center of political opposition.[95] Although Bonhoeffer's involvement with the conspirators is often considered from the second half of 1940 onwards, Dramm convincingly argues that Bonhoeffer had already started to work for the *Abwehr* from October 1939.[96] Oster, Canaris, and von Dohnanyi had been involved in conspiracy for a number of years before they convened in Department Z and Bonhoeffer became involved. Initially their hopes were to have Hitler simply arrested. However, it became clear quite quickly that assassination was the only viable option. The first such attempt was on November 9, 1939. From this followed numerous others. Quite unlike common conceptions, the most difficult but important aspect of the assassination attempts was PR. The conspirators desired to get rid of Hitler, but also to set up a working and just political system in his place. They could not simply leave the country open for anyone to take charge. This required winning over a number of significant political and military figures to their cause. However, once

92. Pugh, *Religionless Christianity*, 40.

93. Schlingensiepen, *Bonhoeffer*, 215, 221.

94. Ibid., 208.

95. Dramm, *Resistance*, 35.

96. Ibid., 22ff.

war had begun, they also needed, if not their support, at least a guarantee from Germany's enemies that they would acknowledge the new government and seek a peace together. The complicating factor was that neither group would move without the other. The German generals would not support the coup without the Allies' guarantee, and the Allies would not offer it until they saw the seriousness of the resistance movement and the prominent names behind it.[97] At the heart of the conspiracy was this delicate but crucial diplomacy. Canaris, Oster, and von Dohnanyi could deal with the negotiations from the German side, but they had very little experience internationally and lacked the appropriate connections. At this point Bonhoeffer enters the picture. Bonhoeffer's time in England and America, as well as his involvement in the ecumenical movement, made him perfect for the task. Consequently, he became one of the *Abwehr's* double agents. On the surface he was sent to gain information about the Allies' movements and alliances, but in reality was communicating to them the intentions and needs of the conspirators. It also solved the problem of conscription. When Bonhoeffer was called up for a medical exam on June 5, 1940, the *Abwehr* were able to have him listed as *UK (Unabkömmlich)*—indispensible.

During this time Bonhoeffer made trips to Switzerland, Norway, Sweden, and Italy for the conspirators, and made contact, most significantly, with Bishop George Bell (whom he had first met in England) and the Dutch Reformed theologian, Willem Visser't Hooft, then general secretary for the World Council of Churches. Bell and Visser't Hooft worked tirelessly to pass on and promote the message from the resistance to the British, with Visser't Hooft also making contact with the Americans. Sadly, it consistently fell on deaf ears. As Dramm comments, on 20th January 1941 Churchill had already issued an unambiguous instruction that the British should remain silent to any such enquiries.[98] Even when presented with a list of reputable names of those involved, this policy was maintained. Nonetheless, assassination attempt after assassination attempt was made, without success.

Hitler's organization of the various state departments made them independent of each other, but also, therefore, in competition with one another. This worked in the conspirators' favor as it allowed them to draw up papers and visas for Bonhoeffer who was considered by other departments an enemy of the state.[99] However, it led to the conspirators' ultimate downfall. The *Abwehr* had always been in conflict with the Reich Central Security Office, who sought to take it over. When a financial discrepancy was discovered at the *Abwehr's* Munich office, this led to the arrest of von Dohnanyi, Bonhoeffer and a number of others. Initially, the charges remained comparatively trivial, and it was hoped that the cases would simply "fizzle out."[100] Bonhoeffer himself ended up being investigated for having avoided the draft. However, following a further failed assassination attempt on

97. Ibid., f87f.

98. Dramm, *Resistance*, 79.

99. Bonhoeffer's position was so unusual that even Barth and colleagues in Switzerland questioned his allegiances as he was able to visit them so often. Cf. Schlingensiepen, *Bonhoeffer*, 261; Dramm, *Resistance*, 112, 155.

100. Dramm, *Resistance*, 232.

20th July 1944, files were discovered that detailed the full range of treason perpetrated by Department Z, and later Canaris' diary. From this there was little hope of rescue.

CONCLUSIONS

Bonhoeffer did not have to detonate a bomb, or pull a trigger. Although Dramm suggests that we cannot finally know how much Bonhoeffer was involved in, or had awareness of, the inner workings of the assassination attempts themselves, it is clear that he believed assassination was the only solution, and that he was working to this end.[101] Without lessening the anxiety of Bonhoeffer's decision, the possibility of its path had already been laid within his ethics. We remember here Bonhoeffer's pronouncements in Barcelona that within the economy of God's will "even murder can be sanctified" (*BBNY*, 367). However, in making his decision, Bonhoeffer made himself terribly alone. Had Bonhoeffer informed the Confessing Church of his intentions it simply would have confirmed their worst fears about him. The Confessing Church remained nationalist, and Lutheran. For Bonhoeffer to be a conscientious objector *and* involved in a political coup—again remembering Luther's declaration that he could think of no possible circumstances in which rebellion could be justified—was beyond outrageous. Even other Christians who were actively involved in the political resistance could not conceive of assassination as ever being justified.

Schlingensiepen's description of Bonhoeffer as a Cassandra to the church is perceptive. Sixty years later, and with a clearer picture of what went on, we can consider Bonhoeffer's predictions to have been right. And yet his calls went consistently unheeded. The heart of his message, beyond all its final applications, was an unqualified obedience to the Word of God spoken anew each day, against any ego-centered idealism, however veiled it might be.

---

101. Cf. Dramm, *Resistance*, 223.

4

Attack on Idealism—Epistemology

Introduction

As described in chapter 3, in *SC* Bonhoeffer nailed his colors to the mast, and stood against the idealist hermeneutic of the likes of Seeberg and Althaus. Bonhoeffer left no doubt in the minds of his readers, dedicating the very first two chapters of his authorship to an energetic critique of German Idealism. Bonhoeffer placed himself in a qualified relationship to Barth and the dialectic school. However, what particularly interests us here are his comments at the end of this section. Here he reveals,

> Our argument is close to [Kierkegaard's] in its critique of the idealist concept of time and reality. I depart from Kierkegaard, however, where he speaks of the origin of the ethical person. For him, becoming a person is an act of the self-establishing I—to be sure in a state of ethical decision. Kierkegaard's ethical person, too, exists only in the concrete situation, but his is not in any necessary relation to the concrete You. His person is self-established rather than being established by the You. In the last analysis, then, Kierkegaard remained bound to the idealist position. (*SC*, 57)

This chapter will compare Kierkegaard and Bonhoeffer's "critique of the idealist concept of time and reality," as well as address Bonhoeffer's criticisms of Kierkegaard. It will be suggested (a) that Bonhoeffer lies in greater proximity to Kierkegaard's critique than his declared "closeness" might suggest, and (b) that Kierkegaard's "self-establishing I" bares far greater similarity to Bonhoeffer's own position and remains, at least in Kierkegaard's mind, beyond idealism. Part 1 will, therefore, address the nature of their epistemological critiques of idealism. Part 2 will then construct a picture of their epistemology that holds the keys to their conceptions of the self.

Before proceeding, a few disclaimers are needed. Although Kierkegaard singles out Hegel for particular criticism throughout his authorship, much recent scholarship has debated whether Kierkegaard was in fact attacking Hegel directly or simple the Hegelianism he experienced in Denmark.[1] Whatever conclusions one might draw, Bonhoeffer was not aware of these questions. Consequently, when considering Bonhoeffer's adoption of Kierkegaard's attack, the use of "Hegel" must be understood in this qualified sense. Secondly, it is beyond the scope of this thesis to appraise the treatment of other authors by either Kierkegaard or Bonhoeffer. This is especially important in the case of Bonhoeffer

---

1. Cf. the debate between Thulstrup and Stewart.

who admits his use of "stylizations" (*AB*, 33) leading, for instance, to something of an amalgamation of Kant, Fichte, and Hegel at the beginning of *SC*. Finally, Bonhoeffer refers to both "German Idealism" as a specific philosophical school, and also "idealism" as a more general form of thought epitomized by Hegelian methodology. Often the lines become somewhat blurred as Bonhoeffer moves from one to the other. In the following discussion, therefore, the most prominent use will be the second, written in the lower case.

PART 1
THE ATTACK

Kierkegaard

At the beginning of *FT*, Johannes de silentio sets the tone for much of Kierkegaard's authorship when he declares that he has neither understood "the System" nor knows whether it really exists (*FT*, 43). And it is at the foot of Hegel that the System, "the momentous march of modern philosophy" (41), is laid. Despite its less than systematic treatment in *FT*, elsewhere Kierkegaard's critique of Hegel and speculative thought can be found on at least two main accounts: 1) its confusion of methodology; 2) its impossible beginnings.

Methodological Confusion

In its zeal to understand everything, speculative thought has failed to appreciate the boundaries of thought and its different forms. At the beginning of both *CA* and *CUP* Kierkegaard reveals the problem of speculative thought to be not its existence but its desire to explain everything through its native method of science and logic. As Haufniensis argues, actuality and logic are mutually exclusive realms. Logic is based on presuppositions about what could be but, unable to deal with the contingency of reality, cannot state what actually is (*CA*, 10). This is picked up in *CUP* where Climacus declares the possibility of a system of logic, but not of existence. Existence, actuality, and its realms of "infinite, personal, impassioned interestedness" (*CUP*, 1:27), cannot be determined, programmed or even anticipated, as all forms of thought are an abstraction from existence, and deal exclusively in the realms of "possibility" (cf. *CUP*, 1:314), "approximation" (cf. 1:41), and therefore, "uncertainty" (cf. 1:38)—what James Collins simply terms the "hypothetical."[2] Far from being objective, all thought is simply the logically uncertain interpretation of the individual, subjective thinker. As Pattison comments, "The thinking subject of philosophy cannot be abstracted from the reality of the existing subject."[3]

To go from thought to action requires making a decision or leap. For Kierkegaard, this decision is a true "movement" within life between these two poles, and is the act by which the individual comes to existentially establish himself (cf. *E/O*, I:475ff.). Without decision and "movement," the person remains a ghost in the realm possibility.

For Kierkegaard, Hegel smuggled the concept of "movement" into his system by describing his method as "dialectical." However, as Haufniensis argues, Hegel's method

2. Collins, *Mind of Kierkegaard*, 140.

3. Pattison, *Philosophy of Kierkegaard*, 21.

is not dialectical as he allows every contradiction to be overcome by "negation" and "mediation" (*CA*, 82). Through such mediation history may be described as "moving" but, correctly speaking, it embodies no "movement." When thought and existence are united, life is simply the logical appropriation of thought into action. No decision is required as everything is explained and obvious. The individual therefore becomes a cog in the world-historical wheel, moving only according to its purposeful revolutions. For logic, everything is decided in advance from the beginning (13), such that movement in logic is a "chimera" (*CUP*, 1:33).

Impossible Beginnings

Secondly, Kierkegaard argues that while existence may be a system, it can only be perceived as such by God, who stands outside of it (1:118). As every individual is within the system, how has speculative thought managed to grasp what that system actually is (1:111)? Specifically, if the system is the absolute, how does one come to know the beginning? To do so must require standing before the beginning, so negating its nature as beginning. Consequently, like movement, the beginning has been smuggled in and the system accepted—but only by turning a blind eye here and there (cf. *CA*, 84; *CUP*, 1:109). As Climacus argues, a system is only a system by its completeness such that "a system that is not entirely finished is a hypothesis, whereas a half-finished system is nonsense" (*CUP*, 1:107). For Kierkegaard, the completeness Hegel claims is only achieved through deception.

Bonhoeffer

As described in chapter 1, an attack on idealism runs throughout Bonhoeffer's work. Indeed, Bonhoeffer's declaration in *SC* of his intention to "confront the Christian ethical concept of person and of basic-relation with that of the idealist-metaphysical concept of person" (*SC*, 53), and to "overcome the idealist concept and replace it with one which preserves the individual, concrete character of the person as absolute and intended by God" (45), stands as the intention of his whole work, presenting the truths of Christianity by "confronting" and "overcoming" their perversion in idealist thought. As we go through Bonhoeffer's authorship up until 1933, we find here a direct and consistent attack on the idealist hermeneutic of the likes of Althaus that Bonhoeffer describes as nothing short of the fallen desire to be *"sicut deus"*—like God.

Hegel and the Plight of Philosophy

Bonhoeffer begins *SC* with a discussion of the German Idealist concept of personhood. Through Kant, Bonhoeffer argues, the knowing "I" has become the starting point of philosophy, perceiving everything through the universal, *a priori* categories of his reason. This universal reason is described as spirit, "the highest universal principle" in which all is encompassed (42), through which the individual becomes most truly "person" in ever more authentic participation (*SC*, 41, cf. *CCIG*, 180). However, according to Bonhoeffer, if all is encountered only through this universal category, contradiction is abolished, and the distinction between subject and object destroyed. As Bonhoeffer comments, "the synthesis of transcendental apperception resolves the opposition of subject and object as well as the I-You relation in the higher unity of spirit" (40). Consequently, in the universal spirit, "the individual loses his value" (42).

Although focusing primarily on Kant, Bonhoeffer levels the same criticisms at Hegel and Fichte, and argues,

> It is the destiny of the human race to be absorbed into the realm of reason, to form a realm of completely similar and harmonious persons, defined by universal reason or by one spirit and separated only by their different activities. Most importantly, however, this union of like beings never leads to the concept of community, but only to the concept of sameness, of unity. (43)

In *AB* the discussion of idealism turns from personality to epistemology, analyzing the interaction between the "act" of thought and the "being" of transcendental forms, addressing the question of the degree to which act may discern true being. While analyzing an ontological perspective through Husserl and Heidegger, Bonhoeffer offers a fuller treatment of a transcendental approach through Kant and Hegel. In marked contrast to *SC*, Bonhoeffer presents an appreciation of Kant in opposition to Hegel. Despite maintaining his earlier criticisms, Bonhoeffer shows deeper respect for Kant's critique of reason, appreciating its limits, and their association with humankind's sin.

Although discarding the terminology of "phenomenal" and "noumenal" for "act" and "being," Bonhoeffer understands Kant as having emphasized act over being, and the impossibility of perceiving the latter uncorrupted by the former. Bonhoeffer agrees and argues that reality is essentially transcendent to reason, which deals purely with the categories of logic, systems, and so possibility (*SC*, 53; *BBNY*, 471f.). Consequently, when everything is transformed in perception, all concepts of "being" must be understood as "in reference to" act, and never simply "through" it (*AB*, 37). Legitimate thought must therefore maintain the resistance of transcendence to thinking (35).

Bonhoeffer describes the temptation of philosophy to go beyond the limits Kant set. For where Kant defined the perceiving "I" as itself perceived only "in reference to" act,[4] Hegel and idealism established the "I" as the concrete, objective beginning and center of thought, ascribing meaning to everything within its perception (39). As Bonhoeffer describes in his 1931 lecture "The Theology of Crisis" the "I," or ego, loses all limits, takes on the nature of God in creating the world around it, and so absorbs all transcendence into itself (*BBNY*, 470f.). Consequently, idealism overcomes the resistance of transcendence to thinking such that being is discerned "through" act (*AB*, 44). However, through this illegitimate move not only has real transcendence been suspended, but also reality destroyed as all that is left is the fabricated system created by the "I" (*AB*, 39; *CCIG*, 178). As Bonhoeffer declares in *SC*, "The point is the *concept of reality* that idealism did not think through thoroughly, and therefore did not think through at all" (*SC*, 46).

---

4. This mirrors arguments made by Karl Jaspers and Gabriel Marcel that in the *cogito* Descartes had failed to ascribe his scepticism to the "I" itself rather than simply the object of the "I's perception (cf. Blackham, *Existentialist Thinkers*, 67).

Bonhoeffer writes favorably of Kant, but also of Heidegger who also emphasized limitations of thought. Here Bonhoeffer interprets act as standing in critical subordination to transcendence and being. Being is neither created, nor fully grasped by thought, but rather discerned through a process of ever critical reflection upon one's state of "thrownness," one's "being bound to a historical situation of existing in the world" (*BBNY*, 394). As such, humankind never breaks out of its concrete existence through which its being can be discerned through authentic living.

Despite Bonhoeffer's favor towards various approaches, all philosophy ultimately falls down at the same point as Hegel: all thought is "imprisoned in itself" (*AB*, 39). Everything is the construct of reason, including the limits one sets to it such that, "In limiting itself it establishes itself" (*BBNY*, 472). Consequently, when Kant argues that transcendence can only be understood "in reference to" reason this limit is itself created by reason (cf. *AB*, 48). Kant has simply not gone far enough and has not escaped idealism. Indeed, Hegel is perhaps more consistent as he simply lets reason loose from these abstract limits. Part of Hegel's own criticism of Kant was the inconsistency of claiming objective limits to delineate reason's inability to perceive objectively (cf. *BBNY*, 472).

The situation is the same for Heidegger, for despite his best efforts Bonhoeffer still concludes, "Ultimately the person himself answers the question about the human being" (*BBNY*, 396). Any form of realism is a fallacy as "reality has to be referred to the interpreting ego, which constitutes reality and which, even though it denies it remains the center of reality" (471).

Even attempts such as those of Eberhard Grisebach, who sought to rescue the transcendent in the form of the human other—confronting the "I" as "subject," invading its being, personality and reason from outside—still falls at the same hurdle as the absolute quality of the Thou that confronts us is still established by the "I" (398). For Bonhoeffer, all philosophy is inevitably a form of idealism. Consequently, despite all efforts, Bonhoeffer concludes, "We notice that we are thrown back firmly onto Hegel" (*NRS*, 57).

Idealism and Sin

Despite his judgment, Bonhoeffer still affirms Kant and Heidegger for their appreciation of reason's limitations. Indeed, Bonhoeffer reveals his sheer distaste for Hegel in describing idealism as laying "violent hands" on the transcendent in contrast to Kant's "modest" methods (*AB*, 40). Hegel has allowed the "I" to "celebrate untroubled the triumph of its liberation" (46), affirming the system as proof of humankind's autonomy and freedom (*BBNY*, 471). Although in itself a speculative point, it is interesting that where Bonhoeffer describes Kant as inevitably falling into the "*cor curvum in se*"—the heart turned in upon itself (*AB*, 46)—so idealism is irrevocably associated with the "*ratio in se ipsam incurva*"— reason turned in upon itself (41). For Bonhoeffer, Kant succumbed to the fallen nature of thought trapped within itself despite his best efforts. In contrast, Hegel embraced this nature and sculpted his thought around it. For Bonhoeffer, Hegelianism is perhaps the perfect philosophical child of fallenness, embracing the "I's creativity, revelling in the 'full power of reason over transcendence'" (37), and turning the "*cor curvum in se*" into its necessary and celebrated form.

In Bonhoeffer's earliest works, idealism is associated with sin. In *CCIG* Bonhoeffer describes idealism as subordinating both the human other and God to the ego (*CCIG*, 178). In "The Theology of Crisis" he goes further to suggest that idealist philosophy is "the most dangerous grasp after God, in order to be like God is and thus to justify man by his own power" (*BBNY*, 473). Bonhoeffer does not deny distinctions in philosophy, nor condemn all philosophy quite this strongly. However, the point remains that no matter what philosophy does, it is still trapped within itself, and so inevitably lord over all that it perceives.

This association of idealism with sin can be seen in *CF*. Although the terms "philosophy" or "idealism" are not used, the description of the fall bears striking resemblance to Bonhoeffer's depiction of idealism. Here Bonhoeffer argues that the real evil of the serpent's question to Eve was that it contained a presupposition that undermined the relationship between creature and Creator, and set the former in judgement on God's concrete word. As Bonhoeffer continues,

> It requires humankind to sit in judgment on God's word instead of simply listening to it and doing it. And this is achieved by proposing that, on the basis of an idea, a principle, or some prior knowledge about God, humankind should now pass judgment on the concrete word of God. But where human beings use a principle, an idea of God, as a weapon to fight against the concrete word of God, there they are from the outset already in the right; at that point they have become God's master, they have left the path of obedience, they have withdrawn from being addressed by God. (*CF*, 107)

The serpent's question essentially made Eve an idealist, promoting a form of knowledge within her by which to judge God's word. Bonhoeffer argues that this "first religious conversation" inspired Eve to speak about God in a way that "passes over, and reaches beyond God" (111), that goes "behind the word of God to procure its own knowledge of God" (116). In agreement with "The Theology of Crisis" Bonhoeffer describes this as humankind's desire to become "*sicut deus*" in gaining knowledge from "the springs of its own life and being" (116).[5]

In his earliest authorship, in the run up to the events of 1933, Bonhoeffer made very clear that he believed the idealist hermeneutic to be nothing less than an expression of humankind's fallenness through which it stands in judgment of God. In the face of the SA and the Nazi student movement, these were bold and brave statements.

Bonhoeffer and Kierkegaard Considered

Similarities between Kierkegaard and Bonhoeffer are already strikingly clear. As we turn to compare their thought we will call to mind the statement with which this chapter started, that Bonhoeffer's own argument is "close to [Kierkegaard's] in its critique of the

---

5. Bethge himself refers to the "original sin of idealism"—Bethge, *Bonhoeffer*, 133.

idealist concept of time and reality" (*SC*, 57). The following analysis will be structured around these two points.

Reality

THE DIFFERENCE BETWEEN THOUGHT AND REALITY

For both thinkers all thought is systematic and universal. It is therefore abstract, standing in permanent exclusivity to reality. The realm, to which it must remain, is logic. Both writers describe philosophy's field of discussion as that of "possibility," for "actuality" stands beyond the realm of logic.

These ideas can be consistently seen from Bonhoeffer's copy of *CUP*. At the beginning Bonhoeffer vigorously marks Kierkegaard's declaration that pure thought "disregards the concrete, the temporal, the becoming of existence and the difficult situation of the existing person" (*AUN*, 1; *CUP*, 1:301). In addition, Bonhoeffer also highlights the realm of pure thought as "possibility" (cf. *AUN*, 14, 16, 20, 26; *CUP*, 1:315, 317, 321, 328), and the danger of pure thinking in promoting a disinterestedness against the passion of existence (*AUN*, 12, 25; *CUP*, 1:131, 327).

In *AB*, these ideas become strikingly clear. Against the possibility of idealist thought, Bonhoeffer comments, "Kierkegaard said, not without justification, that such philosophizing obviously forgets that we ourselves exist" (*AB*, 39). Such statements appear throughout *CUP*. However, Bonhoeffer energetically highlighted and underlined Climacus' declaration that such a thinker "must be absentminded, since he, too, is an existing person" (*AUN*, 1; *CUP* 1:301).

Bonhoeffer expands these ideas a few pages later where he attacks Hegel for having written "a philosophy of angels, but not of human beings as Dasein" (*AB*, 42). Indeed, Bonhoeffer argues that this is seen most profoundly in "the resistance of [such thinkers'] own reality" to their philosophy (42). While clearly reflected in *CUP*, it is interesting to note the argument of *SUD* that such systematic thinkers build a stupendous philosophical mansion and yet continue to live in the kennel (*SUD*, 44).

Bonhoeffer also appears to have been struck by Climacus' argument that "a system of existence cannot be given," and is only potentially possible from the perspective of God (*CUP*, 1:118). Bonhoeffer comments that such a system is only an "eschatological possibility" conceivable by one looking back on it from outside (*AB*, 94).

A FALSE BEGINNING

Kierkegaard argued that Hegel's system essentially fails as it cannot conceive of a beginning from within the system. In *CUP* Bonhoeffer marks his copy where Climacus argues, "An existing person can have gained admission into pure thinking only by a dubious beginning" (*AUN*, 12; *CUP*, 1:313), and again a few pages later where he declares, "Actuality, existence, is the dialectical element in a trilogy, the beginning and end of which cannot be for an existing person" (*AUN*, 14; *CUP*, 1:315). These ideas are reiterated in *CF* in a section entitled "The Beginning." Here, Bonhoeffer declares that one who is within existence cannot know its beginning as to do so would require stepping outside of it. Consequently, "Where the beginning ends, there our thinking stops" (*CF*, 25). These ideas reappear in *Ethics* where Bonhoeffer argues, "While we are still living we are thus ignorant of the limit of our life, namely, death, how could we be able to say what life is in itself?" (*E*, 249). In *CF* the link is then explicitly made with Hegel:

> . . . the thinking of fallen humankind, lacks a beginning because it is a circle. We think in a circle. But we also feel and will in a circle. We exist in a circle . . . The decisive point, however, is that thinking takes this circle to be the infinite, the beginning in itself, and is thereby caught in a *circulus vitiosus* [faulty circle or circular argument] . . .
>
> The Hegelian question how we are to make a beginning in philosophy can therefore be answered only by the bold and violent action of enthroning reason in the place of God. That is why critical philosophy is but a systematic despair of its own beginning, indeed of any beginning. (*CF*, 26)

For both Kierkegaard and Bonhoeffer the system is only visible to God, but thought has enthroned itself in God's place. In "The Theology of Crisis," Bonhoeffer therefore condemns the pretension of a "spectator-knowledge of God" (*BBNY*, 473). In marked similarity, Climacus writes,

> But to God, world history is the royal stage where he, not accidentally but essentially, is the only spectator, because he is the only one who *can* be that. Admission to this theatre is not open to any existing spirit. If he fancies himself a spectator there, he is simply forgetting that he himself is supposed to be the actor in that little theatre and is to leave it to that royal spectator and poet how he wants to use him in that royal drama. (*CUP*, 1:158)

For Climacus, the whole nineteenth century is aimed at viewing everything "from God's point of view" (1:395).

The Difference between God and Man

Behind both writers' thought is the fundamental importance of the difference between God and humankind, which idealism has discarded. Indeed, as Bonhoeffer comments,

> Here, as in the whole of idealism, the inmost identity of I and God, which underlies everything, is merely an expression of the proposition that like is known by like. If God is to come to human beings, they essentially must already be like God. If theology is to grasp the relationship of God and humankind, it can do so only by presupposing a profound likeness of one to the other and finding precisely here the unity between God and human beings. One is like the very God one comprehends. (*AB*, 53)

This charge is repeated in *Christology* where Bonhoeffer makes clear that by making God into an "idea" or the ideal, captive to the mind, dissimilarity between God and humankind is destroyed (*C*, 50ff.). This, again, is Kierkegaard's point: "If God were directly the ideal for being a human being, it would be right to want to express the direct likeness . . . But between God and a human being . . . there is an absolute difference; therefore a person's absolute relationship with God must specifically express the absolute difference, and the direct likeness becomes impudence, conceited pretence, presumption, and the like" (*CUP*, 1:412).

Reflecting a theme of central importance to Bonhoeffer, Kierkegaard argues that God has not come to make humankind divine, but more human. Therefore, "man expresses himself most perfectly when he absolutely expresses the difference" (1:412). Throughout *CUP* Climacus emphasizes this need with the cry, "Let us be human beings" (1:114), not human beings in general, but real, existing human beings (1:120), who express with joy their creaturely humanness with all its quirks (1:493). Although not attached to the obviously Christological interpretation of such places as "Ethics as Formation" (cf. *E*, 94), Kierkegaard mirrors Bonhoeffer's intent when he summarizes, "It is really the God-relationship that makes a human being a human being" (*CUP*, 1:244). The issue of Kierkegaard's affirmation of humanity in its earthly condition will be discussed further in chapter 8.

The Loss of the "I"

Not only has God been lost in the universal but also the "I." Bonhoeffer's claim of the individual subordinated and absorbed into the universal again finds its distinct parallels in Kierkegaard. In *FT* the conflict between the universal and the individual is emphatically stated, for when in Hegel real contradiction is negated, the universal and outward takes priority over the individual and the inward (*FT*, 96ff.). Consequently, "it is the individual's task to divest himself of the determinant of interiority and give it an expression in the exterior" (*FT*, 97). This is further stated in *CUP* where Climacus laments, "To be a human being has been abolished, and every speculative thinker confuses himself with humankind, whereby he becomes something infinitely great and nothing at all" (*CUP*, 1:124). Affirming the contradiction between thought and actuality discussed above, Bonhoeffer underlines Kierkegaard's statement that "the particular cannot be thought, but only the universal" (*AUN*, 24; *CUP*, 1:326), and pays particular attention to the lack of existence that thought presents (*AUN*, 28; *CUP*, 1:330). Bonhoeffer therefore underlines Kierkegaard's declarations that for the existing individual, the abstract pure thought is a "chimera" (*AUN*, 10; *CUP*, 1:310), and "phantom" (*AUN*, 13; *CUP*, 1:314).

Idealism and Sin

It isn't surprising, therefore, that like Bonhoeffer, Kierkegaard speaks of idealism in terms of sin, albeit in a less comprehensive fashion. When "wanting to become objective is untruth" (*CUP*, 1:203), the nature of this objective state is affirmed when he says, "Let us now call the individual's untruth sin" (1:208). Indeed, in the face of existence and subjectivity, Climacus describes idealism as an act of thrusting away from oneself, of keeping at arms length (1:213), and therefore that which stands farthest from the truth by having tried to explain, control, and create it (1:216).

The Confusion of Categories

For both, the problem is not speculative thought itself, but the confusion of categories it promotes. In his copy of *CUP*, Bonhoeffer highlights Kierkegaard's statement that idealism has confused the categories of existence and ethics for abstraction and observation (*AUN*, 18; *CUP*, 320). In particular, Bonhoeffer places two thick lines next to Kierkegaard's comment that existence is annulled when considered in the realm of possibility (*AUN*, 16; *CUP*, 1: 317).

The particular confusion that Bonhoeffer disparages most is that between philosophy and theology. Bonhoeffer repeatedly criticizes idealistic theology, using such examples as Holl (cf. *BBNY*, 417), Scheler (cf. *BBNY*, 393ff.; *AB*, 64ff.), and Brunstäd (cf. *AB*, 52), who unified God with humankind in the universal spirit, perceiving Him through the power of reason in such forms as the conscience, love, or humankind's own nature. Consequently, for Bonhoeffer, in the face of philosophy, theology has lost an understanding of the limits and presuppositions that make it theology, trading them for philosophy's method and description of truth (*CCIG*, 177).

In *CA* Haufniensis conducts a long study on how theology has become a science through ethics and dogmatics, and so, particularly in the former, fails to appreciate the concept of sin. In his own copy, Bonhoeffer boldly underlines both "ethics" (*BA*, 10; *CA*, 16), and "with dogmatics" (*BA*, 12; *CA*, 19), as each subject is considered. However, perhaps Kierkegaard's most in depth discussion occurs in *FT*. Here Johannes comments that to the claims of philosophy, going beyond the immature, subordinate forms of faith and doubt, "Theology sits all painted at the window courting philosophy's favor, offering philosophy its delights" (*FT*, 62). Rather, "Philosophy cannot and should not give us an account of faith, but should understand itself and know just what it has indeed to offer, without taking anything away, least of all cheating people out of something by making them think it is nothing" (63).

For both writers, the importance for theology is to understand its presuppositions against the supposedly presuppositionless philosophical method. This reflects the call throughout *SC* and *AB* that theological issues can only be understood from within themselves and never from a disinterested standpoint.

The Difference between Kant and Plato

A final point of interest is found in Bonhoeffer's description of the movement of thought from Kant to Hegel. Having discussed Kant's limits, and the temptation of philosophy to go beyond them, Bonhoeffer comments, "This second possibility was taken up and elaborated as much in the transition from Socrates to Plato as it was in the turn from Kant to idealism" (*AB*, 39). While the link with Kant and Hegel is more implicit, early in *CUP* Climacus discusses the nature of Socratic thought as emphasizing the existential appreciation of knowledge, against Plato having sought it purely with the mind. Consequently, in marked similarity to Bonhoeffer's words above, Climacus comments, "socrates essentially emphasizes existing, whereas Plato, forgetting this, loses himself in speculative thought" (*CUP*, 1:205).

When one considers that Bonhoeffer's statement appears just after his citation of Kierkegaard that "such philosophizing obviously forgets that we ourselves exist" (*AB*, 39), it is interesting that Climacus continues, "Socrates' infinite merit is precisely that of being an *existing* thinker, not a speculative thinker who forgets what it means to exist" (*CUP*, 1:205). This would appear to be a direct citation of Kierkegaard. Furthermore, it suggests that Bonhoeffer also read the first part of *CUP*, from which this quote is taken, and not simply the second that still exists in his library.

Time

Before going further, Kierkegaard's concept of time needs further elaboration. As discussed above, in contrast to Hegel's simple progression, Kierkegaard sets up the movement or leap of decision as the necessary category for moving between thought and reality. For Kierkegaard, a discontinuity exists between both realms that needs real "transition" rather than "mediation." In *CA* Haufniensis argues that transition is the state of "historical freedom" (*CA*, 82, 85). It is through an understanding of "historical freedom" that Kierkegaard's conception of time becomes clear.

In *CA* section III Haufniensis argues that philosophy has forged the concept of "spatialized-time,"[6] linearly visualized into the periods of past, present, and future. However, such a systematic view is only possible to the external spectator. For those within time the present is in a permanent, ungraspable state of vanishing. Humankind lives not in "spatialized-time" but time as "infinite-succession" (85). Consequently, these linear distinctions are not "implicit in time itself," but applied to time from the outside (85).

In contrast, Haufniensis argues that only when the eternal, as something external to time, establishes a "foothold"—essentially a pause in time's infinite succession—can time and so existence be meaningfully established (85). This point of contact Kierkegaard terms "*Øieblikket*," "the moment," or literally, "the blink of an eye." As Haufniensis argues, "the moment is not an atom of time but an atom of eternity. It is the first reflection of eternity in time, its first attempt, as it were, at stopping time" (88). Only when the eternal intersects time are the past, present, and future injected into the temporal (89). As described in both *CA* and *PF*, in the moment one finds "the fullness of time," for in that blink of an eye the present opens up like a boundless Tardis, containing the eternal within itself (*CA*, 90; *PF*, 18). Although the moment is the present, from the individual perspective it is constantly looking forward. In the words of Eduard Geismar, the moment "wears the aspect of futurity," breaking the present open into limitless possibility.[7] Consequently, in the moment, the individual's "historical freedom" is posited—freedom to be oneself, to grasp hold of one's past, and live in the present with the full freedom of one's future.

However, this freedom also entails decision and anxiety. For Kierkegaard the terms decision, passion, movement, anxiety, consciousness, spirit, moment, and eternity are all intertwined. As described in Kierkegaard's psychological works, the individual is made up of the relationship between his temporal and eternal natures. In their perfect tension,

6. Cf. Taylor, "Time's Struggle."
7. Geismar, *Lectures*, 46.

the individual is described as "spirit." In *JC* Kierkegaard specifies that the individual is constituted by the tension of thought and actuality, and their perfect tension described as "consciousness" (*JC*, 166ff.). Playing on the nuances of the term "Aand," the individual's spirit is his consciousness (169).[8] But Kierkegaard reveals in *JC* that consciousness, spirit, and so the self, are established through passionate decision, the perfect tension of thought and actuality. However, just as theology ruminates over whether obedience precedes faith, Kierkegaard's point is that decision and passion both establish and are the marks of spirit or consciousness.

However, this movement only occurs through the moment, when the individual comes into relation with the eternal within time, and allows it to shine its light on the individual's life and predicament (cf. *SUD*, 44). Most hide themselves in immediacy, to shield themselves from the anxiety that consciousness and the moment inevitably bring (cf. 105). However, as Haufniensis declares, "In the individual life, anxiety is the moment" (*CA*, 81). Without grasping hold of the moment, of the unlimited future for which we are wholly responsible, of anxiety, one can never be spirit, never one's self, never a conscious being.

When we turn to Bonhoeffer, many parallels can be found. Bonhoeffer's own copy of *CA* is littered with highlights and underlinings in the section in which Haufniensis discusses "the moment."

Movement

In *SC*, following his criticism of idealism's lack of reality, Bonhoeffer specifies that "The issue here is the problem of time" (*SC*, 47). Concerning the destruction of contradiction, Bonhoeffer declares, "Kant taught that continuously advancing time was a pure form of the mind's intuition. The result in Kant and in all of idealism is essentially a timeless way of thinking" (47).

For Kierkegaard, once contradiction and therefore also movement are destroyed, time no longer exists. The idealist view of time is simply "stagnation" (*CUP*, 1:312). Bonhoeffer equally discerns the link between time and movement. In his copy of *CUP*, Bonhoeffer marks Climacus' statement that pure thought removes "contradiction" (*AUN*, 5; *CUP*, 1:305), but also his declaration that "The eternal is the continuity of motion, but an abstract eternity is outside motion" (*AUN*, 312; *CUP*, 1:312). At various points, Bonhoeffer therefore argues that in contrast to true existence as "active movement" (*Aktbewgung*) (*NRS*, 52), idealism creates time as a "continuous flow" (*SC*, 48), full of the "immanent quiescent possibilities" of the world-historical (*BBNY*, 391). Consequently, "idealism has no appreciation of movement" (*SC*, 49). For Bonhoeffer, where the world-historical is "static," concrete time constitutes the challenge of decision. Although not using the term "transition," Bonhoeffer underlines its description in *CA* alongside that of "historical freedom" and "the leap," and its meaning is clearly present in his thought (*BA*, 80; *CA*, 85). As he comments,

8. The word Kierkegaard uses is "Aand" which, like "Geist" or "esprit," may take the meaning of either "spirit" or "mind." Curiously, in the Hong and Hong translation of *JC* "mind" is used, where in *SUD* they use "spirit."

> . . . there follows from our concept of time an idea that is quite meaningless for ideal-ism, that *the person ever and again arises and passes away in time.* The person does not exist timelessly; a person is not static but dynamic. The person exists always and only in ethical responsibility; the person is re-created again and again in the per-petual flux of life. (*SC*, 48)

The Moment

For Bonhoeffer this point of decision and ethical responsibility is precisely "the moment." Bonhoeffer therefore writes,

> At the moment of being addressed, the person enters a state of *responsibility* or, in other words, of decision. By person I do not mean the idealists' person of mind and reason, but the person in concrete, living individuality . . . not one existing in timeless fullness of value and spirit, but in a state of responsibility in the midst of time; not one existing in time's continuous flow, but in the value-related—not value-filled—moment. *In the concept of the moment, the concept of time and its value-relat-edness are co-posited.* The moment is not the shortest span of time, a mechanically conceived atom, as it were. The "moment" is the time of responsibility, value-related time, or, let us say, time related to God; and most essentially, it is concrete time. (48)

Alongside the numerous marks Bonhoeffer placed in his copy of *CA*, this would appear to be direct reference to Haufniensis' comment that, "the moment is not properly an atom of time but an atom of eternity" (*BA*, 85; *CA*, 88).

Although Bonhoeffer's description is far less psychological, not only does Bonhoeffer underline Haufniensis' statement that, "In the individual life, anxiety is the moment," but he declares, "idealism has no understanding of the moment in which the person feels the threat of absolute demand . . . Where is there room, then, for distress of conscience, for infinite anxiety in the face of decisions?" (*SC*, 49).

In relation to Bonhoeffer's statements of becoming and anxiety, it isn't surprising that he should boldly highlight Haufniensis' statement that, "to exist, that is, to permeate one's existence with consciousness, simultaneously to be eternal, far beyond it, as it were, and nevertheless present in it and nevertheless in a process of becoming—that is truly difficult (*BA*, 7; *CA*, 308).

Despite the obvious psychological treatment that Kierkegaard grants the moment in *CA*, which receives considerable attention from Bonhoeffer in his copy, Bonhoeffer's own descriptions of anxiety and becoming are far less psychological. However, for both authors real time involves the injection of God into the temporal. As we have seen, Bonhoeffer refers to it as "time in relation to God." This significantly mirrors Kierkegaard's notions of the moment as "time related to God," or rather, "before God." Although differences concerning the medium through which the moment arrives for Kierkegaard will be discussed in Part 2, so this similarity of time "before God" is central to both.

Some Preliminary Remarks

It is clear from the sheer weight of parallels that Bonhoeffer was extremely familiar with Kierkegaard's attack on idealism. This did not come from second hand sources but from his own extensive reading of *CUP*, *CA*, and *FT*. Bonhoeffer has not simply used Kierkegaard's general argument but adopted a weight of Kierkegaard's specific points, covering the breadth of his attack. Furthermore, there are a number of direct, uncited references to Kierkegaard's work drawn from both parts of *CUP* and *CA*. Bonhoeffer's statement that his argument is "close" to Kierkegaard's is an understatement. Kierkegaard's attack on idealism stands at the center of Bonhoeffer's arguments in *SC*, *AB*, and *CF*, and, as will be shown, throughout his whole authorship.

PART 2
THE RECONSTRUCTION

In the quote with which we started this chapter, Bonhoeffer criticizes Kierkegaard for having suggested a theory of personality in which the individual is self-established and separated from the necessity of the concrete You. Consequently, his conclusion is that Kierkegaard has not escaped the idealism he so vehemently criticized. As we turn now from that critique to both writers" positive accounts of epistemology, further light will be shed on these criticisms by comparing their accounts.

Transcendental and Ontological Approaches

For both Kierkegaard and Bonhoeffer, in the moment the individual is forced into decision, establishing him as person. As Bonhoeffer comments, "It is a Christian insight that the person as conscious being is created in the moment of being moved—in the situation of responsibility, passionate ethical struggle, confrontation by an overwhelming claim; thus the real person grows out of the concrete situation" (*SC*, 49).

When for Bonhoeffer the "I" is permanently "imprisoned in itself" (*AB*, 39), in the circularity of its own thinking, so in the moment this ethical claim confronts the individual from outside himself, transcending his mind and acting as its limit. Only when the individual's "intellect is confronted by some fundamental barrier" is this circle broken, and the plight of idealism overcome (*SC*, 45). While this barrier may embody a confrontation of knowledge, for Bonhoeffer it is only a barrier when ethical decision is required (47).

Bonhoeffer clearly demonstrates the strong influence of the I-You school of thought—particularly of Eberhard Grisebach—as it is only a "You" or "person" who provides this ethical claim and so acts as the barrier. Consequently, the individual cannot be discussed atomistically, but only in sociality. As he comments in *CCIG*, "Only personality can limit me, because the other personality has its own demands and claims, its own law and will, which are different from me and which I cannot overcome as such. Personality is free and does not enter the general laws of my thinking" (*CCIG*, 180). Only the "You" embodies true "personality." For Bonhoeffer, "personality" is that which remains a subject to the "I" and never its "object," "never falls into the power of the knowing I," retaining the freedom to reveal or withhold itself (*AB*, 126). In this way the "You" stands as true limit to the "I," and calls it into ethical responsibility.

Bonhoeffer clearly appreciates Grisebach's thought in understanding humankind's essentially social nature, as well as the necessity of transcendent, ethical confrontation. However, for Bonhoeffer it is not the human other but only God who truly embodies personality (*CCIG*, 180), acts as the barrier, and so presents us with an absolute difference in which the barrier can be experienced (*SC*, 49).

The nuance of Bonhoeffer's position is that God in Christ is only met through sociality, and therefore, only in the church-community. As Bonhoeffer writes, "Community with God exists only through Christ, but Christ is present only in his church-community, and therefore *community with God exists only in the church*" (159). For Bonhoeffer this is simply the message of the New Testament and the church as the body of Christ (cf. *SC*, 134ff.; *AB*, 111ff.; *C*, 60), which stands as a mystery of faith (*BBNY*, 407). Consequently, God is revealed through the human other in church-community (*SC*, 55). For whether in the form of preaching, offering of the sacrament, the rites of forgiveness, intercessory prayer, etc., the word of God is always mediated through a human other (*AB*, 121). In ministering the "You" of God through his Word to the "I," the human other becomes transformed into a "You," into real personality. As Bonhoeffer explains,

> *God or the Holy Spirit joins the concrete You; only through God's active working does the other become a You to me from whom my I arises. In other words, every human You is an image of the divine You.* You-character is the essential form in which the divine is experienced; every human You bears its You-character only by virtue of the divine. This is not to say that it is a borrowed attribute to God, and not really a You. Rather, the divine You creates the human You. And since the human You is created and willed by God, it is a *real, absolute, and holy You*, like the divine You. One might then speak here of the human being as the image of God with respect to the effect one person has on another . . . Since, however, one person's becoming You for another fundamentally alters nothing about the You as person, that person as I is not holy; what is holy is the You of God, the absolute will, who here becomes visible in the concrete You of social life. The other person is only a "You" insofar as God brings it about. But God can make every human being a You for us. *The claim of the other rests in God alone; for this very reason, it remains the claim of the other.* (*SC*, 55)

The human "you" becomes the divine "You," such that through Christ the human other is "transposed into a new manner of existence" (*AB*, 114), becomes Christ to me (112), and so an authentic barrier (127). In a phrase that recurs throughout his authorship Bonhoeffer argues, "Through such proclamation of the gospel, every member of the church may and should 'become a Christ' to the others" (113).

Where *SC*, in which most of the foregoing account is found, deals with questions concerning the structure and form of the church-community as revelation, so in *AB* Bonhoeffer takes a step back to argue for the church-community as the bearer of revelation. Here, Bonhoeffer seeks to apply the ecclesiology of *SC* to the currant debate concerning the epistemology of revelation—that is, "How is revelation given to us?" and "How can we, or should we, accept it?" Where the debate had polarized itself once again into transcendental and ontological schools, for Bonhoeffer both failed to take seriously the nature of God's desire concerning revelation, and the nature of the church as its concrete form.

Although his analysis appears to drift somewhat into discussing existentialism more generally, it is Barth who is considered the main figure of the transcendental school. According to Bonhoeffer, the point of greatest importance for Barth is the sovereignty of God found in His freedom, standing unclaimable, untouchable, and "unhaveable" by the individual within his mind (85). God is entirely transcendent, within the realm of the non-objective, and ungraspable. For Bonhoeffer, this is emphasized through Barth's affirmation of Calvin's *finitum non capax infiniti*, where God remains uncontained within the sinful, created order. God may only be known in his revelation through the act of faith, which is both established and sustained in the individual by God himself. Therefore, as Bonhoeffer summarizes, even within faith God is never *given* to humankind, as if he were simply to receive knowledge of God at conversion. Consequently, God is preserved as subject, outside humankind's control (cf. 92).

In Bonhoeffer's account of Barth, God can only be met in the moment of interaction (83). The instant one steps outside of this moment of immediacy, reflection simply holds within it a memory or idea of God, but not God himself. Consequently, as Bonhoeffer argues, for Barth, when theology reflects upon God, it must hold within itself the "critical proviso" of always saying "not-knowing" when it says "knowing," of saying "not-God" when it says "God" (cf. 85, 124), in acknowledgement that knowledge of God is only found in the immediate moment and not as an idea in reflection. Whatever is held afterwards is simply the memory created and controlled by the sinful mind. God's absolute freedom is therefore maintained, unbound to his relationship with humankind (cf. 82). He may grant his revelation one moment, and remove it in the next, leaving behind nothing of himself within humankind's grasp. Theology is only useful if and when God, "from sheer pleasure," chooses to reveal himself through it (87).

For Bonhoeffer, Barth is a direct descendent of Kant and genuine transcendental philosophy, rejecting being as perceivable by the knowing "I" (cf. 55, 91). All knowledge is rather the categorization of the sinful mind, and never the thing in itself. As Bonhoeffer argues, "Epistemologically this signifies that one can speak about the object of knowledge only *in reference to* the knowing subject. Nothing essentially is being said thereby about the being of what exists beyond its being known" (91—author's emphasis). Consequently, it is "existential knowledge," as it is only "known" in the moment when the "I" is placed within this encounter (92, 94–95). Existential knowledge stands in opposition to "systematic knowledge," for where systematic knowledge talks about objectivity, universality etc. so existential knowledge is only possible for the individual in that momentary encounter (95). Only in the decision of faith does the "I" know itself "placed into the truth by Christ in judgment and in grace" (96). Consequently, "Outside the decision, it is 'known truth' but not *truth for me*"—that is, it may be regarded as systematic truth, but never existential truth (96—author's emphasis). Existence, personhood, and authenticity only occur when the individual embraces the truth for himself (97). This is not simple agreement with a concept or object of knowledge, but perceiving, deciding and accepting the absolute claim of God in existential encounter through faith.

These ideas stand in stark opposition to the ontological approach as found in many forms of Christianity. For in such expressions as religious experience, doctrines of the verbal inspiration of Scripture, or the institution of the Catholic Church, the being of God is manifest as "object" (108). For Bonhoeffer, these forms act simply as the means of security by which the "I" finds itself "borne by this something that exists," in subjection and obedience according to its own desire. God is therefore seen as an entity within the field of experience, an object of the mind, removed from any possibility as a barrier.

Bonhoeffer's Criticisms of Barth

It is clear that Bonhoeffer is far more at home with transcendental theology than with the ontological. However, as described in chapter 3, Bonhoeffer also makes clear his distinction from Barth, and qualified appreciation for the contribution of Seeberg and liberal theology more generally concerning the "giveness" of God. Indeed, Bonhoeffer's criticisms of Barth in *AB*, if taken out of context, could seem positively damning.

THE DESTRUCTION OF THEOLOGY

For Bonhoeffer, Barth's ideas offer a fatal blow to theology. By describing God non-objectively, theology is left with no subject matter other than the memories of the existentially perceiving "I." By placing revelation only within the momentary experience of the individual, Barth denies revelation any formal sense of accountability or continuity. As Feil argues, this fundamentally undermines the whole project of theology as "there can be scholarship only where there are concepts of being."[9] Furthermore, Bonhoeffer argues that Barth's limit of the "critical proviso" is simply a "theoretical method" created by the mind, and so a superficial and flawed limit. Theology is regarded as no humbler than any "honorable systematic thinking," and Barth offers no reason why God should use theology as opposed to any other profane discipline (131).

INDIVIDUALISM

Secondly, in Bonhoeffer's mind, Barth's ideas are entirely individualistic, ignoring humankind's social nature, and undermining the church (113). As Sherman rightly points out, Barth is historically something of a "moving target," having undergone many progressions during his long authorship.[10] However, for Bonhoeffer, the early Barth's emphasis on the *non capax infiniti* overwhelmed any possible sanctity to earthly forms. Phillips suggests that Barth considered these forms as simply a manifestation of humankind's rebellious search for security and dominion, particularly those that humankind "endows with moral and spiritual authority."[11] In *Epistle to the Romans*, Barth's only major work until 1927, Bonhoeffer was particularly disturbed by Barth's characterization of the church as an institution of indifference, misunderstanding, and opposition.[12] Indeed, the influence of

9. Feil, *Theology*, 13.
10. Sherman, "Act and Being," 105.
11. Phillips, *Form of Christ*, 160.
12. Ibid., 67.

the *non capax infiniti* was so strong that Feil accuses Barth of holding "a latent acosmic perspective."[13]

God's Freedom

However, perhaps the most significant misunderstanding that Bonhoeffer sees in Barth is the latter's insistence on God's freedom as *from* humankind. In a now famous passage Bonhoeffer writes,

> In revelation it is not so much a question of the freedom of God . . . It is a matter of God's *given* Word, the covenant in which God is bound by God's own action. It is a question of the freedom of God, which finds its strongest evidence precisely in that God freely chose to be bound to historical human beings and to be placed at the disposal of human beings. God is not free from human beings but for them. Christ is the word of God's freedom. God *is* present, that is, not in eternal nonobjectivity but . . . "haveable," graspable in the Word within the church. (90)

God is not free *from* humankind, but free *for* humankind, for it is precisely God's freedom that binds Him to humankind through the church (124). For Bonhoeffer, Barth has essentially aligned himself too strongly with Kant, as the revelation of God in Christ demonstrates God's givenness.[14] It is almost as if Barth has lost sight of Christian first principles and started with a philosophical foundation. As Bonhoeffer describes it, "to leave open a freedom of God beyond the occurrence of salvation is to formalize, to *rationalize*, the contingent positivity of that occurrence" (*AB*, 124; cf. *BBNY*, 407f.).

Bonhoeffer's Ecclesiological Approach

In Bonhoeffer's response to the question of act and being, it becomes clear that God reveals himself as both "haveable" and yet free. Consequently, an adequate answer can only be found in the mediation of transcendence and ontology. In drawing on the conclusions of *SC*, Bonhoeffer argues that this is only possible in the church-community.

For Bonhoeffer, in agreement with Barth, reflection is suspended in faith. For in faith the individual stands open before revelation in the form of the word of God, spoken and ministered through the human other. The "I" is destroyed as creator and controller and rests rather in submission as receiver and accepter to the word of God. Indeed, as Bonhoeffer comments in *CCIG*, faith is "nothing but the act of receiving [the] word of God" (*CCIG*, 183). In this way, through the submission of the 'I's controlling faculties, both God and human other are allowed to be their true nature as persons, freed from the claim the controlling "I" makes upon them. Both divine and human other confront the "I" with their claim, untainted by the understanding and claim of the "I." In this way, the other remains spontaneous, contingent, and utterly free. As Bonhoeffer argues at several points, in faith the other meets the "I" in pure reality, to be either accepted or rejected. Therefore, both divine and human other are met only through belief, and never speculative knowledge (cf. *SC*, 53, 54).

13. Feil, *Theology*, xix.
14. Sherman, "Act and Being," 88.

The being of God on the earth is "Christ existing as church-community" (*AB*, 115; *SC*, 190). Christ may be "in" the church-community as it receives revelation. However, Christ also "is" the church-community. The description of the body of Christ is no metaphor, nor does the church simply represent Christ (*C*, 60; *SC*, 157). Rather, the church-community, as "collective person," bound together through the mutual relations established by and containing the Word of God, *is* Christ (*SC*, 140). Just as in sin humankind had his being in Adam, so now he may rest in the new humanity with his being in Christ.

Bonhoeffer's answer to the conundrum of act and being is found in this ecclesiology as God's being is made "haveable" but also "uncontrollable" through faith. When the act of faith is separate from the being of God, the act remains a rational movement by the individual and lays claim to God's being. However, Bonhoeffer declares that not only is the being of God found in community, but it is only through this being in community, the experience of the barrier through the human other, that faith is created (*AB*, 120). Consequently, one never passes from an act of faith into the being of church-community, but through the act of faith recognizes oneself as already within the being of church-community (122). In this way, the being of God is made "haveable" only through one's participation in the being of Christ. And yet, because this being is only met in the unreflecting act of faith, which has itself been established by, and from within, that being, the control of the "I" is entirely removed. Here act is entirely suspended in being, while for the individual, being is entirely dependent on the act.

Barth Redeemed

Despite strong arguments against Barth, the transcendental approach is redeemed in the being of Christ as church-community. For Bonhoeffer, a more serious ecclesiology overcomes Barth's errors, yet never seeks to undermine the concept of faith, nor remove it from the stringent demands of the transcendental approach. Indeed, in Bonhoeffer's articles and lectures from around this time, where ecclesiology remains essentially untouched, Barth is consistently affirmed, and the act of faith almost exclusively promoted (cf. *BBNY*, 389ff., 462ff.; *CCIG*, 177ff.). In *AB*, having affirmed the centrality of the church-community, Bonhoeffer presents three forms of knowing found within it, the first of which is precisely a "believing" or "existential" knowing (*AB*, 126). The point for Bonhoeffer is not to remove the individual, but rather the individualism upon which the transcendental position is founded (132). For Bonhoeffer, the other two forms of "ecclesial" knowledge—in both preaching and theology—stand in service to the existential, as through the words of preaching "the living person of Christ declares itself in them by disclosing itself to the hearer" (130). When Christ speaks through these words, he speaks his words in the present, about God and sin, "that is, about my sin, in a truly existential way" (131). Consequently, that Christ meets the individual in the moment can never be mediated.

These ideas are affirmed and summarized in Bonhoeffer's 1933 lectures on Christology, in the declaration of Christ as being "*pro me*." Here, the real being of Christ is encountered in his Word spoken to the individual as life-affecting, existence-demanding, within the concrete relations and preaching of the church-community. As Bonhoeffer declares,

> Christ is not as Christ in himself, but in his relation to me. His being Christ is his being *pro me*. This being *pro me* is in turn not meant to be understood as an effect which emanates from him, or as an accident; it is meant to be understood as the essence, as the being of the person himself. This personal nucleus itself is *pro me*. That Christ is *pro me* is not an historical or an ontical statement, but an ontological one. That is, Christ can never be thought of in his being in himself but only in his relationship to me. That in turn means that Christ can only be conceived of existentially, viz. in the community. Christ is not Christ in himself and additionally still in the community. He who is the Christ is the one who is present in the community *pro me*. Luther says: "so it is one thing if God is here, and another if he is there for you" (WA 23, 152). (*C*, 47)

It is only as Christ meets me, speaking to me in the moment through the church-community, that I can "know" Christ—and this only in faith. Any attempt to know the "being" of God in abstraction, in itself, is both useless and godless, and simply conforms to the method of idealism (48).

Bonhoeffer affirms the statement of the transcendent approach that one can speak of the object of knowledge only "in reference to" the knowing subject. This idea is again affirmed in *Discipleship* where Bonhoeffer comments that "knowledge cannot be separated from the existence in which it was acquired" (51). God is therefore only known in the moment of faith, as he existentially meets the individual.

Kierkegaard and the Transcendental Approach

Kierkegaard and Subjectivity

Bonhoeffer's ecclesiology is clearly without any analogy in Kierkegaard. However, both accept humankind's predicament as entrapped within himself, and Bonhoeffer's solution bears striking similarities with Kierkegaard in terms of the necessity of the barrier, as well as in its connection to humankind's sin.

According to Climacus, the individual is somewhat aware of his predicament, as an unknown "beyond" lies forever as a "frontier" to his understanding and plagues his desire for certainty and completeness (*PF*, 44ff.). For Climacus, this frontier defines the absolute difference between God and humankind, forged not as the difference between the infinite and the finite, but between purity and sin, truth and untruth. Although Kierkegaard does not explicitly mention the *cor curvum in se* or the *ratio in se ipsam incurva*, he tacitly agrees by describing the frontier as incomprehensible to humankind's sinful reason.[15] Consequently, that Christ appears as both paradox and absurdity reveals this sinful state (47). Bonhoeffer does not clearly describe the barrier in terms of sin. However, this is suggested in *AB*, and Bonhoeffer connects it with God's judgment, or at least the revelation of humankind's incapacity (*AB*, 126).

For both thinkers, the barrier reveals itself against humankind's reflection as he rests inescapably in untruth. Consequently, the only possible response by the individual is ei-

---

15. It is interesting to note Westphal's suggestion that at the time of the Climacus authorship Kierkegaard began reading Luther's sermon's in earnest and came under their particular influence concerning sin—see Westphal, "Inwardness and Ideology."

ther to reject it as absurd, or to accept it. In acceptance, the individual must therefore suspend his reflection and understanding. However, as Climacus describes, this movement cannot itself be a movement of reflection—such that it is suspended in order that something might occur—as reflection is therefore smuggled back in (*CUP*, 1:113). Rather, it must be rejected for its own sake in recognition of its fallenness. As with our earlier discussion, a movement of passionate decision, a decisive action based in "letting go" of reflection, must be made (*PF*, 43; *CUP*, 1:115). This is the leap of faith.

Although Kierkegaard does not use the term "barrier," nor Bonhoeffer "leap," both stand in agreement. For both, it is only following the suspension of reflection that faith enters into the individual as a gift from God. Although discussed more fully in chapter 6, this agreement can be seen most explicitly in the requirement of a "first step," or a new "setting" or "situation," standing as a deliberate breaking of one's reflection and strength—and so the individual's previous existence in sin—in order that faith may come in from outside (cf. *JFY*, 191; *D*, 62).

As discussed in chapter 2, for Kierkegaard, wars, politics, and all movements of race, nationality, and generation are entirely irrelevant except in their influence on the individual before God. Such issues are potentially fatal distractions from the real issues of the ethical and the ethical-religious, which concern the essential nature and existence of the individual. In *CUP*, Climacus refers to the ethical and ethical-religious as "essential knowledge." Everything else is merely "accidental knowledge," the degree and scope of which is a "matter of indifference" for the individual (*CUP*, 1:197). It is precisely the individual in his most essential nature as "subject" that God desires, honestly and consciously embracing the reality of the world around him, and his place within it (1:131). For Kierkegaard, the definition of this authentic life is one held together by "naïveté"—to know one's limits in terms of what one does and doesn't know—and "primitivity"—a "childlike inwardness" that relates itself and establishes itself before God (*JP*, 1610/*Pap*, VI B 98:45; cf. 85/XI1 A 386, 650/VIII B 82, 654/VIII B 86). However, these terms are in themselves subsumed into the word used most famously in *CUP*: "subjectivity." For in subjectivity, the individual relates himself to his temporal reality in decisive action, and through a leap suspends reflection and the need for secure and conclusive understanding, and enters into faith (*CUP*, 1:33).

For Kierkegaard, faith is the "highest passion of subjectivity" (1:132), such that for the existing individual "passion is existence at its very highest" (1:197). In the face of life's incommensurability and contradictions, in the leap of faith doubt is excluded such that where decision—particularly concerning those issues of infinite importance to one's life such as one's eternal happiness—may present one with the most terrifying uncertainty, in faith, certainty is introduced (*PF*, 84). Indeed, in the moments of the most terrifying uncertainty one finds the potential for the greatest passion, the most significant faith, and so the most profound grasping of one's identity and existence.

Kierkegaard stands in agreement with the transcendental position that objective truth is simply not possible, and declares, "truth is subjectivity." Indeed, Bonhoeffer's statement that "one can speak about the object of knowledge only in reference to the knowing subject" (*AB*, 91; cf. *D*, 51), may be a citation of Kierkegaard's well-known argument that "whatever is known is known in the mode of the knower," once again found in the first part of *CUP* (*CUP*, 1:52). Drawing on our previous discussion, truth as subjectivity is the declaration that truth may only be known through existence, through a "life-view." In *CUP* this position is elaborated to declare, "*Objectively the emphasis is on* what *is said; subjectively the emphasis is on* how *it is said*" (1:202).

Subjectivity as Irrationalism?

Up until this point in Kierkegaard's argument, scholarship appears relatively unified as to the meaning of "truth as subjectivity." However, from here on opinion is more diverse. Before moving on, some of these positions require brief consideration.

That truth is *only* found in appropriation is most heavily stressed by Louis Mackey, who perceives an extreme form of transcendentalism in Kierkegaard. For Mackey, there can be no "being" to knowledge, no objective truth that can be discerned. Consequently, both epistemology and metaphysics are denied. The only form of authenticity available to us is through the mode of our existing. Indeed, in order to mediate this apparent state of "lostness" the individual is forced to create a kind of redemption myth to stabilize and contextualize his existence. It may be argued that this is similar to the opinion of Alasdair MacIntyre. For MacIntyre, Kierkegaard comes at the end of the attempt of the Enlightenment to ground ethics in reason. Consequently, Kierkegaard was forced to present an ethic that divorced itself from reason in order to combat the rise of ethical relativism that stood in the Enlightenment's place. Consequently, the form of the individual life as the exclusive subject of radical choice is the only option open to the individual. Although a little less extreme, Robert Roberts argues that although objective truth is not entirely transcendent, it is at least beyond the possibility of guarantee, and so rendered useless.

These positions do find support in Kierkegaard's thought. Indeed, as Kierkegaard argues in *CUP*, "An objective uncertainty, held fast through appropriation with the most passionate inwardness, is the truth, the highest truth there is for the existing individual" (1:203). Furthermore, Kierkegaard suggests that the person who relates himself correctly to an idol is more in truth than the one who relates himself incorrectly to God (1:201).

This thesis will not go into all of the many possible counter-arguments, but rather highlight several important alternatives.[16] Not only do such irrationalist claims fail to recognize Kierkegaard's assumptions concerning the loving personality of God but, as Hannay argues, their positions find no support from Kierkegaard's work as a whole.[17] Even Climacus, who is a self-confessed agnostic, argues that within humankind there is the "possibility" that "in inwardness is awakened to a God-relationship, and then it is possible to see God everywhere" (1:246). It is clear that this is not meant to be simply the projection of the individual's mind, or the outworking of some kind of "redemption myth," but rather a real interaction with God in terms of his involvement in creation. In this statement we are already far beyond Mackey's limits.

---

16. For arguments against Mackey, Roberts and MacIntyre, see Pojman, *Logic of Subjectivity*; Evans, *Fragments and Postscript*, and "Is Kierkegaard an Irrationalist?"; and Davenport and Rudd, *After MacIntyre*.

17. Hannay, *Kierkegaard and Philosophy*, 105.

God's concrete relationship to humankind can be seen particularly in Kierkegaard's psychology, for God is essentially intertwined in humankind's innermost being as spirit. In a journal entry from 1849, Kierkegaard argues that despite beginning with a few reasons, the power behind a decision is precisely that "under the weight of responsibility before God a conviction comes into existence in him through God" (*JP*, 3608/*Pap*, X1 A 481). Indeed, even though MacIntyre bases his conclusions on *E/O*, these ideas are clearly suggested. As Judge Wilhelm argues,

> In making a choice it is not so much a question of choosing the right as of the energy, the earnestness, the pathos with which one chooses. Thereby the personality is consolidated. Therefore, even if a man were to choose the wrong, he will nevertheless *discover, precisely by reason of the energy with which he chose, that he had chosen wrong*. For the choice being made with the whole inwardness of his personality, his nature is purified and he himself brought into immediate relation to the eternal Power whose omnipotence interpenetrates the whole of existence. (*E/O*, II:171)

Louis Pojman suggests that Kierkegaard may entrust the belief in the objective "what" coming into existence through the correct "how" on an understanding of God as love. Whether this is the full story or not, in *CD* Kierkegaard reflects that God does not leave in ignorance those who truly seek the truth. Consequently, "the need brings with it the nutriment" (*CD*, 244). Concerning *CUP*, Kierkegaard reflected in his journals from later in life,

> In all that is usually said about Johannes Climacus being purely subjective and so on, people have forgotten . . . that in one of the last sections he shows that the interesting thing is that there is a "how" which has a property that when it is present the "what" is also present; and that this is the "how" of faith. Here quite certainly, we have inwardness at its maximum proving to be objectivity once again. (*Pap*, X A 299)

As Climacus himself declares, had Pontius Pilate asked subjectively what truth was he would never have crucified Jesus (*CUP*, 1:230).

Mackey, MacIntyre, and others appear to have stopped their analysis with Kierkegaard's critique of speculative thought, and inferred that Kierkegaard denies both knowledge and truth. However, as Anderson argues, Kierkegaard is not presenting a subjectivism but a polemic against the abstract criteria of objective thought in completeness, necessity, and absolute certainty. Knowledge and truth do not exist in this way. Furthermore, Kierkegaard is not negating reason. As Pojman argues, Climacus uses reason to show reason's inadequacy.[18] Indeed, as will be seen in his later, more religious works, although Kierkegaard argues that reason must be discarded at the crossroads of faith, it is reason that gets the individual to that point in the first place. As can be seen in the concept of the "life-view," Kierkegaard is concerned that the individual authentically embrace his human existence in all its qualities (cf. 1:355). Against the deification of reason, Kierkegaard seeks to restore reason to the arsenal of humankind's faculties. As Climacus argues, "If thinking makes light of imagination, then imagination makes light of thinking, and the same with feeling. The task is not to elevate the one at the expense of the other, but the task is equality, contemporaneity, and the medium in which they are united is existing" (1:348).

---

18. Pojman, *Logic*, 47.

As Climacus again affirms, "for the subjective thinker, imagination, feeling, and dialectics in impassioned existence-inwardness are required. But first and last, passion . . ." (1:350).

Subjectivity and "life-view" are firmly linked. When knowledge is considered as a "*re-spiratio*," as "active passivity," the point is the "how" of breathing, not the "what" of the breath. The individual simply rests in the firm belief that knowledge will reveal itself from God's hand, and affect its truth within him.

Bonhoeffer's Criticisms of Kierkegaard Reconsidered

It is clear that there are many similarities with Bonhoeffer's acceptance of the transcendental view. Kierkegaard's notion of subjective truth is similar to Bonhoeffer's description of "existential knowledge." Bonhoeffer's characterization of the transcendental approach, where we can speak about "the object of knowledge only in reference to the knowing subject" finds strong parallels with Kierkegaard's declaration that "whatever is known is only known in the mode of the knower" (cf. *AB*, 91; *D*, 51; *CUP*, 1:52). For both, there can be no such thing as objective truth or knowledge but only that received by the individual who stands in any relation to what can be called "truth."

Most striking parallels can be found in Kierkegaard's quotation in *CUP* of the final lines of *E/O*: "only the truth that builds up is truth for you" (*E/O (P)*, 609; *CUP*, 1:252). These ideas are further reflected throughout *CD* where Kierkegaard stresses the importance of the question concerning Christianity and the truth, "Is this the way it is for me? (*CD*, 189, cf. 209, 242). In *AB* Bonhoeffer comments, "Outside the decision, it is 'known truth' but not truth for me" (*AB*, 96). In his later lectures Bonhoeffer provides a more Christological interpretation of Christ "*pro me*," and declares, "so it is one thing if God is here, and another if he is there for you" (*C*, 47). It is clear that Bonhoeffer connects this statement with Luther. However, Bonhoeffer's agreement with Kierkegaard is extremely relevant even if a direct connection may only be suggested. As has been argued, Bonhoeffer read both parts of *CUP* before the writing of *SC*. At various points in his life he also shows appreciation of *E/O*. Furthermore, this construction of subjectivity is found in one of the most famous journal articles, written on 1 August 1835, in which Kierkegaard comments,

> What I really need is to get clear about what I am to do, not what I must know, except insofar as knowledge must precede every act. What matters is to find my purpose, to see what it really is that God wills that I shall do; *the crucial thing is to find a truth that is truth for me*, to find the idea for which I am willing to live and die. (*JP*, 5101/ *Pap*, I A 75—author's emphasis)

It is interesting to note that in *EK*, in an entry from 1847, Kierkegaard reveals his joy in discovering that Luther had also quite independently used the formulation, "for you," which Bonhoeffer would have read later in life (*JP*, 2463/*Pap*, VIII1 A 465).

Despite these similarities, given Kierkegaard's association with Barth and the transcendental school, does Kierkegaard equally fall prey to Bonhoeffer's criticisms?

God's Freedom from Humankind

As discussed, there is an essential similarity between Kierkegaard, Bonhoeffer, and Barth with respect to "the moment." Climacus stands in agreement with Barth that Christian knowledge is given ever anew in the moment of faith (cf. *PF*, 64f.). However, lacking from Kierkegaard's subjectivity is an emphasis on the freedom of God. Kierkegaard is equally concerned to protect God's sovereignty from the ravages of idealism. In his journals Kierkegaard describes God as both "infinite majesty" and so "infinite subjectivity," by which he remains "subject," in total control (*JP*, 2570/*Pap*, XI2 A 54). However, in the encounter between God and humankind, it is not the freedom of God that Kierkegaard emphasizes but rather that of the individual. Specifically, Kierkegaard stands close to Bonhoeffer in arguing that the individual only gains true freedom when standing in total submission to God.

Individualism

As for Bonhoeffer's criticisms of Barth's individualism, it is clear that Kierkegaard is extremely individualistic. This issue will be dealt with throughout the coming chapters, and will only be decisively considered in the Conclusion. However, certain points can be made at this point.

It appears that in *SC* Bonhoeffer presents Haufniensis' perception of original sin, albeit stripped of its more psychological context. For both, the doctrine of original sin must combine the responsibility of the individual with the guilt of the race without the one excusing the other. However, most unusual is Kierkegaard and Bonhoeffer's shared desire to redeem Adam and his sin from being considered unique and qualitatively different to the rest of humankind—Bonhoeffer underlines in *CA* the idea of Adam as "a specimen" to the race (*BA*, 56; *CA*, 61). Their answer is that sin did not just enter the world through Adam's sin, but through every sin. Each is qualitatively the same. Consequently, where Haufniensis argues that every sin is essentially a first sin (*CA*, 29ff.), so Bonhoeffer declares, "[Adam's] sin was the 'first' sin. But qualitatively, 'first' sins are the only kind there are" (*SC*, 110).

However, the important issue in their discussion is that of Bonhoeffer's agreement with Haufniensis' assertion that as everyone is like Adam, "the individual is both himself and the race" (*BA*, 23; *CA*, 28). Not only does Bonhoeffer highlight his own copy each time Haufniensis makes such statements, but himself declares,

> The person as synthesis of act and being, is always the two in one: *individual person and humanity . . .*
>
> To speak of the human being as individual person and humanity never in separation but always in unity, is only another way of talking about the human being as act and as being. At no time are human beings one of these alone. (*AB*, 120)

For both writers, the individual bears a social identity in sin—a *peccatorum communio*. Bonhoeffer uses this idea as the justification of the individual's social nature and corporate identity, either "in Christ" or "in Adam" (cf. 113). Kierkegaard does not elaborate on the significance of the corporate nature of sin, and in *CA* there is clearly no description of a transition from the community of sin to a concept of *sanctorum communio*. However, it is distinctly possible that at least the seeds of such an idea rest behind Kierkegaard's thought. When one turns to Kierkegaard's journals of *EK*, one finds the declaration, vigorously highlighted by Bonhoeffer,

> The definition of "Church" found in the Augsburg Confession, that it is the communion of saints where the word is rightly taught and the sacraments rightly administered, this quite correctly (that is, not correctly) grasped only the two points about doctrine and sacraments and has overlooked the first, the communion of saints . . . (*EK*, 148; *JP*, 600/*Pap*, X4 A 246)[19]

Bonhoeffer's argument is that it is natural to move from the *peccatorum communio* to the *sanctorum communio*—that the one presupposes the other. One is left to wonder whether Bonhoeffer would have considered it logical that, even if unspoken, Kierkegaard should also have maintained some sense of *sanctorum communio*. Despite Kierkegaard's silence, it is clear that Bonhoeffer's own understanding of the community was inspired by Kierkegaard as early as *SC*.

An Idealist "I"

However, it is specifically concerning the issue of individuality that one finds the explicit criticism of Kierkegaard that has been the concern of this chapter. Bonhoeffer clearly understands and affirms Kierkegaard's attack and many of its constitutive arguments. However, he suggests that Kierkegaard has not himself escaped idealism as his "I" does not stand in a necessary relation to a concrete "You," but attempts to establish itself (*SC*, 57). For Bonhoeffer, such an individual can never escape himself, and avoids the necessity of the transcendent breaking in. Kierkegaard ultimately falls in the same way as everyone else. However, in what we have already discussed, something of a riposte to this claim has already come through.

As discussed in chapter 1, Kierkegaard has most commonly been considered an individualist. Although it is unclear whether Bonhoeffer had read "The Question of the Single One," here Martin Buber reflects a common position of the I-Thou school, that in separating the individual from the human other into an exclusive relationship with God, Kierkegaard overlooks humankind's social nature and the interrelatedness of the "I" and "You" with God. By removing the "I" from the "You," the "I" loses a part of its relationship with God. These ideas are taken further by Emmanuel Levinas, for whom the issue of alterity is of immense importance. For many, therefore, Kierkegaard's individualism is entirely acosmic and Gnostic. Indeed, although not necessarily agreeing with the charge, James Collins argues that it is easy to see where such a solipsistic interpretation of Kierkegaard comes from, and how he influenced later thinkers of the existential school.[20] This charge is taken up by Mackey in his well known article, "The Loss of the World in Kierkegaard's Ethics." Here Mackey interprets Kierkegaard's individual as only having certainty of his own existence. The human other only comes to him through the mind, not as a "reality"

---

19. Although *EK* was clearly too late to have been considered in the writing of *SC*.

20. Collins, *Mind of Kierkegaard*, 156.

but only as "possibility." The claim of the human other is therefore not real but simply that is accepted by the "I." For Mackey, such normative ethical concepts as temptation and duty are absurd as they are established and accepted by the "I." Consequently, Mackey declares that Kierkegaard is himself an idealist as the limits he sets for the mind are rationally fabricated. For ethics to exist, Mackey argues that the human other must be a concrete reality to the "I" in order for its claim to be meaningful.

Mackey's account clearly bears close relation to Bonhoeffer's. Indeed, one of Bonhoeffer's criticisms of idealism in *SC* is precisely for its inability to see the human other as anything other than a possibility (53). Furthermore, when Feil comments that Bonhoeffer's ecclesiology comes as a reaction against the fact that, "From the middle of the nineteenth century up to Karl Barth, Protestant theology was shaped to a large extent by a latent acosmic perspective," it is likely that he has Kierkegaard in mind as its father.[21] However, as Bonhoeffer does not elaborate on his criticism of Kierkegaard as an idealist, we must ask both how Kierkegaard stands up to the ideas explained above, but also how close Bonhoeffer himself stands to the ideas of Buber and Mackey.

Despite the similarity of his argument and language to that of Bonhoeffer, Mackey's arguments stand in the same line as Grisebach by asserting the transcendent potential of the human other to break in upon the 'I's reality. Consequently, according to Bonhoeffer's criteria, Mackey has also condemned himself to the charge of idealism.

It is clear that Kierkegaard does not emphasize the same ethical potential in the human other as Bonhoeffer. However, when Bonhoeffer's arguments rest on the need for true alterity Kierkegaard essentially agrees. The major error of Mackey's position is in his failure to understand the nature of Kierkegaard's subjectivity as an expectancy towards God's action. The two never stand in separation. As discussed above, the correct "how" brings the "what" with it through God's grace. Mackey's error is to have disjointed subjectivity from the "life-view," and so its definition as "active passivity," forging the condition of the self in expectancy of the transcendent barrier. For Kierkegaard, the barrier can be found through two forms.

The Created Other—When the individual acts through the authentic "how" of passionate decision, so the transcendent "what" breaks in, guaranteed by God's nature. There is little suggestion from Kierkegaard's writing that God acts on his own, injecting himself into the individual experience from out of the blue. Indeed, throughout his life we find Kierkegaard looking for God in the created order, in signs and portents around him. Consequently, although the human other, and indeed the whole created order, remain "possibility" within the movement of the authentic "how," as Mackey perceives, so they also become a real barrier by being used by God in the injection of the "what."

Kierkegaard clearly does not fit within the confines of Bonhoeffer's ecclesiology that suggests that God only forges the *human* other into the transcendent. Rather, the whole of the created order bears this potential. However, Kierkegaard bears marked similarity to Bonhoeffer in terms of how God remains "subject" throughout his encounter with the individual. Where Bonhoeffer argued that in faith the individual gives up the control of

---

21. Feil, *Theology*, xix.

his mind and so receives God's revelation as "subject," so the same movement is found in Kierkegaard's understanding of subjectivity as "life-view." For Kierkegaard, "active passivity" represents the submission of inauthentic reflection in order that knowledge may be revealed by God. It therefore remains outside the control of the individual, and therefore as "subject."

The Personal Other—Alterity is also found within the individual. Kierkegaard's psychology is based on the division of the individual, as both eternal and temporal, infinite and finite, freedom and necessity. Consequently, the individual has the ability to be a barrier to himself. When spirit or consciousness is defined as the relation between these polarities that relates to itself (*SUD*, 43f.), so the individual finds himself in a twofold relationship to both his natures, each one drawing him in different directions. As a result, just as with the human other and the created order, through authentic movement these "others" become an authentic barrier through God's "what."

CONCLUDING REMARKS

Kierkegaard's understanding of such issues as subjectivity, "life-view," the moment, anxiety, decision, and passion are summarized in Climacus' declaration, "But freedom, that is a wonderful lamp. When a person rubs it with ethical passion, God comes into existence for him" (*CUP*, 1:138).

What has been suggested in this chapter's analysis is that in Bonhoeffer's earliest publications of *SC* and *AB*, Bonhoeffer had read and was influenced by *CA*, *FT*, and both parts of *CUP*. The relationship between *SC* and *CA* appears to be particularly strong. Here we find not simply the adoption of such terms as movement, earnestness or passion,[22] anxiety and decision, the relationship between the individual and the universal, the dualism of immediacy and transcendence, but Bonhoeffer adopts Kierkegaard's understanding of "the moment" and original sin as central figures in his own analysis. Bonhoeffer's copy of *CA* is littered with his markings, and *SC* bears witness to this.

It is clear that Kierkegaard was a profound influence on Bonhoeffer's attack on idealism, found most explicitly in *SC*, *AB*, and *CF*. Furthermore, it has also been suggested that the strong existential marks of Bonhoeffer's thought, specifically surrounding the concept of subjectivity, Bonhoeffer's notions of "existential knowing," and knowledge as "*pro me*" find strong parallels in Kierkegaard's thought. Although there are firm links with Luther, when one also considers the notions of God as transcendent barrier and true subject to the individual as rooted in Kierkegaard, these existential notions are simply their logical consequences.

However, it appears at this early stage in his career that Bonhoeffer was working, at least on some level, under the influence of Kierkegaardian stereotypes. Both of Bonhoeffer's criticisms, concerning the self-establishing "I" and Kierkegaard's rejection of the church, play firmly into these perceptions. Furthermore, when they appear as some-

---

22. Bonhoeffer marks his own copy of *CA* particularly concerning "inwardness" and "earnestness" (cf. *BA*, 145, 146; *CA*, 146). In particular, near the end he underlines, "Inwardness, certitude, is earnestness" (*BA*, 150; *CA*, 151).

what throwaway comments, that are left relatively unexplained, the sense one gets is that Bonhoeffer believes that these are criticisms that are widely accepted and need no further elaboration. This chapter has shown that a more considered analysis reveals that according to Bonhoeffer's definitions Kierkegaard does not fall back into idealism, or reject the church. Kierkegaard does not follow Bonhoeffer's stringent presuppositions concerning the church and the exclusivity of revelation, but does preserve transcendence within an authentic, ethically confronting barrier that overcomes the controlling "I." As will be shown in later chapters, as Bonhoeffer gained his own understanding of Kierkegaard these criticisms were overcome. In particular, in chapter 5, quite apart from considering Kierkegaard's interpretation of the *Akedah* as rejecting the church, it will be shown that in *Discipleship* Bonhoeffer used *FT* as the basis of his understanding of mediation and the community.

This chapter has also used Bonhoeffer to ask certain questions of Kierkegaard. These have largely revolved around accusations of irrationalism and individualism—themes that will recur throughout the following chapters. Of particular note is the link between Kierkegaard's understanding of original sin and the *peccatorum communio*. This chapter has suggested that behind Kierkegaard's suggestions of the person as both individual and race one finds roots of the *sanctorum communio*—a theme that Bonhoeffer saw as a logical progression, and used as the root of his own concept of community.

5

Attack on Idealism—Ethics

Introduction

THE INEXTRICABILITY OF EPISTEMOLOGY AND ETHICS IN EXISTENTIAL THOUGHT MEANS that many relevant issues of Kierkegaard and Bonhoeffer's ethics have already been discussed in chapter 4. However, where previous discussion considered the theoretical framework of ethics, so the concern of this chapter is to delve further into its practical outworking.

The particular focus of this discussion will be on Bonhoeffer's use of *FT*. Although a direct reference to *FT* is only found at the very beginning of Bonhoeffer's work, this chapter will argue that its ideas are implicit throughout Bonhoeffer's work.

Of the secondary sources discussed in chapter 1, Stephen Plant emphasizes most strongly the influence of *FT* and, in particular, the "teleological suspension of the ethical." However, his affirmation is marked by the strong proviso,

> Kierkegaard's *Fear and Trembling* proposes that the individual is higher than the community. The consequence of this is that in the duty to love one's neighbor it is not God we meet, but merely the neighbor, since our duty to God can cause us to "suspend" our ethical obligation to our neighbor. For Bonhoeffer, the choice between God and neighbor was false because God meets us in our neighbor. It was true, for Bonhoeffer, that Kierkegaard had correctly turned away from Kant in presenting a critique of philosophical ethics from the biblical point of view: but Kierkegaard had wrongly followed Kant in making the individual central to ethics. For Bonhoeffer . . . individuals meet God in community, not in isolated individualism.[1]

The first half of this chapter will consider the root of both thinkers' ethics in their attacks on idealism, the nature of Bonhoeffer's interaction with the "teleological suspension of the ethical," and their understanding of "ethics" in relation to an absolute duty to God. The second will consider Plant's argument and present a reading of *FT* that suggests far greater parallels than he allows.

---

1. Plant, *Bonhoeffer*, 49.

PART 1

IDEALISM AND THE TELEOLOGICAL SUSPENSION

Kierkegaard

The Realms of the Ethical and the Ethical

What does Kierkegaard actually mean by "ethics"? In such works as *E/O*, *SLW*, and *CUP*, ethics is defended by Judge Wilhelm and Climacus as the mark of authentic existence. However, in *FT* it appears in opposition to Abraham and the way of faith. It is therefore clear that Kierkegaard uses the term "ethics" in (at least) two different ways, marked by the distinction between the ethical as an orientation of life, and that as a moral system. As Calvin Schrag puts it, one must always bear in mind "the crucial distinction between the ethical *as a universal moral requirement* and the ethical *as a manner or mode of existence*."[2] The first is the idealist system that denies contradiction and the incompatibility between thought and action. However, the second is manifest in the concept of passionate decision.

This latter definition stands at the heart of Kierkegaard's "existential" message. In this formulation, the ethical rests lower than the religious in his threefold classification, but is absorbed into the religious, as it is through decision that the individual places his life into the hands of God. Indeed, in *CUP* Climacus argues that the ethical "lies so close [to the religious sphere] that they continually communicate with each other" (*CUP*, 1:162). As C. Stephen Evans concludes, "when purged of its absoluteness and finality [the ethical] reappears as an essential component of the religious life."[3]

As is clear from the preceding chapter, Kierkegaard's attack on idealism is couched in the description of two distinct, exclusive realms of perception that exist side by side. At the beginning of "Preamble from the Heart" Johannes presents the distinction between the "outward and visible world," and the "world of the spirit" (*FT*, 56). Reflecting Paul's description in Col 2:8, the former (also referred to as the "finite" or "temporal" world) is defined according to humankind's sagacity and speculative reason—"the tradition of men, according to the elementary principles of the world."[4] This world stands in opposition to the "world of the spirit," where "there prevails an eternal divine order" (57). Throughout its pages, *FT* describes the battle between these two realms. In his opening speech, Johannes summarizes his argument by declaring that Descartes was right to affirm that whatever God might tell us is "incomparably more certain" than anything else, even if reason should suggest the opposite (41).

Johannes's own predicament bears witness to this distinction. Johannes is neither a man of faith, nor someone who stands outside the "outward and visible world." He is not privy to any special revelation concerning faith and "the System," but is simply one who does not "lack the courage to think a thought whole," to recognize the irreconcilable confrontation and contradiction that occur between these two realms (cf. 60). Johannes

---

2. Schrag, "Notes," 66.

3. Evans, "Telos of Morality," 15.

4. Col 2:8 (NASB).

has the honesty to declare that according to the sagacious, systematic world, Abraham is guilty of attempted murder in its most heinous form. For Johannes this conclusion cannot be mediated. Consequently, one either has to affirm Scripture as incorrect in describing Abraham as the father of faith (and so affirm the judgment of systematic ethics against him) or acknowledge that these systems oppose God (and so submit to the idea that they are ultimately flawed). All attempts to make Abraham acceptable and respectable are ultimately acts of delusion and ignorance (60f.).

Although Johannes can understand this dichotomy, he cannot go any further. In thinking about Abraham he is "virtually annihilated" and "constantly repulsed" (62). The internal logic of each realm is mutually exclusivity to one another. Consequently, as he stands in the finite world, he simply cannot understand the realm of the spirit beyond its formal relationship to the finite. Johannes summarizes his thought best when he comments, "in the temporal world God and I cannot talk together, we have no common language" (64).

As we turn now to a more concrete analysis of faith as presented in *FT* it is this framework that will be borne in mind.

The Knights of Faith and Infinite Resignation

According to the finite world, God's command to sacrifice Isaac went against everything Abraham held dear: against the moral law, his love and responsibility as a father and husband, his hope through Isaac as God's promise, as well as God himself as its author. However, Abraham is not the father of faith because he was obedient. Had Abraham simply been obedient, he would rather have been a "knight of infinite resignation."

KNIGHT OF INFINITE RESIGNATION

The knight of infinite resignation is praised by Johannes as he is armed with an understanding of God, a desire for obedience, and undertakes a movement of spirit (74). However, he is still ultimately bound to the finite world. All of his decisions are "a purely philosophical movement" based on finite reason (77). He is obedient because he understands his eternal validity as spirit, his hope for salvation, and God's nature as love. However, he also understands the consequence of his actions to be Isaac's death by his own hand. The knight of resignation relates to God through resignation rather than faith, for despite his obedience he has resigned himself to this consequence. With such a predicament, Johannes argues that the only way the knight can cope is if he were to reject the whole of the finite realm and to place his hope purely within the eternal (64ff.). In this movement the knight resigns himself to his unhappiness in the temporal world, emotionally detaching himself from it, and looks for his peace and repose in the infinite (74).

KNIGHT OF FAITH

Abraham is obviously obedient. However, instead of believing that he will lose Isaac, the knight of faith recognizes that God commands Isaac's sacrifice, but also that Isaac is his promise for the future. Consequently, he rejects the conclusion of finite reason to believe that both will come true. From the perspective of the finite world, this is clearly absurd. However, when the knight stands in faith, in the "world of the spirit," this absurdity is overcome for here it holds that "for God all things are possible" (75).

Faith is described by Johannes as a "double movement," for the individual must first make a movement of resignation, before rejecting it for the authority of God. As Johannes argues, "[Abraham] admits the impossibility and at the same time believes the absurd" (76). Where in resignation the knight gives up temporality for the eternal, so the knight of faith gains the temporal back again from the eternal. Where the knight of resignation permanently resigns his paternal love, even if Isaac were returned to him, the knight of faith maintains his love throughout and receives Isaac back again in a new way from the eternal (77).

Ironically, although the knight of resignation gives up the finite for the infinite, he still rests in the understanding and systems of finitude. The knight of faith, who embraces the finite, truly lives only in the infinite. Knights of resignation are easily spotted for "their gait is gliding, bold" and they stand out from the world from which they are resigned. However, as affirmed in both *FT* and *CUP*, the knight of faith, in having embraced the world back again, is impossible to recognize, becomes "incognito," and perhaps even resembles a "bourgeois philistine" (*FT*, 67; *CUP*, 1:410). For the knight of faith lives as the infinite in the finite, interacting with temporality, and yet living according to the eternal.

It should be noted that in recent years, commentators such as Lippitt and Cross have criticized this more traditional reading of the "double movement" of faith for holding the movements of resignation and faith together. They argue that both are mutually exclusive, making it untenable for Abraham to believe that he will have to sacrifice Isaac, while at the same time believing that he will not lose him. Cross argues that Abraham acted as though he had faith that he would not lose Isaac, but ultimately believed that he would. Conversely, Lippitt argues that Abraham acted as if he were going to sacrifice Isaac, but never finally believed that God would make him go through with it. However, there is surely a profound irony in rejecting the traditionally unified "double movement" for being essentially "too absurd." Both Lippitt and Cross try to make the double movement plausible and explicable, and fatally undermine its absurdity. Both rationalize Abraham's thought process, and therefore essentially locate him still within the understanding of the finite world. It is unclear that Abraham has faith in either of these formulations. Johannes' point is that even if God had not intervened and Abraham had gone through with the sacrifice, he still would have had faith that he would receive Isaac back again (*FT*, 65).

The Teleological Suspension of the Ethical

In *FT* the ethical is the universal moral requirement to which all must submit. According to Johannes, it is not simply a means to an end, but rather holds its telos within itself. The ethical is itself "good," and therefore, the absolute and ultimate judge (83). Within this concept of the ethical, the individual is subordinate to the universal. Furthermore, Johannes argues that the internal is also defined as unethical as it cannot be universally communicated (96ff.). Rather, faith reveals the individual and the internal over the universal and external (84, 97).

In contrast, Abraham made a "teleological suspension of the ethical." When the ethical holds its telos within itself, through the teleological suspension of the ethical the individual grasps hold of a telos outside of the ethical. In this case, Abraham was obedient to God (88). Johannes presents "tragic heroes" who at first sight commit similar acts of murder but who ultimately act according to a higher expression of the ethical than that maintained in not committing their sacrifices. However, for Abraham, no such mediation is possible. There is no higher expression of the ethical, only the expression of a higher telos.

The submission of the ethical to personal revelation is clearly problematic. Johannes was also aware of the dangers, but believed that the nature of authentic individuality guarded against it. As Kierkegaard experienced in his own life, the paralysing potential of anxiety, the reality of one's sin, of standing against the will of Governance, forces the individual before God's throne in hope for God's grace and mercy (103). When bourgeois philistines live and "rejoice in the security of the masses," the individual lives under the weight of his fear and trembling that every move he makes is a matter of eternity (103). When others find their rest in the universal, "the knight of faith is kept in constant tension," and essentially lives in "absolute isolation," unable to express and explain the grounding of his action (106).

Absolute Duty to God

In holding its telos within itself, the ethical has become the absolute authority and judge. Consequently, "the ethical and a person's eternal blessedness, which is his *telos* in all eternity and at every moment, are identical" (83). Consequently, the ethical has become the divine, and therefore overcomes the individual's relationship with God (89, 96). As Johannes explains,

> The ethical is the universal and as such, in turn, the divine. It is therefore correct to say that all duty is ultimately duty to God; but if one cannot say more one says in effect that really I have no duty to God. The duty becomes duty to God by being referred to God, but I do not enter into relation with God in the duty itself. Thus it is a duty to love one's neighbor; it is a duty in so far as it is referred to God; yet it is not God that I come in relation to in the duty but the neighbor I love. If in this connection, I then say that it is my duty to love God, I in fact only utter a tautology, in so far as "God" is understood in an altogether abstract sense as the divine: i.e. the universal, i.e., duty. The whole of human existence is in that case entirely self-enclosed, as a sphere, and the ethical is at once the limit and completion. Good becomes an invisible, vanishing point, an impotent thought, and his power is to be found only in the ethical, which fills all existence. (96)

In contrast, faith declares that there can only be an absolute relationship to God. The individual "determines his relation to the universal through his relation to the absolute, not his relation to the absolute through his relation to the universal" (97). In discussing this relationship, Johannes alludes to the story of Job in which Job is described as progressing from being one who through his systematic understanding of God had only ever heard of Him, but now comes to see Him.[5] Consequently, in *FT* Johannes describes the "wonderful glory achieved by that knight in becoming God's confident, the Lord's friend, and—to speak really humanly—in addressing God in heaven as 'Thou,' while even the tragic hero only addresses him in the third person" (105). As Climacus affirms in *CUP*, anyone who gives up his individuality for the universal is "selling his relationship with God" (*CUP*, 1:137).

Summary

For Kierkegaard, faith and authenticity are found in an absolute relationship of the individual with the absolute. Within this relationship, the individual leaves behind the supremacy of his rational systems and places his trust in God's understanding and desire. The individual believes that for God all things are possible, and so believes on the strength of the absurd. However, once initiated into faith, into the "world of the spirit," the absurd no longer appears as the absurd, for it is only that according to the judgment of the "outward and visible world." Consequently, as Kierkegaard comments in his journals, "When the believer has faith, the absurd is not the absurd—faith transforms it, but in every weak moment it is again more or less absurd to him. The passion of faith is the only thing which masters the absurd—if not, then faith is not faith in the strictest sense, but a kind of knowledge" (*JP*, 10/*Pap*, X6 B 79).

In the same vein, it is only from the perspective of the finite world that faith is defined according to anxiety. As Kierkegaard argues in "Thoughts Which Wound From Behind," "When faith is seen from its one side, the heavenly, only the reflection of eternal salvation is seen in it; but seen from its other side, the merely human side, one sees sheer fear and trembling" (*CD*, 175). Mooney observes that when such terms as "the absurd" and "the paradox" rarely appear in Kierkegaard's direct, more religious, authorship, so in such non-Christian pseudonyms as Johannes de silentio and Johannes Climacus, they are central concepts. These concepts only have significance for those who rest in the finite world.[6]

Bonhoeffer

At the beginning of *SC*, Bonhoeffer disparages idealism for having forged the ethical as the realm of universal principles the individual is obliged to obey (*SC*, 46). This is reflected again in *Discipleship* where Bonhoeffer argues that through the influence of idealism, the world "has become a rigid, inescapable law of principles" (*D*, 81).

In an address to his congregation in Barcelona entitled "Basic Questions of a Christian Ethic," delivered between his submissions of *SC* and *AB*, Bonhoeffer presents perhaps his most extreme description of ethics as "a child of the earth" (*BBNY*, 360). Divorced from all divine revelation it has become a series of principles concerned with issues of good and evil by which humankind attempts to get to God (363). To fully understand these ideas,

---

5. Job 42:5.

6. Mooney, *Knights of Faith*, 56.

one must delve further into Bonhoeffer's understanding of the fall, which stands at the heart of his ethical theory.

Ethics and the Fall

As described in chapter 4, through the fall and humankind's desire to become *sicut deus* a new knowledge was created with a language that ignored God as its origin and Creator (*CF*, 53). This was not simply different from humankind's old knowledge but a reversal, standing in complete opposition to God (*E*, 301). Most significantly, it became defined according to the language of good and evil. Before the fall, Bonhoeffer suggests that the concepts of good and evil were only theoretical for God who, as the "Good," had no need for them. However, through the fall, they were ripped out of God's hands and corrupted. Consequently, they are no longer the good and evil of God, but rather against Him by which He is judged (302). As Plant argues, "The knowledge of good and evil is not, therefore, knowledge of the good and evil of God, but of good and evil against God."[7] Bonhoeffer therefore proclaims his judgment on humankind, that "In becoming like God man has become a god against God" (302). Bearing this corrupt notion of good and evil, humankind has become the judge of God (308).

Christian Ethics?

For Bonhoeffer, idealist ethics is like the Pharisee who finds meaning only in the judgment of good and evil (309f.). In his refusal to become embroiled in the ethical debate of the Pharisees, Christ reveals God's heart and desire for humankind. According to Bonhoeffer, God has never desired that humankind be good or live according to a universal systems, but for the individual to be in immediate relationship with Him. As Plant argues, "The question 'what is the right thing to do?' did not exist until the Fall because Adam and Eve simply knew and obeyed God's will for them."[8] In "Basic Questions of a Christian Ethic" Bonhoeffer declares that Christianity has no interest in "ethics." Its only concern is to bring humankind back into its original relationship with God, where it knew only God and everything else through Him. In this early address, Bonhoeffer goes so far as to argue, "Christianity and ethics do indeed have nothing to do with one another; there is no Christian ethic and there can be no transition from the idea of Christianity to that of ethics." Consequently, "The primal—let us say, childlike—community between human beings and God stands beyond this knowledge for good and evil; it knows only one thing: God's limitless love for human beings" (*BBNY*, 363). In agreement with Paul Ramsey, Bonhoeffer argues that Jesus actively went out of his way to break the ethical principles of the Pharisees to show his disinterest in them (*E*, 312).[9] For it is only once the individual breaks with the systems of the world, casting off his security and obsession with good and evil, that he can once again become the individual before God. In this way, Bonhoeffer reveals his guarded appreciation of Nietzsche in the need to escape the universal or

7. Plant, *Bonhoeffer*, 90.

8. Ibid., 112.

9. Cf. Ramsey, *Basic Christian Ethics*, 46ff.

herd mentality to go "beyond good and evil" (cf. *BBNY*, 363, 366f.). As he comments in "History and Good," "Through [Idealist principles] human beings do not become stronger and more mature, but only poorer and more suspicious" (*E*, 248).

The Ethical Situation

In the essay "Ethics as Formation," Bonhoeffer argues that the ethical situation in Germany shows the fallacy of ethical systems by revealing their inability to cope (cf. 76). When evil appears in the form of light, when all ethical normality is undermined, when all possibilities of action between a clear good and evil are removed, ethical principles simply serve to bring further confusion and blindness to those who refuse to give them up. In his situation Bonhoeffer saw first hand just how far "ought" stood from "is." Both here and in "After Ten Years," Bonhoeffer describes various ethical systems based on such principles as conscience, duty, freedom, and private virtue (recognisable in such thinkers as Aquinas, Kant, Fletcher, and Hauerwas) and declares their failure in the face of his contemporary situation. Where such systems may be based on the "convictions of a noble humanity," each adherent is left like Don Quixote, charging unprepared into battle for a cause that doesn't exist (80). These systems are for Bonhoeffer like rusty swords that must be replaced. To the question, "Who stands fast?" (*LPP (SCM)*, 4f.) Bonhoeffer answers,

> Only the person who combines simplicity with wisdom can endure. But what is simplicity? What is wisdom? How do the two become one? A person is simple who in the confusion, the distortion, and the inversion of all concepts keeps in sight only the single truth of God . . . Because of knowing and having God, this person clings to the commandments, the judgment, and the mercy of God that proceed anew each day from the mouth of God. Not fettered by principles but bound by love for God, this person is liberated from the problems and conflicts of ethical decision, and is no longer beset by them. This person belongs to God and to God's will alone. The single-minded person does not also cast glances at the world while standing next to God and therefore is able, free and unconstrained, to see the reality of the world. Thus simplicity becomes wisdom. The person is wise who sees reality as it is, who sees into the depth of things. Only the person is wise who sees reality in God. (*E*, 81)

Where God desires the individual to enter into undivided relationship with Him, it is only here that the individual can stand against the ravages of a situation that renders ethical principles useless. For against Quixotic illusions, it is only through the will of God that the individual can grasp the reality of the "concrete situation" (*BBNY*, 377f.).

Responsibility

Obedience to ethical principles denies responsibility as the individual is essentially acting in a way independent of the concrete situation and claim of the human other. Duty "defines what is good exclusively as one's own adherence to principles without any regard for the other person" (*E*, 248). This can be seen for instance in Kant's defence of the principle that one must never lie, to which Bonhoeffer responded in his essay, "What is meant by 'Telling the Truth'?" Here, in the situation where an individual must tell the truth of another's whereabouts to someone who is trying to kill them, Kant argues that the victim's death is merely "accidental" to the truth telling, and not therefore the individual's responsibility.[10] For Bonhoeffer this is simply the evidence of how principled ethics denies the true concept of responsibility, concerned with the reality of the individual's situation (*E* (SCM), 326ff.).

Bonhoeffer's concept of responsibility can be seen mirrored in H. Richard Niebuhr's, *The Responsible Self*.[11] Where Bonhoeffer discards both deontology and consequentialism—described by Niebuhr as "man-the-citizen" and "man-the-maker" respectively—as unable to embrace the full nature of responsibility, so Niebuhr puts forward the concept of "man-the-answerer." This is a useful insight into the nature of responsibility. For as the editors of *Ethics* point out, Bonhoeffer plays on the linguistic connection between the German words *Antwort* ("answer"), *verantworten* ("to answer for"), *Verantwortung* ("responsibility"), and *verantwortlich sein* ("to be accountable") (*E*, 255). For both Bonhoeffer and Niebuhr the concept of responsibility holds within itself the idea of the individual answering to and for the neighbor before God. Indeed, where Niebuhr argues that "man-the-answerer" does what is "fitting" (as opposed to acting in terms of the deontological "right" or the consequentialist "good") so Bonhoeffer has the responsible agent doing what is "appropriate." For both, the only responsible act is that which considers the wholeness of the human other in relation to God's activity. One must consider this other in his "time-full" state, as presenting a claim not simply according to his present, but in the moment that draws the past and future to itself as the "still-present" and the "already-present."[12] Consequently, as Niebuhr summarizes, responsible action is that which asks "What is God doing?" and responds accordingly.[13] In this way Niebuhr affirms Bonhoeffer's declaration that the responsible action is that committed "in accord with reality," embracing the "concrete neighbor in their concrete reality," and seeking beyond absolute principles to discern and enact God's will in their lives (*E*, 261).

Reality

For Bonhoeffer, principled ethics, by which the individual knows in advance what he must do, not only destroys the nature of responsibility, but also denies the personal and loving nature of God in his interactions with humankind (cf. *BBNY*, 365f.). For Bonhoeffer, God interacts with each individual, in every situation, according to their needs and His desires. He has not simply left behind His word to be dutifully fulfilled but demands obedience to the commands "that proceed anew each day from the mouth of God." Consequently, ethics is the individual taking responsibility for his neighbor, manifesting the will of God as it is spoken into the neighbor's concrete existence. Ethics can no more be a system than God himself.

---

10. Kant, "Right to Lie," 123.

11. In many ways, Niebuhr's account appears to be a philosophical reworking of Bonhoeffer's ethics.

12. Niebuhr, *Responsible Self*, 90ff.

13. Ibid., 126.

To define ethics as God's will is to say that it must be in relation to "reality." For when humankind creates a corrupt understanding of the world, so reality is only found in the understanding and will of God. Bonhoeffer vehemently attacks those that would convert Jesus' words into ethical principles as failing to understand the motivation and "reality" behind them. Christ spoke from his divine and inscrutable perspective into the individual's specific, momentary situation (*BBNY*, 363f.; *D*, 77f; *E*, 358f.). Consequently, Christ's words have value in teaching us about who God is and the nature of his will, but not about ethical principles. In a qualified way, Bonhoeffer would agree with Hauerwas that Scripture reveals not what we should do, but rather who we should be, or, as in the case of Niebuhr, presents a "revealed reality" rather than a "revealed morality."[14]

Some commentators, such as Ramsey, have suggested Bonhoeffer's ethics as a form of agapism.[15] Bonhoeffer does speak at length about love. However, love is not a principle upon which ethics can be formulated. Love for Bonhoeffer is simply the nature and will of God. Consequently, to love is simply to manifest and enact God's will (cf. *SC*, 168, 171; *BBNY*, 365; *E*, 334f.). Bonhoeffer therefore avoids describing ethics through love as it runs the risk of distracting the individual from God and converting love into a principle.

There are no principles that mediate God's word, allowing the individual to know in advance what he should do. However, one can come to know God himself, and therefore the orientation of his will. Bonhoeffer argues that God never reveals his unmediated, transcendent nature, but only that presented through Jesus Christ. "Reality" for Bonhoeffer is fundamentally Christological (*E*, 49). Christ reveals that God's will is for humankind to be "accepted, judged, and awakened to new life by God" (92). Consequently, this is the reality to which all ethical discussion must be obedient.

Situationalism and the Divine Order

Alongside the situational nature of God's commands, Bonhoeffer declares, "Principles are only tools in the hands of God; they will soon be thrown away when they are no longer useful" (82). This has led some, such as Joseph Fletcher, to label Bonhoeffer a "situation ethicist." And from a superficial reading, these tenets point in that direction. Indeed, Kelly and Nelson argue that "Basic Questions of a Christian Ethic" reads somewhat as a defence of situationalism due to its less than directional argument (*TF*, 347). However, Bonhoeffer stands apart from situation ethics as described by Fletcher for several important reasons.

THE FORM OF ETHICS

Fletcher derives his situational ethics in large part from Bonhoeffer, and argues that one cannot know in advance what to do but must simply act through love. However, in so arguing he falls into the trap of seeing love in distinction from God and therefore as a principle. Indeed, throughout his account, love appears as a fully comprehensible object, given to humankind to be simply used in each situation. Consequently, Fletcher has lost sight of the simple obedience at the heart of Bonhoeffer's ethical message. This is made clear

14. Hauerwas, *Community of Character*, 59; cf. Gustafson, "Introduction," 23.

15. Cf. Ramsey, *Deeds and Rules*, 118 n. 31.

as Fletcher describes acts of love as intrinsically "good." The whole point of Bonhoeffer's ethics is its disavowal of self-justification and the judgment of good and evil. The irony is that according to Bonhoeffer's definitions, Fletcher is an idealist having converted both love and "the good" into principles. For Bonhoeffer both can only be defined as God himself. Any other formulation simply distracts the individual from relationship with God, placing reliance on an ideal principle rather than a divine person.[16] Bonhoeffer accurately describes Fletcher's situation ethics as like those who believe that they can traverse the ethical minefield of existence with "their very own freedom" by giving up "barren principles" (*E*, 79). However, because their actions are still idealistic—still rooted in their own understanding rather than in the "reality" of God's understanding—they ultimately fall flat.

The Content of Ethics

Bonhoeffer's ethics transcends Fletcher's arrogant antinomianism that, as Ramsey agrees, simply leads to an impractical and destructive arbitrariness.[17] For although Bonhoeffer's ethics may emphasize the momentary situation, it holds within itself a significant content.

As discussed in chapter 4, God is not free *from* but rather *for* humankind. Far from being immune to the activities of humankind, God interacts with them, limiting himself and the ideal height of his divine will. For Bonhoeffer, this is revealed at the end of salvation history in Christ becoming guilty for humankind, but also at the beginning when God brings about the first death in order to clothe Adam and Eve. In this act, God reveals and affirms a new order that embraces humankind in his sinful state, preserving him until Christ's work is fulfilled (*CF*, 139). As described in chapter 3, Bonhoeffer was not uncritical of Luther's *Ordnungen*. However, although Bonhoeffer presents different configurations as to what he considers to be an order—and we remember that in Barcelona *das Volk* was considered as such—Bonhoeffer's reinterpretation in the "orders of preservation," later referred to simply as the "divine mandates," appears throughout his ethical thought at its foundation, preserving humankind from the destructive effects of the fall. Consequently, quite apart from arguing for the unrestrained freedom of the individual from law and principle (as asserted by Fletcher), Bonhoeffer argues that God has bound himself to earthly limitation. This does not undermine the situational aspect of God's will, but simply that God has bound his will to these institutions. In this light the statement that "principles are tools in the hands of God" means something quite different to the interpretation Fletcher ascribes it.[18] For Fletcher there are general "maxims" that can be used in discerning what to do.[19] Likewise, J.A.T. Robinson describes manmade principles that can be useful in ethical reflection.[20] However, for both, these principles can be rejected at any moment should God consider them incompatible with

---

16. Fletcher, *Situation Ethics*, 127.
17. Cf. Ramsey, *Deeds and Rules*, 145ff.
18. Fletcher, *Situation Ethics*, 28.
19. Ibid., 55.
20. Robinson, *Honest to God*, 105ff.

His desire. The point for Bonhoeffer is that not only are these mandates rooted in and established by God's love, but are consistently defended by it.

Bonhoeffer uses Paul's declaration that "The letter kills, the spirit gives life" to interpret Christ's commands (*BBNY*, 368), and applies the same concept to interpret the divine mandates. For Bonhoeffer, life holds within itself an "intrinsic law," based upon God's desire for how it should run (cf. *E*, 271)—as Heinz Tödt describes, "laws that are inherent in life and indispensable for its preservation."[21] Although present in all facets of existence,[22] the mandates are the formal, principled manifestation of this law. However, because of the complexity of life and the limitation of language and conceptual thought, these principles describe the "intrinsic law" but cannot fully encapsulate it. Furthermore, the outward principle may not only fail to describe adequately the "intrinsic law," but actively come against it. Consequently, there are times when telling a lie affirms the truth more than "telling the truth" itself; when the act of rebellion affirms the state more than an obedience that undermines it; when killing affirms the sanctity of life where pacifism becomes its most brutal foe. In most normal situations, the "intrinsic law" and its outward principle stand in direct union. However, under the situation of the "*necessita*," where "responsible action reaches its most profound expression," one's commitment must be to the "intrinsic law" rather than its principled embodiment. For Bonhoeffer, the suspending of an outward principle in obedience to God's will is not a declaration of its worthlessness, but rather the defence and higher expression of that principle. Indeed, quite apart from an antinomianism, according to Bonhoeffer no one has the ability to undermine these mandates and laws of life without paying a severe price. These laws will, in essence, wreak their revenge (cf. *E*, 175f, 272).

The "How" of Simple Obedience

As discussed, the "how" of Bonhoeffer's ethics concerns the individual resting in simple obedience before God with undivided gaze, grasping hold of the word and command of God as it proceeds anew from His mouth every day. As Bonhoeffer argues in *AB* and his lectures on Christology, the living word of God is always spoken in the present for the future, and never as a timeless message to be stored up, converted into a principle, and drawn out according to humankind's wisdom and desire (cf. *AB*, 111; *C*, 49ff.; cf. *NRS*, 162, 165).

For Bonhoeffer, one should not be waiting for an exclusive divine revelation or listening to intuition. There is nothing to suggest that "God forces his way into the human heart" (*E (SCM)*, 22). There is no key that can unlock the voice of God, as this would once again stand in the way of one's direct relationship with God. Rather, as God demands the whole of one's life, Bonhoeffer argues that one must bring together all of one's faculties including reason and reflection in search of God's will—"Heart, intellect, observation, and experience must work together in this discernment" (*E*, 321). Intrinsic to this task is the need to understand the intrinsic laws behind the mandates and natural life. When these

---

21. Tödt, *Authentic Faith*, 166.
22. Cf. Bonhoeffer's discussion of medical ethics in "Natural Life" (*E*, 171ff.).

have been set up and affirmed by divine authority, one cannot be in correspondence with reality without discerning and being in compliance with them (271).

However, this search is never meant to resemble such models as Aquinas' rational conscience, where a decision is based on a survey of available information. As Bonhoeffer argues, "the wise person will seek to obtain the best possible information about the course of events without becoming dependent on it" (81). Rather one's understanding of God's will arrives only through the present, manifest word of God spoken each day.

To the question "How do I know that it is God's word?" no simple answer can be given. As described in chapter 3, the church is to proclaim the Word of God to the world in the "here and now." This comes across particularly strongly in his calls to the ecumenical movement, and when *in statu confessionis*. However, it is clear that there is a difference between the church and the individual and, as Bonhoeffer's own life revealed, a time when one must stand ethically on one's own. These issues are summarized in *Discipleship*, where Bonhoeffer declares, "followers of Jesus are always completely alone, single individuals who can act and make decisions finally only by themselves" (*D*, 135). Indeed, in "Basic Questions of Christian Ethics" Bonhoeffer argues that one does not even have the ability to discuss the content of ethics, as the will of God may be a constant surprise—"From these considerations it follows that one absolutely cannot speak about specific ethical problems from the Christian perspective. There is absolutely no possibility for establishing universally valid principles, since each individual moment lived before God can confront us with completely unexpected decisions" (*BBNY*, 368).

Consequently, despite the presence of the church, there is still no objective criterion by which one can know one's actions to be in accord with God's will. If there were, once again, the relationship with God would be reduced to a principle. That God is speaking to the individual and that he is able to hear it can only be accepted by faith. It is by faith that one receives and acknowledges the Holy Spirit. It is by faith that one understands and accepts God's transformative power such that one may declare, "Jesus Christ has become my conscience" (*E*, 278). It is a faith resting in the knowledge that one is "preserved, held, and guided by the will of God," and the "unity with the will of God that has already been granted" (323). As the individual increasingly undergoes a "metamorphoses" by the power of God's presence, as he comes to "live the life of Christ," so he can know the legitimacy of God's active word within his life.

When the center of Christian ethics is the individual standing in simple obedience before God, everything can only be discerned by the individual himself through faith. However, the anxiety of discerning God's voice is mediated as the more the individual enters this relationship, so the less he is concerned with the concepts of good and evil that judge his actions (*BBNY*, 378). The individual simply submits his actions to God in hope of His grace and mercy, and in faith of His guidance (cf. *BBNY*, 368; *E*, 282, 284).

Kierkegaard and Bonhoeffer Considered

The Two Realms

For both Kierkegaard and Bonhoeffer there are two distinct realms, the one ruled by the Creator, the other by the creature. While explicit in Kierkegaard's work, it runs implicitly throughout Bonhoeffer's. As he argues, through the fall man doesn't simply gain extra knowledge of good and evil, but rather his knowledge is entirely transformed to stand in direct opposition to God—"the knowledge of good and evil means a complete inversion of their knowledge" (*E*, 301). Indeed, when discussing the interaction between Jesus and the Pharisee, Jesus' enigmatic responses are not a deliberate attempt to deceive and confuse the Pharisee, but simply a truthful answer from what Kierkegaard would call the "world of the spirit." For Bonhoeffer, "The Pharisees and Jesus speak on completely different planes" (311).

Bonhoeffer describes the collision as between the "illusion of immediacy" (*D*, 94), and the knowledge of faith. As he describes,

> As those who no longer know good and evil, but only Christ as origin and rec-
> onciliation, human beings will know all things . . . They thus are filled with a new
> knowledge of God, yet no longer as those who have become like God, but as those
> who bear the image of God. They now no longer know anything but "Jesus Christ
> the crucified" (1 Cor 2:2); and in Christ they know all things. All those who know
> not, they have become those who know God alone and, in God, all things. Those
> who know God in God's revelation in Jesus Christ, who know the crucified and
> risen God, know everything in heaven and on earth and under the earth . . . The
> knowledge of the Pharisee was dead and barren, the knowledge of Jesus, and of
> those bound to him, is living and fertile . . . (*E*, 316f.)

According to Climacus, the individual of faith wanders in the world, and yet belongs entirely to heaven (*CUP*, 1:410). Indeed, Kierkegaard argues that within faith there is no longer anxiety or absurdity to faith's leaps as they are seen through a new knowledge (cf. *JP*, 10/*Pap*, X6 B 79; *CD*, 175). In a similar vein, Bonhoeffer argues that what stands out to the Pharisee is Jesus' overwhelming sense of peace as such security should not belong to someone who appears to act arbitrarily, without the certainty of principled guidance (*E*, 313).

However, for both Kierkegaard and Bonhoeffer, this initiation into a new knowledge does not suggest that the individual is suddenly awarded the content of God's understanding. Not only would this turn ethics back into a principle, but it would essentially destroy faith. Rather, the individual becomes initiated into a relationship where both the limits of the "outward and visible world" and the ultimate possibility of the "world of spirit" are understood. The individual remains in a relationship of faith that continually submits itself to God for his will and understanding. In *FT*, Johannes argues that faith is not a matter of a single act, but of repetition. At every moment, Abraham makes a double movement, understanding the impossibility of a certain outcome according to the "outward and visible world," and yet then embracing it in faith on the strength of the absurd. As Johannes argues, "[Abraham] is continually making the movement of infinity" (*FT*, 70).

It is clear that for both Kierkegaard and Bonhoeffer, an understanding of these two realms stands at the heart of their formal understanding of ethics.

Bonhoeffer and Abraham

With this foundation, Bonhoeffer's understanding of Abraham can be more clearly seen. In *Discipleship*, in a chapter entitled "Discipleship and the Individual," Bonhoeffer reveals clearly his indebtedness to *FT* in his analysis of Abraham, and the nature of his obedience to God concerning Isaac.

For Bonhoeffer, all relationships are immediate in the finite realm. Here one is freely allowed to interpret and create the human other through one's own mind. However, in faith, all relationships are mediated by Christ. It is rather only in "reality," through Christ, that a true knowledge of the other can be had.

In "Problema II" Johannes argues that the will of God may stand in total opposition to that of ethical principles such that an act of love appears as an act of hate. To illustrate this, Johannes draws on Luke 14:26, to argue that the manifestation of Christian love may appear to the finite world as hatred. While all the various chapters in *Discipleship* begin with a passage from Scripture, "Discipleship and the Individual" is headed by Luke 14:26 (*D*, 92f.). And the interpretation is essentially the same. For Bonhoeffer, in breaking with the world, resting in isolation, embracing a love for the world which can only be understood and manifested through the mediation of Christ, the individual will act in a way that appears as hatred for the world. Consequently, when Bonhoeffer addresses Abraham, the initial point is precisely Kierkegaard's declaration that, "The moment he is ready to sacrifice Isaac, the ethical expression for what he does is this: he hates Isaac" (*FT*, 101).

For Bonhoeffer, Abraham represents absolute obedience—"[Abraham] receives the call as it is given. He does not try to interpret it, nor does he spiritualize it. He takes God at God's word and is prepared to obey. Against every natural immediacy, against every ethical immediacy, against every religious immediacy, he obeys God's word" (*D*, 97). However, Abraham does not simply obey, as would the knight of infinite resignation, but rather "takes God at God's word" by continuing to trust God's promise through Isaac. As with the knight of faith, he does not reject the temporal realm and his happiness within it, but continues to embrace it. Bonhoeffer does not go into details as to how Abraham thought he would still keep Isaac, except to say that he simply embraces it. However, through this obedience, Bonhoeffer argues that Abraham received Isaac back in a new way:

> Abraham received Isaac back, but he has him in a different way than before. He has him through the mediator and for the sake of the mediator. As the one who was prepared to hear and obey God's command literally, he is permitted to have Isaac as though he did not have him; he is permitted to have him through Jesus Christ . . . Abraham had left everything and had followed Christ, and while he was following Christ, he was permitted to go back to live in the same world he had lived in before. Externally everything remained the same. But the old has passed away; see everything has become new. (98)

Unlike *FT*, Bonhoeffer's interpretation is directly Christological. And yet both present Abraham receiving the finite world back again through the mediation of the infinite, and so Isaac received back in a new way. The point for Johannes is precisely that through the "world of the spirit," through the eyes of faith, not only is anxiety and the paradox of faith overcome (even if at each moment) but everything is seen in a new way, through the mediation of one for whom all things are possible.

This section of *Discipleship* will be discussed more fully in Part 2. However, it is already clear from this brief overview that *FT* formed the backbone to its argument, and was a direct influence on Bonhoeffer's thought.

The Teleological Suspension of the Ethical

Referring back again to Plant's description of Kierkegaard's influence on Bonhoeffer, we must ask, therefore, whether Bonhoeffer does indeed embrace a "teleological suspension of the ethical."

For Johannes, the basis of the teleological suspension is threefold: the negation of ethics as holding its telos within itself, the promotion of the individual above the universal, and the incommensurability of existence against the universal.

God vs. Universal

For both Kierkegaard and Bonhoeffer, idealism presents the union of thought and actuality. The ethical consequence is that everyone can simply know the good and so do it. As Haufniensis comments, "As all ancient knowledge and speculation was based on the presupposition that thought has reality, so all ancient ethics was based on the presupposition that virtue can be realized" (*CA*, 19). Consequently, "Ethics points to ideality as a task and assumes that every man possesses the requisite conditions" to fulfil it (16). The parallels between *SC* and *CA* are once more affirmed as Bonhoeffer declares,

> [Idealist persons] have the dignity to be able to be ethical and, insofar as they are persons, they are obliged to be ethical. The boundary between "ought" and "is" does not coincide with the boundary of the person as a whole . . . [W]ith Kant's "You can, because you ought," the argument abandoned the realm of the ethical transcendence for the immanence of a philosophy of spirit. (*SC*, 46)

For both writers, ethics derived from an "unreal ideology" (*E*, 219ff.) fails to understand the incommensurable and contradictory nature of reality. In *FT*, Johannes attacks the idealist appropriation of Abraham into ethics and declares, "What is omitted from Abraham's story is the anxiety" (*FT*, 28). In the same vein, Bonhoeffer argues, "The idealist knows what he ought to do, and, what is more, he can always do it precisely because he ought. Where is there room, then, for the distress of conscience, for infinite anxiety in the face of decisions?" (*SC*, 49).

For Kierkegaard, ethics holds its telos within itself as there is no higher end to which it points. Although Bonhoeffer does not explicitly use the term "telos," his meaning is the same. As Bonhoeffer declares in reference to Kant in *SC*, it is through the participation in the ethical that the individual finds his fulfilment. In pointing towards itself, for both Kierkegaard and Bonhoeffer, ethics has replaced God.

INDIVIDUAL VS. UNIVERSAL

As Bonhoeffer argues in *SC* as well as *Discipleship*, God's desire is to draw the individual out into total isolation, rather than have him subsumed into the universal. These ideas find their summary in *CUP* where Climacus argues,

> The ethical . . . is predicated on individuality and to such a degree that each individual actually and essentially comprehends the ethical only in himself, because it is his co-knowledge with God. In other words, although in a certain sense the ethical is infinitely abstract, in another sense it is infinitely concrete, indeed, the most concrete of all, because it is dialectical for every human being as this individual human being. (*CUP*, 1:155)

Here the individual stands in concrete responsibility, knowing the ethical only as it is given to him directly by God. In the same way, Bonhoeffer's understanding of ethics is a form of co-knowledge with God, exclusive to that relationship in the moment of concrete responsibility. For both Kierkegaard and Bonhoeffer the Christian is released into a freedom from ethical principles to stand into a real love and obedience to God (cf. *BBNY*, 377; *CUP*, 1:138). This freedom defines the individual.

EXISTENCE VS. UNIVERSAL

For both Kierkegaard and Bonhoeffer, the incommensurability of life destroys the idealist unity between "ought" and "is." For Bonhoeffer, ethical principles simply cannot cope when the extremity of life is revealed. Both *CA* and *CUP* emphasize the anxiety of passionate decision and the desire of idealist thought to "evade some of the pain and crisis of decision" by making everything objective (*CUP*, 1:129). As quoted at the beginning, Johannes argues that, in order to interpret Abraham, idealism excludes the anxiety of his position (*FT*, 28). For Bonhoeffer, real ethical decision understands the concept of anxiety, and finds the way through the terrible path only by the word of God.

Interestingly, both Kierkegaard and Bonhoeffer use the figure of Don Quixote to describe the individual who forges his existence according to ethical principles. For both writers, such an individual lives in the world of illusion that appears preposterous to one living in the realm of reality. Indeed, Climacus further describes him as like one persecuted by a "*nisse*," a temperamental, goblin-like creature who manipulates his victims with illusions and deception to his own mischievous ends (*CUP*, 1:140). As Bonhoeffer argues, by holding to ethical theories, no matter what their nature, such an individual is entering woefully unprepared into a battle he doesn't understand, for a prize that is itself an illusion (*E*, 80).

For Bonhoeffer it is only the individual who combines simplicity and wisdom who stands firm in the heat of ethical battle. Clear parallels can be found in *CUP*. As discussed in chapter 2, Climacus argues that in contrast to the inauthentic "wise" man who believes he has left faith behind to appropriate "real knowledge," the "simple man" is one who, unfettered by his learning, simply accepts the complexities of God and His desire. When the "wise" man becomes bogged down in trying to understand the concepts of paradox and absurdity, etc., so the man of "loveable simplicity" simply accepts them as such (*CUP*, 1:170). Climacus describes the essence of Bonhoeffer's simple wise man, who looses himself from the chains of systems to be able to accept the nature and desire of God, despite its intrinsic inscrutability. The point is emphasized as Climacus then describes authentic wisdom, as found in the "simple wise person." As he summarizes, "The simple wise person will then immerse himself in comprehending the paradox as paradox and will not become involved in explaining the paradox by understanding that it is not a paradox" (*CUP*, 1:228).

In the sections of *CD* that Bonhoeffer himself owned (and indeed throughout the work), the concept of the "simple wise man" is once again prominent (*CD*, 15, 25, 102; cf. 70, 218, 219, 241, 242). Although Kierkegaard here associates this figure with Socrates, the point is still the same as for Climacus. As he describes, the simple wise man is one who sees through the forms of temporality within his existence, is perhaps even ignorant of them, and rather focuses on the things of eternity as they are handed to him within time.

When both the issues of a co-knowledge with God and an incommensurability to life are combined, it is not surprising that Bonhoeffer appears to affirm Johannes' description of Abraham as unable to communicate with anyone about the content of his action. As we have quoted above, Bonhoeffer argues that when ethical normality is discarded, and one is left with the inscrutable will of God standing against ethical principles, "one absolutely cannot speak about specific ethical problems from a Christian perspective" (*BBNY*, 368). For both Kierkegaard and Bonhoeffer, God draws the individual out into profound isolation, of which this silence, forcing the individual into total responsibility for the decisions he makes, is merely its manifestation.

Johannes summarizes the teleological suspension of the ethical when he declares, "In his action [Abraham] overstepped the ethical altogether, and had a higher *telos* outside it, in relation to which he suspended it" (*FT*, 88). In light of the above discussion, it must be affirmed that Bonhoeffer indeed holds to a teleological suspension of the ethical. Bonhoeffer rejects the idea of ethics as holding its telos within itself, and affirms "Telos" as being solely found in relation to reality and the origin. At the beginning of "God's Love and the Disintegration of the World" Bonhoeffer argues,

> The knowledge of good and evil appears to be the goal of all ethical reflection. The first task of Christian ethics is to supersede that knowledge. This attack on the presuppositions of all other ethics is so unique that it is questionable whether it even makes sense to speak of Christian ethics at all. If it is nevertheless done, then this can only mean that Christian ethics claims to articulate the origin of the whole ethical enterprise, and thus to be considered an ethic only as the critique of all ethics. (*E*, 299)

Bonhoeffer's ethics is concerned purely with the telos of the individual as found standing in undivided relationship with God. Where ethics is conceived purely in terms of universal ethical principles, Bonhoeffer essentially argues for its complete destruction. However, where ethical principles do come into play, they have a telos returned to them only as tools in the hands of God to bring about his desire on earth in preservation of humankind.

An Absolute Duty to God

Perhaps the central message of both Kierkegaard and Bonhoeffer's work is that of the individual's absolute duty to God. For Bonhoeffer, nothing must distract one's immediate relationship to God, for the individual "can only know God by knowing God alone" (300). Despite the identity of the church as the body of Christ, the individual's relationship to the Word is not mediated. The only direct relationship the individual ever has is with the Word, who mediates all other relationships. Consequently, when Bonhoeffer affirms the authority of the church (even so far as to suggest its potential to demand the individual's obedience over his intellect or even conscience), he argues that this is still only a "relative authority" over the individual in the face of the "absolute authority" of the word itself (*SC*, 250).

For Bonhoeffer, when knowledge of good and evil stands at the heart of humankind's knowledge against God, so it is reliance on this ethical system that proves most difficult to overcome in order for the individual to enter into absolute obedience with God. For even in relationship with God, the desire to know that one is doing good remains constantly overwhelming. While appearing humble and conscientious, this desire is, for Bonhoeffer, rooted in the desire for self-justification, and stands in the way of one's single-minded relationship with God. The good as a concept must be overcome.

In *CUP*, much the same sentiment is represented. Climacus does not use the term "good," but supports Bonhoeffer's meaning in speaking of "results," "achievements," and the desire for one's acts to have significance for the "world-historical."[23] As he describes, one who holds to these principles inside his relationship with God is like a deceitful lover:

> True ethical enthusiasm consists in willing to the utmost of one's capability, but also, uplifted in divine jest, in never thinking whether or not one thereby achieves something. As soon as the will begins to cast a covetous eye on the outcome, the individual begins to become immoral . . . the individual demands something other than the ethical itself. A truly great ethical individuality would consummate his life as follows: he would develop himself to the utmost of his capability; in the process he perhaps would produce a great effect in the external world, but this would not occupy him at all, because he would know that the external is not in his power and therefore means nothing either *pro* or *contra*. (*CUP*, 1:135)

Subjectivity, for Climacus, is to be able to say to God in divine madness,

> Let me be as if created for the sake of a whim; this is the jest. Yet I shall with utmost strenuousness will the ethical; this is the earnestness. I want nothing else, nothing. O insignificant importance, O jesting earnestness, O blessed fear and trembling! How blessed to be able to fulfil God's requirements while smiling at the demands of the times. How blessed to despair over not being able to do it as long as one does not let go of God! (1:137)

23. Where Bonhoeffer speaks exclusively of "the good" so Kierkegaard, in singling out Hegel as the object of his attack, refers also to "the world-historical" as the object of one's desire for results.

In parallel with Bonhoeffer, Climacus' conclusion is simply that the individual who tries to grasp hold of the results of his actions, to hold onto the good, "is selling his relationship with God" (1:137). As Pattison therefore comments, for Kierkegaard "we must always be hesitant in regarding ourselves as virtuous and in claiming in any given case to have had right on our side."[24]

As described in both "Ethics as Formation" and "After Ten Years" the only way that an individual may "stand fast" (*LPP (SCM)*, 4f.) in the mire of ethical uncertainty, to be able to know what to do when faced with greater or lesser evils, is to stand in absolute obedience and cling to the "commandments, the judgment, and the mercy of God that proceed anew each day from the mouth of God" (*E*, 81). In "The Lilies of the Field and the Birds of the Air" this sense of absolute obedience is clearly affirmed. Here Kierkegaard argues that when faced with the "Thou Shalt" of God there can be no deliberation, but only obedience. To this, Kierkegaard makes the analogy of a child, who does not waste time in deliberating about the command he has been given, but simply obeys and then returns to his "play, fun and the like" (*WA*, 10). Although this work does not appear in Bonhoeffer's library, it is interesting to note that to this analogy of simple obedience Kierkegaard writes, "what the child shall do is a thing that *stands fast* and has nothing whatever to do with deliberation" (*CD (L)*, 322—author's emphasis).

Although this discussion has focussed so far on *CUP*, *CA*, and especially *FT*, as described in chapter 1, Bonhoeffer had gained a comprehensive understanding of *SUD* by the end of 1932. And it is here that one finds perhaps Kierkegaard's clearest rejection of the concepts of good and evil. For here, Anti-Climacus argues that the opposite of sin is not virtue but rather faith (*SUD*, 115). The whole point of Christianity for both Kierkegaard and Bonhoeffer is the individual standing in relation to God. Consequently, the only dichotomy is that between relationship or non-relationship rather than right or wrong, good or evil. For both writers, sin is a state, not an act.

The Mediation of Love

Kierkegaard's understanding of love also bears strong parallels with Bonhoeffer's thought. For both, the nature of love is found in God. As previously described, Bonhoeffer shies away from using the term love, opting rather to simply speak of God, Christ or the Holy Spirit. However, for the same reason, Kierkegaard employs the term all the more, using it to literary effect in place of God. Consequently, when Bonhoeffer speaks of the mediation of God, so Kierkegaard often speaks of love. As argued in chapter 1, Bonhoeffer was extremely familiar with *WL* from as early as *SC*. And here we find a firm description of love's mediating potential. In the section entitled, "Love Abides," Kierkegaard argues that in an authentic relationship, love stands between individuals, supporting and sustaining their relationships (*WL*, 300ff.). Only in this way are these relationships unconditional, and devoid of the claims of the one on the other. Even if one were to fall away from the relationship, Kierkegaard argues that the other would remain unchanged in his love and relationship to them. This bears strong parallels with Bonhoeffer's descriptions in both

24. Pattison, *Philosophy of Kierkegaard*, 123.

Discipleship and *LT* where no direct relationships are allowed but only those mediated by Christ. Only in this way is each individual saved from the egotistical claim of the other.

However, in the upbuilding discourses published on the same day as *FT*, one finds further parallels as Kierkegaard describes the mediating potential of love, not simply in terms of personal relationships, but far more in terms of the very perspective of the individual. For Bonhoeffer, good and evil have been established as the measure by which everything is judged, including God and his actions. In stark agreement, couched in the language of love, Kierkegaard therefore comments, "an evil eye discovers much that love does not see, since an evil eye sees that the Lord acts unjustly when he is good. When evil lives in the heart, the eye sees offence, but when purity lives in the heart, the eye sees the finger of God" (*EUD*, 60).

Although the terminology is different, for both writers, good and evil stand as the foundations of the outward and visible world against the world of the spirit, defined according to the criterion of God or love. In "Ethics as Formation," Bonhoeffer describes further the state of ethical confusion that can be overcome only through God, and seeing clearly through the world of the spirit. So for Kierkegaard it is love that guides and comforts the individual through this confusion—"love remains with a person, and when everything becomes confused for him, when his thoughts rise up accusingly, when anxieties condemningly rear their heads, then love intimidates them and says to them: Just have patience; I will remain with you and witness with you, and my witness will overcome the confusion" (71).

Even if it should feel to the individual as if he had gone astray, love remains and comforts him against these accusations. Indeed, love directs the individual into an absolute relationship with God of simple obedience. For not only does Kierkegaard describe it as taking away both an individual's sense of perfection or imperfection—and so the judgmentalism that comes with a knowledge of good and evil—but directing the individual to an undivided gaze on God (74). As he comments, in ethical action, "when love gives, it does not watch the gift, but keeps its eye on the Lord" (61). In the moment, the individual is not allowed to listen to the voice of righteousness, or judgementalism, of results, for in so doing he loses the voice of love, and so also God. As Kierkegaard summarizes, "the person who thinks of his own perfection does not love, and he who takes his own imperfections into account does not love" (74). Only the one with undivided gaze has love.

It is unclear whether Bonhoeffer read Kierkegaard's *Upbuilding Discourses*. However, the parallels between both writers are striking here, presenting an understanding of idealist ethical systems, forged for the sake of self-righteousness, incapacitated by the reality of life, and overcome only through the mediation of God.

Bonhoeffer and *FT*'s Individual

The key issue behind Bonhoeffer's appreciation of *FT*, and perhaps Kierkegaard in general, is that of the individual. This can be seen from the very beginning. In *SC*, Bonhoeffer affirms that the community is forged through a "plurality of spirits," of individuals led into solitude by the Holy Spirit. As he argues,

> Everyone believes and experiences their justification and sanctification in solitude, everyone prays in solitude, everyone breaks through to the certainty of their own eternal election in solitude, everyone "possesses" the Holy Spirit and Christ completely "for themselves." This solitude, however, is not something done by faith, but is willed by God. It is the solitude of the individual that is a structure of the created order, and it continues to exist everywhere. (*SC*, 162)

As he cites in his footnotes to this passage, it is Kierkegaard he has in mind, "who like few others knows how to speak of the burden of solitude," but concludes that Kierkegaard "comes to reject the concept of the church on that basis" (*SC*, 162 n. 20).

Bonhoeffer's interpretation of *FT* here has already been discussed in chapter 1. What is important here is simply to note the influence of *FT* and its presentation of the individual for Bonhoeffer. This can be seen explicitly throughout Bonhoeffer's authorship. At the beginning of *SC*, Bonhoeffer comes against Heinrich Barth for attempting to make a Kantian notion the root of Kierkegaard's ethics (*SC*, 42 n. 6). While rooted in what Bonhoeffer sees as an attempt to interpret the universality of Kant's ethics as the medium for the individual's real freedom, it is clear that Bonhoeffer is unimpressed by Barth's attempts to undermine Kierkegaard in this way. The aim of Barth's article is to contextualize Kierkegaard through such thinkers as Schelling and Kant. However, in the process it is clear that Kierkegaard's work merges into these other thinkers, and the solitariness of the individual is undermined.[25] When one turns to *CF*, although explicit links with *FT* are not found, the notes taken by Bonhoeffer's Hungarian student, Ferenc Lehel, state that when the concept of the individual is a purely Christian concept, it was "discovered by Kierkegaard" (*CF*, 98 n. 11). Again, in *Discipleship*, it isn't surprising that the section which explicitly draws most heavily on *FT* is entitled "Discipleship and the Individual."

Bonhoeffer is well aware of his difference with Kierkegaard concerning ecclesiology at this early stage. However, it is Kierkegaard's notion of the individual that Bonhoeffer acknowledges as standing at the foundation for his own ecclesiology. People can only enter into true fellowship with the human other once they have been drawn into solitude, into real individuality, from where they reject their own claims on the human other, and receive them back through God and his mediation. In his footnote from *SC* it is curious that Bonhoeffer does not react more strongly against Kierkegaard if he believes him to be rejecting the church. It could be suggested that Kierkegaard's notion of the individual was so important for Bonhoeffer that his criticisms are somehow moderated. For Bonhoeffer, Kierkegaard is the creator and writer of the Christian individual that stands behind true ecclesiology.

Some Preliminary Remarks

Drawing upon the themes of chapter 3, both Bonhoeffer and Kierkegaard forge their ethical theories around the notion of the two realms. For both, ethics and the concepts of good and evil define the outward and visible world in opposition to the mediation of God in the world of the spirit. From this position, the logical progression is to define their thought

---

25. Curiously, despite this overall aim, Barth almost entirely excludes Hegel from his discussion.

in terms of an absolute duty towards God and, ultimately, the concept of the teleological suspension of the ethical. Both positions represent the submission of deified reason to the unlimited possibility of God's will in faith. As discussed in chapter 1, Bonhoeffer was at least familiar with *FT* from the time of *SC*. However, as demonstrated from "Discipleship and the Individual," by 1937 Bonhoeffer had gained an intimate knowledge of it.

PART 2
THE SEPARATION OF GOD AND NEIGHBOR

Concerning the quote with which this chapter began, this analysis agrees with Plant's assertion that Bonhoeffer adopts the teleological suspension of the ethical. However, as further suggested by Plant, does Kierkegaard present a collision between one's duty to the neighbor and a duty to God?

As discussed, despite Bonhoeffer's existential stance, within the mandates, orders, and laws of life there is a fundamental order that stands behind all ethical action, even when the teleological suspension of the ethical is embraced. For some, however, Kierkegaard has no specific content, and actively undermines any attempt at a principled ethics. As Brand Blanshard vehemently argues, "The Kierkegaardian "knight of faith," in electing the "absurd," is divesting himself of the shackles of all insights. But to do that is to be not a saint, but a moral nihilist."[26] Blanshard stands in the line of commentators who understand Kierkegaard as an irrationalist. Without wishing to associate Plant with Blanshard's overall view or form of expression, Blanshard bears similarity to Plant and argues,

> . . . the saint or knight of faith, according to Kierkegaard, is a man whose leading concern is not the welfare of others, but his own "eternal happiness," a description, incidentally that applied to himself . . . What we have in this strange version of Christianity is thus an insistence on the selfish character of the religious motive, combined with an insistence that the values of the Christian life, so far as these can be understood, are provisional only, and may at any time be overridden.[27]

This section will shed further light on Bonhoeffer's adoption of Kierkegaard, and explore whether in fact Kierkegaard in *FT* sets up such an ethical dichotomy between God and neighbor, whether he presents an ethical nihilism, or whether he shares an appreciation of the concrete realm and its order. The discussion will be based around the interpretation of *FT* by Edward F. Mooney. The importance of Mooney's interpretation is not simply that he suggests that *FT* is neighbor-driven, but also that his overall position bears marked similarity to that of Bonhoeffer.[28] Consequently, it will be suggested that not only did Bonhoeffer not interpret *FT* in the way Plant suggests, but that he may have found within it the seeds of his own ethics.

---

26. Blanshard, "Kierkegaard," 118.

27. Ibid.

28. The similarities between Mooney and Bonhoeffer are such that one wonders whether the latter has been an influence on Mooney and his interpretation of *FT*.

Kierkegaard and the Desire for the Human Other

Mooney strongly affirms the collision of the two realms. Reflecting Bonhoeffer's descriptions in *SC* of the fall destroying humankind's relationship with both the human and divine other, Mooney argues that the nature of human relationships in the finite world is defined according to possession, dependence, and a somewhat Nietzschean "will to power." In contrast, God's desire is for individuals to enter into relationship based on freedom, integrity, and faith.[29] Bearing striking resemblance to the tension between unity and solitariness concerning the church in *SC* and man and woman in *CF*, Mooney argues that the relationship of faith is one defined as "independence-in-relationship"[30] and "separateness-in-love."[31] Through the stories of "Attunement," of the mother blackening her breast to wean her child, Mooney sees this central message being forged. The desire of the mother is for her child to grow in both maturity and relationship with her. To continue breastfeeding would simply create a misrelation of dependence and inequality. While Johannes offers no explicit interpretation to this metaphor, Mooney argues it multifariously describes the need for Isaac to be weaned from Abraham, Abraham to be weaned from Isaac, and ultimately, Abraham to be weaned from God.[32]

Through God's command, Abraham is forced to give up his claims on Isaac, God, and the whole of temporality. However, through faith Abraham receives them back again in a new way. Drawing perhaps on the story of Job, when Abraham's relationship with God had been one of dependence, system, and principle, so now Abraham is led into a new and redeemed relationship with God. In the same way, from Abraham's identity as father to Isaac and Isaac's identity as the son of promise, in resignation Isaac is released from Abraham's "immortality project" over him, and through faith receives him back again in a new way, in freedom and maturity.[33]

Mooney's arguments bear striking resemblance to Bonhoeffer's presentation in *Discipleship*. For not only does Bonhoeffer argue that "Abraham received Isaac back, but he has him in a new way than before," but that God's concern was that Abraham not put his trust in Isaac for his future, but rather in God (*D*, 97). Through faith God breaks immediate relationships, placing Christ instead as mediator through whom all things are known. Mooney's argument would seem to be the same, albeit divorced of its Christological manifestation.

Bonhoeffer further argues, "As the one who was prepared to hear and obey God's command literally, [Abraham] is permitted to have Isaac as though he did not have him; he is permitted to have him through Jesus Christ" (97). For Mooney the description of the individual's true relationship with the other is that of "care." This is a summary of the dialectic relationship of "independence-in-relationship." In faith the individual is called at each moment to lose the other in resignation so as to be able to win them back through faith. In "care" the individual is called in each moment to give up the other in grief and

29. Mooney, *Knights of Faith*, 94.

30. Ibid., 31.

31. Ibid., 59.

32. Cf. ibid., 40.

33. Ibid., 59.

loss, and yet at the same moment in joy to receive them back again.[34] Only in this way is the other preserved in freedom apart from the individual's desire to grasp and control him. Through care, Abraham is essentially separated from Isaac, and receives him back only through faith and the new "knowledge" gained through it. Where this has its Christological interpretation in Bonhoeffer, so this mediation can be understood in terms of love for Kierkegaard. For both, however, Abraham receives Isaac back through the mediation of the infinite.

If Bonhoeffer read *FT* according to this interpretation, which seems very possible, not only would he not see an opposition between neighbor and God, but rather find the foundation for his own concept of mediation. For both Bonhoeffer and Kierkegaard, the other can only be loved through God and not in immediacy. Humankind's relationships are mediated through a new understanding gained through faith that establishes the "world of the spirit" within the "outward and visible world." Although it is unclear whether Bonhoeffer read them, in the upbuilding discourses published on the same day as *FT*, Kierkegaard emphasizes God's desire to promote human relations, and further describes the mediation of God in these relationships forging the individual into "God's co-worker in love" (*EUD*, 62).

As argued in chapter 1, Bonhoeffer reveals the influence of *WL* on his ideas of love in *SC*. Here Bonhoeffer's emphasis is that one must not love the neighbor in order to love God, but must really love the concrete neighbor. For Bonhoeffer, Kierkegaard correctly understands the human other, the desire of God for that other, and the responsibility towards the other. Although this interpretation is not unambiguous, as described in chapter 1, it is affirmed as through his reading and use of *FT* Bonhoeffer reveals Kierkegaard to be the foundation for his expressions on mediation and community. Whatever the differences between Kierkegaard and Bonhoeffer in terms of ecclesiology, one cannot doubt Bonhoeffer's understanding and affirmation of Kierkegaard's desire towards the human other.

It should also be pointed out that Bonhoeffer was painfully aware of those who would fight for their own ethical purity over the needs of others. Not only does he describe this as one of the failed groups in "Ethics as Formation" (*E*, 80), but he unleashes his most vehement attack on the church for having adopted this line (*E*, 138ff.; cf. *LPP*, 499ff.). Had Kierkegaard been similarly considered, it seems unlikely he would have escaped undenounced.

Kierkegaard the Nihilist?

A Situational Ethic?

For Mooney one of the main errors commentators have committed is to explain the motivations and consequences of the Abraham story when the essential point of *FT* concerns anxiety, absurdity, and paradox in opposition to systematization. Consequently, Mooney presents something of a deconstruction of God's demand and the nature of Abraham's obedience. As he argues,

---

34. Ibid., 56ff.

> I suggest that we question the premise that has gone virtually unchallenged. Why assume that Abraham has made the *right* choice? I do not mean it would have been better to have rejected God. I mean that we should question the premise that in this crisis there is an objectively correct response. There is a deadlock of considerations—one both *ought* and *ought not* to obey God, and both *ought* and *ought not* to protect Isaac. If this deadlock is massive enough, it will undermine the very *possibility* of there being a correct response.[35]

For Mooney, Abraham is caught in a dilemma in which "the good" cannot be understood, nor the "right" answer discerned. Any mediating claim that he made the right choice undermines the anxiety of Abraham's predicament, and directs him back towards the universal. One cannot therefore make "Always obey God" into a principle as this undermines the whole argument.[36] Drawing on *CUP*, there may be a right answer, but this can only be seen by God. Consequently, the only route out of this predicament is through the authentic "how" of decision standing in superiority to the "what." There can be no principle that gets Abraham out of his dilemma.

For Mooney, the teleological suspension describes "*a terrible deadlock* where inescapable requirements clash. It depicts an ordeal of reason which leaves an individual without comfort or moral assurance or definitive guidance."[37] The teleological suspension simply describes the necessary action of the individual who is presented with an insurmountable dilemma, rather than the principle by which the individual believes himself to be justified in going against ethical principles. Indeed, for Mooney, even the act made in faith cannot aid in justifying its movement against the ethical. There is no "objective justification" by which one can "escape from the dark."[38]

However, by embracing authentically the "how," Mooney argues that the individual becomes transformed. By grasping the teleological suspension, the individual is led further and further into an understanding of his worth as an individual standing higher than the universal and its limits.[39] He becomes endowed with virtues that don't simply equip him with ethical authority, but which propel him towards his "essential humanity." These virtues are "freedom" to be able to choose the line of action, "integrity" to endorse subjectivity as the "properly human goal," and "Trusting Receptivity" or "Faith" to humbly draw to oneself the values of others around him.[40]

For Mooney, the message of *FT* is therefore the acknowledgement of the real dilemmas of existence that overwhelm the limits of ethical principles, the path of the authentic self as found only in subjectivity and not through the universal, but also of the legitimacy of ethical principles within these conditions. Faith does not place itself outside ethics, but rather presents "an advanced ethical position."[41] Just as with all other forms of the tempo-

---

35. Ibid., 65.
36. Ibid.
37. Ibid., 80.
38. Ibid., 81.
39. Ibid., 94.
40. Ibid., 99f.
41. Ibid., 103.

ral, in faith these principles are resigned and received back in a new way. Consequently, faith has "a trusting receptivity, an openness toward the least of finite objects."[42]

Many of the abovementioned concepts are central to Bonhoeffer's ethics. Bonhoeffer affirms not just the inescapable dilemma, and the concern that obedience itself does not get reduced into a principle, but most profoundly, the inability of the individual to find justification for his actions. As discussed, for both Bonhoeffer and Kierkegaard such concerns as "results," "the good," and the "world-historical" are absent from Christian ethics.

Mooney embraces Bonhoeffer's assertion that revelation provides us with an understanding of orientation rather than principles by which we are to act. As he argues, "startling revelations help us *see*. They are not prescriptions to teach us what to *do*."[43]

A Content to Ethics?

Further developing the conclusions of chapter 4 concerning reason, *FT* does not discard ethics but rather affirms ethics within its authentic limits. Kierkegaard is no more a nihilist than an irrationalist. As Evans argues, "The tension between religious faith and the ethical in *FT* is between faith and a form of the ethical life that claims to swallow up faith."[44] Faith essentially redeems the ethical from its corruption in the "outward and visible world." Indeed, for Evans, faith "substitutes a new conception of the ethical for that which underlies prevailing social ethics,"[45] fulfilling "in a more authentic way the ideals that society itself claims to support."[46] According to Mooney and Evans, Kierkegaard not only affirms the presence of ethical principles in the situations in which they are applicable, but argues that even when they are suspended the essence of the principle is still maintained. While not describing the more formal concepts of "mandates" and "orders of creation," for such commentators as Mooney and Evans, Kierkegaard affirms the essence of Bonhoeffer's argument.

For Mooney, the most obvious evidence that Johannes does not promote the annihilation of ethical principles and the order of society is that the knight of faith returns back into society.[47] Such individuals are incognito within their roles as shopmen, maids, or professors. So absorbed are they into the temporal that they may even come to resemble the "bourgeois philistine."

As argued in chapter 4, Kierkegaard's affirmation of the "how" of decision is not at the exclusion of the "what." Rather, through the authentic "how," the "what" comes into existence. In *FT* Abraham is not in relation to an unknown transcendent being, but a known God upon whose nature he bases his actions. The story does not make sense unless, as Johannes describes, God is understood as faithful, loving, and omnipotent. Abraham's decision to be obedient is conditioned by what he knows of God. Through God's promise Abraham had some reason to believe that he would receive Isaac back

42. Ibid., 106.
43. Ibid., 111.
44. Evans, "Telos of Morality," 15.
45. Ibid., 25.
46. Ibid., 24.
47. Mooney, *Selves in Discord*, 45.

again. One must doubt whether Abraham would have acted in obedience if God had commanded that he kill Sarah for whom there was no such "guarantee" of the future. Inherent within Abraham's obedience is faith that Isaac will not ultimately be lost, that God will uphold his promise, that he himself will not end up denying his responsibility as a father. Without this he is simply a knight of infinite resignation.

A Correct Reading?

In using Mooney and Evans this thesis is not affirming their ideas wholesale. Mooney's ideas are not primarily theological and one must question his suggestion that there is essentially no right answer to Abraham's decision. Furthermore, the fear and trembling that Johannes describes is not that applied to the decision as he claims—as has been discussed, even the knight of resignation is obedient—but rather to the requirement of sacrificing Isaac while still believing that he will not be lost. While terrible, the movement of resignation, of giving up the temporal realm, is simple and logical. The difficulty, which annihilates Johannes, is to be obedient while never letting go of the temporal. In addition, it is particularly concerning that Mooney draws so heavily on other Kierkegaardian texts—especially *CUP*. While clearly present in *FT*, does his emphasis on the relational aspect, and specifically the content of nature of faith as "care," come across in the way he emphasizes?

Despite these concerns, in these interpretations we find what is still a highly authentic reading of *FT* that affirms the core content of Bonhoeffer's ethics. When Bonhoeffer read *FT* it can plausibly be argued that he drew the same conclusions from it.

CONCLUDING REMARKS

This chapter has sought to undermine the more stereotyped interpretations of Kierkegaard, and argued that not only are these incorrect, but that Bonhoeffer was himself not a party to them. Although the distinction between "how" and "what" is important for Kierkegaard's work, it does not stand in opposition to a substantial epistemology or ethics. Plant's arguments in particular appear to picture Kierkegaard as a deontologist, bound to the duty of action rather than responsibility towards its content, against the other-preferential teleological ethics of Bonhoeffer. In contrast, Bonhoeffer's reading of *FT* in "Discipleship and the Individual" reveals his affirmation of both human relations and the need for mediation.

For Bonhoeffer's works as a whole, *FT* appears to have been extremely important. Bonhoeffer was clearly influenced by it in terms of notions of the individual and the need for mediation. Both concepts stand at the heart of his ideas on ecclesiology and community. Consequently, Bonhoeffer's understanding of Kierkegaard is far less simple then that suggested by those who describe Bonhoeffer as the communitarian against Kierkegaard the individualist. Although a formal ecclesiology is clearly absent from much of Kierkegaard's work, it is unlikely that Bonhoeffer would have considered the ecclesial opinions that he himself drew from Kierkegaard to be entirely lacking from Kierkegaard's own mind. As Mooney suggests, at the heart of the *Akedah* is not simply individualist issues of faith or obedience, but also God's desire for more perfect community to be established between Abraham and Isaac.

6

Attack on Idealism—Christology and Discipleship

Introduction

THE AIM OF THIS CHAPTER IS TO ANALYZE KIERKEGAARD AND BONHOEFFER'S UNDER-standing of Christology and discipleship. As discussed in chapter 1, the majority of secondary sources have focused on Kierkegaard's influence on Bonhoeffer's *Discipleship*. Here we clearly find some of the richest material. However, in doing so, the discussion has missed one of the most significant areas. In Bonhoeffer's Christology (expressed in both the lecture series conducted in summer 1933, and in his wider writings) we find significant areas of overlap that act as the foundation to *Discipleship* and his authorship from 1932 as a whole. The aim of this chapter is not to abridge its analysis of these two significant areas by placing them within the same chapter, but to show the importance of their relationship and the continuity of Kierkegaard's influence upon them both.

PART 1
CHRISTOLOGY

In the opening "Invocation" of *PC*, Anti-Climacus sets out the key themes of Kierkegaard's understanding of Christology, concerning the historical nature of the incarnation, the requirement of faith, the consequence of contemporaneity, and the inevitable possibility of offense. As we continue analyzing the Kierkegaardian presence in Bonhoeffer's work, it will become clear that these ideas, along with those of the description of Christ as "paradox," "incognito," and "doctrine," stand behind Bonhoeffer's own Christology, and provide the foundation for both his ideas on discipleship and attack on Christendom.

Kierkegaard

History

In relation to the notion of the "two realms," as discussed in previous chapters, Kierkegaard declares in *JFY*, "the world and Christianity have completely opposite conceptions" (*JFY*, 96). Using the story of Pentecost, Kierkegaard describes this dichotomy in terms of sobriety, with each realm appearing as intoxication to the other.

The world holds to facts (97) and probability (99ff.) and by embracing scientific methods considers that it has the authentic grasp of truth. And yet, as Kierkegaard goes on to say, "this deification of sagacity in our day is precisely the idolatry of our age," and the very heart of humankind's intoxication (102). As described in the previous chapters, Kierkegaard's aim is not to discard the categories of sagacity but rather to reinstate them within their rightful limits. This can be found particularly in terms of history. As Climacus argues in *PF*, any form of knowledge derived from history can only be an approximation. Unlike analysis of the present, the past has gone and cannot be honestly represented beyond the categories of doubt and uncertainty (*PF*, 81). Indeed, anyone who claims to apprehend the past, to be an *"historico-philosophus,"* is therefore "a prophet in reverse." The only certainty is that of possibility and prediction (80). Furthermore, as Anti-Climacus argues, history must be considered a "profane science." Unlike the specialized form of "sacred history" (*PC*, 25, 30), history has the ability to make proclamations concerning the natural, temporal world of humankind, but must remain silent concerning issues of the divine and the eternal.

This reinstatement of history is central to Kierkegaard's Christology, for in the face of the incarnation, history must recognize that it encounters a barrier. As Climacus points out in *PF*, by its very nature the eternal has no history (*PF*, 76). Consequently, quite apart from scientific truth, the incarnation must be categorized from the speculative perspective as paradox and offense (cf. *CUP*, 1:208, 596).

Paradox

In *PF* and *CUP* the eternal is by nature paradoxical (1:208). And when the eternal reveals its absolute difference to humankind due to sin (*PF*, 46; *CUP*, 1:208), but also its desire to be reconciled with humankind, its nature as paradox is heightened (*PF*, 47). However, these descriptions do not raise the paradox to the true height of Christianity (*CUP*, 1:561), but remain in what Climacus terms, "Religiousness A."

Religiousness A appears to bear many of the hallmarks of Christianity. Its adherents resign their dependence on the temporal world for happiness in the eternal, they undertake inward transformation in relation to God as the absolute, and they suffer guilt at their failings. However, it cannot embrace the concept of the incarnation. Religiousness A perceives the eternal as lying within and behind existence—"the hidden immanence of the eternal" (1:571)—as both transcendent to the temporal and yet commensurate with it. The eternal is perceived within existence and the task of Religiousness A is inward deepening in relation to it. The eternal does not break into the individual's existence from outside, but the individual performs a transformation within himself based on conviction towards the eternal. Temporal existence, therefore, only has relevance as the medium through which the eternal is perceived and the transformation performed (1:574). Kierkegaard refers to its adherents as the "knights of hidden inwardness" as their religious experience is determined purely internally through the experience of the eternal within themselves, mediated by existence (*CUP*, 1:500ff; *JP*, 2751/*Pap*, IX A 362; *EK*, 60). Religiousness A is therefore a pagan, naturalistic religion, where the eternal is discerned through humankind's own being (*CUP*, 1:557).

The paradox for Religiousness A is found not in the incommensurability between the eternal and the temporal, but rather in the limits of humankind's rational faculties. It is a matter of intelligence, rather than any profound discontinuity between eternal truth and temporal reason (cf. 1:566). Consequently, the paradox expressed in Religiousness A is simply a "relative paradox" (1:217).

The "absolute paradox" that defines Christianity embraces both transcendence and incommensurability. The paradox is not simply the eternal relating to an existence in temporality but the eternal becoming an existence in temporality. As Climacus declares, "The eternal truth has come into existence in time. That is the paradox" (1:209).

When the eternal becomes manifest in time, Christianity, "Religiousness B," "paradoxical religiousness," has been established. As David Law argues, "Eternity is no longer outside existence, undergirding and sustaining it, but is directly present within existence itself."[1] Here the paradox is not simply greater than humankind's understanding but stands in opposition to it—that is, the paradox is itself paradoxical. As described, history and every sagacious science must simply be silent before it. The absolute paradox is therefore the "absurd" (cf. *CUP*, 1:210, 1:557f.).

Following on from the discussion of chapter 5, further strong parallels with *FT* can be found. Like the "knight of infinite resignation," not only does the "knight of hidden inwardness" discard the temporal for the sake of the eternal, but he remains standing in the "outward and visible world," and does not resign his own understanding. Although there are differences between the presentation of faith in Abraham and Religiousness B, both represent the destruction of the "temporal world" for the "realm of the spirit."

Offense

As Kierkegaard discusses at length in *JFY*, "No one can serve two masters, for he must either hate one and love the other or be devoted to the one and despise the other" (*JFY*, 150ff.).[2] Consequently, in the face of the "absolute paradox," one must either react in faith or offense (cf. *CUP*, 1:575, 1:578; *PF*, 49). As discussed throughout the preceding chapters, the error of reason is not its existence but rather the destruction of its limits and the dominion it claims over all categories (cf. *PC*, 31). In his later works Kierkegaard describes this as reason's project of "deification," standing in "continual mutiny against God" (88).

While there is a certain unity between Kierkegaard's various works concerning the nature(s) of the paradox, the issue of offense, discussed over a wide range of his later works, is somewhat nebulous. However, when offense is understood as the reaction of sagacity to both the nature of the paradox and its effects in the world, this should perhaps be expected. In *SUD*, Anti-Climacus describes sagacity's offense at the idea that not only does an individual "have the reality of his being, as a *particular* human being, directly before God," but also "that man's sin should be of concern to God" (*SUD*, 115). Rather,

---

1. Law, *Negative Theologian*, 145.

2. Cf. Matt 6:24.

sagacity places the individual within more general confines of "the race," and argues for an objective understanding of sin, in order to get rid of the concept, "before God." However, this offense would seem to be derivative of sagacity's far deeper concern, that Christianity and its demands are too elevated, "that its standard of measurement is not the human standard," and that it seeks to make people into the extraordinary (116). At a further symptomatic level, Anti-Climacus suggests that the psychological disposition of offense is that of "unhappy admiration," or through its links with envy, "concealed admiration" (118). Such an individual admires the paradox but refuses to resign his own understanding and so embrace it. Anti-Climacus argues that when such an individual "speaks another language" to the paradox, it appears as "something stupid and humiliating" (118).

Indeed, against the desire of sagacity to maintain the status quo, so Kierkegaard argues, "true Christians" are referred to as the greatest and meanest traitors to humankind by those who are offended (*JFY*, 140). Sagacity undertakes a process of levelling in which all extreme demands, anything extraordinary that might show up paltry existence, all life lived "before God," is silenced (119). For sagacity, "moderation, the middle way, the medium size, this is the truth" (161). In *PC* this realm is summarized in the phrase, "to a certain degree" (*PC*, 60). Christianity is simply too extreme.

As Anti-Climacus describes in *PC*, Christ is the offense par excellence for not only does he strike sagacity as the height of vanity by emphasizing his individuality and relationship with God above the universal (85ff.), but as a poor, suffering, and helpless man, he claims to be God (*PC*, 102ff.; cf. *PF*, 32). Beside the nature of Christ, the offensiveness of Christianity is then raised as it demands the individual place his hope for eternal happiness in a historical character, and specifically in this historical character nailed to the cross (cf. *CUP*, 1:578). Religiousness A has no problem in placing its hopes for eternal happiness in the eternal when conceived as the untouchable beyond. But when the eternal itself becomes the paradox by coming into existence, any security concerning one's eternal happiness is dashed. For not only is the historical the realm of factual uncertainty, but the individual in which one must place one's hopes cannot help himself (*PC*, 36ff.).

Incognito

When the paradox is only considered "relative," as in Religiousness A, so there is always the possibility of understanding, of catching a glimpse of the eternal from within temporality (*CUP*, 1:563f.). In contrast, the absolute paradox "cannot and should not be understood"—it always remains the paradox (*CUP*, 1:564; *PF*, 59). It is not a matter of changing one's understanding, but of simply submitting to its limitations (cf. *PF*, 59).

The incarnation is impenetrable to sagacity and speculative thought. There is no way of explaining it according to these systems. History and the scientific method may analyze the physical presence of the man Jesus of Nazareth, and come to certain probable conclusions about the veracity of the historical record. However, they cannot legitimize or explain the claims of his divine nature (*PC*, 26ff.). Such tools are simply not designed for this task. "Sacred history" may describe these claims within the presupposition of faith, but "profane history" must remain silent (30).

In Religiousness A, the eternal is witnessed within temporality but remains entirely untouched by it. However, as the absolute paradox, Christ bears the identity of the eternal and temporal's perfect union. The eternal can neither be separated from the temporal nor seen within it. The glorious Son of God can only be known through the word of the abased Jesus of Nazareth. Christ does not wear his temporal abasement like a cloak, affording one a glimpse of the eternal glory underneath as he walks. Christ is rather the "incognito," whose eternal glory is unrecognisable through his abasement. This incognito cannot be mediated.

Sagacity is not content with this conclusion, and spends its energy trying to find, demonstrate, and prove the claims of Jesus of Nazareth to be God. The opening treatise of *CUP* concerns the fallacy of sagacious thought to prove the truthfulness of Christianity through Scripture, the Living Word of the Church, as well as the results of the last 1800 years. For Climacus, each is meaningless as one is still thrown back, not simply to the words of the abased Jesus of Nazareth, but his nature as abased. The glorious words, "Come here to me, all you who labor and are burdened, and I will give you rest,"[3] as well as the miraculous deeds he performs,[4] still proceed from this abased individual. As Anti-Climacus declares as the opening dialectic of *PC*, the abased Jesus of Nazareth is "the Halt" who brings any possibility of deriving eternal glory from these words or deeds to a dramatic stop (23ff.). The incognito can only be embraced by faith and never simply "known" (33).

Although its deeper nuances will be discussed in the next section, not only is faith required as the condition of belief, but faith is only given to the individual by God himself. Heaven cannot be stormed, nor arrived at through the back gate of Religiousness A.

Doctrine

In proving the claims of Christ and demonstrating the truth of Christianity sagacity desires to convert both into knowledge (cf. 25). In so doing humankind establishes its control and security over its claim to eternal happiness, and destroys the offensiveness of the absolute paradox. As Climacus argues, in faith "every Christian is Christian only by being nailed to the paradox of having based his eternal happiness on the relationship to something historical" (*CUP*, 1:578). When Christ becomes an objective doctrine that is at least glimpsed if not understood, Christianity becomes manageable—"a superficial something that neither wounds nor heals deeply enough" (*PC*, 140). There occurs "the trick of recasting Christ" into a form of "sentimental sympathy" (66). The incarnate Christ becomes separated, his temporal form discarded, and hope placed rather in his eternal nature. Christ becomes an historical character in the past from whom we learn the great truths of eternity (35).

As previously discussed, people relate to an idea through invulnerability, engaging with it at arms length through its captivity in the mind. The same is the case with Christianity as a doctrine. For Kierkegaard Christ must be the paradox as only in this way

---

3. Matt 11:28; cf. *PC*, 11ff.

4. Anti-Climacus argues that miracles are used to draw attention to Christ as the paradox not in any way to prove or demonstrate his divinity—cf. *PC*, 126.

does the individual submit to God in faith and Christ's death result in real transformation of the world. In contrast to an idea, Christianity is an "existence-communication." As Climacus argues,

> Christianity is not a doctrine, but it expresses an existence-contradiction and is an existence-communication. If Christianity were a doctrine, it would *eo ipso* not constitute the opposite of speculative thought but would be an element within it. Christianity pertains to existence, to existing, but existence and existing are the very opposite of speculation . . . Precisely because Christianity is not a doctrine, it holds true, as developed previously, that there is an enormous difference between knowing what Christianity is and being a Christian. With regard to a doctrine, this distinction is unthinkable, because the doctrine is not related to existing. (*CUP*, 1:380)

When the absolute paradox is undermined Christianity is changed from an existence-communication into "an ingenious metaphysical doctrine addressed to professors" (1:579). As Kierkegaard argues in *CD*, "Christianity is regarded as a sum of doctrines; lectures are given on it . . . with the listener's or the learner's relation to it left as a matter of indifference. Basically this is paganism. The essentially Christian is precisely this: the relation to Christianity is what is decisive" (*CD*, 214–25). Under its total control, society has removed its extremity and converted it into security and peace, declaring everyone to be a Christian (*PC*, 35).

Contemporaneity

According to sagacity, the first disciples have a profound blessing and benefit in having been present during Christ's life, teaching, and death. Although eulogizing the first believers, this position also upholds the present believer by presenting a progression to faith and humankind's understanding of God. When Christ becomes objectified and so remains in history, the 1800 years since his death have seen the progressive understanding of the eternal truths that were hidden within him. The present doesn't simply gain its own glimpse of Christ's eternal glory, but benefits from the glimpses of previous generations (56ff.). The first disciples had the benefit of being present with Christ, but the Christians of the present have the benefit of humankind's ever perfecting understanding of him (cf. 128).

However, as Climacus describes at length in *PF*, when Christ remains the absolute paradox, "known" only through faith, one's place in history and physical proximity to him becomes entirely irrelevant (*PF*, 49ff.). For one could be staring him in the face, hearing his words directly from his mouth, and yet, without faith, have no understanding of who he is. Everyone has the same condition through which to see and accept him. Consequently, Christ can no longer be seen as a figure of the past, but rather met in the present. Christ becomes contemporaneous with us. As Anti-Climacus agrees, "His life on earth accompanies the human race and accompanies each particular generation as the eternal history; his life on earth has the eternal contemporaneity" (*PC*, 64).

There can be no first generation of believers, "followers at second hand," or "the latest generation" of believers. There are either those who are contemporaneous with Christ, or those who are offended.

Bonhoeffer

In order to show the influence of Kierkegaard on Bonhoeffer's Christology, whilst also appreciating the progression of Bonhoeffer's thought in this area, the analysis will depart from the form of the previous chapters to analyze Bonhoeffer and Kierkegaard, chronologically through Bonhoeffer's most significant Christological works. These works are Bonhoeffer's 1932 article "Concerning the Christian Idea of God," his 1933 lectures on *Christology*, and *Discipleship*.

"Concerning the Christian Idea of God"

CCIG stands as something of a bridge between his academic theses and the rest of his work, combining the earlier, more philosophical emphasis, with a firm Christology. Bonhoeffer's presentation falls into two sections. The first concerns "God and History," and the second "The Paradoxical God of the Doctrine of Justification."

God and History

Bonhoeffer argues that when God has revealed himself in history, as an individual, as personality, he cannot become sucked into the concept of an idea. Personality is a matter of "once-ness," of revelation and self-disclosure in history. Consequently, "no human attempt can grasp him beyond this history" (*CCIG*, 181). In making Christ into an idea, idealist philosophy forges historical beings into timeless symbols. Consequently, Jesus' life and death become merely the example through which the eternal truths of God become known. This bears striking similarity to Kierkegaard, for whom speculative thought has sought to resign Jesus to his place in history, and discern truths from him, with the help of 1800 years. This is the reduction of Christ into "doctrine." Although Bonhoeffer only appears to use this term in *Discipleship*, in his copy of *CUP* Bonhoeffer highlights two sections in which Kierkegaard describes the transformation of Christianity into "doctrine." The second, as described above, counter-poses Christianity as doctrine and as "existence-communication" (*CUP*, 1:379; *AUN*, 74). However, in the first Kierkegaard declares, "the immediate identifying mark of every misunderstanding of Christianity is that it changes it into a doctrine and draws it into the range of intellectuality" (*CUP*, 1:327; *AUN*, 25). As discussed, Kierkegaard sees speculative thought manipulating and controlling Christianity through the realm of knowledge in order to fit with its desires. Similarly, Bonhoeffer argues,

> The main difference between a so-called revelation in the sphere of idea and a revelation in "once-ness" is that man always will be able to learn a new idea and to fit it into his system of ideas; but a revelation in "once-ness" in a historical fact, in a historical personality, is always anew a challenge to man. He cannot overcome it by pulling it into the system which he already had before. This is the reason why God reveals himself in history: only so is the freedom of his personality guarded. The revelation in history means revelation in hiddenness; revelation in ideas (principles, values, etc.) means revelation in openness. (*CCIG*, 181)

Although Bonhoeffer does not use the term "incognito" here—as he does elsewhere—it is represented in the "hiddenness" of Christ in history, forcing the individual into the leap of faith. As he summarizes a little later, "God entered history in Jesus, and so entirely that he can be recognized in his hiddenness only by faith" (184). For Kierkegaard the incarnation is an indirect communication, a "sign of contradiction," which cannot be directly understood. However, as with Bonhoeffer, it is speculative thought's desire to convert him into directness, into revelation in openness.

According to Kierkegaard history is limited to descriptions of approximation and possibility. Bonhoeffer does not use the same terminology, but presents the same essential point: history cannot provide certainty and so simple acceptance. Rather, "History is the place of decision, nothing else" (182).

Bonhoeffer's arguments resemble Kierkegaard in several different places. On top of the limits of history, the hiddenness of Christ, and the desire of idealism to convert Christ into timeless truth, Bonhoeffer firmly mirrors Kierkegaard in arguing that Christ is only encountered in the decision of faith, in acceptance or rejection. As Bonhoeffer summarizes,

> Decision in its most inward sense is possible only as a decision for or against God. This decision is executed in facing Christ. Within the world of ideas there is no such thing as decision because I always bear within myself the possibilities of understanding these ideas. They fit into my system but they do not touch and challenge my whole existence. Thus, they cannot lead me into the situation of personal decision. (182)

Bonhoeffer's argument is different to Kierkegaard's in emphasizing Christ's nature as "personality" in history, who can be known only through faith. Kierkegaard's specific point is that Christ cannot be known because he is paradox, the eternal within time, and not simply a human being. Because of the limitation of history, Kierkegaard would agree that all historical beings must be related to via faith. Consequently, the difference is not formal but one of emphasis. However, it is also unclear what Bonhoeffer means by "personality" here. As discussed in chapter 4, in *SC* God is true "personality" because he injects himself into the temporal as the eternal and transcendent. If this is his meaning, Bonhoeffer's argument is essentially parallel to Kierkegaard's. This interpretation is backed up later in *CCIG* where Bonhoeffer comments, "being personality, [God] remains in absolute transcendence" (184).

The Paradoxical God of the Doctrine of Justification

Before discussing the true nature of the paradox, Bonhoeffer argues,

> I can know God only if I can effect an act—an act which makes me transcend the limits of myself, which carries me out of the circle of my self-hood in order to acknowledge the transcendent God. While it is obvious that I myself cannot effect such an act, there is nevertheless, such an act, which is executed by God himself, and which is called "faith." (183)

This bears striking linguistic similarity to Climacus' argument in *PF* where he argues,

> How, then, does the learner come to an understanding with this paradox . . . It oc-
> curs when the understanding and the paradox happily encounter each other in the
> moment, when the understanding steps aside and the paradox gives itself, and the
> third something, the something in which this occurs . . . is this happy passion to
> which we shall now give a name, although for us it is not a matter of the name. We
> shall call it *faith*. (*PF*, 59)

As the introduction to Bonhoeffer's discussion of the paradox, it is hard not to see this as a direct reference where, through the submission by the individual of his understanding, God or the paradox "gives itself" to the individual as faith.

Bonhoeffer's description of the paradox is twofold. In agreement with Kierkegaard's notion of the absolute paradox, and Climacus' declaration that "The paradox is that Christ entered into the world *in order to suffer*" (*CUP*, 1:597), Bonhoeffer defines the paradox and argues,

> God himself dies and reveals himself in the death of a man, who is condemned as
> a sinner. It is precisely this, which is the foolishness of the Christian idea of God,
> which has been witnessed to by all genuine Christian thinking from Paul, Augustine,
> Luther, and Kierkegaard and Barth. (*CCIG*, 184)

As discussed in *PF* and *PC*, sagacity is offended by the individual revealing himself to be God in suffering and poverty. While Kierkegaard does not describe this as the paradox itself, as offense it is clearly the effect of the paradox and, therefore, paradoxical. However, at the end of *CCIG* Bonhoeffer qualifies the paradox further declaring that it is only when the individual is in total weakness that God's strength is manifested (185). Once again, Kierkegaard describes how sagacity is offended in finding eternal happiness only in total submission to the crucified Christ.

Christology

In his lectures on *Christology* Bonhoeffer continues many of these themes, and articulates them in a more complete and systematic fashion.

Christ's Transcendence

Bonhoeffer begins by once again describing the attempt of the natural sciences, idealism, and especially Hegel, to grasp hold of the incarnation with their sagacious method. For when Christ is understood as idea, he is absorbed into, and comes under the power of, the human logos (*C*, 28f.). Here again, the incarnation is seen symbolically as the point through which hidden truths are unveiled, recounting a new concept of God or moral doctrine (51). Christ becomes either kept in the past as a figure of history, bequeathing a historical influence, or is taken out of history and essentially spiritualized (43). In such a way he becomes depersonalized, idealized, and transformed into a power (44). However, because Christ comes as Word, as a historical being, he cannot be absorbed into the human logos but becomes its Anti-Logos. In the face of this transcendent personality, one can no longer ask such scientific questions as "What?" or "How?" but only the "Who?" of submission. As Bonhoeffer argues,

> If the Anti-Logos no longer appears in history as an idea, but as the Word incarnate, there is no longer any possibility of incorporating him into the order of man's own Logos. There is in fact only one question left: "Who are you? Speak!" The question "Who are you?" is the question of deposed, distraught reason. But is equally the question of faith: Who are you? Are you God himself? This is the question with which Christology is concerned. Christ is the Anti-Logos. There is no longer any possibility of classification because the existence of this Logos means the end of the human Logos. (30)

When Kierkegaard argues for the impossibility of reason to grasp Christ as the eternal in time, so Bonhoeffer declares, "Jesus is God and it is impossible to argue directly from history to God" (39).

For Kierkegaard, the main distinction between Religiousness A and Christianity is that where the latter truly defined God in terms of transcendence, so the former considers the eternal to be immanent, discernable, graspable within existence. It remains idealistic in allowing reason to perceive God. In just the same way Bonhoeffer argues, "The question 'Who?' is the question of transcendence. The question 'How?' is the question of immanence" (30).

Christ's transcendence sets the tone for the whole of *Christology*, and Kierkegaard's importance to this work is revealed in Bonhoeffer's opening line,

> Teaching about Christ begins in silence. "Be silent for that is the absolute" (Kierkegaard). This has nothing to do with mystical silence which, in its absence of words, is, nevertheless, the soul chattering away to itself. (27)

This is silence before the Word of God, before the "inexpressible." Although it is unclear where this reference comes from, the concept of silence plays an important role throughout Kierkegaard's works, and especially, as discussed in chapter 2, in response to the "busy, clamorous noise" of the mind (*JP*, 2274/*Pap*, III A 5). Bonhoeffer was clearly interested in Kierkegaard's more edifying works, as can be seen from the presence of two volumes of Kierkegaard's discourses in his library. And one is led to ask whether Bonhoeffer may have therefore read Part 1 of *The Lilies of the Field and the Birds of the Air*, which Walter Lowrie entitles simply, "silence" (*CD* (L), 319–32). Here Kierkegaard declares that the Christian must stand before God, before His absolute "Thou Shalt," in silence. Indeed, in the face of humankind's "idle chatter" and his over-willingness to speak, Kierkegaard declares that humankind and God can "hardly converse" (*CD*, 11). Consequently, to pray means to be silent, to become a listener, in fear and trembling to "wait until the one praying hears God," to simply obey God's word (11).

However, Bonhoeffer may also have taken Kierkegaard's notion of silence from *FSE*, still held within his library. Here Kierkegaard argues that the only way to overcome the disease of the world is to "create silence, bring about silence; God's Word cannot be heard, and if in order to be heard in the hullabaloo it must be shouted deafeningly with noisy instruments, then it is not God's Word; create silence!" (*FSE*, 47).

CHRIST'S PROOF

With this in place, Bonhoeffer declares, one cannot discern Christ's divinity from his life. In particular, one cannot derive this understanding from his deeds, as his miracles can only be interpreted through him as a man. As he argues, "I have access to the work of Christ only if I know the person who does this work. It is essential to know the person if the work is also to be known" (*C*, 38). Although his argument is far less fleshed out than Kierkegaard's, it stands in direct parallel with the question of proof and impact of Christ's words and deeds in *PC*. For both authors one cannot get to Christ any other way than through faith. The similarity is further declared as Bonhoeffer argues, everything Christ did was "in the *incognito* of history, in the flesh" (39—author's emphasis).

CHRIST'S INCOGNITO

Bonhoeffer dedicates the last section of his lectures to this important Kierkegaardian concept (110ff.). For both writers, the "incognito" cannot be penetrated by deeds or signs, but only by faith. According to Bonhoeffer, the identity of Christ as the paradox again does not play as strong a role. For Kierkegaard, Christ's words and deeds cannot reveal his divinity because they come from his nature in abasement. This is the paradoxical nature of Christ as "the Halt." For Bonhoeffer, Christ's deeds can only be known once his own identity has been established because as a general rule, an individual's deeds can only be known through the doer (38). It is not, therefore, a phenomenon exclusive to Christ. This would seem to be hand in hand with our concerns in *CCIG*.

Despite this difference, neither writer sees deeds or words as able to penetrate the incognito. As Bonhoeffer argues,

> The Humiliated One is present to us only as the Risen and Exalted One. We know that he is the God-man in incognito only through the resurrection and the exultation. As believers, we always have the incognito as an already penetrated incognito, we have the child in the cradle as the one who is eternally present, the one laden with guilt as the Sinless One. But the converse must also be valid. We cannot get round the scandal by means of the resurrection. We have the Exalted One only as the Crucified, the Sinless One only as the one laden with guilt, the Risen One only as the Humiliated One . . . Even the resurrection is not a penetration of the incognito. Even the resurrection is ambiguous. It is only believed in where the stumbling block of Jesus has not been removed. Only the disciples who follow Jesus saw the resurrection. Only blind faith sees here. They believe as those who do not see, and in this faith they see. (116)

In his own copy of *PC*, Bonhoeffer pays particular attention to Anti-Climacus" argument that Christ's words only proceed from his nature in abasement, and so may only be received by faith (*PC*, 24; *EC*, 18). Here he uses both marginal lines and crosses. Bonhoeffer's argument is more balanced than Kierkegaard's, arguing that one needs to embrace both of Christ's natures equally. However, it could be argued that Kierkegaard's emphasis on Christ's abasement is simply contextual to its abuse at the time. Indeed, Bonhoeffer marks Anti-Climacus's declaration that in the triumph of Christendom, sermons end with

"Hurrah" rather than "Amen" (*PC*, 107; *EC*, 93). Consequently, this may be less a formal difference than a matter of emphasis.

Kierkegaard's influence here can be further substantiated when Bonhoeffer comments, "If a man wishes to be incognito, one insults him if one says to him: I have both seen you and seen through you (Kierkegaard)" (*C*, 113). In his copy of *PC*, it is not surprising that Bonhoeffer places two bold marks in the margin when Anti-Climacus declares, "If Christ is true God, then he also must be unrecognisable, attired in unrecognizability, which is the denial of all straightforwardness. Direct recognizability is specifically characteristic of the idol. But this is what people make Christ into, and this is supposed to be earnestness" (*PC*, 136; *EC*, 120).

CHRIST'S CONTEMPORANEITY

The more systematic appreciation of Kierkegaard's argument can be seen through Bonhoeffer's adoption of the key Kierkegaardian concept of "contemporaneity." As discussed, according to Kierkegaard every individual comes to Christ in the same way through faith. Consequently, Christ is removed from the realm of history and brought into the present, where the individual becomes the one questioned by him. So Bonhoeffer argues,

> Absolute certainty about an historical fact can never be acquired by itself. It remains a paradox. Nevertheless it is constitutive for the church. That means that for the church an historical fact is not past, but present; that what is uncertain is the absolute, what is past is present, and what is historical (*das Geschichtliche*) is contemporaneous (Kierkegaard). (*C*, 74)

Bonhoeffer marks his copy of *PC* with a cross where Anti-Climacus argues that Christ is the same today as he was 1800 years ago, as the abased one (*PC*, 24; *EC*, 18). Bonhoeffer also then highlights a later comment that one cannot have fellowship with Christ unless one has become so contemporary with him as to witness his abasement and risk being offended at him (*PC*, 37; *EC*, 31).

The actual outworkings of Bonhoeffer's understanding of contemporaneity are somewhat unclear. And once again, Bonhoeffer's interpretation appears to differ somewhat from Kierkegaard's. In an earlier passage Bonhoeffer effusively uses the terminology of contemporaneity to describe how Christ is present as a person with us now (*C*, 45). However, his argument is that Christ's humanity causes him to remain in time, and yet his divinity allows him to be "eternally present everywhere" (45). This is clearly not the same as for Kierkegaard.

CHRIST'S OFFENSE

The year before his lectures on Christology, Bonhoeffer wrote a paper entitled, "What is Church?" Here Bonhoeffer essentially summarizes the content of offense for Kierkegaard as he writes,

> The church speaks of miracles because it speaks of God. Of eternity in time, of life in death, of love in hate, of forgiveness in sin, of salvation in suffering, of hope in de-

spair. It does this in full consciousness of the offense of its message, but at the same time in full consciousness of the commission which it cannot resign. (*NRS*, 155f.)[5]

This bears quite significant parallels with Kierkegaard, and one must ask whether Bonhoeffer is drawing on the offense of Christ's nature as the eternal within time from *PF* and *PC*, the offense of the duty to love in all situations from *WL*, the offense of forgiveness of sins from *SUD*, the offense of suffering and "dying to" of *JFY*? Each alternative Bonhoeffer provides reflects specific ideas from Kierkegaard's work.

In returning back to *Christology*, the concept of offense is discussed fleetingly throughout, but does not bear all the hallmarks of Kierkegaard's deeper analysis. For Kierkegaard, it was argued that offense is simply the response of the idealist self to the paradox, and therefore may manifest itself in multifarious ways. However, in contrast to "What is Church?" it is restricted to the humiliation that the God-man undergoes. As Bonhoeffer argues, "The offense caused by Jesus Christ is not his incarnation—that indeed is revelation—but his humiliation" (*C*, 46). For Bonhoeffer, however, this is not simply present in his earthly sufferings, but also through his presence in sacrament (55) and Scripture (76).

Further to this, Bonhoeffer comments,

> Christology is not primarily concerned with the question of the possibility of the union of God and man but rather with the concealment of the presence of the God-man in his humiliation. God is made manifest in the flesh, but concealed as an offense. (55)

When this is added to his statement that the incarnation is revelation rather than humiliation, further light is shed on the issue of the paradox as it is clear that Bonhoeffer does not see the fact of the eternal becoming human to be paradoxical, or even offensive. For Kierkegaard it clearly is. Indeed, Kierkegaard would go so far as to say that because of the infinite distance between God and man, Christ's suffering and humiliation is found in his becoming human, rather than its working out in human suffering (*CUP*, 1:596). The different interpretations of Christ's suffering will be dealt with further in Part 2.

Discipleship

In *Discipleship* we do not find a systematic Christology but rather the Christological insights we have discussed above lie behind Bonhoeffer's thought, with occasional glimpses emerging through different contexts. Most notably, Bonhoeffer's description of Christ revolves around his nature as free personality, in opposition to doctrinal system. Indeed, at least in the first half of the book, the central theme is the idea of "breaking through anything preprogrammed, idealistic, or legalistic," and especially any such concept as "an

---

5. In the DBWE 12 translation "offense" is softened by the word "disconcerts" (*B*, 264). Bonhoeffer uses the word "*Ärgerlichkeit*" (*GS*, III:289). Although this does not have the strength of the term, "*Angriff*," which is often used for that which is "offensive," the meaning for both Kierkegaard and Bonhoeffer is that linked to 1 Cor 1:23. This is revealed in Bonhoeffer's use of "*Ärgerlichkeit*" in his lectures on Christology (cf. *GS*, III:181) where it is translated as "stumbling block" in both the DBWE 12 and Collins editions (cf. *B*, 313f.; *C*, 46—here Bowden also uses "offense").

idea about Christ, a doctrinal system" (*D*, 59). These ideas will be more fully discussed in the next section.

However, in *Discipleship* Bonhoeffer provides greater explanation of an issue that he skirted around in his earlier works. In *PC* Anti-Climacus argues that the consequence of the situation of contemporaneity, of knowing Christ only through faith, is that there can be no advantage to the believer at first hand, relative to the one looking at Christ today. In *Discipleship*, having affirmed once again that "Christ can only be recognized in faith," Bonhoeffer comments,

> But did those first disciples not have an advantage over us in that once they had recognized Christ, they received his unambiguous command from his very own lips and were told what to do? And are we not left to our own devices precisely at this crucial point of Christian obedience? Does not the same Christ speak differently to us than he spoke to them? If this is true, then we would indeed be in a hopeless situation. But it is far from true. Christ speaks to us exactly as he spoke to them. For the first disciples of Jesus it was also not as if they first recognized him as the Christ, and then received his command. Rather, it was only through his word and his command that they recognized him. They trusted in his word and his command, and thereby recognized him as the Christ. (202)

Bonhoeffer couches his discussion in terms of the power of Christ's word, which is absent from Kierkegaard's presentation. However, the essential point is still the same for both writers, that everyone comes to Christ in the same way, without benefit or superiority, and all must become contemporaneous with Christ in order to be truly Christian.

Some Preliminary Remarks

The parallels of Bonhoeffer's thought with Kierkegaard are significant, with clear signs of direct influence throughout. At the time of writing *CCIG* Bonhoeffer appears to have remained influenced by Kierkegaard's more philosophical works. While continuing to use *CUP*, one also finds the first evidence that Bonhoeffer also read *PF*. There is, however, no evidence of Kierkegaard's later, more religious works. This is perhaps striking as in *CCIG* Bonhoeffer's argument reflects the meaning of Christ as the "incognito," but he does not actually use it. Although found in *CUP* (cf. *CUP*, 1:599), it is most clearly discussed in *PC* (*PC*, 127ff.). However, by the time of his lectures on *Christology*, where "incognito" plays a significant role, Bonhoeffer clearly reflects these later works, and *PC* in particular.

What is striking in this area of Christology is that there is very little of Kierkegaard's thought that is not at least adumbrated by Bonhoeffer. Unlike other topics where Bonhoeffer adopts only certain themes, both writers appear to agree across the board in this area. This does not mean that they treat everything in exactly the same way. Indeed, where in *Discipleship* Bonhoeffer bases the confrontation with the individual in Christ's word, Kierkegaard essentially leaves it open to suggest that it is simply the being of Christ as absolute paradox that confronts us and calls us into decision.

However, the differences in such areas as paradox, contemporaneity, and Christ's confrontation of the individual, appear to share a common theme of interpretation. In all these areas, Kierkegaard places their foundation in the being of Christ as the eternal within time: the paradox is simply this union; contemporaneity occurs because the eternal cannot be "known" simply as a historical being; each individual is confronted with the being of Christ as absolute paradox and so has no advantage over any other individual. In contrast, Bonhoeffer consistently searches for a more concrete, less metaphysical reason why these occur, to be able to explain them in terms of a more natural, mechanical process: the paradox is not simply the incarnation but the God-man who suffers; contemporaneity occurs through the different aspects of Christ's union of God and man; the individual is confronted by an authoritative word that draws him into belief.

Despite this change of emphasis, both writers draw upon the same concepts to paint their picture of Christ, and even if the precise explanation for their effects is different, they are both led to the same consequences for the individual before God. It is as if Bonhoeffer has understood Kierkegaard's beginning, end, and the checkpoints along the way, but prefers a different root through them.

Part 2

DISCIPLESHIP

With this foundation, the discussion will now turn to that of discipleship. As previously described, here we find some of the richest material for Kierkegaard's influence. In light of this, our analysis is better served by dividing the area into specific topics rather than trying to deal with the area as a whole. As with the discussion of Christology, the analysis will focus on Kierkegaard, before turning to a comparative analysis of Bonhoeffer and Kierkegaard together.

Cheap Grace

Kierkegaard

As the necessary step preceding faith, Climacus' description of Religiousness A is not entirely negative (1:566–77). However, as will become clear in chapter 7, its consequences can be devastating. As Climacus argues,

> The Religiousness that does not have something dialectical in second place, namely A, which is the individual's own pathos-filled transformation of existence . . . is orientated toward the purely human in such a way that it must be assumed that every human being, viewed essentially, participates in this eternal happiness and finally becomes eternally happy. (1:581)

In Religiousness A everyone has the condition within themselves in order to understand the eternal. Consequently, everyone is assumed to be in relationship with the eternal. To draw upon one of Kierkegaard's most used phrases, through this form of religiosity, "especially in Protestantism, especially in Denmark," everyone is assumed to be a Christian. It is not surprising that here we find one of Kierkegaard's first descriptions of cheap grace as the follower of Religiousness A is described as a "*wohlfeil* [cheap] edition of a Christian"

(1:557). In contrast to Climacus' more restrained treatment, Kierkegaard emphasizes the issue at the beginning of *FSE* and argues,

> Ah, we who still call ourselves Christians are from the Christian point of view so pampered, so far from being what Christianity does indeed require of those who want to call themselves Christians, dead to the world, that we hardly ever have any idea of that kind of earnestness; we are as yet unable to do without, to give up the artistic and its mitigation, cannot bear the true impact of actuality—well then, let us at least be honest and admit it. (*FSE*, 11)

In the face of the absolute paradox and its offensiveness, of the extreme rigorousness of imitation, the secular world has converted Christianity into the palatable affirmation of life in all its peace, comfort, and security. Using a phrase that appears through his journals, in the face of anxiety, the fear and trembling of Christianity, "The world wants to be deceived" (cf. *JFY*, 139; *JP*, 50/*Pap*, V B 14:72).

As described in chapter 2, Danish society does not want to eliminate Christianity because the issue of eternal happiness remains crucial to the individual's security. Consequently, it simply manipulates Christianity to both explain and legitimize people's hopes of heaven and ease their passage into it. As discussed above, "The deification of the established order is the secularization of everything" (*PC*, 91). Consequently, in parallel with the description of Religiousness A, Anti-Climacus refers to Christianity within Christendom as "sentimental paganism" (95).

For Kierkegaard, sagacity has not removed specific doctrines, but altered them through addition and embellishment. A good delusion is the manipulation of truth rather than its abolishment. Consequently, in *CUP* Climacus refers to those who set conditions to faith, adding an inconspicuous "*aber*," and so subtly reducing it from the absolute into the relative. In the same way, in *JFY* Kierkegaard refers to those whose faith is conditioned by such terms as "to a certain degree," "both-and," and "also" (*JFY*, 154). Such people desire the benefits of spirituality, religion, and its promise of eternal happiness, with the joys and security of this world (*PC*, 60). It is, as Kierkegaard argues in *JFY*, the desire to serve two masters (*JFY*, 145ff.), "to have one's mouth full of cake and wanting also to whistle" at the same time (133).

As discussed above, perhaps the most influential force behind this "secularization" or "recasting" (*PC*, 66) of Christianity is its conversion into "doctrine." In this way the absolute paradox is destroyed by being made commensurable with reason and understanding. When Kierkegaard argues that Christ went out of his way to destroy the concept of objectivity in all its forms (cf. *JP*, 4574/*Pap*, XI2 A 366; *EK*, 165), when the very being of Christ as paradox was designed to rob humankind of its own wisdom and sagacity (*PC*, 136ff.), the established order has converted Christianity into it. Everything is considered by way of knowledge and understanding, communicated directly (123ff.), and Christ transformed by either extracting his teachings from him, or converting him into a fantastical, abstract concept (128). In the same way, sin has been converted into an abstract doctrine where it is acknowledged but ultimately robbed of its devastating potential. As previously described, the true nature of sin places the individual "before God" and becomes revealed in its most terrifying height (cf. *SUD*, 115). Through this secularizing process it is acknowledged, but easily overcome. Christianity is no longer offensive (*PC*, 119).

However, when every aspect of Christianity is made into a form of knowledge, it no longer has existential import to be acted upon, but is rather to be considered, understood, and simply acknowledged (*JFY*, 129ff.). As Anti-Climacus comments, "What modern philosophy understands by faith is really what is called having an opinion or what in everyday language some people call 'to believe'" (*PC*, 141).

For Kierkegaard, one of the most dangerous figures is not simply the priest—rewarded by the established order with money, prestige, and applause to keep the masses within the delusion (*JFY*, 140)—but rather the professor who cannot but see Christianity as a doctrine, and so shifts the viewpoint to smuggle Christianity out of the world (195).

In this whole climate Kierkegaard describes Christianity as being "a showpiece for gentle comfort" (*PC*, 62), a "slack and anything but passionate assurance that somehow all of us will certainly be saved" (112), "human compassion" (140), "leniency" (227), coddling and "flabby" (*JFY*, 99), "cowardly sagacity and flabby sensibleness" (102), "mild" and "comfort" (132), "gentle comfort, a kind of insurance for eternity" (190). The effective import of Christianity within Christendom is like the selling of indulgences (*JP*, 2539/*Pap*, X4 A 371; *EK*, 151; cf. *JFY*, 132). Kierkegaard's position is perhaps summarized best when he declares that Christendom has been "pampered and made soft by the lollipop which is called Christianity, enthralled in the delusion of being Christian" (*JP*, 3737/*Pap*, XI2 A 346; *EK*, 166).

Before moving on to Bonhoeffer's understanding of cheap grace, it is worth emphasizing not just the similarities with Kierkegaard's understanding in terms of general content, but also the nature and consistency of Kierkegaard's vocabulary. We have already pointed out how in *CUP* Climacus refers to Religiousness A as a "cheap edition" of Christianity (*CUP*, 1:557). However, this same assertion is found in all the works that have been the focus of our discussion. In *PC* Anti-Climacus comments how Christianity is had at a "cheap price" (*PC*, 60). In *FSE*, Kierkegaard discusses the desire "to become Christian as cheaply as possible" (*FSE*, 16). And in *JFY*, Kierkegaard again repeats Climacus' description of the "cheap edition of what it means to be a Christian" (*JFY*, 189). Upon turning to the journals, and especially those found within *EK*, Kierkegaard not only discusses how men have tried to "get salvation a little cheaper," but declares,

> Luther purchased his situation of appreciation at an infinitely costly price, for fear and trembling and spiritual trials such as his are indeed frightfully costly . . . No doubt one who has the task of reminding people of the Christian demands can purchase at a far cheaper price, for he does not need to be tested by spiritual trials in this way, but then, again, he comes into a situation where he is not appreciated, is not welcome, since this is regarded as rigorousness . . . (*JP*, 2543/*Pap*, XI2 A 301; *EK*, 158)

Although Kierkegaard does not use the term "cheap grace," his notion of "cheapness" is intimately related to the issue of grace, and the price one has to pay for one's relationship with God.

Bonhoeffer

As Kelly argues, "cheap grace" has become something of a catchphrase for Bonhoeffer and *Discipleship*.[6] However, its presence in Kierkegaard has been widely recognized. In the *International Kierkegaard Commentary* to FSE and *JFY* the issue is discussed in three separate articles. Indeed, Craig Hinkson analyzes Kierkegaard's use of "cheap grace" without even referencing Bonhoeffer. David Law, in the same volume, comments that Bonhoeffer's description of cheap grace as on the front line of spiritual battle, "could stand as the epigraph to Kierkegaard's *For Self-Examination*, for Kierkegaard's purpose in this little work is, like that of Bonhoeffer a century later, to expose contemporary Christianity's cheapening of the Gospel and misuse of God's gift of himself in his Son Jesus Christ."[7]

As discussed Kierkegaard's use of financial imagery covers a wide range of his work. Indeed, the very first words of *FT* declare, "Not just in commerce but in the world of ideas too our age is putting on a varitable clearance sale. Everything can be had so dirt cheap that one begins to wonder whether in the end anyone will want to make a bid" (*FT*, 42). As discussed by Kelly and Nickson,[8] Bonhoeffer first used the terminology of cheapness in his 1932 lecture, "Christ and Peace" (*TF*, 94ff.). Although the phrase also appears in Luther,[9] Kelly argues that strong evidence also points towards Kierkegaard. In the interview that marks the end of Kelly's thesis, Bethge pointed towards Vogel and the influence of *EK* on Bonhoeffer's use of the term. However, while *EK* was clearly too late for Bonhoeffer's lecture, this thesis would agree with Nickson to suggest that Bonhoeffer may well have gained the concept from a number of Kierkegaard's other works whose influence was far earlier.[10]

However, what does "cheap grace" actually mean in Bonhoeffer's work? Having described how cheap grace does nothing to change either the world or Christianity, Bonhoeffer writes,

> Thus, the Christian should live the same way the world does. In all things the Christian should go along with the world and not venture (like sixteenth-century enthusiasts) to live a different life under grace from that under sin! The Christian better not rage against grace or defile that glorious cheap grace by proclaiming anew a servitude to the letter of the Bible in an attempt to live an obedient life under the commandments of Jesus Christ! The world is justified by grace, therefore—because this grace is so serious! because this irreplaceable grace should not be opposed—the Christian should live just like the rest of the world! Of course, a Christian would like to do something exceptional! Undoubtedly, it must be the most difficult renunciation not to do so and to live like the world. But the Christian has to do it, has to practice such self-denial so that there is no difference between Christian life and worldly life. The Christian has to let grace truly be grace enough so that the world does not love faith in this cheap grace. In being worldly, however, in this necessary renunciation required for the sake of the world—no, for the sake of grace!—the

6. Kelly, "Kierkegaard as 'Antidote,'" 148.

7. Law, "Cheap Grace," 111.

8. Kelly, "Kierkegaard as 'Antidote,'" 148; Nickson, *Freedom*, 95.

9. Cf. *Rationis Latominae Confutatio* (1521).

10. Nickson, *Freedom*, 96.

Christian can be comforted and secure (*securus*) in possession of that grace which takes care of everything by itself. So the Christian need not follow Christ, since the Christian is comforted by grace! (*D*, 44)

One would be forgiven for thinking this passage was written by Kierkegaard. Part of the reason for quoting this passage in full is so that its deep irony and sarcasm is not lost. Although a speculative point, one wonders how great the influence of Kierkegaard actually is here, for this is not Bonhoeffer's normal, straight talking, earnest style. Where Bonhoeffer can be characterized by simple and direct honesty, it is Kierkegaard who one associates with the more subversive method.

The above quote is further contextualized at the beginning of *Discipleship*, where Bonhoeffer declares,

> Cheap grace means grace as a doctrine, as principle, as system. It means forgiveness of sins as a general truth; it means God's love as merely a Christian idea of God. Those who affirm it have already had their sins forgiven. The church that teaches this doctrine of grace thereby confers such grace upon itself. The world finds in this church a cheap cover-up for its sins, for which it shows no remorse and from which it has even less desire to be set free. Cheap grace is, thus, denial of God's living word, denial of the incarnation of the word of God. (43)

As argued by Murray Rae, each of these claims, of Christianity's conversion into doctrine, of sin being reduced to a general rule, of God's word being denied its living and breathing nature, and the incarnation stripped of its living contemporaneity, are found in Kierkegaard. Indeed, Rae suggests that Bonhoeffer may simply be paraphrasing Kierkegaard.

For both Kierkegaard and Bonhoeffer, the established order desires to escape the true demands of Christianity. As Bonhoeffer therefore argues,

> Discipleship is a commitment to Christ. Because Christ exists, he must be followed. An idea about Christ, a doctrinal system, a general religious recognition of grace and forgiveness of sins does not require discipleship. In truth, it even excludes discipleship; it is inimical to it. One enters into a relationship with an idea by way of knowledge, enthusiasm, perhaps even carrying it out, but never by personal obedient discipleship. Christianity without the living Jesus Christ remains necessarily Christianity without discipleship, and a Christianity without discipleship is always Christianity without Jesus Christ. It is an idea, a myth. (59)

As discussed, for Kierkegaard one does not come into a true and living relationship with an idea, but only one of containment and control. From the perspective of the established order, Jesus Christ must not be allowed to live. Where his contemporaries nailed him to a tree, the present generation nails him to an idea, either extracting his teaching from him or spiritualizing him into a fantastical ideal. In *EK*, Bonhoeffer shows particular attention to two consecutive sections entitled "Imitation." In the first, Bonhoeffer underlines Kierkegaard's declaration that to the secular mind, "social morality approximates the existential" (*JP*, 1912/*Pap*, X4 A 500; *EK*, 144). In the second, Bonhoeffer underlines in four separate sections the notion of Christ's conversion into "idea," marking the first with double exclamation marks. As Vogel points out, the above quote appears to be a direct reference to *EK*.[11] For where Bonhoeffer discusses the nature of Christ as "an idea, a myth," so Kierkegaard writes that imitation "really provides the guarantee that Christianity does not become poetry, mythology, and abstract idea" (*JP*, 1904/*Pap*, X4 A 354; *EK*, 145).

For Bonhoeffer, the situation with Scripture is much the same, with God's living word transformed into an instructional document. Its unconditional character to command has been entirely displaced. When we bear in mind the longer passage quoted above and then read Kierkegaard's description in *FSE*, the parallels become strikingly clear:

> Fie on me if I were to be so vain! To think about myself and to say "It is I" is, as we scholars say, the subjective, and the subjective is vanity, this vanity of not being able to read a book—God's Word!—without thinking that it is about me. Should I not abhor being vain! Should I be so stupid as not to abhor it when I thereby also make sure that God's Word cannot take hold of me because I do not place myself in any personal (subjective) relation to the Word but on the contrary—ah, what earnestness, for which I am then so highly commended by men—change the Word into an impersonal something (the objective, an objective doctrine, etc.), to which I—both earnest and cultured!—relate myself objectively. (*JFY*, 36)

So strong is Kierkegaard's faith in the power and authority of Scripture to command and penetrate the individual's life that he speaks of his fear of reading Scripture—"to be alone with Holy Scripture! I dare not!" (*FSE*, 31).

With respect to the idealizing of sin, Bonhoeffer argues that a misunderstanding has occurred concerning the application of grace as forgiveness. Instead of being granted by Christ through the process of one's life and repentance, grace has been taken to be a "principled presupposition," and so unconditionally received. Instead of radical discipleship being its necessary presupposition, grace is now no longer dependent on action, allowing the world to stay as it is. Discipleship therefore becomes irrelevant.

In the next paragraph, Bonhoeffer directly references Kierkegaard with respect to a schoolboy who takes as a presupposition for himself the conclusion of Faust that we can know nothing (*D*, 51). The idea is that conclusions can only be reached through the path of presuppositions, and not adopted from elsewhere. When Bonhoeffer places the word "conclusion" in quotation marks, the editors of DBWE 4 suggest that Bonhoeffer is at least in part getting this idea from the journals of *EK* where Bonhoeffer underlined in his copy the word "conclusion" in a story about an illiterate innkeeper who adopts the conclusion of an academic who suggests that "it is not scholarship that matters" (*JP*, 2543/*Pap*, XI2 A 301; *EK*, 158). However, this idea reappears in several places for Kierkegaard. In *PC*, while talking about the place of the church in Christendom, and the assumption that what is manifest is the "church triumphant" as everyone is Christian, Kierkegaard comments,

> . . . what has mainly contributed to the fallacy of the Church triumphant is that the truth of Christianity has been interpreted as the truth in which there is a difference between result and way, or the truth of Christianity has been interpreted as a result . . . (*PC*, 209)

11. Vogel, "Christus als Vorbild," 299.

In another entry from *EK* Kierkegaard comments that in Christendom, "instead of faith we substitute an assurance about faith" (*JP*, 1135/*Pap*, X2 A 207; *EK*, 89). As with Bonhoeffer, the issue is the confusion of the result of discipleship for that which is generally received.

The aim of the established order is to make the Christian "live the same way the world does," to maintain the status quo by rejecting the extraordinary. For Kierkegaard, this is termed becoming "homogeneous" with the world (cf. *JFY*, 194; *JP*, 2760/*Pap*, X4 A 531; *EK*, 143). In *JFY*, Kierkegaard therefore argues that sagacity demands that Christianity "be brought into harmony with the rest of our life," and its absurd demands reduced (*JFY*, 155). In *EK*, Bonhoeffer marks the margin where Kierkegaard comments, "Once the objection against Christianity . . . was that it was antihuman—and now Christianity has become humanity" (*JP*, 4209/*Pap*, X4 A 126; *EK*, 136).

Before moving on, it is worth pointing out a theme hidden within the sarcasm of Bonhoeffer's opening quotes. For the world, the desire of the individual to be extraordinary is attacked as pure vanity. In *Discipleship* Bonhoeffer argues against those who reject discipleship and harden their hearts to the call of God "under the appearance of humble faith" (*D*, 67). For Kierkegaard, the established order relies upon its "humility"—"we have fabricated the notion that to think about oneself is—just imagine how sly!—vanity, morbid vanity" (*FSE*, 36). Again, the voice of the admirer declares, "The apostle, the disciple, is the extraordinary. God forbid that I be so immodest as to claim or crave to be such a personage. No, I am modestly and humbly content with something less" (*JP*, 1901/*Pap*, X4 A 340; *EK*, 138). In *EK*, the link is explicitly affirmed as Bonhoeffer underlines Kierkegaard's declaration that in secularity, "we interpret rigorousness as pride" (*JP*, 1904/*Pap*, X4 A 354; *EK*, 145). In this way, all are kept, or keep themselves, within the security if their spirituality without threatening the status quo.

Suffering and Imitation

Kierkegaard

As discussed, Christ is heterogeneous with the world. Consequently, his life was defined by suffering. For Anti-Climacus Christ's abasement is unrivalled, standing, as it were, behind the human race, at the base of human suffering (*PC*, 238ff.). Drawing again on themes discussed in Part 1, according to Kierkegaard Christ's suffering goes far beyond its physical side. In *CUP*, Climacus argues that when the "paradox is that Christ entered the world *in order to suffer*," this suffering is constituted by his adoption of human form (*CUP*, 1:597). It is irrelevant whether Christ came as a servant or emperor, as each is equally humiliating (1:596). In *FSE*, Kierkegaard argues even when people offered him their praise, Christ will rather have heard the cry, "Crucify!" (*FSE*, 60). In being heterogeneous with the world, Christ had to use his powers against himself, promoting his identity as offense. Furthermore, with each step he also made the path of discipleship narrower and narrower (61ff.). Consequently, in both his nature and task, the suffering increased.

As discussed, when Christ is converted from his historical abasement into doctrine and loftiness, one does not need to relate to him with existential investment and submission. As a result, Christ gains "admirers" but not followers (*PC*, 237). In such a relationship, an admirer relates to the lofty Christ through the imagination, as if watching him in a play from the safety of the stalls, "detached from any actual relation to danger" (244). An admirer of Christ is, like Judas, essentially a traitor, for Christ is only found in his abasement (cf. 246). For Kierkegaard, Christ did not come to be a symbol but the "prototype" of human existence. The only relationship required is that of "following" or "imitation" (238). In becoming an imitator, the follower must take on the life of Christ and stand in heterogeneity with the world, facing the same persecution and suffering that Christ underwent. For Kierkegaard, a follower must therefore be a martyr. As he argues in his journals, "every true Christian, is a martyr" (*JP*, 481/*Pap*, IX A 51; *EK*, 44).

Reflecting once again on the nature of Religiousness A, in the journals published in *EK* Kierkegaard argues that the only place in Christendom where even a hint of Christianity can be found is with the "quiet one's among the people," the religious of "hidden inwardness." Again Kierkegaard argues that such individuals are not decisively Christians, but rather tiny fragments of Christians, because "their lives are not exposed to double danger" (*JP*, 2751/*Pap*, IX A 362; *EK*, 60). The significance of the "double danger" is that the individual does not simply suffer internally—as with the knight of "hidden inwardness"—but also externally. Religiousness A is like an internal monastery. Religiousness B is the full injection of one's life "before God," within the world. To the understanding of sagacity, this description of Christianity is the highest treason against humankind (*JFY*, 141).

In *FSE*, it is only through this homogeneity with the world that true life is established through the spirit. The individual must go through death, a "dying to" forged through imitation, in order for new life to be born within him (*FSE*, 76).

Bonhoeffer

For both Kierkegaard and Bonhoeffer Christianity has been corrupted by the doctrinization of Christ. And so, as we have seen Kierkegaard argue concerning the absurdity of existential investment in an idea, Bonhoeffer declares,

> Discipleship is commitment to Christ. Because Christ exists, he must be followed. An idea about Christ, a doctrinal system, a general religious recognition of grace or forgiveness of sins does not require discipleship. In truth, it even excludes discipleship; it is inimical to it. One enters into a relationship with an idea by way of knowledge, enthusiasm, perhaps even by carrying it out, but never by personal obedient discipleship . . . A Christianity in which there is only God the Father, but not Christ as a living Son actually cancels discipleship. In that case there will be trust in God, but not discipleship. (*D*, 59)

Discipleship, for Bonhoeffer, is not an option to be worked out, but rather a commandment to be obeyed (47). In his copy of *PC*, it is not surprising that Bonhoeffer marks Anti-Climacus' declaration that Christ's call is "the absolute" (*PC*, 62; *EC*, 56).

However, discipleship does not simply involve obedience but the transformation of the individual. This is a central theme for Bonhoeffer's *Discipleship*, in which he dedicates an entire chapter to the introduction of the Sermon on the Mount. As he declares,

> How are disciples different from non-believers? What does "being Christian" consist of? At this point the word appears toward which the whole fifth chapter [of Matthew's Gospel] is pointed, in which everything already said is summarized: what is Christian is what is *"peculiar," perisson*, the extraordinary, irregular, not self-evident. (*D*, 143)

To be a disciple is to be "the extraordinary," separate from the world, and dedicated purely to Christ. As can be seen from the previous discussion in this chapter, the term "extraordinary" is central to Kierkegaard's later work. Consequently, as noted by Vogel in agreement with Kelly and Feil, "From [Kierkegaard] comes the term "the extraordinary," from him the sharp criticism that in Lutheranism discipleship has become conformed to the world."[12] The term appears throughout *EK*,[13] and Bonhoeffer marks his copy of *PC* where Anti-Climacus discusses Christ's nature as the extraordinary (*PC*, 42; *EC*, 36). The term was so influential on Bonhoeffer that he entitled a whole section of *Discipleship*, "The Enemy—the 'Extraordinary'" (*D*, 137–45). For both writers, the defining characteristic of the extraordinary is "heterogeneity" with the world. For just as Christ stood in opposition to society so too the disciple.

Bonhoeffer does not use the term "imitation," but its sense is clearly felt throughout. Indeed, Vernard Eller argues without reference to Bonhoeffer that *"Nachfolge"* should not so much be translated as "discipleship," but rather "imitation."[14] As a further suggestion towards a more Kierkegaardian interpretation, as discussed in chapter 1, Bonhoeffer's close friend Franz Hildebrandt revealed that at the time of writing *Discipleship*, Bonhoeffer had been reading the article on Kierkegaard in *Die Religion in Geschichte und Gegenwart* and, further, had been inspired by it to use the term *"Nachfolge"* as his title.[15]

As described, Bonhoeffer shows particular attention to the entries of *EK* that deal with "imitation." When discussing the perversion of Christianity in secularity, Bonhoeffer underlines Kierkegaard's statement that, "the guarantee of distinction between theatre and Church is "imitation," its earnestness, and the sobriety involved in making men into single individuals" (*JP*, 1904/*Pap*, X4 A 354; *EK*, 145). Furthermore, in his copy of *JFY*, Bonhoeffer boldly marks in the margin a paragraph in which Kierkegaard declares the role of the "prototype," and in particular, "The highest is: unconditionally heterogeneous with the world by serving God alone, to remain in the world and in the middle of actuality before the eyes of all, to direct all attention to oneself—for then persecution is unavoidable" (*JFY*, 169; *ASA*, 549).

The necessity of the disciple suffering in imitation of Christ plays a central role in both writers' work. While discussing Jesus' teaching to his disciples Bonhoeffer comments, "so Jesus has to make it clear and unmistakable to his disciples that the need to suffer now applies to them, too. Just as Christ is only Christ as one who suffers and is rejected, so a dis-

---

12. Vogel, "Christus als Vorbild," 301.

13. *JP*, 3153/*Pap*, X3 A 276, *EK*, 117; *JP*, 1914/*Pap*, X4 A 556, *EK*, 127; *JP*, 1913/*Pap*, X4 A 521, *EK*, 128; *JP*, 1901/*Pap*, X4 A 340, *EK*, 138; *JP*, 2760/*Pap*, X4 A 531, *EK*, 143; *JP*, 1090/*Pap*, X4 A 652, *EK*, 156; *JP*, 2047/*Pap*, X5 A 121, *EK*, 162.

14. Eller, *Radical Discipleship*, 383.

15. Prof. Daphne Hampson, in correspondence with the author, January 8, 2009.

ciple is a disciple only in suffering and being rejected, thereby participating in crucifixion" (*D*, 85). Indeed, "suffering becomes the identifying mark of the follower of Christ" (89). According to Bonhoeffer, the definition of discipleship is "being bound to the suffering Christ" (89). It is not surprising that Bonhoeffer's copy of *PC* is heavily marked in sections concerning suffering (*PC*, 108–10; *EC*, 93–96). The parallels are particularly prominent in the section, "Discipleship and the Cross," where not only is suffering defined in terms of a heterogeneity with the world, but of dying to the world. As Bonhoeffer comments,

> The first Christ-suffering that everyone has to experience is the call which summons us away from our attachments to this world. It is the death of the old self in the encounter with Jesus Christ. Those who enter into discipleship enter into Jesus' death . . . Whenever Christ calls us, his calls leads us to death. (*D*, 87)

As with Kierkegaard, it is only through death that the individual, in analogy to baptism, comes to life (88).

In his own copy of "The Gospel of Sufferings," Bonhoeffer pays particular attention to the section, "The Joy of it that the School of Sufferings Educates for Eternity," which focuses on Heb 5:8—"Although he was a son, he learned obedience from what he suffered" (*UDVS*, 248–63). Bonhoeffer marks in the margins three of the final paragraphs, and in particular the section in which Kierkegaard argues that just as Christ himself had to learn obedience from his suffering, so it must be the same for the disciple (263).[16] Although less Christologically grounded, it should also be pointed out that Bonhoeffer owned a copy of *CD*. In Parts 1 and 2, "The Cares of the Pagans" and "States of Mind in the Strife of Suffering," Kierkegaard counter-poses the necessary sufferings of the disciples with the rewards of eternity, arguing that what might appear externally as the greatest anxiety is rather the greatest peace (*CD*, 3–159).

At the end of *Discipleship*, Bonhoeffer once again returns to the subject of suffering and summarizes his position:

> The form of Christ on earth is the *form of death* of the crucified one. The image of God is the image of Jesus Christ on the cross. It is into this image that the disciple's life must be transformed. It is a life in the image and likeness of Christ's death (Phil 3:10; Rom 6:4f.). It is a crucified life (Gal 2:19) . . . Having died to the flesh and to sin, Christians are now dead to this world, and the world is dead for them (Gal. 6:14). (*D*, 285)

This could easily be a summary of Kierkegaard's thoughts on the subject. But further issues embellish the parallels. For in "Discipleship and the Cross," not only is the form of the suffering Christ described as an "offense" to both the secular world and the church (85), but Christ's path is described as the "narrow road" (176). Perhaps more convincingly, Bonhoeffer describes the disciples suffering as standing apart from the suffering of the world by the nature of being "voluntary" (85). The nature of the "voluntary" is a major theme within Kierkegard's work, and in particular concerning suffering. In *FSE*, Kierkegaard distinguishes the nature of the suffering life to argue that not every narrow way leads to heaven. Rather, what makes the suffering of the disciples stand out is the free-

---

16. *UDVS*, 263.

dom of their suffering. As he comments, "That which distinguishes the Christian narrow way from the common human narrow way is the voluntary" (*FSE*, 67). This is affirmed again in "Thoughts Which Wound from Behind" where the concept of the "voluntary" plays an important role. Here Kierkegaard argues,

> Christianity is indeed the religion of freedom, and precisely the voluntary is essentially Christian . . . God can take everything away from a human being, but he has left it up to the individual to give up everything, and this is exactly what Christianity requires. (*CD*, 179)

In the same way, Bonhoeffer not only describes Christ as setting his disciples free to enter into suffering (*D*, 85), but places this as the distinguishing mark in distinction to human self-denial and random suffering (86). In *EK*, Bonhoeffer marks up an entry entitled, "The Voluntary," in particular where Kierkegaard describes the voluntary nature of Christ's suffering. However, Bonhoeffer provides an exclamation mark in the margin when Kierkegaard juxtaposes the suffering of the individual against sagacity, mocking those who would declare spiritual struggle to be "tempting God" (*JP*, 4950/*Pap*, X3 A 43; *EK*, 102).

Both Bonhoeffer and Kierkegaard embrace an extremely high concept of discipleship in terms of its demand and the repercussions within the world. However, both hold equally high notions of God's sustaining grace. As Bonhoeffer argues,

> Jesus' commandment is harsh, inhumanly harsh for someone who resists it. Jesus commandment is gentle and not difficult for someone who willingly accepts it. "His commandments are not burdensome" (1 John 5:3). Jesus' commandment has nothing to do with forced spiritual cures. Jesus demands nothing from us without giving us the strength to comply. (*D*, 39)

And again,

> [Jesus'] yoke and his burden is the cross. Bearing the cross does not bring misery and despair. Rather, it provides refreshment and peace for our souls; it is our greatest joy. Here we are no longer laden with self-made laws and burdens, but with the yoke of him who knows us and who himself goes with us under the same yoke. Under his yoke we are assured of his nearness and communion. It is he himself whom disciples find when they take up their cross. (91)

These passages directly resemble a section from *JFY* in which Kierkegaard describes the individual who is crushed by the height of Christ's demands because he "has placed himself in a wrong place and receives the pressure in a wrong place and the requirement crushes him instead of humbly exerting pressure that lifts up in joy over and in bold confidence through grace" (*JFY*, 153). As Kierkegaard continues,

> In the physical world it is indeed the case that lifting can be done by means of a weight—thus if someone mistakenly thought he was supposed to lift the weight instead of being lifted by the weight—well, then he is crushed. But it would not be due to the weight but to him. So it is with the unconditioned requirement; if I am supposed to lift it, I am crushed. But this is not the intention of the Gospel. Its intention is that by means of the requirement and my humiliation I shall be lifted, believing

and worshipping—and then I am light as a bird. What lifts up more, the thought of my own good deeds or the thought of God's grace? (153)

As argued throughout this study, the central structure behind Kierkegaard and Bonhoeffer's thought is the presence of two realms, of the mutual exclusivity of Christianity and sensibleness. Consequently, God's commands are impossible from the perspective of sagacity, but from the viewpoint of God and imitation, are lighter than all the comforts of the world. For the burden is the cure against the corrupt life forged by humankind's sagacity. Further parallels can be found in this analogy. For where Bonhoeffer speaks of true "healing" as opposed to "forced spiritual cures," so Kierkegaard argues that Christianity is not a bungling "quack doctor," but that which truly cures over time with the aid of eternity (*FSE*, 80). It is interesting to note that Bonhoeffer pays close attention to the discussion of suffering and spiritual trial in *PC*, and in particular highlights the declaration, "The possibility of offense lies in the contradiction that the remedy seems infinitely worse than the sickness" (*PC*, 107–10; *EC*, 93–96).

As Kierkegaard argues, sagacity accuses Christianity and its demands of treason against human beings (*JFY*, 141). However, as will be discussed at length in the next chapter, both Kierkegaard and Bonhoeffer present Christianity as the firm affirmation of humanity in its earthly existence.

Luther

Kierkegaard

As described in his later works, Kierkegaard's analysis of faith and obedience begins with Luther. Although Kierkegaard appears to have come to Luther later in his life, Craig Hinkson goes so far as to claim that not only was Kierkegaard unique amongst his contemporaries in the profundity of his understanding of Luther, but "provided the impetus for the retrieval of the historical Luther and rediscovery of the heart of his theology by modern Luther research."[17]

In *FSE*, *JFY*, and *EK*, Kierkegaard sets out a historical analysis of the corruption of Christianity into its cheap state drawing on Luther and his relation to the Middle Ages. For Kierkegaard, the Middle Ages began as an authentic movement towards imitation. Individuals left the world and entered the monastery to set up a heterogeneity with the world. However, before long, a scale was established in Christendom, praising the extraordinary Christianity of the monastics, while legitimizing its lower forms as found among the masses. For Kierkegaard, there are no such people as "extraordinary Christians," but rather Christians, who are the extraordinary. The extraordinary describes the relationship with the world, not that within Christianity (*JFY*, 192). This scale simply served sagacity, creating both vanity and works righteousness within the monastery and ease for the rest by suggesting that by definition not everyone could be the extraordinary (*FSE*, 16). In a journal entry within *EK*, Kierkegaard suggests that the reason why the monasteries were so easily corrupted was that they were not so

17. Hinkson, "Real Martin Luther," 38.

much imitating Christ but simply copying him, turning his teaching and actions into principles and law (*JP*, 1893/*Pap*, X3 A 776; *EK*, 116).

It was into this context that Luther stepped and proclaimed salvation through grace alone. The point was not to undermine works, but to redress the balance. As Kierkegaard argues, "His life expressed works—let us never forget that—but he said: A person is saved by faith alone" (*FSE*, 16; cf. *JFY*, 193). But for Kierkegaard this is partly where the problem lies. Luther's life expressed works to the height of suffering, and yet his teaching concerned grace. Consequently, when he died, his followers simply adopted his teaching as doctrine but not his life (*JFY*, 193). Once again, as described above, these followers confused the result for a presupposition. As Kierkegaard describes,

> . . . they did not do as Luther did, *come* to faith *from* an exaggeration with regard to works, but started out immediately with faith, which "naturally" everyone has. (*JFY*, 194)

Consequently, concerning Luther's followers,

> Here again we see how infinitely important it is in respect to the essentially Christian to take the proclaimer along. For they took Luther's doctrine about faith—but Luther's life, that they forgot. (*JP*, 2140/*Pap*, X3 A 672; *EK*, 121)[18]

The journal entries of *EK* are littered with descriptions of Luther and his actions against "works righteousness," as well as formulations of arguments found throughout *FSE* and *JFY*. However, especially in his later life, Kierkegaard believed that Luther was at least in part to blame for the way his teaching was used. A full treatment of Kierkegaard's perceptions of Luther will not be attempted here. However, it is worth highlighting certain aspects, as discussed especially in *EK*.

For Kierkegaard, Luther was simply not dialectical enough. Consequently, he actually proclaimed a gospel of comfort (cf. *JP*, 486/*Pap*, IX A 292; *EK*, 61). According to Kierkegaard, Christianity is dialectical, as both the fountain of joy and peace, but also the source of suffering for the Christian. Luther, according to Kierkegaard, declared that where evil and suffering are created by the devil, so peace and joy are of God—that "the fruit of godliness is that everything goes well" (*JP*, 2531/*Pap*, X3 A 605; *EK*, 122). For Kierkegaard this is simply "Jewish piety" (*JP*, 2531/*Pap*, X3 A 605; *EK*, 122). Ultimately, Kierkegaard argues that Luther was too caught up in the secular world. For not only was he "ensnared in the idea that it is godliness to be made happy in this life" (*JP*, 4220/*Pap*, X5 A 115); *EK*, 160), but was also guilty of founding a party (*JP*, 2047/*Pap*, X5 A 121; *EK*, 162), and "mistaking secular victory for godly victory" (*JP*, 4699/*Pap*, X5 A 38; *EK*, 163).

Furthermore, Kierkegaard believed that Luther was himself too extraordinary. Consequently, he suggests that Luther didn't understand that almost no one else was like him and able, through humble spirituality and fear and trembling, to balance the embracing of the world while still essentially rejecting it. It was, therefore, inevitable that his ideas would be perverted. As Kierkegaard suggests at the beginning of *FSE*, the secular mental-

---

18. Cf. *JP*, 2512/*Pap*, X2 A 448, 2531/X3 A 605, 1447/XI2 A 130; *EK*, 97, 122, 175).

ity became aware of Luther, and used him to promote indulgence (*JP*, 1901/*Pap*, X4 A 340; *EK*, 138) and cheap grace (*FSE*, 16).

Bonhoeffer

Bonhoeffer's use of Kierkegaard in interpreting Luther and the Middle Ages is clear. The appropriate sections from both *EK* and *JFY* received considerable attention from Bonhoeffer and are heavily highlighted. In particular, Bonhoeffer's copy of *JFY* remains relatively free of marks until Kierkegaard discusses Luther, from which point every page bears vigorous highlighting and exclamation marks.

At the beginning of his analysis, like Kierkegaard, Bonhoeffer describes how from its authentic start by people wanting to follow Christ's commandments, manifesting itself as a "living protest against the secularization of Christianity," the monastery became a part of the cheap grace it intended to reject (*D*, 46ff.). Concerning the introduction of meritoriousness and corruption of the monasteries Bonhoeffer explains,

> For now monastic life became the extraordinary achievement of individuals, to which the majority of church members need not be obligated. The fateful limiting of the validity of Jesus' commandments to a certain group of especially qualified people led to differentiating between highest achievement and lowest performance in Christian obedience. This made it possible, when the secularization of the church was attacked any further, to point to the possibility of the monastic way within the church, alongside which another possibility, that of an easier way, was also justified. (47)

The parallels are strikingly clear when compared to Kierkegaard's argument in the journals of *EK*,

> Haggling can be done in two ways: either by being freed from the requirement or by being declared the extraordinary. Christendom came to consist of these two kinds: either Christians who were completely exempted from "imitation" (these are actually not Christians, and it should be noted that this is only an approximation of Christianity) or Christians who did strive in the direction of imitation but gained the title of extraordinary Christians—and this untruth had the result that neither was Christian. It was the secular mentality which conquered here. In general, men wanted to get rid of imitation—and yet be Christians. Thus there was no other way but to let those who expressed "imitation" advance to "the extraordinary" in order to be rid of them and be able to continue to be Christians with a secular peace of mind. And "the extraordinary" found pleasure in this recognition—again the secular mentality. (*JP*, 1914/*Pap*, X4 A 556; *EK*, 127)

For both writers, not only did the monastic movement become the extraordinary, but it justified secular Christianity.

As we have seen Kierkegaard argue, Bonhoeffer declares that Luther in no way "proclaimed a dispensation from obeying Jesus' commandments in the world" (*D*, 49). He proclaimed grace, but his life expressed the most rigorous discipleship. And so Bonhoeffer writes,

Luther knew that this grace had cost him one life and daily continued to cost him, for he was not excused by grace from discipleship, but instead was all the more thrust into it. Whenever Luther spoke of grace, he always meant to include his own life, which was only really placed into full obedience to Christ through grace. He could not speak of grace any other way than this. (49)

Following the same historical theory as Kierkegaard, Bonhoeffer therefore also argues that Luther's proclamation was adopted but not his lifestyle:

Luther said that grace alone did it, and his followers repeat it literally, with the one difference that very soon they left out and did not consider and did not mention what Luther always included as a matter of course. Yes, he no longer needed to say it, because he always spoke as one whom grace had led into a most difficult follow-ing of Jesus. (50)

With each step, Bonhoeffer's argument follows the same pattern as that of Kierkegaard. Consequently, it is at this point that Bonhoeffer draws in further the issues of cheap grace and, at the same point in the argument as with Kierkegaard, declares that in ignoring Luther's life, his disciples confused grace as the result of one's life for grace as its presuppo-sition. Just as we have seen both Kierkegaard and Bonhoeffer reject the acceptance of life's "conclusions" as rather "principled presupposition," so in his copy of *EK* Bonhoeffer not only underlines "as a result" in relation to Luther's acceptance of grace, but accompanies it with two exclamation marks in the margin.

Faith and Obedience

Kierkegaard

As Kierkegaard describes, one of the reasons why Luther's doctrines were taken up as they were was because the secular mentality refused to believe that one could coherently maintain faith and works together. In doing so, it therefore failed to take seriously the extremity of Christianity's demand. As Kierkegaard expresses it in *FSE*,

Christianity's requirement is this: your life should express works as strenuously as possible; then one thing more is required—that you humble yourself and confess: But my being saved is nevertheless grace. (*FSE*, 17)

In this respect, Luther's own life was a declaration of this possibility. The two must always be held together in balance. It is not simply a matter of the will, but also the nature of faith to demand its expression in works. Drawing further from Luther, Kierkegaard argues that "faith is a restless thing" (17), "the pulse in your life," which bears witness to itself through action (18). Consequently, faith always leaves one with the question that Kierkegaard places in the mouth of Luther,

To what end has faith, which you say you have, made you restless, where have you witnessed for the truth, where against untruth, what sacrifices have you made, what persecution have you suffered for Christianity, and at home in your domestic life where have your self-denial and renunciation been noticeable? (18)

However, according to Kierkegaard, the connection between faith and obedience also permeates the stage before belief. Although implicit in much of his writing, the journals of *EK* are littered with Kierkegaard's affirmation of free will in the face of predestination. Kierkegaard is extremely keen to emphasize the true height of grace, but not at the expense of the individual's possibility for decision. As discussed, subjectivity demands the correct "how" and not just the "what." There must therefore be a concrete and real human "how" somewhere in the process of salvation. For Kierkegaard, its lack is pure fatalism (cf. *JP*, 4551/*Pap*, X2 A 301; *EK*, 95). Without subjectivity, there can also be no concept of the voluntary, defining Christian suffering in homogeneity to the suffering of the world (cf. *JP*, 4950/*Pap*, X3 A 43; *EK*, 102). Furthermore, there can be no concept of costly grace as there cannot be any presuppositions upon which grace can then enter as the "result."

As described in both *EK* and *JFY*, before faith can be given, a "situation" must be created within the individual in order for that faith to come in. This situation must be enacted by the individual, as a movement against his reason. When we take on board Kierkegaard's understanding of the two realms, of the exclusivity of the understanding of God to that of humankind's reason, it comes quite naturally to say that in order for the word of God to be understood, the individual must have lowered his rational guard, submitting it, even just for a moment, to the message being heard. Only in that way can the truth of the message be considered, and faith be granted. Contrary to most thought, therefore, Kierkegaard argues that knowledge is imparted through obedience, creating the situation, but not before. Therefore, to have faith one must act. The relationship between faith and obedience is emphasized again when Kierkegaard argues that it is only obedience through imitation that can destroy doubt within the individual (cf. *FSE*, 67). For when faith rests in the ground beyond reason, so the only way to get back there from the rational state of doubt, is to once again act and create a situation through which faith might return.

Bonhoeffer

Kierkegaard's influence can be seen in Bonhoeffer's treatment of faith and obedience, and in particular the need for a "situation" to be created by the individual for faith to occur. In *JFY*, Kierkegaard argues,

> To such a person [who wants to be a follower] [Jesus] said something like this: Venture a decisive act; then we can begin. What does that mean? It means that one does not become a Christian by hearing something about Christianity, by reading something about it, by thinking about it, or, while Christ was living, by seeing him once in a while or by going and staring at him all day long. No, a *setting* (*situation*) is required—venture a decisive act; the proof does not precede but follows, is in and with the imitation that follows Christ. That is, when you have ventured the decisive act, you become heterogeneous with the life of this world, cannot have your life in it, come into collision with it. Then you will gradually be brought into such tension that you will be able to become aware of what I am talking about. (*JFY*, 191)

To this section Bonhoeffer places some of his most enthusiastic and erratic marks, including lines and large crosses in the margin.

These ideas are further discussed, in a passage from *EK* that is particularly picked up by Vogel.[19] Here Kierkegaard further comments,

> Usually it is presented this way: first one must have faith and then existing follows . . . We have taken this very much to heart and have abolished [authentic] existence—since faith is much more important to be sure. The matter is quite simple. In order to have faith, there must first be existence, an existential qualification. This is what I am never sufficiently able to emphasize—that to have faith, before there can even be any question about having faith, there must be *the situation*. And this situation must be brought about by an existential step on the part of the individual. (*JP*, 1142/*Pap*, X4 A 114; *EK*, 140, author's emphasis)

Although Vogel was not aware of this, once again, Bonhoeffer covers the margin with both lines and an exclamation mark.

The direct parallels in Bonhoeffer's work are strikingly clear. At the beginning of the chapter, "The Call to Discipleship," Bonhoeffer argues that to the call of Christ, the disciples did not make a confession of faith but rather an obedient deed. For Bonhoeffer, obedient action must precede faith, in the form of what Bonhoeffer terms a "first step." As in Kierkegaard, the content of this step is the creation of a new situation that separates the individual from their previous existence. As Bonhoeffer therefore argues,

> Following Christ means taking certain steps. The first step, which responds to the call, separates the followers from their previous existence. A call to discipleship thus immediately creates a new *situation*. (*D*, 61—author's emphasis)

Bonhoeffer argues that this step puts the believer in a situation from which he can believe. For in this situation the individual is removed from his place of security, the calculable realm, the realm of limited possibilities (*D*, 58). For the gospel message centeres on the absolute paradox, and so requires that the individual lower his reason and sagacity even to be able to attend to the content of faith. It is, consequently, only after this step has been taken that faith has the ability to enter in. As with Kierkegaard, it is only in this situation that the individual has a hope of understanding what the call might mean. As Bonhoeffer therefore summarizes, "Now all bridges had to be burned and the step taken to enter into endless insecurity, in order to know what Jesus demands and what Jesus gives" (62).

Consequently, with regard to the commonplace statement "only the believers obey," Bonhoeffer agrees with Kierkegaard that "only the obedient believe" (63). It is not surprising that in his copy of "The Gospel of Sufferings" Bonhoeffer placed brackets around the passage,

> Only suffering educates for eternity, because eternity is in faith but faith is in obedience, but obedience is in suffering. Obedience is not apart from suffering, faith is not apart from obedience, eternity is not apart from faith. In suffering obedience is obedience, in obedience faith is faith, in faith eternity is eternity. (*CD*, 263)

The first step of obedience must occur in order for faith to enter in. According to Bonhoeffer there is no definition as to what it must be, other than that it draws the individual out of

---

19. Vogel, "Christus als Vorbild," 299f.

his previous existence. That could include the rich man giving up his wealth, the alcoholic giving up his alcohol. Or it may simply be a matter of the individual deciding to enter a church. This is the act of obedience before faith. However, when Kierkegaard argues that only imitation can destroy doubt, so Bonhoeffer's advice to someone who claims they cannot believe is "be obedient." For both, faith will follow from that act.

To further cement the influence of Kierkegaard on Bonhoeffer in this area, it should be noted that in *EK*, where the concept of the "situation" is described, Kierkegaard then goes on to discuss the story of the rich young man. As Kierkegaard comments,

> Take an example, the rich young ruler. What did Christ require as the preliminary act? He required action that would shoot the rich young ruler out into the infinite. The requirement is that you must venture out, out into water 70,000 fathoms deep. This is the situation. (*JP*, 1142/*Pap*, X4 A 114; *EK*, 140)

Not only did Bonhoeffer mark his copy at this point, but to end his own discussion of the "first step" it is to the rich young ruler that Bonhoeffer also turns (*D*, 69). For it is in Christ's decree that he should sell all his possessions, give his money to the poor, and then follow Christ, that this individual finds the first step required of faith.

Drawing up ideas discussed in chapter 4, for both Kierkegaard and Bonhoeffer, not only is obedience required for faith to exist, but it is only through obedience that doubt can be overcome. As Bonhoeffer argues, those who are plagued by doubt, who have lost belief, or claim they cannot hear the command of God, have hardened their hearts through disobedience. Such individuals hide behind cheap grace and undermine the power and authority of God's words by grasping hold of it themselves, applying blanket forgiveness to their own sins. Consequently, Bonhoeffer advises the pastor met by such a person to halt all futile conversation with them and to simply demand that they be obedient. As Bonhoeffer declares, "At this point, Christ appears on the scene; he attacks the devil in the other person, who until then had been hiding behind cheap grace. At that point everything depends on the pastors having both sentences ready: only the obedient believe, and only the believer obeys" (*D*, 68).

Likewise, in both *FSE* and *JFY* Kierkegaard argues that without imitation doubt cannot be overcome (*FSE*, 68–69; *JFY*, 190–91). For both Kierkegaard and Bonhoeffer, the doubting individual strives to understand God on his own, through his own conditions, his own understanding. Bonhoeffer relates this to cheap grace and the individual remaining essentially in control. In a similar vein, Kierkegaard describes the individual as seeking to overcome his doubt with "reasons," to enter into faith through his own understanding. However, as he describes in both *JFY* and "Thoughts Which Wound From Behind," this is like using the enemies" own weapons, of betraying the very thing one sought to defend (*JFY*, 191; *CD*, 190). Consequently, it simply creates a vicious cycle, where "a kind of doubt has been opened up that Satan himself cannot combat but does indeed invent, a kind of doubt that is impossible to combat because to combat it actually requires one to go over to its side" (*CD*, 190). In "The Gospel of Sufferings" Kierkegaard makes a similar point arguing that through obedient suffering the individual is protected from doubt. Here Bonhoeffer marks the margins of his own copy where Kierkegaard argues,

... as soon as unrest begins, the cause is that you are unwilling to obey; but suffering will help you to obey. Therefore, when there is suffering, but also obedience in suffering, you are being educated for eternity; then there is no impatient hankering in your soul, no restlessness, neither of sin nor of sorrow. Just as the cherubim with the flaming sword stood guard to keep Adam from returning to paradise, so also suffering is the guardian angel who keeps you from slipping out again into the world. (*UDVS*, 259)

Unconscious Discipleship

Before finishing, one of Bonhoeffer's most distinctive marks of discipleship will be discussed in relation to Kierkegaard. In the previous chapter, the issue of the single-minded relationship to God was analyzed in terms of its ethical context. However, its most striking feature is Bonhoeffer's assertion that at its height, discipleship becomes unconscious for the individual (cf. *D*, 146ff.). For Bonhoeffer, when one's gaze is finally fixed on God, without distraction from oneself or the world around, then the questions of being and doing which occupy our minds will cease, and the disciple will simply be and do without thinking. It is the aim that the individual should become Christ. This image can be seen in Tolstoy's short story, "The Three Hermits." Here a bishop from the mainland meets three old men (who have spent their lives in isolation) on a desert island. Realizing that they have been starved of doctrine and authoritative guidance, he embraces his pastoral duty and attempts to teach them the Lord's Prayer. After considerable effort, the Bishop finally leaves, and as he mulls over his experience that night on the bow of the boat, suddenly sees the hermits running towards him across the water. Upon reaching the boat they confess that they have already forgotten the words, and request his further aid. Tolstoy sought to juxtapose the knowledge of the Bishop with the simple relationship of the hermits. When the concept of the two realms is considered, the point becomes especially clear. For the Bishop, living still within the sagacious systems of society and the church, walking across the water is impossible. However, the hermits, in their simple and undivided relationship with God, are so filled with the "world of the spirit," of God's understanding of what is "possible," that they are not even aware of anything strange. There is no suggestion that Bonhoeffer necessarily read this story. However, it is an example of Bonhoeffer's unconscious discipleship, where the *cor curvum in se* has been overcome, and one's light is visible to everyone but oneself, for whom it is entirely hidden. Bonhoeffer's position is perhaps summarized in his declaration that one must know only Christ, even to the rejection of knowing oneself—"self-denial means knowing Christ, no longer knowing oneself. It means no longer seeing oneself, only him who is going ahead" (*D*, 86).

Within Bonhoeffer's thought, the issues of the undivided gaze and an absolute duty come together in "unconscious discipleship." As discussed in previous chapters, these ideas he shares with Kierkegaard. So in chapter 5 it was demonstrated that in his actions the individual must not consider at all the issues of "good" or "right" but simply keeps in mind the person and will of God. These ideas are further discussed in *JFY* where Kierkegaard argues that instead of trying to understand a divine command or piece of knowledge, one must rather immediately embody it in action. As he argues, "According to Christianity, then, the only person who is completely sober is the person whose understanding is action. And so it ought to be. Your understanding must *immediately* be action. Immediately!" (*JFY*, 120). In "The Lily of the Field and the Bird of the Air," this is described as like the child who does not waste time on fruitless deliberation but simply obeys (*WA*, 10). Again, in a short journal entry from *EK*, Kierkegaard attacks those in the meritorious Middle Ages who have become "important" through their actions, and argues, "Christianity believes that the Christian should be so spiritual that he should do such things as easily as if they were nothing" (*JP*, 2710/*Pap*, X2 A 464; *EK*, 99). For one resting in the world of the spirit, in which all things are possible for God, fruitless reflection must be overcome as it can only stand in the way of obedience.

These examples point towards a similarity of "doing" with respect to unconscious discipleship, but do not address the more fundamental issue of "being," of the individual's internal state and self-consciousness. However, points can be found to this effect.

As previously discussed, Kierkegaard emphasizes that one can only serve one master. The individual's being must be "before God," such that he "at every moment relates first to God, serving him alone" (*JFY*, 170). However, in *SUD* these ideas are taken further and one gains a sense of the individual's being lost in God. Anti-Climacus declares, "This then is the formula which describes the state of the self when despair is completely eradicated: in relating to itself and in wanting to be itself, the self is grounded transparently in the power that established it" (*SUD*, 44). When despair is understood as an imbalance of self, so it can be defined in terms of self-awareness. Although despair is not described in quite the same sensate language as anxiety, despair must be considered as a form of awareness of the self and the disquiet of its imbalance. Indeed, when despair is at its most extreme the individual experiences the most terrible self-awareness. If we make this the center point of a scale, the extreme in one direction is the total ignorance of being in despair, which Anti-Climacus ascribes to the majority. Here the individual is described as being ignorant of the self, resting in a state of spiritlessness, and essentially only a hair's breadth away from being mere animals. However, when one considers the other extreme, when God destroys despair and the individual rests transparently in him, although Kierkegaard is not clear, one must consider that the individual again loses a sense of self by rooting his gaze, not in the immediacy and distractions of life, but in God himself. When the self reaches perfect equilibrium with itself, does it depart from the individual's mind? Does the concept of "transparency" suggest this disappearing from view? This is not to deny the self—in "The Lilies of the Field and the Birds of the Air" Kierkegaard describes the need to be "present to oneself" (*WA*, 39)—but rather to suggest that in its new found wholeness it no longer remains an object of one's consciousness.

Further suggestions can be made from Kierkegaard's edifying works. In the sections of *CD* that Bonhoeffer owned, Kierkegaard argues that the Christian, like the lilies and the birds, is freed from the earthly anxieties of the pagans because he is "ignorant" of the earthly conditions that bind them (*CD*, 27–29). Kierkegaard's point is that whether the individual is physically rich or poor, he rests in every moment in the will of God. Such an individual is therefore ignorant of his earthly condition and invested only in that of God. Referring back to the issue of reflection, Kierkegaard once again affirms that "with increased knowledge increased care" (34). In contrast, the Christian "craves only to be satisfied with God's grace" (64), which is here specifically defined as God's will (65).

Perhaps the most significant example of this ignorance can be seen in the example of "the woman who was a sinner" in "Three Discourses at the Communion of Fridays." Kierkegaard describes the story of Luke 7, where a women enters a crowded house of a Pharisee house in order to anoint Jesus and seek his forgiveness. Kierkegaard argues that because this woman loved Jesus, she came to hate herself because of her sin (*WA*, 138). Consequently, she forgot every consideration for herself and entered the Pharisees house in order to search for Jesus. At this point, she became ignorant of everything other than this immediate relationship. However, the point of concern for us here is what follows. Upon receiving forgiveness, Kierkegaard argues that all that remained was her love for Jesus, and so she then forgot even herself. As she sat at Jesus' feet Kierkegaard reveals,

> She has forgotten herself completely, forgotten the setting with all its disturbing elements . . . but she weeps, and as she weeps she forgets herself. O blessed tears of self-forgetfulness, when her weeping does not once remind her anymore of what she is weeping over; in this way she has forgotten herself completely.
>
> But the true expression of loving much is just to forget oneself completely. If one remembers oneself, one can, to be sure, love but not love much; and the more one remembers oneself, to the same degree one loves less. She has forgotten herself completely. (*WA*, 140)

In order to discern these ideas in Kierkegaard one must piece them together from across Kierkegaard's authorship. However, there is clearly a sense of unconsciousness to both the being and doing of the individual who rests perfectly "before God" in the "world of the spirit." Bonhoeffer's understanding is derived from presuppositions he shares with Kierkegaard. Consequently, when one combines Kierkegaard's attack on idealism and the deification of reason, the distraction of immediacy, the demand of the individual to serve one master and stand perfectly "before God," and to make the leap of faith in every action, does one simply arrive at unconscious discipleship?

CONCLUDING REMARKS

It is clear that many of Bonhoeffer's central themes from *Discipleship* find parallels in Kierkegaard. This is particularly the case when one considers the influence of *FT* as discussed in the previous chapter. However, what is particularly striking is the influence of Kierkegaard on Bonhoeffer's Christology. Drawing on our continued theme, both writers sought to extract Christ from the hands of idealist thought, rejecting the notion of Christ as "idea" or "doctrine." While embracing the differences of their interpretation, many of Bonhoeffer's central descriptions of Christ's nature as paradox, incognito, offense, and contemporaneity are directly rooted in Kierkegaard's thought.

As both writers emphasize the notion of "imitation," the issues of Christology are foundational to their thoughts on discipleship. Consequently, in failing to take seriously Kierkegaard's Christological influence, many of the secondary sources fail to recognize the scope of his influence in this area. This chapter has shown the extent to which

Bonhoeffer drew on such works as *EK*, *CUP*, *PC*, *FSE*, and *JFE*—all of which are evidenced in Bonhoeffer's library—but has also suggested that from as early as the beginning of 1931 Bonhoeffer came into contact with the arguments of *PF* concerning Christ's nature as paradox, and his incongruous presence in history. Furthermore, from the division between the philosophical *CCIG* and the clearly theological *Christology*, it appears that by 1933 Bonhoeffer had also come under the influence of *PC*.

In comparing Bonhoeffer to Kierkegaard, this chapter has also raised questions about the nature of self-consciousness in Kierkegaard's work. It has been suggested that Kierkegaard contains at least the seeds of an unconscious discipleship, if not necessarily the fruits.

7

Attack on Christendom

Introduction

THE FINAL SUBSTANTIVE CHAPTER OF THIS THESIS FOCUSES ON THE RELATIONSHIP BE-
tween Kierkegaard and Bonhoeffer's most provocative writings concerning their attacks
on Christendom. While highlighting their clear parallels, by drawing together many of the
themes that have already been discussed, this chapter will suggest that these attacks represent not the unfortunate end to otherwise profound careers, but the fulfilment of their
earlier thought. To this end, this chapter will set out both writers' thought independently
before finally turning towards their comparison.

PART 1
KIERKEGAARD AND BONHOEFFER'S ATTACKS

Kierkegaard

As described in chapter 1, Kierkegaard's final attack has often been disparaged. Such commentators as Bain and Allen suggest that Kierkegaard's attack was written out of a com-
bination of "brooding unhappiness" and "aristocratic pride,"[1] a "bitterness and tumult of
spirit"[2] that, influenced by Schopenhauer, simply presented an acosmic pessimism against
the true gospel of Christ.[3] If others are not so direct, the substantial lack of secondary
source material that deals with such works as *The Moment* points towards a subordination
of these later works. Other than biographical accounts, which by nature must deal with
the period, there are only a handful of pieces that critically concern this final attack. Even
here the verdict is often far from positive.[4]

In contrast, this thesis argues that these final thoughts stand as the progression and
fulfilment of Kierkegaard's earlier thought, most importantly through the events of 1848.
As described in chapter 2, through this year Kierkegaard became more clearly aware of
his task and his foe, transforming his writing from its more general polemical style into a

---

1. Allen, *Kierkegaard*, 106.
2. Bain, *Kierkegaard*, 115.
3. Ibid., 119.
4. Cf. Law, "Anti-Ecclesiology."

frontal assault. As outlined, this "transformation" occurred through various stages, from his "direct pseudonymity" in Anti-Climacus, through his direct authorship, and into *The Moment*. In order to more fully appreciate this progression, the analysis will move through each of these stages.

The Road to 1848

A LITERARY REVIEW

As Eduard Geismar comments, the ideas presented in Kierkegaard's writings are not the new ramblings of a "sick man," but rather "that which he had been conversant with for many years, as the entries of his diaries show."[5] When one turns to *LR* this becomes clear. Although published in March 1846, and couched within far more subtle and discursive language, one finds the seeds of Kierkegaard's frustrations concerning Christendom and the church. Of particular importance to our study is Kierkegaard's association of the clergy with the concept of a "life-view," but also with the impending revolution. In *LR* one finds Kierkegaard rooting the essential elements of his attack on Christendom with a theme that summarizes and runs through his previous authorship, but also with the spiritually calamitous socio-political events he saw before him.

As described in chapter 2, *LR* represents a polemic against Denmark's "revolutionary" climate, defined as "essentially *sensible, reflective, dispassionate, eruptive in its fleeting enthusiasms and prudently indolent in its relaxation*," and so lacking any sense of a "life-view" (60). Of particular importance for our present discussion, however, is the connection Kierkegaard makes between the "life-view" and speech. Armed with a "life-view," Kierkegaard argues that a speaker not only "persuades" his listener towards the truth, but causes himself to drop out (16ff., 30). As he clarifies, "persuasion is not a matter between two persons, but the pathway in the life-view, and leads one into the world that that view creatively sustains" (17).

In contrast, the present age is described as endlessly speaking, and yet never communicating, of "*letting everything remain but slyly defrauding it of its meaning*" (68). While arguing that this is true politically in the desire to create the illusion of revolution without its dangers, Kierkegaard declares that this is particularly true of the spiritual state of Christendom—"One can let the entire Christian terminology stand, but in the private knowledge that it is not supposed to mean anything decisive. And there will be no call to repent since, after all, one isn't tearing anything down . . . No, one quite innocently wants to let the established order stand—but while being increasingly aware, in a reflective knowledge that it *isn't* standing" (72).

Although subtle, Kierkegaard clearly aims his thoughts at the clergy in terms of their speech and image. According to Kierkegaard, the priests' words are essentially correct, but so devoid of passion and inwardness that they have been rendered meaningless. Their lives neither back up what they say, nor persuade individuals towards the truth. Rather, they direct them towards the speaker himself. In contrast to their vestments and regalia,

---

5. Geismar, *Lectures*, 84.

their pounding of the pulpit, Kierkegaard therefore writes, "If you have listened properly to a sermon brim-full of inwardness, even if your gaze has been fixed on the pastor, you will find it impossible to describe the pastor's appearance" (30). In Kierkegaard's mind, the words of the clergy are so lacking in inwardness that they point the listener towards the speaker. However, the speaker lacks such inwardness, any sense of an existential "I," that the listener comes away believing they have been listening to an anonym (93).

For Kierkegaard, the clergy reveal their lack of a "life-view" or any sense of "epistemological respiration." As will be shown, it is the notion of a "life-view" that underlies many of Kierkegaard's criticisms of Christendom, and especially the clergy, in his later works.

CHRISTIAN DISCOURSES

Published only a month after the Danish "revolution," *CD* represents an unusual stage in Kierkegaard's attack: while in one way extremely guarded, it contains one of Kierkegaard's most sarcastic and pointed polemics. Kierkegaard essentially sets the scene in Part 1 by mocking Christendom in Denmark as simply a veiled paganism where all are proclaimed Christians (cf. *CD*, 11–12). These ideas are then picked up in Part 3, "Thoughts that Wound From Behind," where Kierkegaard presents a still guarded, but clearly forceful, attack that holds within it many of the central themes of these later works. These include the offensiveness of Christianity (179), the need for honesty against insincerity (167, 184, 185, 187), the desire of Christendom to defend the Gospel (189–90), to convert it into proofs (202–13) and doctrine (214), of the clergy preaching tranquillity and security (163–64, 202), valuing honour and esteem (227), and a fixed income and permanent job above sacrifice (182). In perhaps his most extreme statement, Kierkegaard argues not only that in contrast to its proclaimed triumph, Christianity remains militant within Christendom (229), but that should Christ return to Christendom he would once again be crucified (229).

Kierkegaard was well aware of the extremity of his message at this time, and his journals bear witness to his anxiety at having published Part 3 with the rest of his discourses, shifting first one way and then another as to whether *CD* would have been too mild without it (cf. *JP*, 6111/*Pap*, VIII1 A 559; 6112/ VIII1 A 560; 6121/ VIII1 A 590; 6125/ VIII1 A 602). It is perhaps not surprising that *CD* caused such consternation and has such a curious tone as it falls between his indirect communication, and his desire (or compulsion) to become more direct. *CD* represents Kierkegaard's escalating frustrations full to bursting within his old, indirect method, without the release afforded either by Anti-Climacus, or his final direct method.

Although the tone and language is different to that of *LR*, and Kierkegaard does not here use the concept of a "life-view," his description of the clergy in *CD* represents the lack of passion and inwardness of the "present age" in their tranquil preaching, revealing their substitution of sacrifice, decision, and commitment for security, a wage, and the *status quo*. In *CD*, Kierkegaard argues that when people go to church they want to hear an orator of eloquence (*CD*, 164–65), someone who may pound the pulpit with heartfelt declarations of how they would give everything up if it were asked of them (185). However, as with *LR*, this is simply the desire to let everything stand while removing its meaning: the clergy will not substantiate their words with their lives.

Personal Confessions and the New Pseudonym

THE SICKNESS UNTO DEATH

Despite the various forms of despair described in *SUD*, Anti-Climacus argues that each is rooted in the attempt to lose oneself in the illusory security and peace of immediacy (*SUD*, 55). This attempt has been so successful that by far the most common form of despair is the ignorance of being in despair (73ff.). This is the state of spiritlessness where even the boundaries between man and beast, demarcated by despair itself, have become blurred (45). Bound to this spiritlessness, Anti-Climacus therefore declares that Christendom is nothing but "paganism" (75).

As discussed in chapter 6, Christendom is not simply a form of secular paganism for having removed Christianity's essential characteristics of offense and imitation, but is far worse as a wilful corruption of it (77). Where in paganism the name of "god" is still treated with reverence, so in Christendom it has been transformed into the most common of words (148, 150), stripping God of his authority and replacing his unconditional command with human sagacity (148f.). Consequently, while paganism is simply the sin of being ignorant of God, and therefore not a sin "in the strictest sense," for Anti-Climacus Christendom is a sin "before God" (80f.).

For Anti-Climacus, Christendom is "not only a miserable edition of Christianity, full of misprints that distort the meaning and of thoughtless omissions and emendations, but an abuse of it in having taken Christianity's name in vain" (134). Consequently, not only is everyone assumed to be a Christian, but the call to ministry has been converted into the passing of an exam. A priest is now nothing more than a "livelihood" and "official appointment" (135).

PRACTICE IN CHRISTIANITY

In *PC*, Anti-Climacus expands upon these themes, including the destruction of offense (cf. *PC*, 99), the transformation of Christianity into "sentimental paganism" (cf. 95), the universalization of "faith" (cf. 99, 112), and the deification of the established order (cf. 88ff.). Consequently, "established Christendom is like sheer meaninglessness" (112). Just as with the relationship between Jesus and Peter in Mat 16:23, so Anti-Climacus argues that in relation to Christianity, Christendom only has in mind the things of men (119).

Of particular stress in *PC* is not simply the "paganization" of Christianity, but rather its "secularization." Christianity has become related to society as "culture" or "civil justice" (112), such that the church rests at the center of Danish society enjoying both peace and influence as the church triumphant of which all are members (cf. 211). Indeed, the sermons of such a church "could more appropriately end with "Hurrah" than with "Amen"" (107). However, through the imitation of Christ, Anti-Climacus argues that the only true church is the church militant that stands in heterogeneity to the secular world, and therefore struggles for its place there (201ff.). Not only does Christendom believe that it has triumphed over the world, but it has essentially abolished Christ by simply appropriating his merits and achievements—that is, people are deluded into believing that "Christendom is Christ" (107). For Anti-Climacus this is rather the sign that the world has won, for now the church no longer exists but simply the world (223).

In Part III, Anti-Climacus's presentation of Christendom resembles Religiousness A as not only has it universalised salvation (so destroying faith's confession as a distinctive characteristic), but converted the strenuousness of the Christian life into hidden inwardness (so remaining indiscernible and uninvasive within life) (252f.).

The Point of View of My Work as an Author

The essential ideas of the Anti-Climacus literature are heavily reflected in *PV*. Here Christendom is described as an "intellectual paganism" (*PV*, 78), "the caricature of true Christianity, or a monstrous amount of misunderstanding, illusion, etc., mixed with a sparing little dose of the true Christianity" (80). Christendom is simply an "illusion" (cf. 23, 41ff.), in which people live out an aesthetic existence (43), where universal salvation has made ethical responsibility superfluous (48).

Up until this point in our analysis, Kierkegaard's polemics have remained somewhat general, discussing a homogeneity with the world. However, in *PV* Kierkegaard unleashes a direct attack on both the position and motives of the clergy. As he argues,

> The objection I have repeatedly made privately against those who ordinary proclaim Christianity in Christendom is that they, themselves surrounded and safeguarded by all too many illusions, do not have the courage to make people aware. That is, they do not have sufficient self-denial in relation to their cause. They are eager to win adherents, but they want to win them—because this strengthens their cause—and therefore are not scrupulously careful about whether they in truth become adherents or not. This in turn means that in a deeper sense they have no cause; they relate themselves selfishly to the cause they do not have. Therefore they do not actually risk going out among the people or abandoning illusions in order to make a genuine idea-impression, because they have a dim notion that it is truly a dangerous matter to make people aware. (51)

Not only are the clergy therefore deceived, but they deliberately affirm this illusion for their own personal gain.

The Direct Communication

For Self-Examination

As we enter the second period following 1848 it is clear that the urgency and gravity of the situation in Christendom has become far more pressing on Kierkegaard's writing. Kierkegaard opens *FSE* by declaring that those who call themselves Christian in reality have no idea of the earnestness that such a title requires (*FSE*, 11). However, Christendom is not simply a caricature of true Christianity that "arouses a restlessness" (21), but rather "the stillness of death, a dying out" (20).

As described in chapter 2, still within this more direct period, Kierkegaard was painfully aware of overstepping his authority as a writer. Consequently, in *FSE* he reaffirms his identity as one "without authority," describing the true height of Christianity, and yet disowning the project of reformation (21f.). In accord with *PC*, he declares his desire to simply make people take notice.

Judge For Yourself!

Drawing on themes discussed in *PC*, in *JFY* Kierkegaard argues that by transforming Christianity into the world that holds "completely opposite conceptions" (*JFY*, 96ff.), its premises and demands have been reversed, confusing the finite for the infinite, the eternal for the temporal, the highest for the lowest (123). So great is this transformation that not only is Christendom at best a form of "Jewish piety" in which the suffering life of imitation has been removed, but Christendom has completely forgotten what Christianity is (187). Indeed, by having replaced suffering with respectability, the true height of Christianity can only appear as the greatest cruelty and torture. The distinction is so great that Kierkegaard comments, "The ordinary kind of Christianity is: a secularized life, avoiding major crimes more out of sagacity than for the sake of conscience, ingeniously seeking the pleasures of life—and then once in a while a so-called pious mood. This is Christianity—in the same way as a touch of nausea and a little stomachache are cholera" (202).

In contrast to revealing the presence of Christianity through "true self-denial and renunciation of the world," Kierkegaard affirms that the clergy are simply professionals. Indeed, their staggering number actually suggests that Christianity no longer exists (124). However, despite their ignominious roles, Kierkegaard reserves his most fearsome words for the category of the "reformer." Chapter 2 described Kierkegaard's profound dislike of the inauthentic Danish revolutionaries. In the same way, Kierkegaard argues that the most frightful of confusions is created when someone tries their hand at spiritual revolution, without the calling, life-view, or authentic life of suffering to back it up (131). In the last paragraphs of the book, Kierkegaard therefore declares that anyone who dabbles in reforming is "more corrupting than the most corrupt established order" (212).

It is no surprise that despite venturing out into direct communication, Kierkegaard once again refuses to be a reformer, stating at the end that his own form of Christianity is merely an approximation. As he affirms, "I belong with the average among us" (208). Indeed, he even suggests that he would find an authentic witness for the truth quite unbearable (113). His role, rather, is to reveal what the ideal should be. For it is only once the confusion has been swept aside that people may come "to truth and salvation and Christianity" (126). Kierkegaard demands society's confession rather than reformation, demanding only what he himself is able to perform (cf. 135). Consequently, "if there is no such [reformer] among us, then let us hold to the established order; let us see the error of our ways, let each one individually confess before God how far behind we are in Christianity . . ." (212).

In this much-shortened autobiographical account, Kierkegaard reflects many of the points already discussed in *PV*. However, recalling his emphasis on the "common man" (see chapter 2), Kierkegaard juxtaposes the life of Christendom with that of the authentically religious sphere. Specifically, Kierkegaard argues that the religious needs to be connected to reflection, and yet equally to be "completely taken back out of reflection into simplicity" (*PV*, 7). As he summarizes, "one does not reflect oneself into Christianity but reflects oneself out of something else and becomes, more and more simple, a Christian" (7).

However, in agreement with the rest of the authorship from this period, Kierkegaard once again affirms that his task is "'*Without Authority*' **to make aware** of the religious, the essentially Christian" (12).

The Moment and Later Writings

Fædrelandet

Following the publication of his new, direct authorship, Kierkegaard remained silent for over three years. As discussed in chapter 2 this was at least in part to afford Mynster and the church the time to make a confession. Indeed, reflecting back in an article from April 1855 Kierkegaard declares that *PC* was written as a defense of the established order, to provoke it into making its confession in order to submit to God's grace (*M*, 69). However, the established order continued its relationship with sagacity. Consequently, Kierkegaard broke his silence in 18 December 1854 declaring, "and now that Bishop Mynster is dead I am able and willing to speak" (3). What followed was a series of scandalous articles, published in the popular newspaper, *Fædrelandet*.

Mynster's death afforded Kierkegaard both the possibility and the opportunity for his final polemic. In a eulogy given by Prof. Hans L. Martensen, who would later become his successor, Mynster was described as standing in the "holy chain" of "authentic truth-witnesses," armed with a faith evident "not only in word and confession but in deed and truth" (3). That this was uttered by someone who Kierkegaard loathed is not irrelevant to hiss vitriol. But what Martensen declared was clearly and directly the very opposite of what Mynster and Christendom embodied for Kierkegaard. For as we have seen discussed in chapter 6, to have faith, to become a witness or imitator of Christ, means to suffer in heterogeneity with the world (cf. 5, 10). The first point of Kierkegaard's redefining of Mynster was therefore to declare that while not necessarily doctrinally wrong, Mynster's preaching was a scaling down of the essentially Christian elements of the New Testament (4, 17). As we have seen, Kierkegaard himself benefited from Mynster's teaching. However, while perhaps being full of compassion and benediction, Mynster proclaimed a message of peace rather than repentance, which for Kierkegaard amounted to ecclesial malpractice and self-indulgence (18).

However, Kierkegaard believed that Mynster didn't even live up to his own selective proclamation (4). As he declares, "his sermon on Sunday he either did not recognize or dared not or would not acknowledge on Mondays" (13). Rather, because of "worldly-sagacity," to avoid having to step out of his peace and comfort, Mynster refused to live according to his own rhetoric. For Kierkegaard, therefore, this is the reason why Mynster remained silent while the events of 1848 occurred (4). Kierkegaard seems to suggest that had Mynster even been obedient to his own preaching he perhaps would not have felt obliged to begin his attack (13).

The situation in Christendom is one of peace and enjoyment where all are Christians, assured of their salvation (42). Here the clergy avoid the essentially Christian "either/or," to embrace a "both/and" that claims both the title of "truth witness" and a life of ease (cf. M, 10f., 20ff., 26). This, however, is an illusion, as ludicrous as to talk of "a virgin with a flock of children" (10), or to call "a parade ground manoeuvre a war" (26). Kierkegaard declares that everyone wants to be deceived (45). However, this deception has become so great that not only does Christendom not embody or proclaim Christianity (28), but within this realm "Christianity does not exist at all" (35). As Kierkegaard declares, "the human race is now at an age when it literally will be true that there no longer exists or is born one single individual who is able to be Christian in the New Testament sense" (34). For Kierkegaard, the life and worship of the church are simply making a fool of God (30f.). Consequently, he declares his refusal to participate in any way (49).

This is a key moment as it marks Kierkegaard's first direct movement against the established order. However, once again he continues to maintain his role as one "without authority," rejecting the role of "reformer" (40). Indeed, Kierkegaard suggests that as Christianity no longer exists, and Christendom is now the opposite of New Testament Christianity, there is nothing left to reform (39). In the article entitled, "What Do I Want?" Kierkegaard therefore declares, "Very simply—I want honesty" (46). For Kierkegaard, as long as a confession is made the clergy can remain paid professionals in the service of the state (47). Indeed, the clergy are "as competent, respectable, and worthy a class in society as any other" (53). However, should the clergy maintain the illusion, they immediately become the most dangerous heretics for true Christianity (6).

While gaining a certain emphasis, most of this material does not depart from the previous, post-1848 writings. However, in the last two articles before Kierkegaard begins *The Moment*, a far greater strength and direction can be discerned. In the article, "This Must Be Said, So Let It Be Said," Kierkegaard encourages others in no uncertain terms to take part in his boycott of the church—"*Whoever you are, whatever your life is otherwise, my friend—by ceasing to participate . . . in the public divine service as it now is . . . you always have one and a great guilt less—you are not participating in making a fool of God by calling something New Testament Christianity that is not New Testament Christianity*" (73). This is by far the most invasive movement made thus far, and one is brought to question whether Kierkegaard is beginning to trespass into the territory of "reformation." Kierkegaard is still not saying what should constructively occur within Christendom, but is clearly beginning to take his active destruction to a new level. Indeed, in an addendum to the same article, Kierkegaard actually argues for the separation between church and state (75).

In the final article before *The Moment*, these thoughts are developed as he declares the church to be more concerned with finances than religion. Consequently, as "stockholders," the clergy not only keep the establishment going, but perhaps even keep silent about the truth of Christianity for the sake of their own pockets (85).

By the end of this period of *Fædrelandet* articles, one can already begin to see the traces of what can be called a "negative reformation" in which Kierkegaard rejects the task of rebuilding Christianity, but rather attempts to sweep away the structures that stand in its way. And yet, in terms of the relationship between church and state, how distinct are these two movements?

The Moment

As his attack became more defined and pointed, it seems likely that Kierkegaard felt obliged to move his thoughts from between the sheets of *Fædrelandet* to his own journal, of which ten editions were produced. However, he picks up where he left off. So in *The Moment* No.1 Kierkegaard not only denounces the clergy for having discarded the "either/or" of authentic Christianity for its "both/and," demanding everything "to a certain degree" (*M*, 91ff., 302, 355), but declares that the state has made Christianity's existence impossible (95). For by employing the clergy the state not only destroys the possibility of heterogeneity with the world, but also gives these professional stockholders a vested interest in maintaining the situation (95).

Throughout the editions of *The Moment* Kierkegaard describes the clergy as "parasites" (160), "wolves" (160), "swindlers" (161), "criminals" (166), "forgerers" (166), "soul-sellers" (171), "oath-bound liars" (245), "perjurers" (255), "hypocrites" (302), "cannibals" (321), "thieves" (325), "huckstering knaves" (340), etc. And his frustration grows as the pamphlets proceed. As discussed in chapter 6 concerning cheap grace, Kierkegaard continues to use a financial theme with perpetual frequency, describing the clergy as selling grace and eternity for the sake of their own security (cf. 47, 64, 109, 113, 135, 158, 171, 181, 231, 256, 287, 299, 352). By the end of No. 7, therefore, Kierkegaard argues that there are no honest clergy, as to stay within the established order, to tow the party line, is dishonesty and a betrayal of Christianity (255). Even if the individual clergyman should agree with Kierkegaard, by remaining within the established order they simply reinforce the situation, and all for the sake of self-preservation.

In the final edition of *The Moment*, Kierkegaard argues that the true role of the clergy is to "do everything to make every human being eternally responsible for every hour he lives, even for the least thing he undertakes," to make everyone into individuals before God (350). However, they have done the very opposite, demanding that people come to them for knowledge, before coddling them with cheapened Christianity. Instead of affirming individual responsibility, they have entirely undermined it. As Law comments, "In summary, for Kierkegaard the pastor is the most fundamental and pernicious denial of the essentially Christian."[6] Consequently, Kierkegaard's final words, addressed to the common man, once again call for a boycott:

> But one thing I beseech you for God in heaven's sake and by all that is holy: avoid the pastors, avoid them, those abominations whose job it is to hinder you in even

6. Law, "Anti-Ecclesiology," 96.

> becoming aware of what true Christianity is and thereby to turn you, muddled by
> gibberish and illusion, into what they understand by a true Christian, a contributing
> member of the state Church, the national Church, and the like. Avoid them . . . (347)

At this point we must again address the issue of how Kierkegaard conceives his task. In this last declaration Kierkegaard has again become involved in the movements of Christendom, in the "negative reforming" discussed at the end of his *Fædrelandet* articles. In this final edition of *The Moment*, Kierkegaard once again declares that as one who does not call himself a Christian his task is to declare the truth of the situation in Christendom by revealing the true height of Christianity (341; cf. 212). However, a subtle but profound shift has occurred between *The Moment* and his earlier writings. Previously Kierkegaard's task was to demand that Christendom make an admission. Indeed, there was a certain redemption within Kierkegaard's mind for the clergy once this is done. However, within *The Moment* the concept of honesty appears only twice: in No.5 Kierkegaard presents a list of Christian characteristics, one of which is honesty; in No.7 he argues that the easiest way for hypocrisy to be avoided is to make an admission (226). Not only are these the only two references that resemble Kierkegaard's original demand for a "confession," but are themselves no longer phrased as demands but statements of fact. The reason for this appears to be that Kierkegaard now believes that as Christianity no longer exists in Christendom, and that Christendom actively inhibits Christianity from coming into being, an admission is no longer possible. In the *Fædrelandet* articles, Kierkegaard argued that there was no longer any Christianity to reform within Christendom, and so the only thing possible was therefore a confession. It now appears that the time for the latter solution has now also disappeared. At the end of *JFY* Kierkegaard argued that the established order should continue until an authentic reformer is found. While his heightened call for a boycott appears at the end of *The Moment*, so now in No.4 Kierkegaard clearly sets out a call for "negative reformation" in terms of the relationship between church and state and the form and activity of the church once removed from the state. So he argues,

> This whole junk heap of a state Church, where from time immemorial there has
> been, in the spiritual sense, no airing out—the air confined in this old junk heap has
> become toxic. Therefore the religious life is sick or has expired, because, alas, pre-
> cisely what worldliness regards as health is, Christianity, sickness, just as, inversely,
> Christian health is regarded by worldliness as sickness.
>
> Let this junk heap tumble down, get rid of it; close all these boutiques and
> booths, the only ones that the strict Sunday Observance Act exempted . . . and let us
> once again worship God in simplicity instead of making a fool of him in magnificent
> buildings. Let it again become earnestness and cease to be play . . . (158)

Here we find the most significant sense of a "negative reformation" as Kierkegaard calls for the destruction of the established church to which he declares, "Yes, let it happen. What Christianity needs is not the suffocating protection of the state; no, it needs fresh air, persecution, and—God's protection" (158). This falls far beyond the boundaries of his auditing task, and yet stands in consistency with his concerns over the events of 1848.

An understanding of Kierkegaard's frustration with the clergy, their actions and motivations, all that has been outlined above, must come from an understanding of the events of 1848. As he declares in his journals from 1851, "When a society goes to pieces the way it did in '48, it is not the fault of the kings and nobility—but is essentially the fault of the clergy" (*JP*. 4193/*Pap*, X3 A 746; *EK*, 37). Lying behind Kierkegaard's accusations in *The Moment* is the belief that when the religious situation in Denmark required radical religious reform, so this was entirely undermined by the false "revolution" that occurred. In line with Kierkegaard's aesthetic theory of the "life-view," the form of knowledge as "*respiratio*," as well as his hope for the common man, so Kierkegaard desired such individuals to authentically come to an awareness of the need for reform themselves. Not only did the revolutionaries destroy the possibility of this process by falsely creating and defining this need, but they then provided its false solution. Furthermore, this was all done not out of concern for the common man but purely for the sake of the clergy themselves and the church, that both should weather the revolutionary storm with their finances and influence intact.

And yet, Kierkegaard's desire and hope for the common man is not entirely lost. At the end of his last *Fædrelandet* article, Kierkegaard argues that the common man can understand very clearly the dichotomy needed between Christianity and the world, and certainly "much more easily and much better than demoralized pastors and a corrupt upper class" (84). As outlined in chapter 2, the issues of eternity that surround the essential "either/or" are far better understood by the simple than the wise. So at the very end of *The Moment* No.10 Kierkegaard declares,

> You common man! The Christianity of the New Testament is something infinitely high, but please note that it is not high in such a way that it pertains to differences among people with regard to talents etc. No, it is for all. Everyone, unconditionally everyone—if he will unconditionally, will unconditionally hate himself, will unconditionally put up with everything, suffer everything (and everyone can indeed do that if he will)—then this something infinitely high is accessible to him.
>
> You common man! I have not segregated my life from yours, you know that; I have lived on the street, am known by all. Furthermore, I have not become somebody, do not belong to any class-egotism. So if I belong to anyone, I must belong to you, you common man, you who nevertheless at one time, enticed by someone who, making money on you, gave the appearance of desiring your welfare, have been willing enough to consider me and my life ludicrous, you who least of all have reason to be impatient over or should be unappreciative of my belonging to you, something the more elite have rather than reason to be because I definitely have not joined them but have kept only a loose relation to them. (346)

From this platform Kierkegaard therefore beseeches them, "avoid the pastors" (347).

Bonhoeffer

Although forged throughout his theology, Bonhoeffer's frontal assault on Christendom appears in his final prison letters through his ideas of a "religionless Christianity." Although Macquarrie rather uncharitably refers to these thoughts as "tentative and obscure gropings," they are clearly "thoughts in progress" whose implications, consequences, and even meaning in general was perhaps not fully visualized by Bonhoeffer.[7] This section will analyze Bonhoeffer's letters and seek to organize his wandering thoughts into a coherent whole, contextualized by his earlier works. This will be organized first to discuss the nature of religion in the world, and secondly with the specific responsibilities of the church itself.

Religionless Christianity in a World Come of Age

THE NATURE OF CHRISTIANITY AND "RELIGION"

A plethora of catchphrases have been drawn out of Bonhoeffer's *LPP* such as "religionless Christianity," the "world come of age," God as the "*deus ex machina,*" the "secret discipline," Barth's "positivism of revelation" etc. These ideas appear throughout his letters and are picked up, dropped, expanded upon, and altered according to where his thoughts led him. However, a helpful place from which to start is the first of his main "theological" letters, sent to Eberhard Bethge on 30 April 1944, prefaced with the warning, "What might surprise or even worry you would be my theological thoughts and where they are leading" (*LPP*, 362).[8] Here we find discussion of the concept of the "religious *a priori*."

Bonhoeffer begins his first substantial argument by suggesting that the Christian religion has for the last 1,900 years rested on the false belief that for all people there is such a thing as a "religious *a priori*," that humankind is by nature endowed with an innate perception of God. As described in chapter 3, Reinhold Seeberg presented a somewhat experiential theology that placed *a priori* knowledge at the heart of its hermeneutic. In *AB*, Bonhoeffer directly criticized his former tutor for having argued that there is an "unmediated perception of, or contact with, God on the part of human beings" (*AB*, 57). Although the context of his discussion was different, in *LPP* Bonhoeffer took up these same criticisms to argue that the church has forged its identity as the answer to the need that this *a priori* creates, and sought to become the authority to which all people look for explanation of themselves and the world around them.

Within his analysis, Bonhoeffer creates an important distinction between Christianity and "religion." As Wüstenberg clearly demonstrates, Bonhoeffer does not have a consistent "theory of religion" running throughout his thought, but employs religion both positively and negatively.[9] However, Bonhoeffer's critical use of "religion" was significantly influenced by Barth. Mirroring the discussion of Barth's criticisms of "theology" in *AB* (as discussed in chapter 4), in *Church Dogmatics* Barth argues that although it may be redeemed and used by God, "religion" is the flawed and sinful endeavour of humankind to grasp hold of God.[10] Consequently, in *AB*, Bonhoeffer argues

---

7. Macquarrie, *God and Secularity*, 38.

8. Eberhard Bethge was Bonhoeffer's biographer, student, and closest friend. He was also married to Bonhoeffer's niece, Renate. Bethge was one of the most important characters in Bonhoeffer's life as a confidant and sounding board for his growing theology. Almost all the letters in *LPP* are between Bethge and Bonhoeffer.

9. Wüstenberg, *Theology of Life*, 26.

10. Cf. Barth, *Church Dogmatics* I/II, 280ff.

that Seeberg's use of a religious *a priori* as this "unmediated perception of, or contact with, God" makes revelation into an immediate object interpreted by the *cor curvum in se* (*AB*, 57f.). Not only does Bonhoeffer charge Seeberg with having turned away "from pure transcendence toward idealism," but declares that through the religious *a priori*, "revelation must become religion" (57f.). The point at the beginning and end of Bonhoeffers's theology, in both *AB* and *LPP*, is that revelation has become "religion," where the truths of Christianity have become interpreted and forged through the light of humankind's own mind rather than that of God. As described in chapter 3, this is the idealist hermeneutic of Althaus and so many others during that time.

In *LPP* Bonhoeffer describes "religion" as like a garment that covers Christianity and presents or interprets it in a very particular way through such categories as "metaphysics" (*LPP*, 364, 372), "the inner life" (364, 455), and "individualism" (372). Metaphysically, God is portrayed as a strong, transcendent figure, standing beyond the world as its creator and definer. Inwardly, humankind is divorced from his earthly existence by having spirituality driven away from his external life into the confines of his inner life. Individualistically, humankind is separated from the people around him, and his concerns directed away from his ethical freedom in responsibility for others, into a responsibility for his own purity and salvation. Each of these perspectives divide the eternal realm from the temporal, driving the individual away from the world and his own abilities into a reliance on the church and its understanding of both the spiritual and temporal realms. Not only has the church forged its own identity around the religious *a priori*, but forged humankind around its own thought, binding him ever more fully to the church. Most significantly for Bonhoeffer, God has himself become forged into a *"deus ex machina,"* as the answer to the questions and ambiguities of existence.

In humankind's more primitive state, this framework of power and influence was never substantially challenged. However, not only has humankind become more enlightened, and aware of his own abilities, but Bonhoeffer questions whether the religious *a priori* ever existed in the first place. Consequently he asks, "Yet if it becomes obvious one day that this 'a priori' doesn't exist, that it has been a historically conditioned and transitory form of human expression, then people really will become radically religionless—and I believe that this is already more of less the case . . . what does that then mean for 'Christianity'?" (363).

The situation is particularly perilous as when God as the *deus ex machina* has been made to stand in direct relation to humankind's own knowledge, so with each movement in this direction He is made to lose ground, to be pushed out of humankind's life. For Bonhoeffer, the world has "come of age" and reveals the corruption of religion and so the church.

Eller attacks Bonhoeffer at this point to argue that, unlike Kierkegaard, his attack is temporally conceived, relevant only now that the world has come of age.[11] However, what this fails to realize is that the situation reveals that the church was wrong all along for having forged these identities in such a way. For not only was humankind never to be

---

11. Eller, *Radical Discipleship*, 329.

so undermined in his abilities, but God was never meant to have been conceived as the answer to his weakness.

The Nature of Christianity and the World

Bonhoeffer's thoughts must be understood as orientated around his experiences in prison, for here he not only witnessed the secular mentality of humankind through his fellow prisoners, but also came to a profound understanding of "worldliness." Throughout his letters the reader is given a glimpse into Bonhoeffer's loneliness and piercing desire to have fellowship with his fiancée, family, and Bethge. With each letter, gift or visit he received one gets a sense of Bonhoeffer's joy. While in prison, he was constantly reminded of his separation from those he loved, missing the marriage of Bethge to Renate his niece, and the birth and baptism of his great nephew and namesake Dietrich Bethge. Most significantly, he missed his fiancé, Maria von Wedermeyer, with whom he become betrothed just three months before his arrest. Throughout this time, therefore, Bonhoeffer became more and more aware of his deep spiritual yearning for the "natural" experiences of life. So in a letter from December 1943, written as Bonhoeffer prepared for his first Christmas in prison, he writes, "One should find and love God in what God directly gives us; if it pleases God to allow us to enjoy an overwhelming earthly happiness, then one shouldn't be more pious than God and allow this happiness to be gnawed away through arrogant thoughts and challenges and wild religious fantasy that is never satisfied with what God gives" (228).

These thoughts re-emerge a month later as Bonhoeffer suggests that the church should embrace Kierkegaard's "aesthetic existence" to provide an understanding and authenticity to freedom found in art, education, friendship, music, play, etc. (268). Should the church remain attached to an "ethical existence" it will remain exclusively caught up in the piety of religious fantasy. Indeed, a little while later he argues against Nietzsche's aesthetic theory that he believes polarizes beauty into either classical or demonic forms, to embrace the beauty that is "simply earthly" (331).

The emphasis on "worldliness" was powerfully influenced by the priority that Bonhoeffer afforded the Old Testament during his time in prison. From the Old Testament Bonhoeffer gained a strong sense of God's establishment and involvement in the world, and the earthly, communal nature of its message. In a message that was particularly poignant for its time, Bonhoeffer argues that the Christian religion has become corrupt at least in part through its divorcing of the New Testament from the Old. Through a denial of the world in favor of a super-spirituality, as Dumas argues, "Without its Hebraic rootage, Christianity is subtly transformed—initially into gnosticism, and more recently into idealism."[12] As Bonhoeffer therefore writes,

> By the way, I notice more and more how much I am thinking and perceiving things in line with the Old Testament; thus in recent months I have been reading much more the Old than the New Testament. Only when one knows that the name of God may not be uttered may one sometimes speak the name of Jesus Christ . . . Whoever

---

12. Dumas, *Theologian of Reality*, 144.

wishes to be and perceive things too quickly and too directly in New Testament ways is to my mind no Christian. (157)

In *CF* Bonhoeffer set forth a somewhat Christological reading of the Old Testament. In contrast, in *LPP* Bonhoeffer affirms the interpretation of the New Testament through the Old. However, the sense of worldliness is certainly no stranger to his earlier work. As described in chapters 3 and 5, at the heart of Bonhoeffer's thought is the involvement in humankind's sinful existence through the orders of preservation or mandates. Indeed, running throughout such essays as "Natural Life" and "Heritage and Decay" is the concept of the "ordering power" of life that works within nature and frustrates all attempts to subdue it. Throughout Bonhoeffer's Christological writing we find the nature of the incarnation as revealing not simply the "No" of God's condemnation, but also the profound "Yes" of Christ as truly human, as the "*ecce homo,*" calling humankind into true humanity. In both Dumas and Feil's overviews of Bonhoeffer's work the central unifying theme is that of "reality" and the explicit rejection of an antinomian position. However, the issue that arises most frequently in *LPP* is the distinction between the "ultimate" and the "penultimate" discussed in Bonhoeffer's essay, "Ultimate and Penultimate Things" (*E,* 146ff.). Here Bonhoeffer comes against those who would either proclaim ultimate, eternal concerns to the expense of penultimate, earthly issues, or those who would simply separate both realms from each other. Rather, Bonhoeffer argues that the penultimate things of our earthly existence find their meaning and legitimation through the ultimate that defines and establishes them. For Bonhoeffer, salvation does not raise us out of our earthly life, but releases us into it.

As both Bethge and Kelly point out, Bonhoeffer came under the influence of Nietzsche at an early stage in his career, and this can perhaps be seen most significantly in "Nietzsche's tremendous plea for the earth and for loyalty to its creatures."[13] Although his conclusions are clearly at odds with Bonhoeffer, Nietzsche's leitmotif of humankind's liberation from the unnatural, inauthentic, and predominantly "Christian" bondage stands in direct continuity with Bonhoeffer's thoughts. For Nietzsche, Christianity is not simply "hostile to life,"[14] but creates an illusion in the place of reality.[15] Within this illusion, therefore, Christianity is "hatred of *mind,* of pride, courage, freedom, *libertinage* of mind . . . hatred of the *senses,* of the joy of the senses, of joy in general,"[16] hatred of all that is natural to man.[17] In relation to the incarnation as the divine "Yes" to humankind it is striking that Nietzsche argues that through Christianity the concept of God has become "degenerated to the *contradiction of life,* instead of being its transfiguration and eternal *Yes!*"[18]

---

13. Bethge, "Life and Theology," 27.

14. Nietzsche, *Twilight,* 52.

15. Ibid., 137.

16. Ibid., 143.

17. Ibid., 137.

18. Ibid., 140.

In relation to "religion" as forged through the *cor curvum in se*, Kelly points towards the influence of Feuerbach who described religion as merely the "projection of man."[19] And in relation to his criticisms of Seeberg and Hegel, Wüstenberg argues that for Bonhoeffer, any concept that has revelation becoming religion is "ultimately idealistic."[20] Dumas agrees and suggests that the catastrophe occurred for Bonhoeffer when Christianity became more closely linked to neo-Platonic idealism than to the Old Testament.[21] Interestingly, in *Beyond Good and Evil*, Nietzsche directs his argument in the same direction, suggesting not only that "Christianity is Platonism for 'the people,'"[22] but that to strap the New Testament of weak mercy and inwardness onto the earthly Old Testament to form a single book is a "sin against the spirit."[23]

Bonhoeffer clearly appreciated Nietzsche's understanding of Christianity's frustration of the authentically human. The difference is simply that for Bonhoeffer what Nietzsche is riling against is not Christianity but rather "religion." For it is religion, the idealistic interpretation of Christianity, that has undermined humankind, and stands in opposition to the truly Christian God who shouts his "Yes" at the truly human life.

RELIGIONLESS CHRISTIANITY—THE RENEWED RELATIONSHIP

In *Redeeming Nietzsche*, Fraser comments, "Nietzsche's message is not just that there is no God, but that the very idea that human life requires some source of meaning external to itself is both false and ultimately degrading."[24] Similarly, Bonhoeffer not only argues that the world has come of age and that humankind has lost its religious *a priori* but, in a qualified sense, that humankind does not need God to fulfil his earthly potential. Humankind has been created and released to live, think, and create without the overwhelming intervention of God. In order to sustain itself and its presentation of God as the *deus ex machina* Bonhoeffer argues that religious Christianity has emphasized the issues of sin and guilt, in order to reaffirm a need to which it can respond. For Nietzsche, Christian faith is purely concerned with the issue of an "over-ripe, manifold and much-indulged conscience."[25] Furthermore, Christianity has actually developed the concepts of guilt, punishment, and the entire "moral world-order" as a weapon against the march of science and humankind's maturity.[26] Indeed, Nietzsche rejects the whole area of psychology as it "has hitherto remained anchored to moral prejudices and timidities."[27] In this light, Bonhoeffer attacks both existential philosophers and psychotherapists as offshoots of Christianity, who force people into their sins, and "prove to secure, contented, and

19. Kelly, "'Non Religious' Christianity," 125; cf. *LPP*, 478.

20. Wüstenberg, *Theology of Life*, 42f.

21. Dumas, *Theologian of Reality*, 153.

22. Nietzsche, *Beyond*, 32.

23. Ibid., 80.

24. Fraser, *Redeeming Nietzsche*, 73.

25. Nietzsche, *Beyond*, 75.

26. Nietzsche, *Twilight*, 177.

27. Nietzsche, *Beyond*, 53.

happy human beings that they are in reality miserable and desperate and just don't want to admit that they are in a perilous situation, unbeknown to themselves, from which only existentialism or psychotherapy can rescue them" (*LPP*, 427, cf. 450, 457).

Religion for Bonhoeffer is therefore not simply a garment placed over Christianity, but has become the condition of salvation, the hoop through which everyone must jump, the barrier between the world and truth. For Bonhoeffer the question of religion is Paul's question of circumcision, and must be dealt with in the same way. As Bonhoeffer declares, "Freedom from περιτομη [circumcision] is also freedom from religion" (366). Religion must be removed as not only is it incomprehensible to secular humankind, but it has been revealed to be false.

The question that Bonhoeffer must therefore answer is what Christianity legitimately looks like, and how it can be manifest to a world come of age. This question is not an entirely new one to him. In the opening paragraph of *Discipleship* Bonhoeffer questions,

> Behind the daily catchwords and battle cries needed in the Church Struggle, a more intense, questioning search arises for the one who is our sole concern, for Jesus himself. What did Jesus want to say to us? What does he want from us today? How does he help us to be faithful Christians today? It is not ultimately important to us what this or that church leader wants. Rather, we want to know what Jesus wants . . . It is not as if our church's preaching were no longer God's word, but there are so many dissonant sounds, so many human, harsh laws, and so many false hopes and consolations, which still obscure the pure word of Jesus and make a genuine decision more difficult. We surely intend our preaching to be preaching Christ alone. But it is not solely the fault of others if they find our preaching harsh and difficult because it is burdened with formulations and concepts foreign to them. (*D*, 37)

Although Bonhoeffer did not consider the answer in terms of a total rejection of "religion," the question and its context within the world are the same. What then is true Christianity, and how can one authentically proclaim it?

As described, idealist religion has painted Christianity according to certain ideas: a belief in God as omnipotent and transcendent, of God as the answer to life, of humankind's identity forged in his weakness and guilt, of the separation of the eternal from the temporal, the internal from the external. Bonhoeffer's contention is that on each point, Christianity is entirely the opposite. When Nietzsche argued that Christianity had warred against the strong and "*higher* type of man," in favor of the sickly,[28] Bonhoeffer argues that religion has sought to make God strong and humankind weak. In contrast, the essence of Bonhoeffer's religionless Christianity is to stress the strength of humankind orientated around God's weakness.

For Bonhoeffer, God does not set himself up against the world, but rather steps into it, and affirms it through the incarnation. Furthermore, it is not simply a matter of affirming his earthly life, but also humankind's potential and maturity within it. For Bonhoeffer, the concept of the "world come of age" is clearly positive. Quite apart from trying to draw humankind out of it, God's desire is to drive humankind into a more authentic inhabitation of it. As he declares throughout *Ethics*, Christ did not come to make people more di-

---

28. Cf. Nietzsche, *Twilight*, 129.

vine, but more human. God has established the world and its order through the mandates, and has given humankind life in abundance. Humankind does not obviously need God in his day-to-day life. In contrast to religion's assertion that humankind cannot live without God as its answer, Bonhoeffer argues that humankind needs to live, "*etsi deus non daretur*"—even if there were no God (*LPP*, 476). In a now famous passage Bonhoeffer argues,

> [W]e cannot be honest unless we recognize that we have to live in the world—"etsi deus non daretur." And this is precisely what we do recognize—before God! God himself compels us to recognize it. Thus our coming of age leads us to a truer recognition of our situation before God. God would have us know that we must live as those who manage our lives without God. The same God who is with us is the God who forsakes us (Mark 15:34!). The same God who makes us to live in the world without the working hypothesis of God is the God before whom we stand continually. Before God, and with God, we live without God. (479)

Bonhoeffer is not suggesting that humankind does not ultimately need God, nor is he undermining the consequences of sin in both its eternal and social sense.[29] Rather, Bonhoeffer is arguing against the concept of God as a necessary "working hypothesis" without which life is meaningless (478). God desires humankind to be released into his life armed with his own potential and creativity, within the orders that God has set in place.

God must not be seen as the answer to life but rather as its meaning—the one presupposes distinction, the other unity. In the guise of the *deus ex machina* God has more and more been pushed to the extremities of life. The point for Bonhoeffer is that God does not interact with the world through omnipotent, transcendent strength, but rather through weakness. God revealed his power not through a subjection of the world but through submitting to it. God does not transcendently exist at the extremities of life looking in, present only in the religious "answers," but rather at the very center, in amongst life. So Bonhoeffer declares,

> God consents to be pushed out of the world on to the cross; God is weak and powerless in the world and in precisely this way, and only so, is at our side and helps us. Matt 8:17 makes it quite clear that Christ helps us not by virtue of his omnipotence but rather by virtue of his weakness and suffering! This is the crucial distinction between Christianity and all religions. Human religiosity directs people in need to the power of God in the world, God as deus ex machina. The Bible directs people toward the powerlessness and the suffering of God; only the suffering God can help. (479)

In just the same way, the strength and calling of true Christianity is not to rule over the world in separation from it, but rather to stand alongside God in his suffering, to partake of it within the world, to be Christ in the world. Christians are not called to adopt a spiritual identity in opposition to the world, but rather to become truly human. As Woelfel points out, the heart of Bonhoeffer's concerns in a religionless Christianity can be found in the essay "Ethics as Formation."[30] Here Bonhoeffer argues, "The church's concern is not religion, but the form of Christ and its taking form among a band of people" (*E*, 97).

---

29. Cf. *SC* where sin has corrupted both divine and social relationships.

30. Woelfel, "Bonhoeffer's Portrait," 340f.

Drawing heavily on the issues of ethics and discipleship already discussed in chapters 5 and 6, Bonhoeffer argues against the systematization of Christianity through ethical and religious programs, to declare that what it means to be a Christian, what it means to be the church as the body of Christ, is to be in undivided relationship with the living Christ to embody his will and desire for the world. All human ballast must be discarded for the sake of that relationship. In a powerful passage Bonhoeffer therefore declares,

> The form of Christ is one and the same at all times and in all places. The church of Christ is also One throughout all generations. Still, Christ is not a principle according to which the whole world must be formed. Christ does not proclaim a system of that which would be good today, here, and at all times. Christ does not teach an abstract ethic that must be carried out, cost what it may. Christ was not essentially a teacher, a lawgiver, but a human being, a real human being like us. Accordingly, Christ does not want us to be first of all pupils, representatives and advocates of a particular doctrine, but human beings, real human beings before God. Christ did not, like an ethicist, love a theory about the good; he loved real people. Christ was not interested, like a philosopher, in what is "generally valid," but in that which serves real concrete human beings. Christ was not concerned about whether "the maxim of an action" could become "a principle of universal law," but whether my action now helps my neighbor to be a human being before God. God did not become an idea, a principle, a program, a universally valid belief, or a law; God became human. That means that the form of Christ, though it certainly is and remains one and the same, intends to take form in real human being, and thus in quite different ways. (*E*, 98)

This passage summarizes Bonhoeffer's religionless thought. For as he writes in his letters,

> Being a Christian does not mean being religious in a certain way, making oneself into something or other (a sinner, penitent, or saint) according to some method or other. Instead it menas being human, not a certain type of human being, but the human being Christ creates in us. It is not a religious act that makes someone a Christian, but rather sharing in God's suffering in the worldly life. (*LPP*, 480)

When humankind's autonomy, creativity, and potential are affirmed by God this has implications for the way in which Christianity and the gospel message are therefore proclaimed. Firstly, its content will no longer stand in condemnation to humankind's life but redeem it and affirm it. Secondly, it will not appeal to humankind's weakness but rather to his strengths. Thirdly, it will not disrespect humankind's ability to consider its message and so to choose. As a final point, it will respect the progression of humankind's journey towards God and the different pathways that this may take.

For Bonhoeffer there had been several attempts to reformulate Christianity in light of a critique of religion, but each had fallen down by failing to understand the nature of Christianity and its affirmation of the world come of age. Bonhoeffer turns his attention to Barth whom he praises for being the first to properly critique religion. However, For Bonhoeffer, Barth's critique is not concerned with individual concepts themselves, of combing through Christianity to discern its religious elements, but rather a simple, epistemological statement. Religion is never weeded out from Christianity, but everything is simply redeemed through God's choice in using it. Barth offers no guidance to the nuances of the Christian faith, the priority of its ethics or doctrines, or their significance for secular existence. Everything is lumped in together for full acceptance or rejection. This, Bonhoeffer refers to as Barth's "like it or lump it" theology (373). Bonhoeffer therefore accuses Barth or presenting a "positivism of revelation" (364, 429). This complex term is further explained in Bonhoeffer's "Outline for a Book"—in which he planned to expand and explain these preliminary "religionless" thoughts—where he argues, "Karl Barth and the Confessing Church have encouraged us to entrench ourselves persistently behind the "faith of the church," and evade the honest question as to what we ourselves really believe" (502). Barth has once again re-established religion as the hoop through which the world must jump rather than the message of hope and affirmation that reaches out to humankind in his own existence.

The dangers of Barth's understanding for Bonhoeffer are twofold. Firstly, it fails to understand that there are "degrees of knowledge and degrees of understanding" within faith, to grasp the reality of humankind's relationship with God and its progression, as well as to admit that such degrees of faith and knowledge can be found within authentic, secular existence. Secondly, it fails to protect the deep mysteries of Christianity from profanation and exhaustion through constant repetition and superficial familiarity. Therefore, Bonhoeffer argues, "an 'arcane discipline' must be re-established, through which the mysteries of the Christian faith are sheltered against profanation" (373).

Bonhoeffer's criticisms of Barth strongly mirror those discussed in chapter 4 concerning God's transcendence. For Bonhoeffer, Christianity is not a belief or understanding whose principles are free from humankind, but created for humankind. Christianity is not concerned with eternal, immutable truths that humankind must somehow grasp from out of his existence, but truths that are designed for humankind within his existence. Like God, Christianity reaches down into humankind's existence and not the other way round.

At the end of the sermon written for the baptism of Dietrich Bethge, Bonhoeffer explains the nature of the church's proclamation and its root in Christ,

> It is not for us to predict the day—but the day will come—when people will once more be called to speak the word of God in such a way that the world is changed and renewed. It will be in a new language, perhaps quite nonreligious language, but liberating and redeeming like Jesus' language, so that people will be alarmed and yet overcome by its power—the language of a new righteousness and truth, a language proclaiming that God makes peace with humankind and that God's kingdom is drawing near. (390)

Unlike Bultmann's programme of demythologization, Bonhoeffer's point is not that Christianity needs to be modernized to embrace contemporary existence (cf. 372, 430), but that, when removed from its religious interpretation, it is by nature relevant. To convert the Gospel would remain as much an idealist endeavor as the religious interpretation. Rather, it is a matter of re-submitting to God's voice in Scripture to hear its profound relevance and affirmation of life.

The Church in a World Come of Age

For Bonhoeffer, concrete action can only come from obedience to the present command of Christ. However, in the present situation Bonhoeffer believed that that voice could no longer be heard. As described in chapter 3, the task of the church in relation to the state is to question the state concerning its actions, bind the wounds of its victims, and finally to bring it to a grinding halt. For Bonhoeffer, the church had fulfilled none of its responsibilities. Most importantly, it had fought for its own survival instead of those who were falling victim all around it. When religious Christianity is defined according to a divine superiority and immutability towards humankind's existence, a separation from the world, a false understanding of strength, so Bonhoeffer believed that these ideas manifested themselves in the actions of the church. In contrast to a church that stands by God in his suffering, giving itself to humankind, in the heat of battle the church had seen itself as an end that needed to be protected above all else. Rather, as de Lange argues, "the church is to be for others just as Jesus was."[31] As Bonhoeffer argues in "Christ, Reality, and Good,"

> The church can only defend its own space by fighting, not for space, but for the salvation of the world. Otherwise the church becomes a "religious society" that fights for its own interest and thus has ceased to be the church of God in the world. So the first task given to those who belong to the church of God is not to be something for themselves, for example, by creating a religious organization or leading a pious life, but to be witnesses of Jesus Christ to the world. (*E*, 64)

As de Lange describes,

> Herein lies a significant cause of the disappointment of Bonhoeffer in the direction "his" Confessing Church took. It stood up for itself. With great difficulty and display of courage it established its own space in a totalitarian state. But it did not put its commitment to the service of others whose humanity was being violated outside the walls of the church. It stood up for itself but did not, as Bonhoeffer did by his participation in political resistance, stand up for Germany in general and for the Jews in particular.[32]

As described in chapter 3, it was in part because of the church's failure that Bonhoeffer became politically involved.[33] To the specific content of the religionless interpretation of Christianity Bonhoeffer therefore admits at the end of the baptism sermon,

> In these words and actions handed down to us, we sense something totally new and revolutionary, but we cannot yet grasp it and express it. This is our own fault. Our church has been fighting during these years for its self-preservation, as if that were an end in itself. It has become incapable of bringing the word of reconciliation and redemption to humankind and to the world. So the words we used before must lose their power, be silenced, and we can be Christians today in only two ways, through prayer and in doing justice among human beings. All Christian thinking, talking, and organizing must be born anew. (*LPP*, 389)

31. de Lange, *Waiting*, 29.

32. Ibid., 28.

33. Cf. Bethge, "Life and Theology," 69.

As Woelfel argues, "word and action are inseparable for Bonhoeffer."[34] Therefore, not only was it impossible for the church to hear Christ's words to the world, but its own words had become deformed and meaningless because of its actions.

Bonhoeffer's perceptions of the church appear to change over the course of his life, and especially while in prison. Anticipating the "cheap grace" of *Discipleship*, in *SC* Bonhoeffer criticizes the church for becoming like theatres, pandering to its audience with soothing music and joyful words (*SC*, 94). In *Christology*, Bonhoeffer further attacks the church for its elitist message and vision, such that "for the working-class world, Christ seems to be settled with the church and bourgeois society" (*C*, 35). By the end of 1940 and the essay "Guilt, Justification, Renewal," Bonhoeffer's understanding of the church's failure was very different. Here, over a number of pages, he outlines the guilt of the church, for such reasons as having made its message unclear and timid, misusing the name of Christ, and undermining God's orders within the world. However, its consistent theme is its guilt for having coveted its own security and peace, for having silently looked on while the people all around it were exploited, slandered, brutalized, oppressed, hated, and murdered. "The church was mute when it should have cried out, because the blood of the innocent cried out to heaven" (*E*, 138). As described in chapter 3, for Bonhoeffer this was most significantly found in the church's failure concerning the question of the Jews.

Following the continued silence of the church, following his involvement in the failed assassination attempt, following his arrest, Bonhoeffer's perception changed. In an earlier letter from the end of 1943 this is suggested as Bonhoeffer comments to Bethge, "'Lies' are the destruction of and the enmity against the real as it is in God; whoever tells the truth cynically is lying. By the way, I miss worship so remarkably little. What is the reason for this?" (*LPP*, 223). Bonhoeffer doesn't ever rescind his earlier ecclesiology. However, as revealed in the baptism sermon, for the time being the church has lost its identity. Like the Israelites forced to walk the desert for forty years, entering the promised land only after its unfaithful generation had given way to the new, so Bonhoeffer stresses the importance of the next generation for the renewed identity of the church. Until that moment, the church must re-establish the works of Christ before His words may be heard and the power of their proclamation restored.

Throughout Bonhoeffer's letters, there is a sense that an understanding of the actual content of a religionless interpretation of Christianity lies finally beyond his grasp. Whether this is because of the communal guilt of the church is not clear. However, as Christ's words are always spoken "*hic et nunc*," as Bonhoeffer looks forward to this as yet unknown society, he cannot yet know Christ's command. What is clear is that the religionless interpretation will embody the desire of Christ in proclaiming words, not simply of relevance, but of liberation and redemption for people within their lives. One senses that, in contrast to religion's concept of God's strength, the power of these words to shock the individual will be forged in part through the empathy of Christ, having experienced all of humankind's weakness and pain. In opposition to the immutable words of religion

---

34. Woelfel, "Portrait," 340.

that places the onus on humankind to understand them, not only will the truly Christian words be understandable, but they will be words of understanding.

The words themselves remain elusive to Bonhoeffer. However, in the "Outline for a Book" Bonhoeffer describes the life and form of the renewed church, standing in affirmation and consistency with its message:

> The church is church only when it is there for others. As a first step it must give away all its property to those in need. The clergy must live solely on the freewill offerings of the congregations and perhaps be engaged in some secular vocation [Beruf]. The church must participate in the worldly tasks of life in the community—not dominating but helping and serving. It must tell people in every calling [Beruf] what a life with Christ is, what it means "to be there for others" . . . It will have to see that it does not underestimate the significance of the human "example" . . . the church's word gains weight and power not through concepts but by example. (382)

PART 2
THE ATTACKS CONSIDERED

Kierkegaard and Bonhoeffer Considered

As discussed in chapter 1, Bonhoeffer owned a substantial number of Kierkegaard texts, the majority of which concern his final attack on Christendom. Indeed, two of the editions contained collections from *The Moment*. Although it is unclear at what point Bonhoeffer read them, they were clearly on Bonhoeffer's radar from an early stage, having been recommended to him by his friend and fellow student, Richard Widmann, while he was writing *SC*.[35]

Throughout his letters Bonhoeffer makes reference to a plethora of writers who have been picked up and discussed by commentators as sources of inspiration. However, apart from more general comments, such as from C. B. Armstrong that "The reaction against orthodox beliefs and religious practices received an immense impulse from Kierkegaard," Kierkegaard appears to have been sidelined, appearing rather as an "also ran."[36] So in Wüstenberg's substantial work on *LPP* and its influences, Kierkegaard is referenced only once in a list of authors that Bonhoeffer also read while in prison.[37] Even Kelly, who is to date the most substantial commentator on Kierkegaard's influence, doesn't mention him in his various articles on Bonhoeffer's later works, preferring instead to concentrate on such figures as Nietzsche and Feuerbach.[38]

Part of the reason for this omission may well be simply that although Kierkegaard is famous for having made an attack on the church, its actual content is far less familiar. It may also be that in *LPP* one finds some of the greatest differences between Bonhoeffer and Kierkegaard. Indeed, if one did not know of Bonhoeffer's earlier appreciation of

---

35. Bethge, *Bonhoeffer*, 82.

36. Armstrong, "Without Religion," 176.

37. Wüstenberg, *Theology of Life*, 100.

38. Cf. Kelly, "'Non Religious' Christianity."

Kierkegaard, a superficial reading might suggest Kierkegaard as a prime object of his critique.

Some Critical Observations

METHODOLOGICAL CONSIDERATIONS

Both writers understood their tasks in very different ways. While Bonhoeffer attempted to express the future form of Christianity, so Kierkegaard explicitly sought to avoid doing so. This presents an immediate barrier to comparison.

However, a second issue arises from potential incompatibilities between Bonhoeffer's earlier works and the incomplete thoughts of *LPP*. The issue of cheap grace clearly plays a strong role in both writers' attacks on Christendom. However, a dichotomy exists between Bonhoeffer's conception of the church as pandering to the ease of life through the watering down of the gospel on the one hand, and its apparent desire to force people into their sins and to separate itself from the world on the other. Does Bonhoeffer consider the church to be claiming members through emphasizing their guilt, but then keeping them happily within its fold by offering them grace and discipleship at a bargain price? When comparing Kierkegaard and Bonhoeffer's attacks on Christendom, one must ask whether Bonhoeffer has changed his emphasis on worldliness, from what Hopper would describe as a more acosmic stance in *Discipleship* to the embracing of the world in *LPP*. For Kierkegaard, the movement of Christendom is purely in one direction, towards worldliness.

SUFFERING AND THE OLD TESTAMENT

In July 1944 Bonhoeffer writes, "Now, should one oppose the cross with the OT blessing? That is what Kierkegaard did. This turns the cross and/or suffering into a principle, and this is precisely what gives rise to an unhealthy Methodism that denies suffering its quality of contingency within divine providence" (*LPP*, 492). For Bonhoeffer, Kierkegaard's assertion that discipleship and imitation require suffering removes the individual from God's will and converts suffering into a principle. Whether or not Bonhoeffer is interpreting Kierkegaard correctly,[39] in *EK* Kierkegaard reveals the difference that their thoughts were taking concerning suffering and the Old Testament. As Kierkegaard writes,

> It is not easy to have both the Old and the New Testament, for the O.T. contains altogether different categories. What, indeed, would the N.T. say about a faith which believes that it is going to be well off in the world, in temporality, instead of giving this up in order to grasp the eternal. Hence the instability of clerical discourse, depending on whether it shows forth the Old or New Testaments. (*JP*, 206/*Pap*, IV A 143; *EK*, 8)

For Bonhoeffer, Kierkegaard separated the Old Testament from the New rather than interpreting the New through the Old in a direct line of consistency. However, this once again

---

39. In Kierkegaard there appears to be a tension between theory and practice, such that he would assert that in theory one is obedient to God for whatever he should desire—suffering or pleasure—but that in practice, the imitation of Christ in relation to the world will mean suffering.

suggests a shift in Bonhoeffer's thought as in *CF* he interprets the Old Testament through the New.

Religiousness

As has already been discussed in chapter 3, something of an explanation towards the shift in Bonhoeffer's thought can be seen when Bonhoeffer looks back over his life and writes, "I thought I myself could learn to have faith by trying to live something like a saintly life. I suppose I wrote *Discipleship* at the end of this path. Today I clearly see the dangers of that book, though I still stand by it" (*LPP*, 486). At that stage in his life at least, Bonhoeffer believed that he manifest something of a religious spirit by trying to make himself something—such as "a saint, converted sinner, or a churchman"—rather than simply embracing the life and path that God desired for him (486). As has been argued by Feil and Hopper, it is this shift that is the foundation of Bonhoeffer's move from the potentially anti-worldly perspective of *Discipleship* to the worldliness of *LPP*. Not only is no such movement present for Kierkegaard but, as Feil and Hopper argue, Bonhoeffer's transition may represent a move away from him.

Sin

For Bonhoeffer, the religious spirit can be found manifest in the desire to knock the individual into his sin before granting him the gift of grace. It is difficult not to sense Kierkegaard's presence when Bonhoeffer particularly refers to existential philosophy and psychotherapy as being its main culprits. Indeed, sin for Kierkegaard is the main impetus behind salvation and so the proclamation of Christianity. Sin stands as the root of his understanding of anxiety and despair, and is the natural impetus behind humankind's desire and need for God. As he argues in *EK*, "Remove the anguished conscience, and you may as well close the churches and turn them into dance halls. The anguished conscience understands Christianity" (*JP*, 2461/*Pap*, VII1 A; *EK*, 16).

Despite the apparent contradiction between Bonhoeffer and Kierkegaard on this point, the issue is far more nuanced. Kierkegaard's point is not simply based on Christianity as the answer to the need for sin, but rather that Christianity can only be understood by the individual through an understanding of his own sin. Furthermore, he argues—linked perhaps to his assertions in *SUD* that most people are unaware of themselves being in a state of despair—that awareness of one's sin is not something that the individual naturally knows, but must rather have revealed to him. Consequently, "It is therefore entirely consistent for Luther to teach that a person must be taught by a revelation concerning how deeply he lies in sin" (*JP*, 2461/*Pap*, VII1 A 192; *EK*, 16).

Bonhoeffer is not clear about when and how sin is to be used within the Gospel proclamation. This has provoked major criticism of his later ideas. In *The Abolition of Religion*, Morris interprets Bonhoeffer as seeing salvation coming through the self-fulfilment of an authentic earthly existence, rather than through repentance and confession. In relation to Bonhoeffer's emphasis on the Old Testament promoting the idea of a holy worldliness, Morris therefore laments, "It is distressing that so eminent a theologian and so brave a martyr as Bonhoeffer should in his last days concentrate on the Old Testament to such an extent that Christ is brought in only to confirm what has already been discovered in the Old Testament."[40] Consequently, Morris wonders whether Bonhoeffer's ideas should be seen not as a "religionless Christianity" but rather a "religionless Judaism." Morris does not take into account the context of religionless Christianity to Bonhoeffer's wider work. And it is clear that Bonhoeffer is certainly not trying to get rid of sin, nor the idea that Christianity can only be understood through the concept of it. However, despite the ambiguity of his thought, it appears that he is steering—whether consciously or not—away from Kierkegaard and Luther on this matter.

Parallels and Influence

Despite these differences, there are a number of important parallels and potential points of influence that suggest that Kierkegaard stands very much behind Bonhoeffer's attack. In order to understand this better the central issues of Bonhoeffer's concept will be analyzed one by one before turning to the theory of a religionless Christianity as a whole.

THE RELIGIOUS A PRIORI

Although discussed in very different ways to Bonhoeffer, Kierkegaard's thought revolves around the notion of a religious *a priori*, revealed through the concept of despair, but in the most part, lost to each individual. As discussed above, the most common form of despair is "the despair which is ignorant of being despair" (*SUD*, 73). Consequently, such individuals have lost their understanding of themselves as spirit and, therefore, a true knowledge of themselves before God.

For Kierkegaard, the loss of the religious *a priori* is clearly negative. Furthermore, by the time of writing *The Moment*, Kierkegaard suggests that the final movement into spiritlessness has occurred, such that the ability to become a Christian or to embrace the authentically religious life is no longer possible (*M*, 34, 158).

Kierkegaard's position therefore raises several questions. First, does Bonhoeffer believe that humankind is by nature a-religious or has simply lost touch with his *a priori* potential, as for Kierkegaard? Bonhoeffer asks what would happen if the religious *a priori* were discovered to be a "historically conditioned and transitory form of human expression," that doesn't exist, but ultimately neither provides the answer nor affirms whether this is even possible (cf. *LPP*, 363). In his earlier works Bonhoeffer stands in line with Luther and Kierkegaard in terms of the conscience and the more general psychological realm that suggests some form of *a priori* knowledge. However, has this been rejected? Secondly, one must ask whether Bonhoeffer considers the loss of this *a priori* positively or negatively. It is clear that its loss has effected humankind's ability to "come of age" and escape the unhelpful clutches of the church but, if it has simply been lost, is this positive *in itself*? Once again, Bonhoeffer does not provide a comprehensive answer.

---

40. Morris, *Abolition*, 109.

Worldliness

In contrast to Bonhoeffer's notion of a holy worldliness, Kierkegaard has been charged with presenting a decidedly anti-worldly perspective. This can be seen, for instance, in many of the irrationalist interpretations that have been discussed in preceding chapters. Indeed, one suspects that Kierkegaard is the prime suspect of Feil's claims that Bonhoeffer is reacting against the "latent acosmic perspective" of the nineteenth century.[41] In terms of *The Moment*, however, Law goes so far as to suggest that in the end Kierkegaard not only totally rejected the church as a concept, but that his dismissal of the world suggests a form of gnosticism. As he summarizes, "Kierkegaard seems to come close to a Gnostic view of God's relation to the world according to which the world is irredeemably evil and the task of the Savior is to allow the select few to escape from it. Indeed, in the final editions of *The Moment* Kierkegaard seems to be advocating what we might call Christian nihilism or Christian masochism."[42]

The Moment is full of such declarations as, "Christianity is the renunciation of this world" (*M*, 226). However, to suggest that Kierkegaard is presenting a Gnostic gospel is to ignore the concept of the "two realms" that has been argued runs throughout his thought. These realms are not separated in terms of areas of life, but rather the interpretation of life. Consequently, when Kierkegaard speaks of the renunciation of the "world" he is referring to the human interpretation and understanding of the world, not that described and determined by God.

Law is himself influenced by Bonhoeffer, and his criticisms are laced throughout with Bonhoefferian language, particularly concerning the nature of the incarnation as the affirmation of "the human." However, the irony must surely be that Bonhoeffer is perhaps himself drawing on Kierkegaard for such statements. In "Ethics as Formation" Bonhoeffer describes Christ as *"ecce homo,"* as the example and affirmation of humankind's temporal existence. In direct similarity Kierkegaard therefore comments in *EK*, "Everything Christ expresses belongs essentially to a Christian's life. He who does not express this *ecce homo* is really not a true Christian" (*JP*, 1847/*Pap*, IX A 82; *EK*, 46).

For Kierkegaard, Christ is the prototype for Christian imitation, making people more truly human rather than divine. Alongside the evidence provided in chapter 4 concerning *CUP*, when we turn to *FSE* and *JFY* these ideas are clearly affirmed. Kierkegaard argues that when Christianity is revealed to its highest, people will decry that it is "treason against being human" (*JFY*, 141, cf. 177). However, this is simply the opinion of an intoxicated world. For in reality, the world creates "half-humans" (99), the person who "scarcely resembles a human being" (97). In contrast, true Christianity is that which affirms the human, and directs it to its intended state. So Kierkegaard exhorts,

> This is how . . . you are to read God's Word, and just as, according to superstition, one can conjure up spirits by reading incantations, in the same way you will . . . read a fear and trembling into your soul so that, with God's help, you will succeed in *becoming a human being,* a personality, rescued from being this dreadful nonentity

41. Feil, *Theology*, xix.
42. Law, "Anti-Ecclesiology," 102.

into which we humans, created in the image of God, have been bewitched, an imper-
sonal, an objective something. (*FSE*, 43—author's emphasis)

Kierkegaard's whole psychological writing is forged around the idea that the individual
only becomes spirit or self when he is "grounded transparently in the power that established it" (*SUD*, 44). It should come as no surprise therefore that this is most truly manifest
through the guidance and imitation of Christ. These ideas are affirmed in the sections of
CD that Bonhoeffer himself owned. Here Kierkegaard argues that in the face of the rigors
of authentic Christianity, *the* temptation that comprises the many is "by doing away with
God, to cease to be a human being . . . to sink below the animal" (*CD*, 35). A little later
Kierkegaard affirms, "To slay God is the most dreadful suicide" (67). For Kierkegaard,
the whole idealist method of trying to deal with Christ is simply the destruction of one's
nature as human.

In a later section of *JFY* human existence in its labor within the world is affirmed.
As Kierkegaard argues, humankind must learn from the lilies and the birds to work in the
world with all his might, and yet to trust in God for every need and the direction his life
takes, understanding that it is really God who works through him. To this Kierkegaard
therefore declares, "Man, man, callous understanding, will you never learn from the bird
to lose your senses in order to become a human being!" (*JFY*, 184). The image of the lilies
and the birds, and the desire for the truly human to be found in divinely submitted work
within the world, is essentially represented through the aesthetic ideas of the "life-view"
and knowledge as "*re-spiratio*." For here truth and knowledge are received neither through
abstract thought nor transcendent revelation, but rather as a gift of God through the authentic saturation of oneself in the world. So Kierkegaard comments in *LR*, in relation to
the life-long process of the life-view, "we seem to lack the patience to learn in this way
what it is to be human, and to renounce the inhuman" (*LR*, 9).

The point is once again the conflict of the two realms within the world, and
Kierkegaard's desire to strip away that created by humankind's mind for that of God.
For in the latter the truth of real existence is found. This thesis has already concentrated
on the importance of the common man for Kierkegaard's thought, and it is the simplicity attached to such a life that placed the common man in such favor. In contrast to the
"bourgeois-philistines" who embody spiritlessness (cf. *JFY*, 199), the common man has
the ability to understand the truth for he is unbridled from the visible and outward world
of corruption and intoxication. In *FSE* Kierkegaard points towards the twelve disciples as
embodiments of the common man, whose simple, honest life, in contrast to that of the
Pharisees, allowed them the ability to understand and embrace Christ (*FSE*, 86). However,
for Kierkegaard such individuals are not isolated examples of what humankind should
be, but rather embodiments of human existence in its concrete form. For when in previous chapters it has been argued that it is the common man who understands the "either/
or" of life, the concept of contradiction, and so the ability to be passionate and decisive,
Kierkegaard argues that this is the true standard of "culture." So he argues, "The age of
revolution is essentially passionate, for which reason it essentially possesses *culture*. For
the degree of essential culture is the resilience of inwardness. A maidservant genuinely

in love is essentially cultured; a common man with his mind vigorously and passionately made up is essentially cultured" (*LR*, 54). What is important for Kierkegaard is not an abstract concept of "true humanity" but rather a "true humanity" found through "true existence" and the imitation of Christ.

Bonhoeffer's concept of "worldliness" is far more pronounced and defined than Kierkegaard's. However, the essential traits are the same. For Bonhoeffer it is equally a matter of simplicity before God, having cast aside the manmade strictures that lead one astray. In "Ethics as Formation" we have already seen the importance of the man of "simplicity and wisdom," who has divorced himself from ethical theories to rest unflinchingly in God's will. When we turn to *LPP* the issue is essentially the same. Here Bonhoeffer describes the importance of both "simpleness" as a gift from God, and "simplicity" as an intellectual and ethical endeavour, but each as marks of authentic Christianity in their ability to submit to God's understanding (*LPP (SCM)*, 212). So Bonhoeffer argues in one of his later letters, "simplicity is an intellectual achievement, one of the greatest" (385).[43]

Although it is unclear whether Bonhoeffer read *LR*, the parallels between Kierkegaard and Bonhoeffer are further emphasized as Bonhoeffer reflects Kierkegaard's definition of "culture" as bound to passionate decision. As Bonhoeffer remarks, "The only thing clear to me about the whole problem is that "culture" [Bildung] that fails you in a time of danger isn't culture. Culture must be able to face danger and death" (*LPP*, 194). Despite their different examples, their definitions of culture are essentially the same, as that bound to passionate decision and personal investment.

One of the major concerns over Law's opinions is found in his interpretation of Kierkegaardian suffering. In his analysis of "cheap grace," Law suggests that for Kierkegaard, "Christian discipleship consists in witnessing for the Gospel *against* the society in which the Christian lives."[44] Law therefore describes suffering and confrontation with the world to be initiated by the disciple himself. However, for Kierkegaard, suffering is not something sought out, but rather received by the disciple simply through expressing a life of imitation that stands in difference and so opposition to the world. In the example Law uses in our first quote above, Christ's miracles can be reconciled with a Kierkegaardian concept of suffering in that Christ received suffering because of his miracles. For Kierkegaard, to perform Christian love, Christian peace, Christian security means that one will face suffering because of the world's reaction to it, rather than because of the action in itself. For Kierkegaard, Christian suffering is a matter of reconciling the peace that Christ reveals in his life with the sword revealed through his proclamation.[45]

In contrast to Law, Daniel Jenkins argues that in Kierkegaard's work we find such an affirmation of the world that "it is Kierkegaard who has given us the classic picture of 'holy worldliness.'"[46] Indeed, although he does not make any suggestions of influence, Jenkins'

---

43. In DBWE 8, the juxtaposition is between "naïveté" and "simplicity." Although there is no evidence that he read them, Bonhoeffer's discussion here bears striking resemblance to the distinction Kierkegaard makes in his journals between "naïveté" and "primitivity" (cf. *JP*, 1610/*Pap*, VI B 98:45).

44. Law, "Cheap Grace," 135.

45. Cf. Matt 10:34.

46. Jenkins, *Beyond Religion*, 18.

whole thesis is founded on Bonhoeffer and Kierkegaard. Jenkins quotes large sections of *FT* to argue that in the knight of faith we find this picture of worldliness, where the knight "realizes the universally human" in everything he does. For unlike the knight of infinite resignation, who rejects the world in order to embrace the infinite, the knight of faith receives finitude back again, converted and redeemed through the infinite. He is one who "purchases every moment that he lives, 'redeeming the seasonable time' at the dearest price; not the least thing does he do except on the strength of the absurd . . . at every moment making the movement of infinity" (*FT*, 69). Indeed, "This man takes pleasure, takes part, in everything, and whenever one catches him occupied with something his engagement has the persistence of the worldly person whose soul is wrapped up in such things" (68).

These ideas are affirmed in *EK*, where Kierkegaard comments, "Faith hopes for this life also, but, note well, by virtue of the absurd, not by virtue of human understanding; otherwise it is only common sense, not faith" (*JP*, 5/*Pap*, IV A 108; *EK*, 7). Although bearing in mind the criticisms discussed in chapter 5, Jenkins' position is the same as that of Mooney, presenting the mediation of God in allowing Abraham to receive the whole world back again. For Mooney, *FT* presents the basis of a firm social theory.

How does this picture fit with the descriptions of *The Moment*? The portrayal in Kierkegaard's later works of the Christian in the world, the suffering he faces, and the heterogeneity of his life with that of the world, stand in contrast to that of the knight of faith who is unrecognisable within the world. However, the discrepancy is not found in the description of the knight of faith, but rather in that of the world in its reaction to the knight of faith. For once again, the issue of suffering is not that created by the individual against the world, but rather by the world against the individual. What this describes, therefore, is that in *The Moment* we find the same sense of worldliness as in *FT*, the same sense of embracing the world and living according to one's human nature, except that now Kierkegaard believes that the world will not allow the knight its enjoyment.

It is clear that Bonhoeffer's presentation of the world in *LPP* differs from that of *Discipleship*. However, the arguments that *Discipleship* and *LPP* are in strong counterposition to each other, and that it is from Kierkegaard that Bonhoeffer particularly gained his anti-worldly perspective, have been overplayed. One must ask how it is that Kierkegaard maintained his affirmation of the simple life of the common man throughout his life alongside what Feil and Hopper consider his acosmic ideas. Although it is unclear that Bonhoeffer would not have known the full extent of Kierkegaard's understanding of the common man, the worldliness of *LPP* bears marked similarity to it.[47] For both authors the life of simple wisdom is the life intended and ordained by God through which He is met. In contrast to Morris, this life aids the individual's relationship to God not because of a pantheistic meeting of God in it, but that through its simplicity the individual remains perpetually open to God.

As discussed in chapter 3, Bonhoeffer's oft-quoted reflections on *Discipleship* from *LPP* do not reflect a rejection of its content but rather Bonhoeffer's own mentality at the

---

47. From the works Bonhoeffer owned only *CUP* and *The Moment* contain Kierkegaard's thoughts on the matter.

time of writing. Given Bonhoeffer's understanding of the need to continually surrender one's mastery of life, every retrospective will consider one's past to have been that
of piety, religion, and mastery. Furthermore, Bonhoeffer was familiar with Kierkegaard's
more humanist tendencies before *Discipleship*. Indeed, as has been suggested in previous
chapters, Bonhoeffer gained not only the foundation for his understanding of community
from Kierkegaard but also, as seen through the interpretation of *FT* and represented in
Discipleship, its actual content.

There is a difference between Kierkegaard and Bonhoeffer concerning worldliness,
but it is less a formal difference as one of emphasis. As described, the juxtaposition between the life of the knight of faith in *FT* and that represented in *The Moment* is that
where in *FT* Kierkegaard believed that the individual was simply called to live out whatever life God chose for the individual, so in *The Moment* he believed that that life would
necessarily involve suffering because of the reaction of the world. It can be suggested that
for Bonhoeffer the movement has been reversed. In *Discipleship* Bonhoeffer essentially
argued that we are to live out the life God defines for us, so in *LPP* he suggests that this suffering may not necessarily be a forgone conclusion. Bonhoeffer's rejection of his religious
mentality in *Discipleship* was the rejection of the idea that suffering was that inevitability, and perhaps the sign of one's Christ-like life. The difference between *Discipleship* and
LPP, and therefore between Kierkegaard and Bonhoeffer, is simply a matter of suffering
as a "necessary conclusion." How then does Kierkegaard hold these two lives together,
of both the common man and of the necessity of suffering? The answer may simply be
that he did not consider the life of the common man to be lived in the same world as
that of persecuting society. Not only does Kierkegaard declare that his attacks are against
bourgeois society and not the common man, but he also considered escaping his battle by
disappearing into the country.

The World Come of Age

What has been argued throughout this thesis is that Kierkegaard is not an irrationalist, nor
interested in acosmic ends. Kierkegaard's works perpetually attack sagacity and speculative thought. However, his polemic is specifically only against its misuse. Christianity and
sagacity are mutually exclusive, but this does not necessarily undermine sagacity in itself.
Furthermore, Kierkegaard is well aware of the progression that humankind has undergone
since the enlightenment. In *JFY*, Kierkegaard describes "the change that has occurred in
the human race through increasing enlightenment and culture and liberation from all
unworthy pleasures," and declares, "Who will deny that this world has changed! For the
better? Well, that remains a question" (*JFY*, 155).

For Bonhoeffer, the world come of age is revealed in its confrontation with religious
Christianity, in having "outgrown" the explanations and presentations with which it was
plied and controlled. In the same way, Kierkegaard places humankind and his "maturity"
in relation to the church's explanation of God, and argues that the sagacity of the church
now finds itself confronted by the world's sagacity. So he argues,

> . . . the [church's] sagacity in deceiving has encountered an equally great sagacity in seeing through it. Period. This is the halt. The hard-earned working capital of three hundred years has been used up, ladies and gentlemen. No new deception can be squeezed out of it; nothing more can be extorted from it, because the sagacity in seeing through the deceptions has become just as great. The working capital has been used up; this is the financial statement. (130)

While he does not develop or particularly use the concept, at least on some level for Kierkegaard the world has "come of age." He remains extremely ambiguous as to whether this can be described as a good movement, but a movement it is nonetheless. As described, for both writers the most authentic life is that of simplicity. Consequently, even for Bonhoeffer, it is unclear whether this newfound maturity is positive in itself. For Bonhoeffer it does stand as a movement of humankind's autonomy, and therefore his God-given dignity. However, Kierkegaard would perhaps argue that this new "maturity" remains still an idealist movement of the crowd rather than as the expression of personal autonomy. For both, however, it has at least seen through the deception of religious Christianity.

The Defense of God

For Bonhoeffer, God has been forged into the *deus ex machina*, as the answer to life's questions and needs. However, this has arisen because of the growth in humankind's maturity, in the face of which, Bonhoeffer argues, "we leave room for God only out of anxiety" (*LPP*, 366). The abuse of existential philosophy and psychotherapy has already been mentioned. To this Bonhoeffer adds the endeavour of Christian apologetics that has done all it can top undermine humankind's self-confidence and "persuade the world that has come of age that it cannot live without 'God' as its guardian" (426f.). Religious Christianity has therefore confronted humankind's knowledge so as to undermine it and to place God in the remaining void (450). However, as a counter-measure, it seems, Bonhoeffer also suggests that God has been more firmly moved into the "internal" realm, away from the clutches of humankind's mind. So he comments, "God's being pushed out of the world, away from public human existence, has led to an attempt to hang on to God at least in the realm of the 'personal,' the 'inner life,' the 'private' sphere. And since each person has a 'private' sphere somewhere, this became the easiest point of attack" (344).

Ultimately, for Bonhoeffer, religious Christianity has sought to defend God in order to keep him alive within the world. These ideas find strong parallel in Kierkegaard. As Anti-Climacus argues in *SUD*,

> One can see how extraordinarily (supposing any extraordinariness remains)—how extraordinarily stupid it is to defend Christianity, how little knowledge of humanity it betrays, how it connives if only unconsciously with offense by making Christianity out to be some miserable object that in the end must be rescued by a defense. It is therefore certain and true that the person who first thought of defending Christianity in Christendom is *de facto* a Judas No.2; he too betrays with a kiss, except his treason is that of stupidity. To defend something is always to discredit it . . . Yes, the person who defends [Christianity] has never believed in it. If he does believe, then the en-

thusiasm of faith is not a defense, no, it is the assault and the victory; a believer is a victor. (*SUD*, 119)

Throughout Kierkegaard's later works, the issue of the church's desire to defend God and Christianity reappears. And for both Kierkegaard and Bonhoeffer it is perhaps the greatest sign of humankind's idealistic appropriation of God, moulding and weaving Him in order to resuscitate His presence in the world. No greater sign can be given of God having become an idea at the expense of His being.

For Kierkegaard, Christianity has been defended in at least two ways in order to make it compatible with the world's newly-matured sagacity (*JFY*, 155). First, Christianity has been converted into humankind's reason in order to be explained and proven. At the beginning of *PC*, Kierkegaard describes at length Christendom's attempts at demonstrating the truth of Christ in terms of his historical existence as well as the results of his life over the last 1,800 years. These attempts are blasphemy undermining his nature as supernatural by placing him under the natural judgment and examination of historical scholarship (cf. *PC*, 25f.). However, secondly, Christianity has been made comfortable and palatable. In *WL*, Kierkegaard describes how Christendom has removed the concept of offense in order that it might be better accepted (*WL*, 198–204). This is further clarified in *PC* where Anti-Climacus argues that Christendom has destroyed Christ's identity as person, by converting him into an idea in order to overcome the problems of contemporaneity (cf. *PC*, 206). Both the movements to prove Christ and to convert him into an idea have destroyed the power of his witness by undermining his authority and then allowing the "believer" to relate to him by way of knowledge rather than obedience. Christendom has destroyed the power of Christ's "Thou shalt" in both its authority and demand (cf. 230f.). As Anti-Climacus comments,

> They defended Christianity; there was never any mention of or use of authority; this "You shall" was never heard, lest it arouse laughter. They defended Christianity and said, "Do not reject Christianity; it is a gentle teaching, containing all the gentle consolations that everyone can easily come to need in life. Good Lord, life is not always smiling, we all need a friend, and such a friend is Christ. Do not reject him; he is kindly disposed toward you." (*PC*, 231)

However, the irony of the situation is that Christendom has succeeded in achieving the complete opposite of a defense by playing it into the hands of its enemies. By converting Christianity into an idea, faith is actually undermined by doubt. Kierkegaard argues that the moment Christianity became an idea, became converted in the realm of reason, so it allowed itself to be judged by reason. Such a movement therefore played Christianity into the hands of its enemy (230).

As described in chapter 6 concerning the relationship between faith and obedience, these ideas are summarized in "Thoughts that Wound from Behind," where Kierkegaard argues that by removing the authority of the message, doubt has been created by releasing the individual into fruitless reflection. In destroying the need for passionate decision, of making the first movement of obedience, the individual not only begins to doubt the truth but, by trying to combat it with reason and proofs, simply creates more doubt. Consequently, Kierkegaard argues,

> [A] kind of doubt has been opened up that Satan himself cannot combat but does indeed invent, a kind of doubt that is impossible to combat because to combat it actually requires one to go over to its side—that is, to conquer it one must oneself betray Christianity. In the Christian sense, the only weapon against doubt is, "Be still," or, Luther-like, "shut your mouth!" Doubt, however, says, "Get involved with me, fight me—with my own weapons." (*CD*, 190)

These ideas are affirmed in *PC* where Anti-Climacus writes concerning sagacity's understanding of the overly extreme commands of Christianity—"Then a perhaps well-meaning human sagacity began the sorriest of all enterprises—to betray Christianity by defending it. At that the devil secretly laughed and said to himself: Well, now I can sit back and relax, because the game is won" (*PC*, 230). For both Kierkegaard and Bonhoeffer religion has sought to defend Christianity, but by converting it into reasons, an idea, it has effectively sold it to its enemies. In "Thoughts that Wound from Behind," Kierkegaard argues that, like the Philistines to Samson, Christendom has betrayed Christianity and removed its strength (*CD*, 213). The point for both writers is that the power of the gospel lies in the personality of God, in the absolute demand of obedience, in the offense and paradox of Christ's life. It is this that has the ability to overcome and transform the individual away from the chains of his heart and mind turned in upon themselves. "God" should never have to do head-on battle with science, ethics, politics or any other earthly form. Its power is rather to wound from behind.

The Secret Discipline

As a counter-measure against religion, Bonhoeffer argues that the church must understand the notion of the "*Arkandisziplin*" or "secret discipline." In a somewhat Hauerwasian way, Jenkins argues that this term signifies the need for the church to hide away its exclusive, "religious" forms from the view of those who cannot understand them, in order to simply let its works of service speak.[48] However, as argued by William Nichols, this fails to take seriously the corruption that the mysteries of revelation have received from within the church.[49] In addition to the perversion of the *deus ex machina* Bonhoeffer argues that through the positivism of the church, the mysteries and sacred teachings of Christianity have become altered, exhausted, and taken in vain by constant and uncritical preaching, rather than protected in their true nature as mysteries. In Bonhoeffer's mind, it is not revelation that must be changed in order for it to become more understandable to us but, should this even be possible, we who must change in order to be able to understand it.

The most common way this manifests itself is in the use of the name of God. As Bonhoeffer reflects on the Old Testament he is struck by the idea that "the Israelites *never* say the name of God aloud" (*LPP*, 189). Consequently, he suggests that "only when one knows that the name of God may not be uttered may one sometimes speak the name of Jesus Christ" (213). In Christendom the names of God and Jesus Christ have become corrupted and meaningless. For Bonhoeffer, the dignity of the religionless person is found in part by the fact that he is more honest than the religious person because God remains a

---

48. Jenkins, *Beyond Religion*, 36.
49. Nicholls, *Systematic*, 221.

real and pure concept to him. Bonhoeffer comments that he has trouble speaking the name of God to religious people because "somehow [that name] doesn't ring true for me here, and I feel a bit dishonest saying it," so he can mention God's name to those with no religion without qualms (366). Indeed, while reading Otto's *The Gods of Greece*, Bonhoeffer suggests to Bethge that he finds something extremely attractive in the image of these foreign gods, and far less offensive than certain brands of Christianity, because they demand faith from the depth of human experience, and not from its weakness (440).

In a remarkably similar way, in *SUD* Kierkegaard comments,

> . . . while paganism mentioned God's name with some awe, with a healthy respect for the mysterious, and most often with great solemnity, in Christendom God's name is the word that occurs most often in everyday speech, and incontestably the word to which least meaning is attached and that is used with least care, because this pitiable revealed God . . . has become all too well known a personage to the population at large, who now do him an incalculable great service by going once in a while to church, where they are also commended by the priest who thanks them on God's behalf for the honour of the visit, and confers on them the title of piety, while making a few gibes at the expense of those who never do God the honour of going to church. (*SUD*, 148)

Likewise, in "Thoughts that Wound from Behind," Kierkegaard describes the way in which the call of God has been undermined and made insignificant by the monotony of its repetition (*CD*, 165). In *EK*, not only does Kierkegaard continue to speak of Christianity's language becoming "meaningless or topsy-turvey," but he frequently makes the contrast with paganism and the dignity with which it carried its own language and self-esteem (*JP*, 661/*Pap*, IX A 232; *EK*, 56).

As described above, it is clear that Bonhoeffer and Kierkegaard differ in terms of their appreciation of the Old Testament. However, Kierkegaard's perception is far more nuanced than suggested, for in parallel with Bonhoeffer, in *EK* Kierkegaard affirms the dignity of the Old Testament in terms of its address of God. As he comments,

> . . . religion assumes a certain silly solemnity in which there is no meaning and the name of God is named with the same empty veneration elicited by the ink-stand which in the supreme court represents the king. In our age, therefore, a simple and natural effusion of the religious becomes almost blasphemy, and the manner in which one in the Old Testament permitted himself to address God would scandalize, as something unseemly and in conflict with ritual, and yet those men certainly maintained a completely different, deep respect for God. (*JP*, 1330/*Pap*, IV A 106; *EK*, 6)

Kierkegaard does not discuss a "secret discipline," or suggest any formal method that should be applied. However, in keeping with Bonhoeffer's thought, once again in *EK* he suggests several times that it would be better if Christianity were not proclaimed than as it is done now (*JP*, 675/*Pap*, X2 A 19; *EK*, 85), and that the power of Christianity would become manifest through its silence. As he argues, "If it really ever happened that the proclamation of Christianity was silenced, its time would surely come again, instead of an appearance which is now maintained by the pitiable thing palmed off as Christianity" (*JP*, 4168/*Pap*, X2 A 240; *EK*, 91).

The Preaching of the Church

Following on from the previous point, for both Kierkegaard and Bonhoeffer there is a fundamental problem with the preaching of the church. Although Bonhoeffer is far less assertive than Kierkegaard in his criticisms, given the strength with which he described the authority of the church's preaching in his earlier works, it was of real frustration and sadness that the church had so easily betrayed this calling. For both writers, the essential error is the way in which the words of the minister have not been backed up by his life. Consequently, they have become meaningless. While this criticism runs throughout Kierkegaard's later works, for Bonhoeffer the issue is twofold. First, according to his attack on idealism, in the paper "What is Church?" Bonhoeffer argues that the preaching of the church has been taken over by sagacity, misusing the name of God and making Him into "a plaything, the false idol of human beings (B, 263). These ideas are backed up at the very beginning of *Discipleship* where he declares, "It is not as if our church's preaching were no longer God's word, but there are so many dissonant sounds, so many human, harsh laws, and so many false hopes and consolations, which still obscure the pure word of Jesus . . ." (*D*, 37). As described in the SCM edition, the preaching of the church has become overlaid with "so much human ballast" (*D* (SCM), 29).

Secondly, the church's words have become meaningless through its (in)actions. While in *Discipleship* Bonhoeffer still felt that the church had the ability to speak, so by the time of his imprisonment, Bonhoeffer believed that this was no longer the case. This is made strikingly clear in the sermon for the baptism of Dietrich Bethge. Here Bonhoeffer reveals that the present generation must now remain silent until a new generation arrives that gains the ability once again to hear God's voice and so speak to the world.

For both Kierkegaard and Bonhoeffer the church had become sick. As quoted at the beginning, Kierkegaard describes Christendom as like a confined hospital in which the air has become toxic and the whole religious life sick or expired (*M*, 158). The only solution is to let the whole building collapse to let fresh air in. Reflecting Bonhoeffer's earlier, far less extreme position, in "What is the Church?" Bonhoeffer argues that the air in the church has "become quite stale" and what is needed is a "reformer" to open the window (*B*, 263). By the time of his imprisonment Bonhoeffer's description would bear even greater similarity to Kierkegaard.

The Suffering of God

Before concluding our discussion, it is worthwhile turning once again to Heinrich Vogel. In his brief analysis, Vogel draws attention to similarities between Bonhoeffer's poem, "Christians and Pagans," and a passage from Kierkegaard's journals, entitled "Ascending Forms of Religiousness":

"Christians and Pagans"

1. Men go to God when they are sore bestead,
Pray to him for succour, for his peace, for bread,
For mercy for them sick, sinning, or dead;
All men do so, Christian and unbelieving.

2. Men go to God when he is sore bestead,
Find him poor and scorned, without shelter or bread,
Whelmed under weight of the wicked, the weak, the dead;
Christians stand by God in his hour of grieving.

3. God goes to every man when sore bestead,
Feeds body and spirit with his bread;
For Christians, pagans alike he hangs dead,
And both alike forgiving. (*LPP*, 348)

"Ascending Forms of Religiousness"

(A) The individual relates to God so that it may go well with him on earth—consequently to profit from the God-relationship in an earthly sense.

(B) The individual relates to God in order to be saved from sin, in order to triumph over his inclinations, in order to find in him a merciful judge—consequently in such a way that the relationship becomes altogether undialectical and the individual alone has benefit from this relationship.

(C) It is required that the individual must confess in word and in deed (self-denial, renunciation of finite aims) the faith in which his salvation lies, but the confession will have the result that the individual suffers, humanly speaking makes himself unhappy. This is where the dialectical aspect of gaining benefit from the God-relationship comes in; in his weak moments the God-relationship must appear to him to be a misfortune and a detriment since, humanly speaking, he would be rid of a lot of suffering by omitting the confession, the words of the confession as well as the deeds of the confession . . . (*JP*, 4459/*Pap*, X2 A 318; *ZFG*, 29)

This journal does not appear in any of the works within Bonhoeffer's library but, as Vogel points out, is found in the journal collection, *ZFG*, published in 1938, which he considers Bonhoeffer may have read.[50] Vogel does not suggest that these passages are the same, but argues that from both their form and progression influence is powerfully suggested.

CONCLUDING REMARKS

When Kierkegaard and Bonhoeffer's attacks on Christendom are considered as a whole, it is clear that certain presuppositions do not agree. While Kierkegaard may affirm that humankind has essentially lost his religious *a priori*, it is in a very different sense to Bonhoeffer. Where Kierkegaard argues that Christendom is a part of the loss of this *a priori*, so for Bonhoeffer Christendom stands in juxtaposition to the loss of the religious *a priori*, and acts in reaction against it. Indeed, one wonders whether in both these instances Bonhoeffer has in fact changed direction from his previous works, arguing against their psychological presuppositions, as well as such notions as the cheapening of Christianity that Kierkegaard more consistently follows through into his attack.

---

50. Vogel, "Christus als Vorbild," 301–2.

However, from this point striking parallels can be seen. Despite their differences concerning the direction of Christendom, both hold within their thought a sense of the world having "come of age," and agree on the failures of the church. Not only has the church taken the name of God in vain and cheapened the gospel message but, perhaps most importantly, it has not taken up its responsibility and fought for those around it. For both Kierkegaard and Bonhoeffer, the church has simply fought for its own survival. For both writers, this fight can be found both in the historical journey of the church, altering the Gospel message and seeking to defend Christianity against humankind's knowledge and potential, but also in their specific contexts in terms of the revolution of 1848 and the Second World War. In many ways, for both writers the specific events that they witnessed were merely the outworking of the church's historical nature.

In terms of the future, both writers appear to have been limited in what they felt they could say. Kierkegaard's limits were perhaps self-imposed, but despite his desire to go further, Bonhoeffer felt that the future was not open to his view. However, for both a halt had been reached, a division between the past and the future. For both Kierkegaard and Bonhoeffer this halt is manifest in two ways. First, in giving up its responsibility and undertaking its corruption the present church had become incapable of any further service. Consequently, a new generation is required. In his earlier *Fædrelandet* articles, Kierkegaard argued that should the possibility of a confession no longer be possible, then "everything must be burst so that in this nightmare individuals who are able to bear New Testament Christianity might once again come into existence" (*M*, 34). These thoughts are taken further in *JFY* where he comments,

> . . . this is the situation, Christianity has reached the point where it must be said: So now I am going to begin all over again from the beginning. Is there no one, then, whom I can move to overcome his disposition and be willing to understand what Christianity is, that to proclaim Christianity is to make sacrifices, to be willing to suffer. If there is such a one or if there are several such, then Christianity will once again begin to become power, something that "this doctrine" has not been for ages, something it never could be either, if being a Christian (not only being a pastor or professor) were to become a livelihood, a secular career. (*JFY*, 130)

However, secondly, for both writers the form of Christianity in the next generation must also be different. Bonhoeffer is far more specific in his understanding of the non-religious interpretation of Christianity. However, the central tenets are equally present in Kierkegaard. In *EK* Kierkegaard declares, "It is a matter neither more nor less than an auditing of Christianity; it is a matter of getting rid of 1,800 years as if they had never been" (*JP*, 6168/*Pap*, IX A 72; *EK*, 45). What is needed is a return to simplicity, divorced from the layers of pomp and circumstance that Christendom has lain over the top. As he argues, "let us once again worship God in simplicity instead of making a fool of him in magnificent buildings" (*M*, 158).

When one considers the issue of the two realms for both writers, the nature of their reinterpretations becomes clear. The point is not to modernize Christianity, to alter it in some way—as has been considered by such thinkers as J. A. T. Robinson and the "death of God" school—but rather to return it to the "realm of the spirit," to strip away the ballast that has been placed upon it over the last 1,800 or 1,900 years, and to return it to its rightful meaning. When one of the central themes of both writers' work is an attack on idealism, this sense of reinterpretation stands as its natural conclusion. For both writers, true Christianity is counter culture when it is understood as the idealism of the two ages. Although it is unclear whether he read it, missing as it is from his collection of *CD*, one is left to wonder what Bonhoeffer would have thought of Kierkegaard's definition of Christianity found in his title, "Thoughts that Wound from Behind." Against the Philistine desires of Christendom and proposed defense of Christianity, Kierkegaard declares, "Christianity is the attacker—in Christendom, of course, it attacks from behind" (*CD*, 162; cf. 216, 223). The desire behind both Kierkegaard and Bonhoeffer's representations of Christianity is to replace it in opposition to the "Christianity" of sagacity and the "outward and visible world." Both writers consider the strength and authority of Christianity to be bound to what is considered by this world as its weakness. For both, the authority of Christianity undermines all attempts to defend oneself against it. It is simply that which demands a decision.

In the face of their mutual desires, one is left to ponder what Kierkegaard and Bonhoeffer therefore considered this new, purified Christianity would look like. Little is provided by way of an answer. What is clear is that for Bonhoeffer, it will be essentially worldly. What is entirely unclear is that this position stands in formal counter-position to Bonhoeffer's earlier thought, but also to Kierkegaard. As has been argued, such a view rests upon a Kierkegaardian stereotype, and not on his work as a whole, or the specific works that particularly influenced Bonhoeffer.

Kierkegaard clearly does not formalize the disparate themes of his writing into a coherent theory of "religionless Christianity." Indeed, despite describing the dignity of humanity, the need for Christianity to be stripped away of its false clothing, and for a return to simplicity, Kierkegaard does not tie these issues together to suggest the need for a reinterpretation to Christianity that speaks into life. Nor is there necessarily a sense of Christianity as *for* humanity within his earthly life. However, perhaps undermined by his refusal to reform, these issues are clearly present within his ideas, and one is simply left to wonder what Kierkegaard would have thought of Bonhoeffer's formalization and desire for reformation.

The significance of Kierkegaard for Bonhoeffer's final work is difficult to quantify. Of the isolated ideas Bonhoeffer presents in *LPP*, it is only the issues of the defense of the Gospel, as well as direction concerning the preaching of the church, that we can say Bonhoeffer directly borrowed from Kierkegaard. Much of our argument has therefore focussed on similarities rather than influence (when we consider the question of Bonhoeffer as a Kierkegaardian reformer in the Conclusion, this will prove of particular use). However, other than the potential discrepancies mentioned, Bonhoeffer's attack stands in essential unity with his previous work. Consequently, it is not simply the specific issues dealt with in *LPP* that describes Kierkegaard's influence, but the issues that led Bonhoeffer to this point. As we turn now to our conclusion further light will be shed on this question.

8

Conclusion

"Already one hundred years ago Kierkegaard said that Luther today would say the opposite of what he said back then. I think that is true—*cum grano salis*." (*LPP*, 173)

Influence

IT SHOULD BY NOW BE CLEAR THAT PREVIOUS RESEARCH ON THE RELATIONSHIP BETWEEN Kierkegaard and Bonhoeffer has not taken seriously the full extent of Bonhoeffer's knowledge and use of Kierkegaard. Although it is impossible to say at what point Bonhoeffer read some of the works found within his library, nor to what extent he read those works or sections he did not annotate, from our analysis tentative suggestions can be made for many of them.

1. *Concluding Unscientific Postscript*: although only Part 2 can be found in his library, there is strong evidence to suggest Bonhoeffer was familiar with both parts from the writing of *SC* (1927).

2. *The Concept of Anxiety*: *CA* clearly played a particularly important role in *SC* (1927).

3. *Works of Love*: although embracing the ambiguity of Bonhoeffer's interpretation, as discussed in chapter 1, it is cited in *SC* (1927).

4. *Fear and Trembling*: again, while the full extent of Bonhoeffer's interpretation is somewhat unclear, it is cited in *SC* (1927). A firm grasp of *FT* can be seen, however, in *Discipleship* (1937).

5. *Philosophical Fragments*: although not conclusive, *CCIG* (1931) suggests Bonhoeffer's knowledge of *PF*.

6. *The Sickness Unto Death*: Bonhoeffer shows a firm grasp of *SUD* in his lecture series "Theological Psychology" (1932).

7. *Practice in Christianity*: from its marked absence from *CCIG* (1931) but presence in *Christology* (1933) it can be suggested that Bonhoeffer became familiar with *PC* during this gap.

8. *For Self-Examination/Judge For Yourself!*: these works are clearly used in *Discipleship* (1937). However, from Bonhoeffer's reference to Kierkegaard and silence in *Christology* (1933) it can be suggested that Bonhoeffer was familiar with *FSE* at this point.

Both are found within the same volume (*ASA*) but one cannot say whether the whole volume was read at the same time.

9. *Der Einzelne und die Kirche*: clear evidence can be found from the time of *Discipleship* (1937).

10. *Either/Or*: explicit reference to *E/O* is only found within *LPP* (1944). However, in the Barcelona lecture, "Jesus Christ and the Essence of Christianity," one also finds a reference to Christ's demand that "we commit to him in an abrupt either-or" (*BBNY*, 342). That Bonhoeffer gave a copy to Bethge in 1935 certainly suggests Bonhoeffer's appreciation of it at an early stage.

11. *Im Zwange des freien Gewissens*: as suggested by Vogel, Bonhoeffer may have been familiar with this journal collection as he wrote the poem "Christians and Pagans" (1944).

12. *A Literary Review*: the evidence for Bonhoeffer's knowledge of *LR* is perhaps the weakest, bound to their shared definition of "culture," as discussed by Bonhoeffer in *LPP* (1944).

13. *The Moment*: textual evidence is not substantial for Bonhoeffer's use of *The Moment* before *LPP*. However, he was clearly aware of it as early as 1925 through the letter of his colleague, Richard Widmann. It is also reproduced, either whole or in part, in both *EK* and *ASA* and so may follow the same time line as for these.

As has been shown throughout the previous chapters, Bonhoeffer gained a substantial knowledge of Kierkegaard over the course of his life. Furthermore, Bonhoeffer's understanding progressed over his authorship, from a somewhat stereotyped perspective in *SC* to a fully fledged appreciation in his later works. One of the main errors made by many of the secondary sources is to have simply taken Bonhoeffer's perspective and criticisms of Kierkegaard in *SC* and applied them to the rest of his work.

Bonhoeffer's library is clearly helpful in understanding Bonhoeffer's appreciation. However, as has been shown, it does not tell the whole story. First, the library contains works that it has been impossible to chronicle, such as *EL*, *T*, and *ACR*. Secondly, it also does not contain many of the works that played a significant role in our analysis, such as *WL* and the highly influential *FT*. Finally, our analysis has also raised questions concerning Bonhoeffer's possible appreciation of other works. This is the case, for instance, with "Thoughts Which Wound from Behind," omitted from the selection of *CD* that Bonhoeffer owned. As discussed in chapter 7, here one finds many parallels between Kierkegaard and Bonhoeffer concerning their attacks. However, here Kierkegaard also discusses how truth has been made insignificant by over-repetition (*CD*, 165), the nature of suffering and that bound to the voluntary (178–80), the issue of the two realms and the sagacious incomprehensibility of life as seen through faith (175), the interplay between faith and obedience (263), the important of salvation *for me* (189) and, indeed, the whole subversive definition of Christianity as "wounding from behind."

A further work that deserves consideration is "The Lilies of the Field and the Birds of the Air." In each of its three sections, Kierkegaard appears to summarize the essential tenets of Bonhoeffer's notion of discipleship. Kierkegaard discusses the individual standing in silence before God (*WA*, 10ff.), quietening the noise of his own mind (24f.), undermining the ambiguities of his deliberation with simplicity (32f.), listening to the voice of God in joy and obedience (36ff.), and finding both himself and God anew in the moment (39). Although the work focuses on the individual standing before God, Kierkegaard also defends the true nature of society, bound by his understanding of the individual (43f.).

Bonhoeffer was clearly appreciative of Kierkegaard's edifying work as can be seen by his reading of *EL* and *ACR*. One might wonder whether he was also familiar with these further works. "The Lilies of the Field and the Birds of the Air" was certainly published in its own volume in German by Bärthold as early as 1885. However, it is difficult to confirm their influence as Kierkegaard's discourses tend to repeat material found in his later works, many of which are in Bonhoeffer's library.

A Question of Community

One of the major tasks of this thesis has been to overcome the stereotypes that have created barriers to understanding the Kierkegaard and Bonhoeffer's relationship. These have revolved around Kierkegaard being portrayed as an irrationalist, acosmist, Gnostic, and individualist. While there are passages in Kierkegaard that might be interpreted in these terms, it has been shown that they do not fit with an overview of Kierkegaard's work and, most importantly, an overview of the Kierkegaard works Bonhoeffer himself owned and read. The criticism of Kierkegaard as an individualist is most pertinent to a comparison with the highly ecclesial Bonhoeffer. However, in discerning the nature of Kierkegaard and Bonhoeffer's relationship, one must go beyond the simple, literal comparison of their writings to compare them as individuals. One must draw again upon the quote discussed in chapter 1 and quoted at the beginning of this chapter, and ask whether in Bonhoeffer's context "Kierkegaard would say the opposite of what he said then."

In nineteenth-century Denmark, the problem for Kierkegaard was not the existence of the church or the community, but rather the loss of the individual. However, as affirmed by Stephen Plant, the issue for Bonhoeffer was quite the opposite.[1] As described in chapter 3, German theology came under the strong influence of Adolf von Harnack and the scientific, historical-critical approach, had essentially discarded the church. If Kierkegaard was presenting a dogmatic affirmation of the individual at the expense of the church or community then the answer to our question must be that Kierkegaard would not have changed his position or emphasis. However, as the previous chapters have emphasized, this is certainly not the reading of Kierkegaard that was obvious to Bonhoeffer. In *EK* Kierkegaard wrote concerning the difference between "the Crowd" or "Public" and "Community,"

> In the "public" and the like the single individual is nothing; there is no individual; the numerical is the constituting form and the law for the coming into existence of a

---

1. Plant, *Bonhoeffer*, 55.

generatio aequivoca; detached from the "public" the single individual is nothing, and in the public he is, more basically understood, really nothing at all.

> In community the single individual is; the single individual is dialectically decisive as the presupposition for forming community, and in community the single individual is qualitatively something essential and can at any moment become higher than "community," specifically, as soon as "the others" fall away from the idea. The cohesiveness of community comes from each one's being a single individual, and then the idea; the connectedness of a public or rather its disconnectedness consists of the numerical character of everything. Every single individual in community guarantees the community; the public is a chimera. In community the single individual is a microcosm who qualitatively reproduces the cosmos; here, in a good sense, it holds true that *unum noris, omnes*. In a public there is no single individual and the whole is nothing; here it is impossible to say *unum noris, omnes*, for here there is no one. "Community" is certainly more than a sum, but yet it is truly a sum of ones; the public is nonsense—a sum of negative ones, of ones who are not ones, who become ones through the sum instead of the sum becoming a sum of the ones. (*EK*, 94; *JP*, 2952/*Pap*, X2 A 390)

It is unclear whether Bonhoeffer would have read this journal entry before its publication in *EK*. However, it bears striking resemblance to Bonhoeffer's description of "the mass" in *SC*, and the interplay between the individual and the community. Bonhoeffer shows the significant parallels when he comments, "By viewing the individual person in a primal state as an ultimate unit who is created by God's will—but also by seeing individual persons as real only in sociality—we interpret their relations to one another, which are built upon their difference, as willed by God" (*SC*, 84).

As discussed in chapter 7, Kierkegaard and Bonhoeffer share the definition of "culture" as that bound to passionate action. Kierkegaard continues his description in *LR* by discussing the nature of such a society, arguing,

> When the individuals (severally) relate essentially and passionately to an idea and, on top of that, in union essentially relate to the same idea, that relation is perfect and normal. The relation singles out individually (each has himself for himself) and unites ideally. In the essential inward directedness there is that modest reticence between man and man that prevents crude assumption . . . Thus individuals never come too close to each other in a brute sense, just because they are united at an ideal distance. The unanimity of the singled-out is the band playing well orchestrated music. If, on the other hand, individuals relate to an idea merely on masse (that is, without the individual, inward-directed singling out), we get violence, unruliness, unbridledness . . . (*LR*, 55)

Bonhoeffer's understanding of community is equally rooted in the individual, united at an ideal distance to the human other through the mediation of Christ. These ideas are backed up at the very end of "The Lilies of the Field and the Birds of the Air" where Kierkegaard explicitly rebukes the poet who blames "society" for stopping people from being obedient to God, wishing rather to rest in the isolation of the birds and the lilies (*WA*, 43f.).

This thesis has argued that part of the importance of Kierkegaard for Bonhoeffer, and most certainly in *SC*, is that Kierkegaard's notion of the individual is the foundation for Bonhoeffer's concept of community. It has also been suggested that Kierkegaard's notion of love in *WL*, the concept of mediation in *FT*, and the relationship of the individual to the race in the concept of original sin in *CA*, all undermine the full disassociation of communality and ecclesiology from Kierkegaard's ideas. Many of Bonhoeffer's views on community and ecclesiology are the logical progression of the presuppositions that he shared with Kierkegaard. Despite his earlier statement in *SC* that Kierkegaard rejected the church because of his individualism—although it has also been suggested in chapter 1 that this interpretation of the relevant passage from *FT* is unjustified—once his knowledge grew it is far from obvious that Bonhoeffer would have considered Kierkegaard in this light. This notion is backed up by an entry from *EK* entitled "The Church" where Kierkegaard argues,

> The definition of "Church" found in the Augsburg Confession, that it is the communion of saints where the word is rightly taught and the sacraments rightly administered, this quite correctly (that is, not correctly) grasped only the two points about doctrine and sacraments and has overlooked the first, the communion of saints (in which there is the qualification in the direction of the existential). Thus the Church is made into a communion of indifferent existences (or where the existential is a matter of indifference)—but the "doctrine" is correct and the sacraments are rightly administered. This is really paganism. (*EK*, 148; *JP*, 600/*Pap*, X4 A 246)

It is scarcely surprising that Bonhoeffer marked his copy of *EK* with two dark marginal lines and an exclamation mark next to this entry. If in *SC* Bonhoeffer believed that Kierkegaard had rejected the church, from 1937 this interpretation was no longer possible.

A final piece of evidence from Bonhoeffer's own library can be presented as pointing not only towards Kierkegaard's affirmation of the church, but also the possibility that he could have changed his stance in relation to Bonhoeffer's context. Once again in *EK* Kierkegaard remarks,

> Solomon's judgment may be applied to the Church. It was clear that the true mother was the one who would rather give up the child than have half. So it is with the Church, the true mother: it would rather let go of the individual, let him still live, than have half of him—and spiritually it is just as impossible to have a half person as it is physically. (*EK*, 103; *JP*, 596/*Pap*, X3 A 54)

For Kierkegaard, the true church is that which desires to keep the whole individual or nothing at all, rather than to take whatever it can in fear for its own survival. Within this single statement of Kierkegaard's we find not only a positive ecclesiology, but also a suggestion of the desire for the church to release humankind from its clutches into its own life. This bears striking parallels with Bonhoeffer's thought in *LPP*, releasing humankind into its own natural life rather than keeping hold of it at any cost. Once again, it is no surprise that Bonhoeffer marked his own copy of *EK* with several thick lines at this point.

At the beginning of his life, Kierkegaard's views were radically different concerning the church to those of his final attack. In a journal article from 1838 Kierkegaard comments,

> There are on the whole very few men who are able to bear the Protestant view of life. If the Protestant view is really to become strengthening for the common man, it must either structure itself in a smaller community (separatism, small congrega-

tions, etc.) or approach Catholicism, in order in both cases to develop the mutual bearing of life's burdens in a communal life, which only the most gifted individuals are able to dispense with. Christ indeed has died for all men, also for me, but this "for me" must nevertheless be interpreted in such a way that he has died for me only insofar as I belong to the many." (*JP*, 1976/II A 223)

One would be forgiven for thinking that this was written by Bonhoeffer rather than Kierkegaard. Near the beginning of his life, Kierkegaard showed a far greater concern for both a formal ecclesiology but also for the church itself. In a letter to his childhood friend, Emil Boesen, he comments, "the more I think about our motto: '*A church stands at the distance*,' the more I also feel the truth of what you once remarked, that it had come considerably closer" (*LD*, 54). Even though Kierkegaard rejected a direct communication even at this early stage in his life, these words represent his desire that the church should indeed come closer to impact the lives of its members, and in particular the common man. The question that must remain open is whether Kierkegaard ultimately maintained these desires into his later life.

To summarize: Kierkegaard did not emphasize the individual at the expense of the church, but rather fought against the church for the sake of the individual. It has been shown that Bonhoeffer did not finally see Kierkegaard in a stereotypical light, and suggested that Kierkegaard himself would have reacted differently to Bonhoeffer's own context.

Bonhoeffer the Reformer?

In comparing Kierkegaard and Bonhoeffer as individuals we must return to the question raised in both chapters 1 and 7. Although the path that the church should take remained hidden to his gaze, Bonhoeffer wanted to help in the process of reformation. In contrast, Kierkegaard rejected this role, and declared in 1849 concerning his task,

> All communication of truth has become abstract; the public has become the authority; the newspapers call themselves the editorial staff, the professor calls himself speculation; the pastor is meditation—no man, none, dares to say I. But since without qualification the first prerequisite for the communication of truth is personality, since "truth" cannot possibly be served by ventriloquism, personality had to come to the fore again. But in these circumstances, since the world was so corrupted by never hearing an I, it was impossible to begin at once with one's own I. So it became my task to create author-personalities and let them enter into the actuality of life in order to get men a bit accustomed to hearing discourse in the first person. Thus my task is no doubt only that of a forerunner until he comes who in the strictest sense says: I. But to make a turn away from this inhuman abstraction to personality—that is my task. (*JP*, 6440/*Pap*, X1 A 531)

Kierkegaard considered himself to be a forerunner, who prepared the way for one who would come after him to be the "reformer" (*JFY*, 211-13) or "missionary" (*JP*, 2004/*Pap*, VIII1 A 482; *EK*, 32) that he could never be. In relation to such a figure, Kierkegaard saw his task "to escort him, the reformer, step by step, never leaving his side, in order to see if he step by step is in the character, is the extraordinary"—to strengthen or undermine the reformer, relative to his authenticity and motivation (*JFY*, 211).

Kierkegaard further defines the role of the reformer when he comments in *EK*, "When he, the missionary, comes, he will use this category [of the single individual]. If the age is waiting for a hero, it waits in vain; instead there will more likely come one who in divine weakness will teach men obedience—by means of their slaying him in impious rebellion, him, the one obedient to God" (*JP*, 2004/*Pap*, VIII1 A 482; *EK*, 32).

Finally, in an ambiguous reference that reflects on Luther but also speaks into this mysterious future character, Kierkegaard declares at the very end of *JFY*, "When the Church needed a reformation, no one reported for duty, there was no crowd to join up; all fled away. Only one solitary man, the reformer, was disciplined in all secrecy by fear and trembling and much spiritual trial for venturing the extraordinary in God's name" (*JFY*, 213). In the light of these passages, is Bonhoeffer a Kierkegaardian "reformer"? To answer this question one must consider Kierkegaard's idea of reformation in terms of both content and form.

The content of Kierkegaard's understanding of reformation is extremely vague as Kierkegaard refused to enter into such a project himself. But certain points can be discerned. As described above, Kierkegaard declares that the reformer will use the category of the single individual, and lead people in obedience. Drawing on his attack on Christendom, this must go hand in hand with an admission of guilt, and a confession of one's weakness. As described in the previous chapters, Bonhoeffer fulfils each of these criteria. Despite his profound thoughts concerning the nature of community and the authority of the church, the foundation of Bonhoeffer's theology is that of the single individual, drawn away from direct relationship with others into the mediation of Christ, bound to undivided relationship with God. Bonhoeffer's ethics can perhaps be best described as "simple obedience," listening to the command of God as it proceeds from His mouth anew every day. As Bonhoeffer considered the church he was led to write "Guilt, Justification, Renewal"—an essay dedicated to personal and collective repentance for the guilt of the church, in desire for its renewal. Furthermore, like Kierkegaard, Bonhoeffer was also deeply struck by Paul's words concerning the thorn in the flesh, and founded his notion of discipleship and a striving for God's command on weakness.

Beyond these more theoretical ideas, one must also consider the full extent of Kierkegaard's "negative reformation," and so his ideas concerning the relationship between church and state. For Kierkegaard, to imitate Christ in the world infers persecution and suffering. It is therefore inconceivable that anyone could take up such a role while in the pay of the state. At the end of *JFY* Kierkegaard argues that the situation must not change while authentic reformation is impossible. However, it is clear that Kierkegaard saw the need for a break between church and state, and that within the manifesto of the reformer. Vernard Eller has argued that Kierkegaard's desire for such a separation is endemic of his movement towards pietistic religion and ecclesiology. However, this fails to take seriously Kierkegaard's Lutheran background and the central premise of the *Zweireichlehre*. When understood in this context, Kierkegaard's desire is no more than a call for the reaffirmation of Lutheran principles, which saw the church and state as equal yet distinct orders.

Not only was this distinction clearly affirmed by Bonhoeffer, but it lies at the heart of his attack on the Nazi state and the church.[2]

To fully appreciate the figure of the "reformer" one must also draw on the wealth of Kierkegaard's other works, including such themes as "subjectivity," the promotion of the "how" over the "what," and the concept of "active passivity," that run throughout Kierkegaard's work. For Kierkegaard, the reformer must live in the guise of the extraordinary, to stand in heterogeneity with the world as the peculiar, to embody the true revolutionary spirit of passion, to found words on existential decision and commitment. It is to be like Luther, to report for duty when reformation is needed, to be disciplined in all secrecy by fear and trembling and spiritual trial. It is, in the words of Geismar, to be the "martyr prophet,"[3] in the image of Christ, "embodying in Himself a divine love for all humankind, crucified in pathological hatred by human beings whom He loved."[4] It is clear that Bonhoeffer would have met Kierkegaard's critical gaze in these respects.

Kierkegaard refused to discuss reform, and Bonhoeffer felt that it was somehow beyond his gaze. However, the passage in which Bonhoeffer ventures the most sheds light on his similarity with Kierkegaard in both content and form. In "Outline for a Book," written in Prison and discussed in chapter 7, Bonhoeffer writes,

> The church is only the church when it exists for others. To make a start it should give away all its property to those in need. The clergy must live solely on the free-will offerings of their congregations, or possibly engage in some secular calling. The church must share in the secular problems of ordinary human life, not dominating, but helping and serving. It must tell men of every calling what it means to live in Christ, to exist for others . . . It must not under-estimate the importance of human example . . . it is not abstract argument, but example, that gives its word emphasis and power. (*LPP*, 382)

Kierkegaard's ecclesiology, and "negative reformation," cannot definitively state whether he would have agreed with all of these points. His own work is certainly not as forthright concerning either the church or the individual being "for others." However, his frequent attacks on the clergy with respect to their wages, declarations about the responsibility of the church to fight for the people around it, and his desire for the common man must at least point us in this direction. Most importantly, in declaring that "it is not abstract argument, but example, that gives [the church's] word emphasis and power," Bonhoeffer has summarized the issue at the heart of Kierkegaard's thought. For both Kierkegaard and Bonhoeffer, everything concerns the ability to say "I," and that before God.

FINAL REMARKS

Kierkegaard and Bonhoeffer clearly come from different contexts that had profound effects upon their work. As described in the conclusion to chapter 7, Bonhoeffer departs

---

2. For Bonhoeffer, the most profound sign of corruption was in the appointment of Ludvig Müller as Reich Bishop.

3. Geismar, "Søren Aabye Kierkegaard," 250.

4. Geismar, *Lectures*, 73.

somewhat from Kierkegaard's influence when considering the attack. However, it is precisely in their final attacks that one finds the greatest difference concerning their contexts. For Kierkegaard, society had lost itself in the ease of life, denying the strenuousness of the gospel message, and was using the church as a source of comfort. Kierkegaard's emphasis on the individual was against society's promotion of the mass, the importance of sin against personal interestedness, suffering against security, and the spiritual extremity of the New Testament against the worldly comfort of the Old Testament. Bonhoeffer on the other hand was met with a very different situation. Theology had become individualized at the expense of the church. The church was fighting against the rise of secularism with an emphasis on sin. Furthermore, in the heat of Germany under Nazi rule, Bonhoeffer witnessed the undermining of humankind's creatureliness by both those who sought to deify humanity (cf. Aryans), and those who sought to deny it (cf. a Gnostic super-spirituality)—each caught up in responsibility for the massacre of millions of people by acts commission or omission. Consequently, by the time of *LPP* Bonhoeffer emphasized the church alongside the individual, and the affirmation of humankind's creaturely existence as expounded in the Old Testament alongside the New. Both writers clearly went along different paths concerning their attacks.

And yet what has been argued here is that both writers not only started in the same place, but also sought the same ends. Like a bridge over a still river, they are the mirror of each other. Furthermore, their departures from one another are more a matter of emphasis than, for want of a better phrase, "doctrinal truth." There is no suggestion in either attacks that their views on epistemology, ethics, or discipleship radically changed. Furthermore, the final writings of both authors are the fulfilment of their attacks on idealism, seeking to release Christianity into the "world of the spirit" from its shackles in the "outward and visible world." Both held to the responsibility of unleashing Christianity and the church back into its true power in order that it might once again speak authoritatively into people's lives.

Despite their differences, Bonhoeffer embodies the character of a Kierkegaardian reformer. At the beginning of the thesis it was argued that Bonhoeffer wrote from within Kierkegaard. At the end of the thesis we might suggest in addition that Bonhoeffer was "escorted" through his life by Kierkegaard.

Bibliography

Primary Sources

Søren Aabye Kierkegaard

WORKS BY KIERKEGAARD IN ENGLISH

Kierkegaard's Writings. 25 vols. Edited and Translated by Howard V. Hong, Edna H. Hong, Julia Watkin, Reidar Thomte, and Henrik Rosenmeier. Princeton, NJ: Princeton University Press, 1978–2002.

Christian Discourses, Etc. Translated and edited by Walter Lowrie. Princeton: Princeton University Press, 1974.

Either/Or. Translated and edited by Alastair Hannay. London: Penguin, 1992.

Fear and Trembling. Translated by Alastair Hannay. London: Penguin, 1985.

A Literary Review. Translated by Alastair Hannay. London: Penguin, 2001.

The Sickness Unto Death. Translated by Alastair Hannay. London: Penguin, 1989.

Søren Kierkegaard's Journals and Papers. 7 vols. Translated and edited by Howard V. Hong and Edna H. Hong. Bloomington: Indiana University Press, c1967–c1978).

WORKS BY KIERKEGAARD IN GERMAN

Abschliessende unwissenschaftliche Nachschrift: Teil 2, *Gesammelte Werke* 7. Translated and edited by Christoph Schrempf. Jena: Diederichs, 1910.

Ausgewählte christliche Reden. Translated by Julie von Reincke. Giessen: A. Topelmann, 1923.

Der Begriff der Angst, Gesammelte Werke 5. Translated and edited by Christoph Schrempf. Jena: Diederich, 1923.

Einübung in Christentum, Gesammelte Werke 9. Translated and edited by Christoph Schrempf. Jena: Diederichs, 1924.

Der Einzelne und die Kirche. Translated and edited by Wilhelm Kütemeyer. Berlin: Kurt Wolff Verlag/Der Neue Geist Verlag, 1934.

Entweder-Oder, ein Lebensfragment. Translated by Otto Gleiß. Dresden: Ungelenk, 1927.

Das Evangelium der Leiden. Christliche Reden. Translated by Wilhelm Kütemeyer. München: Chr. Kaiser, 1933.

Furcht und Zittern: Wiederholung, Gesammelte Werke 3. Translated and edited by H. C. Ketels, H. Gottsched und Christoph Schrempf. Jena: Diederichs, 1909.

Die Krankheit zum Tode, Gesammelte Werke 8. Translated and edited by Christoph Schrempf. Jena: Diederich, 1911.

Sören Kierkegaards agitatorische Schriften und Aufsätze: 1851 bis 1855, Sören Kierkegaards Angriff auf die Christenheit, Erster Band: Die Akten. Translated and edited by Christoph Schrempf and August Dorner. Stuttgart: Frommanns, 1896.

So spricht Sören Kierkegaard; aus seinen Tage- und Nächtebüchern ausgewählt. Translated and edited by Robert Dollinger. Berlin: Furche, 1930.

Die Tagebücher. Translated and edited by Theodor Haecker. Innsbruck: Brenner, 1923.

Im Zwange des freien Gewissens: Gedanken über Gott und Mensch aus den Tage- und Nächtebüchern. Translated and edited by Robert Dollinger. Berlin: Furche, 1938.

Bibliography

WORKS BY KIERKEGAARD IN DANISH

Papirer, Vols I-XI. Edited by P. A. Heiberg, V. Kuhr and E. Torsting. Kiøbenhaven: Gyldendal, 1909–1948.

Dietrich Bonhoeffer

WORKS BY BONHOEFFER IN ENGLISH

Dietrich Bonhoeffer Works. 16 vols. Edited by Wayne Whitson Floyd Jr. et al. Minneapolis: Fortress, 1998–present.
Christology. Translated by John Bowden. London: Collins, 1974.
"Concerning the Christian Idea of God." *The Journal of Religion* 12:2 (April 1932) 177–85.
The Cost of Discipleship. Translated by R. H. Fuller. London: SCM, 1959.
Ethics. Translated by Neville Horton Smith. London: SCM, 1998.
Letters and Papers from Prison. Edited by Eberhard Bethge. London: SCM, 1971.
Love Letters from Cell 92: Dietrich Bonhoeffer, Maria von Wedermeyer. Translated and edited by Ruth-Alice von Bismarck and Ulrich Kabitz. London: Harper Collins, 1994.
No Rusty Swords: Letters, Lectures, and Notes, 1928–1936. Translated and edited by Edwin H. Robertson and John Bowden. London: Collins, 1965.
The Prison Poems of Dietrich Bonhoeffer. Translated and edited by Edwin Robertson. Guildford, Surrey: Eagle, 1998.
A Testament to Freedom: The Essential Writings of Dietrich Bonhoeffer. Translated and edited by Geffrey B. Kelly and F. Burton Nelson. San Francisco: HarperSanFrancisco, 1990.
True Patriotism: Letters, Lectures, and Notes, 1939–1945. Translated and edited by Edwin H. Robertson and John Bowden. London: Collins, 1973.
The Way to Freedom: Letters, Lectures, and Notes, 1935–1939. Translated and edited by Edwin H. Robertson and John Bowden. London: Collins, 1966.

WORKS BY BONHOEFFER IN GERMAN

Dietrich Bonhoeffer Werke. 16 vols. Edited Eberhard Bethge et al. Munich: Chr. Kaiser, 1986–99.
Gesammelte Schriften. 4 vols. Edited by Eberhard Bethge. Munich: Chr. Kaiser, 1958–61.

Secondary Sources

Adams, Robert. "Kierkegaard's Arguments Against Objective Reasoning in Religion." *Monist* 60 (1977) 228–43.
Ake, Stacey Elizabeth. "'As We *Are* So We *Make*': Life as Comparison in Søren Kierkegaard and Dietrich Bonhoeffer." *Kierkegaard Studies Yearbook* (1999) 293–309.
Allen, E. L. *Kierkegaard: His Life and Thought*. London: Stanley Nott, 1935.
Althaus, Paul. *The Ethics of Martin Luther*. Philadelphia: Fortress, 1972.
———. *The Theology of Martin Luther*. Philadelphia: Fortress, 1966.
Altizer, Thomas J. J. *The Gospel of Christian Atheism*. London: Collins, 1967.
Altizer, Thomas J. J., and William Hamilton. *Radical Theology and the Death of God*. Middlesex: Penguin, 1968.
Anderson, Thomas C. "Kierkegaard and Approximation Knowledge." In *International Kierkegaard Commentary: Concluding Unscientific Postscript*, edited by Robert L. Perkins, 175–84. Macon, GA: Mercer University Press, 1997.
Armstrong, C. B. "Christianity Without Religion." *Church Quarterly Review* 165 (1964) 175–84.
Backhouse, Stephen G. "Completing the Vision: Søren Kierkegaard's Pseudonymous Texts and *Attack upon Christendom*." M.A. diss., McGill University, 2003.
Bain, John A. *Søren Kierkegaard: His Life and Religious Teaching*. London: SCM, 1935.

Barrett, Lee C. "Faith, Works, and the Uses of the Law: Kierkegaard's Appropriation of Lutheran Doctrine." In *International Kierkegaard Commentary: For Self-Examination and Judge For Yourself!*, edited by Robert L. Perkins, 77–110. Macon, GA: Mercer University Press, 2002.

———. "Subjectivity is (Un)Truth: Climacus' Dialectically Sharpened Pathos." In *International Kierkegaard Commentary: Concluding Unscientific Postscript*, edited by Robert L. Perkins, 291–306. Macon, GA: Mercer University Press, 1997.

Barth, Heinrich. "Kierkegaard, der Denker." *Zwischen den Zeiten* 4:3 (1926).

Bedell, George C. "Kierkegaard's Conception of Time." *Journal of the American Academy of Religion* 37:3 (1969) 266–69.

Beiser, Frederick C., editor. *Cambridge Companion to Hegel*. Cambridge: Cambridge University Press, 1993.

Bentley, James. *Martin Niemöller*. Sevenoaks, Kent: Hodder & Stoughton, 1984.

Bergman, Marvin. "Teaching Ethics and Moral Decision-Making in the light of Dietrich Bonhoeffer." In *A Bonhoeffer Legacy*, edited by A. J. Klassen, 367–82. Grand Rapids: Eerdmans, 1981.

Bethge, Eberhard. *Dietrich Bonhoeffer: A Biography*. Rev. ed. Minneapolis: Fortress, 2000.

———. *Dietrich Bonhoeffer: Theologe, Christ, Zeitgenosse*. Munich: Chr. Kaiser, 1967.

———. *Dietrich Bonhoeffer: Theologian, Christian, Contemporary*. London: Collins, 1970.

———. *Friendship and Resistance: Essays on Dietrich Bonhoeffer*. Grand Rapids: Eerdmans, 1995.

———. "Bonhoeffer's Assertion of Religionless Christianity—Was He Mistaken?" In *A Bonhoeffer Legacy*, edited by A. J. Klassen, 3–11. Grand Rapids: Eerdmans, 1981.

———. "The Challenge of Dietrich Bonhoeffer's Life and Theology." In *World Come of Age*, edited by Ronald Gregor-Smith, 22–87. London: Collins, 1967.

Bialas, Wolfgang, and Alsion Rabinbach, editors. *Nazi Germany and the Humanities*. Oxford: Oneworld, 2007.

Blackham, H. J. *Six Existentialist Thinkers*. London: Routledge & Kegan Paul, 1952.

Blanshard, Brand. "Kierkegaard on Faith." *Personalist* 49 (1968) 5–23.

Bloom, Harold. *The Anxiety of Influence*. Oxford: Oxford University Press, 1997.

Bowden, John, and James Richmond. *A Reader in Contemporary Theology*. London: SCM, 1967.

Buber, Martin. *Between Man and Man*. London: Routledge, 2002.

Bukdahl, Jørgen. *Søren Kierkegaard and the Common Man*. Translated by Bruce H. Kirmmse. Grand Rapids: Eerdmans, 2001.

Caputo, John D., and Gianni Vattimo. *After the Death of God*. New York: Columbia, 2007.

Collins, James. *The Mind of Kierkegaard*. Princeton, NJ: Princeton University Press, 1953.

Cox, Harvey. *The Feast of Fools*. Cambridge, MA: Harvard University Press, 1969.

———. *The Secular City*. London: SCM, 1967.

Crites, Stephen. *In the Twilight of Christendom*. Chambersburg, PA: AAR, 1972.

Cross, Andrew A. "Fear and Trembling's Unorthodox Ideal." *Philosophical Topics* 27:2 (1999) 227–54.

Croxall, T. H. *Glimpses and Impressions of Kierkegaard*. Welwyn, Herts: James Nisbet, 1959.

Daise, Benjamin. *Kierkegaard's Socratic Art*. Macon, GA: Mercer University Press, 1999.

Dallago, Carl. "Augustine, Pascal und Kierkegaard." *Der Brenner* 6:9 (April 1921).

Davenport, John, and Anthony Rudd, editors. *Kierkegaard After MacIntyre*. Chicago: Open Court, 2001.

De Gruchy, John, editor. *Cambridge Companion to Dietrich Bonhoeffer*. Cambridge: Cambridge University Press, 1999.

———. *Dietrich Bonhoeffer: Witness to Jesus Christ*. London: Collins, 1988.

Dramm, Sabine. *Dietrich Bonhoeffer and the Resistance*. Minneapolis: Fortress, 2009.

Dumas, André. *Dietrich Bonhoeffer: Theologian of Reality*. London: SCM, 1971.

Dumbach, Annette, and Jud Newborn. *Sophie Scholl and the White Rose*. Oxford: Oneworld, 2006.

Dunning, Stephen N. "Kierkegaard's Systematic Analysis of Anxiety." In *International Kierkegaard Commentary: The Concept of Anxiety*, edited by Robert L. Perkins, 7–33. Macon, GA: Mercer University Press, 1985.

Dupré, Louis. *Kierkegaard as Theologian: The Dialectic of Christian Existence*. New York: Sheed & Ward, 1963.

———. "Of Time and Eternity." In *International Kierkegaard Commentary: The Concept of Anxiety*, edited by Robert L. Perkins, 111–31. Macon, GA: Mercer University Press, 1985.

Dru, Alexander. "Introduction." In *Journal in the Night*, by Theodor Heacker. London: Harvill, 1949.

Eller, Vernard. *Kierkegaard and Radical Discipleship: A New Perspective*. Princeton, NJ: Princeton University Press, 1968.

Elrod, John. *Kierkegaard and Christendom*. Princeton, NJ: Princeton University Press, 1981.

Ericksen, Robert P. *Theologians Under Hitler*. New Haven: Yale University Press, 1985.

Evans, C. Stephen. "Faith as the Telos of Morality: A Reading of *Fear and Trembling*." In *International Kierkegaard Commentary: Fear and Trembling and Repetition*, edited by Robert L. Perkins, 9–27. Macon, GA: Mercer University Press, 1993.

———. "Is Kierkegaard an Irrationalist? Reason, Paradox and Faith." *Religious Studies* 25 (1989) 347–63.

———. *Kierkegaard on Faith and the Self: Collected Essays*. Waco, TX: Baylor University Press, 2006.

———. *Kierkegaard's "Fragments" and "Postscript": The Religious Philosophy of Johannes Climacus*. Atlantic Highlands, NJ: Humanities, 1983.

Feil, Ernst. *Die Theologie Dietrich Bonhoeffers*. Munich: Chr. Kaiser, 1971.

———. *The Theology of Dietrich Bonhoeffer*. Translated by Martin Rumscheidt. Philadelphia: Fortress, 1985.

Fendt, Gene. "Whose 'Fear and Trembling'?" In *International Kierkegaard Commentary: Fear and Trembling and Repetition*, edited by Robert L. Perkins, 177–91. Macon, GA: Mercer University Press, 1993.

Fenger, Henning. *Kierkegaard: The Myths and their Origins*. Translated by George C. Schoolfield. New Haven: Yale University Press, 1980.

Fiddes, Paul. *Past Event and Present Salvation*. London: Darton Longman & Todd, 1989.

Floyd, Wayne. "Encounter with an Other: Immanuel Kant and G. W. F. Hegel in the Theology of Dietrich Bonhoeffer." In *Bonhoeffer's Intellectual Formation*, edited by Peter Frick, 83–120. Tübingen: Mohr/Siebeck, 2008.

Fletcher, Joseph. *Situation Ethics*. London: SCM, 1966.

Foley, Grover. "Religionless Christianity." *The Christian Century* 80 (11 September 1963) 1096–9.

Fraser, Giles. *Redeeming Nietzsche: On Piety and Unbelief*. London: Routledge, 2002.

Frick, Peter, editor. *Bonhoeffer's Intellectual Formation*. Tübingen: Mohr/Siebeck, 2008.

———. "Friedrich Nietzsche's Aphorisms and Dietrich Bonhoeffer's Theology." In *Bonhoeffer's Intellectual Formation*, edited by Peter Frick, 175–200. Tübingen: Mohr/Siebeck, 2008.

Gardiner, Patrick. *Kierkegaard*. Oxford: Oxford University Press, 1988.

Garff, Joakim. "The Eyes of Argus: The Point of View of Points of View on Kierkegaard's Work as an Author." In *Kierkegaard: A Critical Reader*, edited by Jonathan Ree and Jane Chamberlain, 75–102. Oxford: Blackwell, 1998.

———. *Søren Kierkegaard: A Biography*. Translated by Bruce H. Kirmmse. Princeton, NJ: Princeton University Press, 2005.

———. "'What Did I Find? Not My I'—On Kierkegaard's Journals and the Pseudonymous Autobiography." *Kierkegaard Studies Yearbook* (2003) 189–201.

Geismar, Eduard. *Lectures on the Religious Thought of Søren Kierkegaard*. Minneapolis: Augsburg, 1937.

———. *Sören Kierkegaard: seine Lebensentwicklung und seine Wirksamkeit als Schriftsteller*. Göttingen: Vandenhoeck & Ruprecht, 1929.

———. "Søren Aabye Kierkegaard." *Die Religion in Geschichte und Gegenwart: Handwörterbuch für Theologie und Religionswissenschaft* (1927–1931) 247–51.

Gibellini, Rosino. *The Liberation Theology Debate*. London: SCM, 1987.

Gill, Jerry H., editor. *Essays on Kierkegaard*. Minneapolis: Burgess, 1969.

———. "Kant, Kierkegaard and Religious Knowledge." In *Essays on Kierkegaard*, edited by Jerry H. Gill, 58–73. Minneapolis: Burgess, 1969.

Glebe-Møller, Jens. "Recollecting One Who Is Dead—An Interpretation of Søren Kierkegaard's Funeral." *Kierkegaard Studies Yearbook* (2004) 525–35.

Golomb, Jacob. *In Search of Authenticity: From Kierkegaard to Camus*. London: Routledge, 1995.

Gouwens, David J. *Kierkegaard as Religious Thinker*. Cambridge: Cambridge University Press, 1996.

Green, Clifford J. "Bonhoeffer's Concept of Religion." *Union Seminary Quarterly Review* 19:1 (1963) 11–21.

———. "Human Sociality and Christian Community." In *Cambridge Companion to Dietrich Bonhoeffer*, edited by John de Gruchy, 113–32. Cambridge: Cambridge University Press, 1999.

Green, Ronald M. *Kierkegaard and Kant: The Hidden Debt*. Albany: State University of New York Press, 1992.

Gregor-Smith, Ronald, editor. *World Come of Age*. London: Collins, 1967.

Grimsley, Ronald. *Søren Kierkegaard and French Literature*. Cardiff: University of Wales Press, 1966.

Guignon, Charles, editor. *Cambridge Companion to Heidegger*. 2nd ed. Cambridge: Cambridge University Press, 2006.

Gustafson, James, and James T. Laney, editors. *On Being Responsible*. London: SCM, 1969.

———. "Introduction." In *The Responsible Self*. Louisville: Westminster John Knox, 1963.

Gutiérrez, Gustavo. *A Theology of Liberation*. Translated by Sister Caridad Inda and John Eagleson. London: SCM, 2001.

Haecker, Theodor. *Journal in the Night*. Translated by Alexander Dru. London: Harvill, 1949.

———. *Kierkegaard the Cripple*. Translated by C. Van O. Bruyn. New York: Philosophical Library, 1950.

———. *Søren Kierkegaard*. Oxford: Oxford University Press, 1937.

———. "Vorwort." In *Die Tagebücher*, by Søren Kierkegaard. Innsbruck: Brenner, 1923.

Hamilton, William. "Dietrich Bonhoeffer." In *Radical Theology and The Death of God*, edited by Thomas J. J. Altizer and William Hamilton, 118–23. Harmondsworth: Penguin, 1966.

———. "The Letters are a Particular Thorn." In *World Come of Age*, edited by Ronald Gregor-Smith, 131–60. London: Collins, 1967.

Hannay, Alastair. *Kierkegaard: A Biography*. Cambridge: Cambridge University Press, 2001.

———. *Kierkegaard and Philosophy: Selected Essays*. London: Routledge, 2003.

———. "Kierkegaard's Journals and Notebooks as Interpretive Tools for the Published Works." *Kierkegaard Studies Yearbook* (2003) 189–201.

Hannay, Alastair, and Gordon D. Marino, editors. *Cambridge Companion to Kierkegaard* Cambridge: Cambridge University Press, 1998.

Hauerwas, Stanley. *A Community of Character*. Notre Dame, IN: University of Notre Dame Press, 1981.

———. *The Hauerwas Reader*. Edited by John Berkman and Michael Cartwright. Durham: Duke University Press, 2001.

Haynes, Stephen R. *The Bonhoeffer Phenomenon: Portraits of a Protestant Saint*. Minneapolis: Fortress, 2004.

Heschel, Susannah. "For 'Volk, Blood, and God': The Theological Faculty at the University of Jena During the Third Reich." In *Nazi Germany and the Humanities*, edited by Wolfgang Bialas and Alison Rabinbach, 365–98. Oxford: Oneworld, 2007.

Hinkson, Craig Q. "Will the Real Martin Luther Please Stand Up! Kierkegaard's View of Luther vs. Evolving Perceptions of the Tradition." In *International Kierkegaard Commentary: For Self-Examination and Judge For Yourself!*, edited by Robert L. Perkins, 37–76. Macon, GA: Mercer University Press, 2002.

Hirsch, Emanuel. *Kierkegaard-studien*. Gütersloh: Der Rufer, 1930.

Hodgson, Peter C. *GWF Hegel: Theologian of Spirit*. Edinburgh: T. & T. Clark, 1997.

Hopper, David H. "Bonhoeffer's 'Love of the World', 'the Dangers of that Book', and the Kierkegaard Question." Paper presented to the Bonhoeffer Group, American Academy of Religion Annual Meeting, 1989.

———. "Metanoia: Bonhoeffer on Kierkegaard." *Metanoia* [Prague] 2:3 (1991) 70–75.

Janik, Allan. "Haecker, Kierkegaard and the Early Brenner: A Contribution to the History of the Reception of *Two Ages* in the German-speaking World." In *International Kierkegaard Commentary*: *Two Ages*, edited by Robert L. Perkins, 189–222. Macon, GA: Mercer University Press, 1984.

Jehle, Herbert. "Dietrich Bonhoeffer on War and Peace." In *A Bonhoeffer Legacy*, edited by A. J. Klassen, 362–66. Grand Rapids: Eerdmans, 1981.

Jenkins, Daniel. *Beyond Religion*. London: SCM, 1962.

Jespersen, Kund, J. V. *A History of Denmark*. Translated by Ivan Hill. Basingstoke: Palgrave Macmillan, 2004.

Jones, W. Glyn. *Denmark: A Modern History*. London: Croom Helm, 1986.

Kant, Imanuel. "On a Supposed Right to Lie from Altruistic Motives." In *On Being Responsible*. London: SCM, 1969.

Kelly, Geffrey B. "Bonhoeffer's 'Non Religious' Christianity: Antecedents and Critique." *Bijdragen* 37 (1976) 118–48.

———. "Bonhoeffer's Theology of History and Revelation." In *A Bonhoeffer Legacy*, edited by A. J. Klassen, 89–130. Grand Rapids: Eerdmans, 1981.

———. "Bonhoeffer's Theology of Liberation." *Dialog* 34:1 (Winter 1995) 22–29.

———. "The Influence of Kierkegaard on Bonhoeffer's Concept of Discipleship." *The Irish Theological Quarterly* 41:2 (1974) 148–54.

———. "Kierkegaard as 'Antidote' and as Impact on Dietrich Bonhoeffer's Concept of Christian Discipleship." In *Bonhoeffer's Intellectual Formation*, edited by Peter Frick, 145–66. Tübingen: Mohr Siebeck, 2008.

———. *Liberating Faith: Bonhoeffer's Message for Today*. Minneapolis: Augsburg, 1984.

———. "Revelation in Christ: A Study of Dietrich Bonhoeffer's Theology of Revelation." PhD diss., Université Catholique de Louvain, 1972.

Kelly, Geffrey B., and F. Burton Nelson. *The Cost of Moral Leadership: The Spirituality of Dietrich Bonhoeffer*. Grand Rapids: Eerdmans, 2003.

Kirmmse, Bruce H. *Encounters With Kierkegaard: A Life as Seen by His Contemporaries*. Princeton, NJ: Princeton University Press, 1996.

———. *Kierkegaard in Golden Age Denmark*. Bloomington: Indiana University Press, 1990.

Klassen, A. J., editor. *A Bonhoeffer Legacy: Essays in Understanding*. Grand Rapids: Eerdmans, 1981.

Krötke, Wolf. "Dietrich Bonhoeffer and Martin Luther." In *Bonhoeffer's Intellectual Formation*, edited by Peter Frick, 53–82. Tübingen: Mohr/Siebeck, 2008.

Kütemeyer, Wilhelm. "Vorwort." In *Der Einzelne und die Kirche*, 5–33. Berlin: Kurt Wolff, 1934.

Laney, James T. "An Examination of Bonhoeffer's Ethical Contextualism." In *A Bonhoeffer Legacy*, edited by A. J. Klassen, 294–313. Grand Rapids: Eerdmans, 1981.

Lange, Frederik de. *Waiting for the Word: Dietrich Bonhoeffer on Speaking About God*. Grand Rapids: Eerdmans, 1999.

Law, David. "Cheap Grace and the Cost of Discipleship in Kierkegaard's *For Self-Examination*." In *International Kierkegaard Commentary: For Self-Examination and Judge For Yourself!*, edited by Robert L. Perkins, 111–42. Macon, GA: Mercer University Press, 2002.

———. "Christian Discipleship in Kierkegaard, Hirsch, and Bonhoeffer." *Downside Review* 120:421 (2002) 293ff.

———. *Kierkegaard as Negative Theologian*. Oxford: Clarendon, 1993.

———. "Kierkegaard's Anti-Ecclesiology: the Attack on 'Christendom', 1854–1855." *International Journal for the Study of the Christian Church* 7:2 (2007) 86–108.

Lee, Seung-Goo. "The Antithesis between the Religious View of Ethics and the Rationalistic View of Ethics in *Fear and Trembling*." In *International Kierkegaard Commentary: Fear and Trembling and Repetition*, edited by Robert L. Perkins, 101–26. Macon, GA: Mercer University Press, 1993.

Leon, Arnold E. *Secularization: Science without God?* London: SCM, 1967.

Levinas, Emmanuel. "Existence and Ethics." In *Kierkegaard: A Critical Reader*, edited by Jonathan Ree and Jane Chamberlain, 26–37. Oxford: Blackwell, 1998.

Lippitt, John. *Kierkegaard and Fear and Trembling*. London: Routledge, 2003.

Littell, Franklin H. "The Question: Who is Christ for Us Today? Bonhoeffer's History, Church, and World." In *The Place of Bonhoeffer*, edited by Martin E. Marty. Westport, CT: Greenwood, 1962.

Lohff, Wenzel. "Rechfertigung und Ethik." *Lutherische Monatshefte* 2 (1963) 311–18.

Lohse, Bernard. *Martin Luther: An Introduction to his Life and Thought*. Edinburgh: T. & T. Clark, 1987.

———. *Martin Luther's Theology: Its Historical and Systematic Development*. Edinburgh: T. & T. Clark, 1999.

Lowrie, Walter. *Kierkegaard*. Oxford: Oxford University Press, 1938.

———. "Preface" and "Introduction." *Attack on Christendom*. Princeton, NJ: Princeton University Press, 1968.

MacIntyre, Alasdair. *After Virtue*. 2nd ed. London: Duckworth, 1992.

———. *A Short History of Ethics*. London: Routledge Classics, 2002.

Mackey, Louis. "Kierkegaard and the Problem of Existential Philosophy." In *Essays on Kierkegaard*, edited by Jerry H. Gill, 31–57. Minneapolis: Burgess, 1969.

———. *Kierkegaard: A Kind of Poet*. Philadelphia: University of Pennsylvania Press, 1971.

———. "The Loss of the World in Kierkegaard's Ethics." *Review of Metaphysics* 15:4 (1962) 602–20.

Macquarrie, John. *God and Secularity.* London: Lutterworth, 1968.

Malik, Habib. *Receiving Søren Kierkegaard: The Early Impact and Transmission of His Thought.* Washington, DC: The Catholic University of America Press, 1996.

Marsh, Charles. *Reclaiming Dietrich Bonhoeffer: The Promise of His Theology.* Oxford: University Press, 1994.

Marty, Martin E. *The Place of Bonhoeffer.* Westport, CT: Greenwood, 1962.

Matheson, Peter. *The Third Reich and the Christian Churches.* Edinburgh: T. & T. Clark, 1981.

McCarthy, Vincent A. "Schelling and Kierkegaard on Freedom and Fall." In *International Kierkegaard Commentary: The Concept of Anxiety,* edited by Robert L. Perkins, 89–110. Macon, GA: Mercer University Press, 1985.

Meyer, Dietrich, and Eberhard Bethge, editors. *Nachlass Dietrich Bonhoeffer.* Munich: Chr. Kaiser, 1987.

Minear, Paul S., and Paul S. Morimoto. *Kierkegaard and the Bible: An Index.* Princeton, NJ: Princeton University Press, 1953.

Mooney, Edward. "Exemplars, Inwardness, and Belief: Kierkegaard on Indirect Communication." In *International Kierkegaard Commentary: Concluding Unscientific Postscript,* edited by Robert L. Perkins, 129–48. Macon, GA: Mercer University Press, 1997.

———. *Knights of Faith and Resignation: Reading Kierkegaard's Fear and Trembling.* New York: State University of New York Press, 1991.

———. *Selves in Discord and Resolve: Kierkegaard's Moral-Religious Psychology from Either/Or to Sickness Unto Death.* London: Routledge, 1996.

Morris, Leon. *The Abolition of Religion: A Study in Religionless Christianity.* London: InterVarsity, 1964.

Moses, John A. *The Reluctant Revolutionary: Dietrich Bonhoeffer's Collision with Prusso-German History.* New York: Berghahn, 2009.

Mynster, J. P. *Meddelelser om mit Levnet.* Kiøbenhavn: Gyldendalste Boghandlings Forlag, 1854.

———. *Prædikener paa alle Søn- og Hellig-Dage i Aaret.* Vol. 1. 4th ed. Kiøbenhagen: Gyldendal, 1845.

Nicholls, William. *Systematic and Philosophical Theology.* Middlesex: Penguin, 1969.

Nickson, Ann L. *Bonhoeffer on Freedom: Courageously Grasping Freedom.* Burlington, VT: Ashgate, 2002.

Niebuhr, H. Richard. *The Responsible Self.* San Francisco: Harper & Row, 1978.

Nietzsche, Friedrich. *Beyond Good and Evil.* Translated by R. J. Hollingdale. London: Penguin, 2003.

———. *Ecce Homo.* Translated by R. J. Hollingdale. London: Penguin, 2004.

———. *Thus Spoke Zarathustra.* Translated by R. J. Hollingdale. London: Penguin, 2003.

———. *Twilight of the Idols/The Anti-Christ.* Translated by R. J. Hollingdale. London: Penguin, 2003.

Ott, Heinrich. *Reality and Faith: The Theological Legacy of Dietrich Bonhoeffer.* Translated by Alex A. Morrison. London: Lutterworth, 1971.

Pangritz, Andreas. *Karl Barth in the Theology of Dietrich Bonhoeffer.* Translated by Barbara and Martin Rumscheidt. Grand Rapids: Eerdmans, 2000.

———. "Dietrich Bonhoeffer: 'Within, not Outside the Barthian Movement.'" In *Bonhoeffer's Intellectual Formation,* edited by Peter Frick, 245–82. Tübingen: Mohr/Siebeck, 2008.

———. "Who is Jesus Christ for Us Today?" In *Cambridge Companion to Dietrich Bonhoeffer.,* edited by John de Gruchy, 134–53. Cambridge: Cambridge University Press, 1999.

Pattison, George. "'Before God' as a Regulative Concept." *Kierkegaard Studies Yearbook* (1997) 70–84.

———. "Kierkegaard and Imagination." *Theology* 87 (1984) 6–12.

———. *Kierkegaard and the Crisis of Faith.* London: SPCK, 1997.

———. *Kierkegaard, Religion, and the Nineteenth-Century Crisis of Culture.* Cambridge: Cambridge University Press, 2002.

———. *Kierkegaard: The Aesthetic and the Religious.* London: Macmillan, 1992.

———. *The Philosophy of Kierkegaard.* Chesham: Acumen, 2005.

Perkins, Robert L., editor. *International Kierkegaard Commentary.* Macon, GA: Mercer University Press, 1984–2007.

Peters, Timo Rainer. "Orders and Interventions: Political Ethics in the Theology of Dietrich Bonhoeffer." In *A Bonhoeffer Legacy,* edited by A. J. Klassen, 314–29. Grand Rapids: Eerdmans, 1981.

Phillips, J. A. *The Form of Christ in the World: A Study of Bonhoeffer's Christology.* London: Collins, 1967.

Piety, M. G. "The Reality of the World in Kierkegaard's *Postscript*." In *International Commentary: Concluding Unscientific Postscript*, edited by Robert L. Perkins, 169–86. Macon, GA: Mercer University Press, 1997.

Plant, Stephen J. *Bonhoeffer*. London: Continuum, 2004.

———. "'In the Sphere of the Familiar': Heidegger and Bonhoeffer." In *Bonhoeffer's Intellectual Formation*, edited by Peter Frick, 301–27. Tübingen: Mohr/Siebeck, 2008.

Plekon, Michael. "Introducing Christ into Christendom: Reinterpreting the Late Kierkegaard." *Anglican Theological Review* 64 (1983) 327–52.

———. "Kierkegaard, the Church and Theology of Golden-Age Denmark." *Journal of Ecclesastical History* 34:2 (1983) 245–66.

Pojman, Louis P. *The Logic of Subjectivity*. University of Alabama Press, 1984.

Poole, Roger. *Kierkegaard: The Indirect Communication*. Charlottesville: University Press of Virginia, 1993.

———. "The Unknown Kierkegaard: Twentieth-century Receptions." In *The Cambridge Companion to Kierkegaard*, edited by Alastair Hannay and Gordon D. Marino, 48–75. Cambridge: Cambridge University Press, 1997.

Prenter, Regin. "Dietrich Bonhoeffer and Karl Barth's Positivism of Revelation." In *World Come of Age*, edited by Ronald Gregor-Smith, 93–130. London: Collins, 1967.

Pugh, Jeffrey C. *Religionless Christianity: Dietrich Bonhoeffer in Troubled Times*. New York: T. & T. Clark, 2008.

Purkarthofer, Richard. "'Suppose I would Die Tomorrow'—Possible Uses of Kierkegaard's Journals and Notebooks for Research." *Kierkegaard Studies Yearbook* (2003) 202–13.

Quinn, Philip L. "Kierkegaard's Christian Ethics." In *The Cambridge Companion to Kierkegaard*, edited by Alastair Hannay and Gordon D. Marino, 349–75. Cambridge: Cambridge University Press, 1997.

Rades, Jörge Alfred. "Kierkegaard and Bonhoeffer." PhD diss. chapter, University of Aberdeen, 1988.

Rae, Murray. "Kierkegaard, Barth, and Bonhoeffer: Conceptions of the Relation Between Grace and Works." In *International Kierkegaard Commentary: For Self-Examination and Judge For Yourself!*, edited by Robert L. Perkins, 143–68. Macon, GA: Mercer University Press, 2002.

Ramsey, Paul. *Basic Christian Ethics*. London: SCM, 1950.

———. *Deeds and Rules in Christian Ethics*. London: University Press of America, 1983.

———. "Existenz and the Existence of God: A Study of Kierkegaard and Hegel." *The Journal of Religion* 28:3 (1948) 157–76.

———. "Forward." In *The Death of God: The Culture of Our Post-Christian Era*. New York: George Braziller, 1967.

———. "Two Concepts of General Rules in Christian Ethics." *Ethics* 76:3 (1966) 192–207.

Rasmussen, Larry. "The Ethics of Responsible Action." In *Cambridge Companion to Dietrich Bonhoeffer*, edited by John de Gruchy, 206–25. Cambridge: Cambridge University Press, 1999.

Ree, Jonathan. *Heidegger*. New York: Routledge, 1999.

Ree, Jonathan, and Jane Chamberlain, editors. *Kierkegaard: A Critical Reader*. Oxford: Blackwell, 1998.

Roberts, Robert. "Thinking Subjectively." *International Journal of Philosophy of Religion* 11:2 (1980) 71–92.

Robertson, Edwin, editor. *The Prison Poetry of Dietrich Bonhoeffer*. Guildford: Eagle, 1998.

Robinson, J. A. T. *Honest to God*. London: SCM, 1963.

Saez Tajafuerce, Begonya. "Kierkegaardian Seduction, or the Aesthetic 'Actio(nes) in Distans.'" *Diacritics* 30:1 (2000) 78–88.

Schlingensiepen, Ferdinand. *Dietrich Bonhoeffer 1906–1945*. Edinburgh: T. & T. Clark, 2010.

Scholder, Klauss. *The Churches and the Third Reich*. 2 vols. London: SCM, 1987–88.

Schrag, Calvin. "Note on Kierkegaard's Teleological Suspension of the Ethical." *Ethics* 70:1 (1959) 66–68.

Schrempf, Christof. "Einleitung." In *Sören Kierkegaards agitatorische Schriften und Aufsätze: 1851 bis 1855, Sören Kierkegaards Angriff auf die Christenheit, Erster Band: Die Akten*. Stuttgart: Frommanns, 1896.

Selby, Peter. "Christianity in a World Come of Age." In *The Cambridge Companion to Dietrich Bonhoeffer*, edited by John de Gruchy, 226–45. Cambridge: Cambridge University Press, 1999.

Sherman, Franklin. "The Methods of Asking the Question Concerning Jesus Christ: Act and Being." In *The Place of Bonhoeffer*, edited by Martin E. Marty. Westport, CT: Greenwood, 1962.

Sponheim, Paul. *Kierkegaard on Christ and Christian Coherence*. London: SCM, 1968.

Stewart, Jon. *Kierkegaard's Relations to Hegel Reconsidered*. Cambridge: Cambridge University Press, 2003.

Swenson, David. "Editor's Introduction." In *Lectures on the Religious Thought of Søren Kierkegaard*. Minneapolis: Augsburg, 1937.

Tame, Kim. "And Finally, A Religionless Christianity Today." *Expository Times* 118:5 (2007) 260.

Tanner, Michael. *Nietzsche*. Oxford: Oxford University Press, 2000.

Taylor, Mark C. "Time's Struggle with Space: Kierkegaard's Understanding of Temporality." *The Harvard Theological Review* 66:3 (1973) 311–29.

Thulstrup, Niels. *Kierkegaard and the Church in Denmark*. Copenhagen: Reitzel, 1984.

———. *Kierkegaard's Relation To Hegel*. Translated by George L. Stengren. Princeton, NJ: Princeton University Press, 1980.

Tödt, Heinz Eduard. *Authentic Faith: Bonhoeffer's Theological Ethics in Context*. Translated by David Stasson and Ilse Tödt. Grand Rapids: Eerdmans, 2007.

Tolstoy, Leo. *Walk in the Light and Twenty-Three Tales*. Translated by Louise and Aylmer Maude. Maryknoll, NY: Orbis, 2003.

Vahanian, Gabriel. *The Death of God: The Culture of Our Post-Christian Era*. New York: George Braziller, 1967.

Van Buren, Paul. *The Secular Meaning of the Gospel: Based on an Analysis of its Language*. London: SCM, 1963.

Vogel, Heinrich Traugott. "Christus als Vorbild und Versohner: eine kritische Studie zum Problem des Verhältnis von Gesetz und Evangelium im Werke Sören Kierkegaard." PhD diss., Humboldt-Universitat, Berlin, 1968.

Walsh, Sylvia. *Living Christianly: Kierkegaard's Dialectic of Christian Existence*. University Park: Pennsylvania State University Press, 2006.

———. "Subjectivity vs. Objectivity: Kierkegaard's Postscript and Feminist Epistemology." In *International Kierkegaard Commentary: Concluding Unscientific Postscript*, edited by Robert L. Perkins, 11–31. Macon, GA: Mercer University Press, 1997.

Wannenwetsch, Bernd, editor. *Who Am I? Bonhoeffer's Theology Through His Poetry*. London: T. & T. Clark, 2009.

Watkin, Julia. *Kierkegaard*. London: Geoffrey Chapman, 1997.

Watts, Michael. *Kierkegaard*. Oxford: Oneworld, 2003.

Weikart, Richard. *The Myth of Dietrich Bonhoeffer: Is His Theology Really Evangelical?* San Francisco: International Scholars, 1997.

Wesson, Anthony. "Bonhoeffer's Use of Religion." *London Quarterly Review* 2:4 (1970) 43–53.

Westergaard, Harold. *Economic Developments in Denmark*. Oxford: Clarendon, 1922.

Weston, Michael. *Kierkegaard and Modern Continental Philosophy*. London: Routledge, 1994.

Westphal, Merold. *Becoming a Self*. West Lafayette, IN: Purdue University Press, 1996.

———. *Kierkegaard's Critique of Reason and Society*. Macon, GA: Mercer University Press, 1987.

Wilde, Frank-Eberhard. *Kierkegaard and Speculative Idealism*. Copenhagen: Reitzels, 1979.

Willmer, Haddon. "Costly Discipleship." In *Cambridge Companion to Dietrich Bonhoeffer*, edited by John de Gruchy, 173–89. Cambridge: Cambridge University Press, 1999.

Woelfel, James. "Bonhoeffer's Portrait of the Religionless Christianity." *Encounter* 28 (1967) 340–67.

Wüstenberg, Ralf K. *Bonhoeffer and Beyond: Promoting Dialogue Betweeen Religion and Politics*. Frankfurt am Main: Peter Lang, 2008.

———. *A Theology of Life: Dietrich Bonhoeffer's Religionless Christianity*. Grand Rapids: Eerdmans, 1998.

Wüstenberg, Ralf K., and Stephen Plant, editors. *Religion, Religionlessness and Contemporary Western Culture: Explorations in Dietrich Bonhoeffer's Theology*. Oxford: Peter Lang, 2008.

Young, Josiah. "Dietrich Bonhoeffer and Reinhold Niebuhr: Their Ethics, Views on Karl Barth, and African-Americans." In *Bonhoeffer's Intellectual Formation*, edited by Peter Frick, 283–300. Tübingen: Mohr/Siebeck, 2008.

Zimmermann, Wolf-Dieter, and Gregor-Smith, Ronald, editors. *I Knew Dietrich Bonhoeffer*. London: Collins, 1966.

Index of Names

Subject Index